Lending Credibility

Lending Credibility

The International Monetary Fund and the Post-Communist Transition

Randall W. Stone

PRINCETON UNIVERSITY PRESS
PRINCETON AND OXFORD

Published by Princeton University Press, 41 William Street, Princeton, New Jersey 08540

In the United Kingdom: Princeton University Press, 3 Market Place, Woodstock, Oxfordshire OX20 1SY

ISBN 0-691-09528-0 (cloth: alk. paper)
       0-691-09529-9 (pbk.: alk. paper)

British Library Cataloging-in-Publication Data is available

The publisher would like to acknowledge the author of this volume for providing the camera-ready copy from which this book was printed.

This book has been composed in LATEX by Branislav L. Slantchev.

Printed on acid-free paper.

www.pup.princeton.edu

Printed in the United States of America

10 9 8 7 6 5 4 3 2 1

To Martha, Henry, Sophia, and William, with love

Contents

List of Figures   xi

List of Tables   xiii

List of Acronyms   xv

Preface   xix

1   Introduction   **1**
   1.1   The Strategy of Transition: Inflation and Democracy   6
   1.2   What Would We Like the IMF to Do?   10

I   Models and Data   **13**

2   A Formal Model of Lending Credibility   **15**
   2.1   The Model   21
   2.2   The Equilibrium   22
   2.3   Hypotheses Derived from the Formal Model   26
   2.4   Conclusions   27

   Appendix: A Formal Model of Lending Credibility   **29**

3   Studying IMF Effectiveness   **39**
   3.1   Previous Research   39
   3.2   Critiques Raised in the Literature   46
   3.3   New Critiques   48
   3.4   Research Design   49
   3.5   Conclusions   58

4   An Empirical Test of the Model   **59**
   4.1   Models of IMF Lending Decisions   60
   4.2   Covariates of the Duration of Punishment Intervals   61
   4.3   Covariates of Program Suspensions   67
   4.4   Models of Policy Variables   73
   4.5   Conclusions   84

II History   87

5 Poland   89
  5.1 The Balcerowicz Plan   90
  5.2 The Extended Fund Facility   99
  5.3 The Second Stand-by Agreement   106
  5.4 Poland's Turn to the Left   109
  5.5 Conclusions   114

6 Russia   116
  6.1 The Window of Opportunity Closes: 1992   118
  6.2 The First Stand-by Agreement, July 1992   120
  6.3 The Systemic Transformation Facility: May 1993   126
  6.4 The STF Renewal, April 1994   128
  6.5 The Second Stand-by Arrangement, April 1995   136
  6.6 The Extended Fund Facility, February, 1996   138
  6.7 The Third Stand-by, July 1998   153
  6.8 The Fourth Stand-by, July 1999   158
  6.9 Conclusions   164

7 Ukraine   169
  7.1 From Hyperinflation to Market Reform, 1992-1994   170
  7.2 The Systemic Transformation Facility, 1994   177
  7.3 The First Stand-by, 1995   179
  7.4 The Second Stand-by, 1996   183
  7.5 The Third Stand-by, 1997   190
  7.6 The Extended Fund Facility, 1998   196
  7.7 Conclusions   207

8 Bulgaria   209
  8.1 False Starts, 1990-1994   210
  8.2 The Origins of the Crisis, 1995-1996   217
  8.3 Consolidation under the Currency Board   227
  8.4 Conclusions   231

9 Conclusion   233
  9.1 Research Design   234
  9.2 Policy Implications   239

Appendixes   243

A Data   245

B   Statistical Methods   **250**
    B.1   Multiple Imputation   250
    B.2   Duration Models   254

C   List of Interviews   **262**

Bibliography   **266**

Index   **279**

Figures

1.1   Inflation and GDP Growth   8

2.1   The Stage Game   22

4.1   Country Variations in Expected Duration of Punishment Intervals   65

4.2   Effects of Variables on Expected Duration of Punishment Intervals   66

4.3   Country Variations in Expected Duration of Programs in Good Standing   71

4.4   Effects of Variables on Expected Duration of Programs in Good Standing   72

7.1   IMF Financing, NBU Reserves and Domestic Credit in 1995   182

Tables

1.1   Effects of Inflation on Growth and Quality of Life   7

3.1   International Accounts   41
3.2   Policy Variables   42
3.3   Growth, Savings, and Investment   43
3.4   Quantitative Studies of Conditionality Programs   44

4.1   Durations of Punishment Intervals   62
4.2   Durations of Programs in Good Standing   68
4.3   Effects of Foreign Aid on Policy Variables   76
4.4   Effects of Punishment Duration on Policy Variables   82

5.1   1990 Targets and Results   96
5.2   Sejm Election of October 27, 1991   103
5.3   Sejm Election of September 19, 1993   110

7.1   PriceWaterhouseCoopers Audits of Reported NBU Reserves   194

A.1   Correlations of U.S. and non-U.S. Foreign Aid   249

B.1   Assumptions and Implications of Missing Data   251
B.2   Government Duration Models   257
B.3   Analysis of Duration of Programs in Good Standing   258
B.4   Analysis of Duration of Punishment Intervals   260

Acronyms

ASI	American Statistics Index
AWS	Solidarity Electoral Action
BBWR	Non-Party Bloc for Reform
BNB	Bulgarian National Bank
BSP	Bulgarian Socialist Party
CBR	Central Bank of Russia
CIS	Commonwealth of Independent States
CMEA	Council for Mutual Economic Assistance
CPSU	Communist Party of the Soviet Union
CSFB	Credit-Suisse First Boston
CUP	Central Planning Agency
EBRD	European Bank for Reconstruction and Development
EFF	Extended Fund Facility
EMS	European Monetary System
EU	European Union
FIMACO	Foreign Investment Management Company
FSB	Federal Security Service
GDP	Gross Domestic Product
GEE	Generalized Evaluation Estimator
GKO	Short-term State Obligations (Russian treasury bonds)
G-7	Group of Seven Industrialized Countries
HIID	Harvard Institute for International Development
IBRD	International Bank for Reconstruction and Development (World Bank)
ICPSR	Intercollegiate Consortium for Political and Social Research
IFS	International Financial Statistics
IMET	International Military Education and Training
IMF	International Monetary Fund
ITAR-TASS	Russian Information Agency
KGB	Committee for State Security
KLD	Liberal Democratic Congress
KPN	Confederation for an Independent Poland
KPRF	Communist Party of the Russian Federation
LDPR	Liberal Democratic Party of Russia
LHS	Left-hand side
MAE	Monetary and Exchange Department of the IMF

M0	Base money, a narrow measure of the money supply
M2	A broad measure of the money supply
MRF	Movement for Rights and Freedom
MVF	International Monetary Fund (in Russian)
NAFTA	North American Free Trade Agreement
NATO	North Atlantic Treaty Organization
NBP	National Bank of Poland
NBU	National Bank of Ukraine
NDA	Net domestic assets (of a central bank)
NIR	Net international reserves (of a central bank)
NIS	Newly Independent States
NSZZ "S"	Independent, Self-Governing Trade Union "Solidarity"
OA	Official Assistance
ODA	Official Development Assistance
OECD	Organization for Economic Cooperation and Development
OLS	Ordinary Least Squares
OMRI	Open Media Research Institute
PBE	Perfect Bayesian Equilibrium
PC	Center Alliance
PL	Peasant Alliance
PPPP	Polish Beer Lovers' Party
PSL	Polish Peasant Party
PUWP	Polish United Workers' Party (Communist Party)
RAO	Joint Stock Company (in Russian)
RFE/RL	Radio Free Europe/Radio Liberty
RHS	Right-hand side
SBA	Stand-by Arrangement
SBU	Security Service of Ukraine
SDR	Special drawing rights
SdRP	Social Democracy of the Republic of Poland
SDS	Union of Democratic Forces (in Bulgarian)
SLD	Alliance of the Democratic Left
SOE	State-owned enterprise
STF	Systemic Transformation Facility
TASS	Telegraph Agency of the Soviet Union
UD	Democratic Union
UDF	Union of Democratic Forces (SDS in Bulgarian)
UES	Unified Energy System
UP	Union of Labor
UPR	Union of Real Politics
USAID	United States Agency for International Development
USMil	United States military aid
USSR	Union of Soviet Socialist Republics

UW	Union of Freedom
VAT	Value Added Tax
WAK	Catholic Electoral Alliance
ZChN	Christian National Union

Preface

I embarked on this project five years ago not with the intention of providing policy guidance but simply to study the influence of an important international institution that seemed to me poorly understood by the scholarly community. At the time, the International Monetary Fund (IMF, or simply the Fund) was a likely focus for academic conferences but not for congressional hearings or street protests in Washington. Most of the undergraduates I taught had no idea what the IMF was until they took my course, nor could they have distinguished it easily from the rest of the alphabetical flotsam that clutters syllabi in international political economy, such as WTO, IBRD, ECB, OECD–all of which are important institutions in their own right, of course. East Europeans, on the other hand, along with citizens of developing countries, recognized the significance of my topic immediately. Indeed, in the course of my travels across the region I have often been asked which agency I worked for: the IMF or the CIA?[1] The IMF quickly lost its obscurity in the United States, largely as a result of the events related in this book. Subsequently, I have been asked to address Sunday school classes, groups of concerned students, and gatherings of officials in Washington and Moscow. I have discovered some important things, and they are relevant to the practical concerns of churchgoers, students, and policymakers, but this is not primarily a book of policy advice. This is a work of political science, and its objective is to train the best tools available to social science on an important substantive question in order to see what we can learn in the process.

It is not easy to write about the IMF without taking sides. When I mention at Washington cocktail parties that I am writing a book about the IMF and the post-Communist transition, I am invariably asked the question, "Are you for or against?" My standard reply is that I am in favor: I think the post-Communist transition was a pretty good idea. Flip rejoinders aside, my position on the IMF is more supportive than critical on balance, and I hope that, as devastating as my criticisms may seem, they will be seen in time as constructive. I believe that both the extreme Right and the extreme Left are fundamentally mistaken about the IMF. It is neither simply an example of the abuses of big government, nor simply the executive committee of international finance that represses efforts to ameliorate the situation of the poor. In principle, the IMF has an important role to play in improving government policy, which can greatly improve the

---

[1] My truthful answer, that I was an independent researcher working on a book, was often met with skepticism.

lot of the poorest of the global poor. In practice, it has played a constructive role in a number of post-Communist countries, which has, in fact, benefited the poor.

This is the starting point for a barrage of criticism that I address to the IMF, as well as the motivation for the hope that inspires my most important policy recommendation. The IMF is effective only in countries from which it can credibly threaten to withdraw support. In the work that follows, I show that the credibility of the IMF's bargaining position depended on the international influence of the target countries. Countries that were very influential—in particular, those that received the most foreign aid from the United States—were treated very leniently and, consequently, were much less likely to follow IMF advice. The IMF can lend credibility to governments sorely in need of it, but only when the conditions attached to its own lending are credibly enforced. Thus, countries that were influential enough to convince the United States government to pressure the IMF to be lenient derived much less benefit from their interactions with the Fund than ordinary countries that lacked such leverage.

For countries like Russia, as a result, international influence became a strategic liability rather than an asset. In a crowning irony, the same can be said about the ultimate exponent of such influence, the United States. For the United States, the most important policy goal in the post-Communist region in the 1990s was the consolidation of democracy and a market economy in Russia. The U.S. government's continual efforts to shield Russia from the rigor of IMF conditions, however, compromised Russia's efforts at market reform, and the prolonged economic transition that resulted ultimately undermined the basis of democratic legitimacy in the most important country in the region. The United States gained a number of short-term concessions from Russia in return, but the long-term cost of this policy was disastrous. Influence is not always an advantage; indeed, the United States would have achieved a much better outcome had it been unable to influence the IMF. Consequently, my most important piece of policy advice is this: As is true of central banks, international financial institutions can only be effective to the extent that they are independent of political authorities. The IMF is a tremendous force for farsighted economic management in small countries, but it will remain a deficient tool for managing the affairs of the large countries that are most important to the international system as long as it remains dependent on the policies of a small number of powerful countries.

I have accumulated many debts in the process of completing this project. The greatest is to my colleagues and students, past and present, at the University of Rochester. In particular, I learned a great deal from my colleagues Jeff Banks, Randy Calvert, John Duggan, Curt Signorino, and Dave Weimer, without which the technical parts of this book would have been much less effective. Bing Powell and John Mueller were also very generous with a junior colleague, and this book is better for my many conversations with them. Colleagues at other institutions have also been very helpful at key junctures. In particular, I wish to thank Chris Achen, Jim Alt, Leslie Armijo, Tom Biersteker, Doug Blum, John Carey, Jerry Cohen, Matt Evangelista, Jim Fearon, Geoff Garrett, Joe Grieco, Steve Hanson, Joel Hellman, Yoi Herrera, John Jackson, Juliet Johnson, Miles Kahler, Barb Koremenos, Gary King, Herbert Kitschelt, Bob Keohane, Mark Kramer, Charles Lipson, Lisa Martin, Vladimir Popov, Ronald Rogowski, Duncan Snidal, Josh Tucker, Celeste Wallander, Tom Willett, David Woodruff, Kim Marten Zisk, and five anonymous reviewers for their helpful comments and constructive criticism. While some of them disagree with much that I have written, their arguments have surely improved the final product. For any errors and omissions that remain—other than those recorded in the current accounts of the countries in this study—I have only myself to blame.

The many people who generously helped with technical details, coding data, making connections with interview subjects, and in other ways are too numerous to list but have my gratitude. Chuck Myers and Roger Haydon offered valuable suggestions for revisions, and Rita Bernard did a very thorough and professional job of copyediting the manuscript. Norma Koenig generously read the entire manuscript and made numerous suggestions that improved it. Judith and Robert Martin have my thanks for hosting me in Washington on numerous occasions, and Judith (aka Miss Manners) has my gratitude and admiration for thinking of the title. When she heard my working title (which I sensibly decline to reveal now), she told me that it "simply would not do." Within five minutes she had suggested *Lending Credibility*. Naturally, I accepted her advice with good grace.

The research on which this book is based was supported by grants from the National Science Foundation (SES-9974663), the Social Science Research Council, the National Council for Eurasian and East European Research, the Skalny Center for Polish and Central European Studies at the University of Rochester, the Watson Institute for International Studies at Brown University, and by a year of leave generously granted by the University of Rochester.

I am deeply indebted to the research assistance of a number of talented Ph.D. students at the University of Rochester: Timothy Carter, Chris Kamm, Iulia Kazdobina, Kalina Popova, Branislav L. Slantchev, and Robert Walker. This project reflects their hard work and dedication. For their significant contributions, Timothy Carter, Chris Kamm, and Kalina Popova are listed as coauthors of Appendix B: Statistical Methods.

Early versions of some of the research for this book were presented at various annual meetings of the American Political Science Association, the International Studies Association, and the American Association for the Advancement of Slavic Studies; at conferences sponsored by the Program on New Approaches to Russian Security (PONARS), by the Watson Institute for International Studies at Brown University, and by Jagiellonian University in Krakow, Poland; and in talks at the University of Chicago, Harvard University, the Uni-

versity of Rochester, Brown University, and Duke University. I am thankful
for all the comments and suggestions that were made by members of the au-
dience in each of these forums. Many of these filtered into the final product,
even though I cannot always recall where they originated.

I gratefully acknowledge the permission of MacMillan Press to republish
portions of a chapter I wrote for a volume edited by Leslie Elliott Armijo, *Financial Globalization and Democracy in Developing Countries* (1999). Portions of this chapter reappear in altered form in chapters 1, 2, and 6.

My deepest gratitude goes to my wife, the Rev. Martha Koenig Stone, whose
support and confidence never cease to amaze me, and to my children, Henry,
Sophia, and William. They have tolerated my long absences, have always
welcomed me home with joy, and have made the effort worthwhile.

Lending Credibility

1

Introduction

WITH THE END of the Cold War, the International Monetary Fund (IMF) emerged as the most powerful international institution in history. The Western countries designated the IMF as their primary vehicle for funneling aid to the countries that had emerged from the ruins of the Soviet empire and made it responsible for creating a strategy for interacting with them. That strategy, as it gradually unfolded, was ambitious: nothing less than the economic transformation of every society in the region. The early years after the collapse of the Soviet bloc were heady ones for the IMF: A vast new territory was becoming integrated with the world economy, international capital movements were rising to the top of the political agenda in Central Europe and Eurasia, and multilateral lending agencies were beginning to figure prominently in cabinet meetings and parliamentary debates. The Fund eventually signed loan and conditionality agreements with every country of the former Soviet Union and Eastern Europe except Serbia and Turkmenistan. Even as this ambitious institutional strategy took shape, however, questions were raised about whether the instrument was equal to the task. Can an international institution really hope to exercise influence in a nation's domestic affairs? If it does so, will that influence be beneficial?

Formal international institutions are the peculiar innovation of the advanced industrial democracies, which have relied on these institutions since World War II as a central pillar of their effort to impose order on the anarchy of international politics. In the aftermath of the worst war the world has ever known, the United States and its allies had sought to promote international cooperation by creating an impressive architecture of international institutions: the United Nations, the International Monetary Fund, the World Bank, the General Agreement on Tariffs and Trade, the European Economic Community, and numerous specialized agencies. The Cold War between the United States and the Soviet Union quickly became the focus of attention in the international system, and it redefined many of the purposes of these institutions. Still, whenever the United States and its allies tried to foster cooperation after World War II, they created international institutions. International institutions became an essential part of the relations among these countries, and a broad consensus on the rules that they embodied helped to foster an unprecedented blossoming of coordinated action across a variety of issue areas.

The International Monetary Fund is an unusual international institution because it has some enforcement powers. International institutions generally rely on convention, normative suasion, modest efforts at monitoring, and decentralized collective action to promote cooperation. To be sure, the Fund extends carrots, not sticks, when it attempts to influence government policies. However, it signs intrusive agreements with governments that regulate sensitive aspects of their domestic and international economic policies; it typically does so when countries are particularly vulnerable and dependent on international financing; and it threatens to withdraw support if its detailed policy prescriptions are not observed. This enforcement mechanism would seem to give the IMF a significant edge over gentler international institutions.

Two strong traditions in international relations shed doubt on the ability of international institutions to influence public policy. The first, commonly known as realism, emphasizes the priority of security concerns, the overriding interest of states to assert their autonomy from foreign control, and the tendency for international norms or rules to be manipulated by powerful countries for their own purposes. According to this perspective, the IMF is likely to find that borrowing countries are unwilling to submit to its tutelage and that powerful donor countries will subvert its objectives in order to advance their own. The second perspective emphasizes the importance of domestic constraints and argues that economic policy involves distributive and redistributive issues that go to the heart of politics. If political coalitions and alignments are fundamentally about economic policy, there are severe limitations to what foreign intervention in these matters can achieve.

This book argues that both perspectives are right, up to a point: International power and interests constrain what the IMF can achieve; so do domestic power and interests. Nevertheless, I will argue that the IMF plays an important role in the nexus between power, interests, and policymaking, and exerts a significant influence over national policies. The effects of domestic and international constraints can obscure IMF influence in quantitative and qualitative studies if we fail to take them into account. However, carefully studying both sets of constraints reveals the very important role the IMF has played in the post-Communist countries.

If it is true—and it is—that IMF conditions are often violated and inconsistently enforced, that the IMF has made a number of mistakes in managing the economics of transition, and that countries have misused IMF funds in sometimes spectacular and intricately fraudulent schemes, this still does not answer the question: Has the IMF exerted a meaningful influence over economic policies in these countries? To answer this question, we have to do more than simply measure the economic policies of countries in transition against the

ideal of IMF performance criteria or merely catalogue the Fund's tactical errors and the instances of corruption. In this book I do both in great detail; but
to answer the question, we have to examine the counterfactual: What policies
would have been followed without the involvement of the IMF?

In some sense, of course, we can never know. The IMF was a feature of
the international system into which the post-Communist countries were born,
and its existence shaped the incentives they faced as they sought to define economic policies right from the beginning. We cannot remove the IMF from
the equation and restart history from 1990. However, there are three ways in
which one can do meaningful counterfactual analysis that can shed light on the
effect that the IMF has had on the post-Communist transition. First, one can be
rigorous about what effects one ascribes to the causal variable, and explore the
influence it has in an abstract formal model. Second, statistical analysis with
a large sample enables one to make certain kinds of counterfactual inferences.
Third, detailed studies of relations between the IMF and several borrowing
countries can fill in the context, the actors' expectations, and the intermediate
causal links that, on balance, lead us to believe certain causal inferences and
reject others. In this book, these three approaches form the legs of a tripod that
supports a causal argument. Without any one of these supports—analytical
rigor, generalizable inferences, or contextual knowledge—the structure becomes unstable and the argument untenable. In combination, each approach
complements the others by supplying pieces of the puzzle that the others cannot.

The first step in my research design is to define the effects that IMF intervention is expected to have, and the precise conditions under which it is
supposed to have them. To do this I develop a formal model that specifies the
hypothesized relationships among the IMF, international capital markets, and
borrower countries. The key innovation of the model is that the IMF is treated
as a strategic actor that seeks to defend its reputation for enforcing conditionality, but suffers from credibility problems. In the model I assume that every
actor is sophisticated about the strategies and beliefs of the other actors, so they
all anticipate that IMF programs will not always be properly implemented, that
countries will sometimes find it advantageous to cheat, and that the IMF will
sometimes find it difficult to hold them accountable. Nevertheless, IMF programs affect the economic policies of the borrowing countries, and because of
this they influence capital flows to those countries. The results of the formal
model can be thought of as a possibility theorem. They show that even in a
messy world where things often do not go as planned, it is still possible for
an imperfect institution like the IMF to exert influence. The IMF can still lend
credibility, even if the credibility of its lending is in question. The model spells
out the kind of influence that the Fund is expected to have—both over countries' policies and over market expectations—and it defines the conditions that
limit that influence because of the Fund's own credibility problems.

The second step is to subject the hypotheses that the model advances to quantitative tests. Testing these hypotheses requires a data set with novel features: one that allows the analyst to control for the political factors that influence countries' abilities to stabilize their economies, and that measures country policies and IMF responses with sufficient precision to untangle the causes from the effects. With the help of several research assistants, I have compiled a data set designed for this purpose. The result is a unique statistical database that comprises monthly economic and political time series for twenty-six countries over the decade of the 1990s. Using a variety of statistical methods that are explained in the text for the layperson, and with more technical detail in an appendix, I estimate models to explain IMF strategies, government longevity, government policies, and market expectations. To foreshadow, I find that the IMF does have a significant effect on government policies but that this effect is mitigated whenever the IMF cannot credibly threaten to impose lengthy punishments, namely, in large countries and countries that receive substantial amounts of foreign aid from the United States. As the model predicts, countries that are harder to punish are punished for shorter periods, and the reduced severity of the IMF's response significantly increases their propensity to pursue inflationary policies. Conversely, however, these pessimistic conclusions imply an optimistic one. In order to be vastly less effective in some countries, the IMF must be vastly more effective in others; indeed, in small countries and those without recourse to U.S. intervention, the IMF plays a very critical role in moderating the incentives that fuel inflation and in establishing credibility for stabilization policies.

The third step is to check the plausibility of general conclusions by plunging back into the details. A detailed study of the bilateral relations between the Fund and particular countries, based on interviews with policymakers, negotiators, and Fund officials, can go beyond the thin description accessible in statistical form. Participants can be asked counterfactual questions and asked to share their own hypotheses about which variables caused which effects, based on the accumulation of years of experience. This book is based on extensive field research in Russia, Ukraine, Poland, Bulgaria, and the IMF headquarters in Washington, D.C. Readers of the detailed country studies may find that the picture that emerges confirms the broad-strokes critiques of the Fund as an ineffective organization; indeed, there are numerous anecdotes that could be used as cautionary tales. In part, this is a matter of whether the reader chooses to view the glass as half full or half empty. I believe that what emerges is a picture of an organization that has remarkable influence in spite of the fact that it is working against tremendous odds. Certainly, the case studies in this volume suggest that the Fund should be humble about offering advice and that our expectations of success in difficult cases should be modest. However, they also demonstrate that the deck was terribly stacked against reform in most of these countries and that the IMF was almost always a relevant player—sometimes the only relevant player—lobbying for economic reform. In some cases, when circumstances were right, the IMF did exactly what the model predicts: It tipped the balance of incentives in favor of a long-run strategy of fiscal and monetary restraint, and reinforced the credibility of governments that presided over fragile capital markets. Even in cases where IMF programs failed and ultimately had to be abandoned, the Fund typically exercised a significant influence over policies.

The primary focus of this book is on the effectiveness of the IMF at influencing government policies. However, a prior question that must have occurred to the reader is whether it is normatively desirable for the IMF to exercise influence, and I turn to this question before proceeding with my argument. Critics of unbridled capital markets and the "Washington Consensus" that supports them worry that international institutions and global capital flows may so constrain economic policies during the transition that weak democratic institutions are swept away by popular discontent. Furthermore, they argue, the IMF's neoliberal economic prescriptions of tight monetary and fiscal policies, deregulating the economy, and lowering the barriers to the "creative destruction" wreaked by markets—stabilization, liberalization, and privatization—represent a naïve application of standardized recipes to a much more complex reality. In the felicitous Russian aphorism, it is easy to turn an aquarium into fish soup, but only God can reconstitute the aquarium.

To the contrary, I argue that the basic thrust of the policies urged by the international financial institutions was, in fact, correct. At this point, I want to distinguish carefully between the basic strategy of transition and the specific tactical choices that were made in particular countries. By tactical choices I mean operational decisions on which economic theory does not yet provide straightforward guidance, such as the best ways of targeting exchange rates, the ideal method of privatization, and the optimal sequence of structural reforms. The Fund supported programs in countries that chose a wide range of approaches to these issues, but in some cases IMF staff promoted specific policies that turned out very poorly. We have learned things about economic transitions over the last ten years that would have made it possible to make better choices, had we known them earlier. On the other hand, the key IMF strategy for reform was clear: Accelerate the full spectrum of market reforms as much as possible, and lead with rapid macroeconomic stabilization and liberalization. This appeared to be a rather risky strategy from the vantage point of 1990. After a decade of experience, however, it is clear that this was the strategy best suited to promoting economic growth and consolidating democracy in post-Communist countries, because inflation has such disastrous consequences during the transition.

1.1 THE STRATEGY OF TRANSITION: INFLATION AND DEMOCRACY

Critics of austere, anti-inflationary policies in post-Communist countries point to the apparent success of gradual reform in China, and to the enormous human costs and political instability associated with neoliberal policies in Latin America.[1] The image that captures the imagination is Adam Przeworski's "J-curve," which describes a trade-off between the short-term and long-term pain of the transition.[2] As countries enter the reform process, they adopt austerity measures that reduce output, cut social transfers, and create unemployment, moving down into the "valley of the transition." The more rapidly this is done, the more quickly comes the recovery—but at what cost? What if the misery of the transition is so intense that popular patience is exhausted and democratic institutions are swept away? Perhaps a flatter "J-curve" would be preferable, one that spreads the transition over a longer period but reduces the depth of the recession.

The evidence of the last ten years is that there is, in fact, no such trade-off.[3] Instead, the post-Communist countries that succeeded in quickly bringing inflation under control suffered a smaller drop in output than those that continued to endure the ravages of inflation.[4] They attracted foreign investment and began to grow, laying the groundwork for long-term prosperity and political stability. Economies that failed to tame inflation declined more precipitously and continued to decline long after the transition had been completed in more successful countries. In addition, the low-inflation countries maintained a much less skewed distribution of wealth and income, maintained more social services, and sustained a higher quality of life. Table 1.1 summarizes the data by presenting the results of bivariate regressions of growth, foreign direct investment, income inequality, the United Nations' Human Development Index, and life expectancy on inflation, using a variety of methods. Each row represents a variable that is affected by inflation, and the columns represent a series of econometric models for assessing the effects. The analysis uses all available annual data for post-Communist countries from 1990 through 1999.

The significance of these results is that countries with higher inflation grew

---

[1] Note that there are some good reasons for questioning whether Chinese-style gradualism would have been successful in the more highly developed countries of Eastern Europe and the former Soviet Union (Woo 1994).

[2] Przeworski 1991, p. 163.

[3] Hellman 1998.

[4] This is consistent with a large quantity of scholarship that shows that inflation leads to lower rates of growth in gross domestic product (GDP) (Kormendi and Meguire 1985, Grier and Tullock 1989, Barro 1991, De Gregorio 1992, Roubini and Sala-i-Martin 1992). Levine and Renelt (1992) criticize the robustness of some of these findings; Gylfasson and Herbertsson (1996), Andres, Domenech and Molinas (1996), and Andres and Hernando (1997) find that the negative correlation between inflation and growth is robust to changes in the specification of the model.

Table 1.1: Effects of Inflation on Growth and Quality of Life.

	n	OLS	Robust SE	Fixed Effects[a]	Random Effects
			Inflation (in 1,000%)		
GDP Growth	135	−5.34**	−5.34*	−4.43**	−4.93**
		(1.02)	(2.45)	(1.06)	(1.00)
Foreign Direct Invest. (% GDP)	132	−.797**	−.797*	−.694*	−.717*
		(.293)	(.167)	(.282)	(.270)
Income Inequality (Gini Coeff.)	52	5.97**	5.97**	1.14	5.97**
		(2.06)	(.46)	(.81)	(2.02)
Human Develop. Index	82	−.026*	−.026**	−.0086	−.01
		(.011)	(.0076)	(.0055)	(.0055)
Life Expectancy	131	−.47	−.47	−.012	−.011
		(.032)	(.031)	(.011)	(.011)

$^*p < .05; ^{**}p < .01$, two-tailed tests

[a] F-tests reject the hypothesis that all fixed effects are equal to zero at the .01 level for each of the equations.

more slowly, or declined more rapidly, and attracted less foreign direct investment. Furthermore, it was the poor rather than the relatively wealthy who suffered most from inflation: High inflation caused income inequality to increase. There is also some evidence that high inflation caused countries' scores to decline on the United Nations' broadest scale of the quality of life, the Human Development Index. This captures a wide range of factors, such as health care, education and nutrition as well as per capita income. Inflation may cause life expectancy to decline as well, but these data cannot prove this to be the case. Figure 1.1 presents the relationship between growth and inflation in graphical form using the same data.

Taming inflation was the most urgent task facing post-Communist countries, because high levels of inflation threatened to derail all other aspects of their reform programs. All these countries faced a substantial jump in prices when they abolished price controls, and most accelerated inflation by continuing to subsidize state-owned enterprises. High inflation is a self-fulfilling prophecy: The longer it persists, the more stubborn inflationary expectations become, and the more difficult it becomes to restore confidence in the currency. Meanwhile, financial instability distorts economic decisions and, in particular, increases the risks for investors. In addition, a high level of inflation has proven to be a profoundly destabilizing force in politics. While the costs

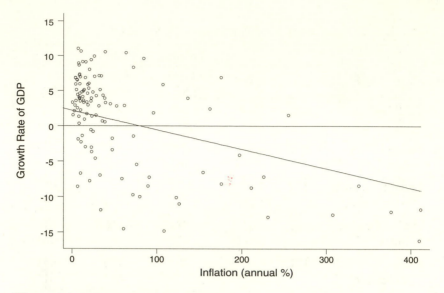

Figure 1.1: Inflation and GDP Growth.

of inflation have been vividly demonstrated in developing countries such as Argentina and Brazil, inflation has the potential to be even more devastating in post-Communist countries, for three reasons.

First, inflation and the policies that lead to high levels of inflation—loose credit, budget deficits, and government subsidies—warp the incentives of firms, preventing industrial restructuring. Firms make choices about whether to make costly investments in future competitiveness or to engage in lobbying activity, and when the latter is relatively inexpensive and lucrative, they fail to restructure. This is particularly costly in post-Communist countries, because the structure of production inherited from central planning is highly inefficient. The evidence indicates that controlling inflation contributes substantially to industrial restructuring.[5] Countries that succeed in controlling inflation and restructuring industry, in turn, experience higher rates of growth.

Second, inflation undermines the confidence of international investors. Recent research shows that inflation significantly depresses capital flows to developing countries and leads to higher real interest rates.[6] International investment provides foreign exchange, technology transfers and management expertise. Foreign investment takes on critical significance for post-Communist countries, because it determines the success of privatization programs and represents the best hope for rapid industrial restructuring. In the most successful

[5]Berg 1994.
[6]Pindyck and Solimano 1993; Sobel 1997.

Central European countries, foreign direct investment has made a substantial contribution to export-led growth and has turned centrally planned dinosaurs into modern, competitive firms. In countries like Russia, on the other hand, potentially lucrative investments remained mired in political risk and economic uncertainty.[7]

Third, high inflation leads to a skewed distribution of wealth. The evidence for the post-Communist countries is striking, as Table 1.1 demonstrates. Econometric studies of developing countries have led to the same conclusion: High inflation leads to increased inequality.[8] This observation clashes with widespread assumptions about the distributional effects of inflation, but there is a good reason: These assumptions are largely based on the American experience in the nineteenth century, which was unique in important respects. The Left in America has long assumed that inflation was good for the poor and bad for the rich, because it deflates the real value of debt. Since the poor in America tended to be in debt and the rich tended to hold the debt, it was clear whose interests were served by a policy of tight money and a strong currency. In William Jennings Bryan's phrase, the common folk of America were being crucified on a "cross of gold." The Left understood its interests properly in nineteenth-century America; but the inflationary strategy of the Populists was only attractive because there were no low-cost alternatives to holding dollar-denominated assets, labor was virtually unable to engage in collective bargaining, and the government provided no transfer payments. Once the wealthy become able to shelter their assets from the inflation tax at low cost, it is no longer possible to use it to redistribute their wealth. Meanwhile, if labor has any bargaining power, inflation is disadvantageous because it shifts the status quo in favor of management. Nominal wage bargains become less valuable, and indexation becomes a concession that management makes grudgingly in return for something else of value. Finally, if government makes transfer payments, inflation erodes their value. Again, if policymaking is a bargaining process, inflation shifts the status quo away from the beneficiaries of transfer payments, who face dwindling real payments.

The transition countries are unusually prone to the inegalitarian effects of inflation, because the combination of inflation with far-reaching structural reform and political instability creates opportunities for nonproductive activities that generate a great deal of profit, usually at the expense of the state. For example, Russian banks made most of their profits in the early years of the transition by taking subsidized credits from the Central Bank of Russia, investing in foreign currency, and repaying the credits after the ruble fell.[9] Similarly, high rates of inflation and access to subsidized credits for the privileged

[7] Halligan and Teplukhin 1996; Watson 1996.
[8] Crisp and Kelly 1999.
[9] Åslund 1995; Treisman 1998.

few led to the pervasive pattern of manager ownership, frequently referred to as "*nomenklatura* privatization," that has tarnished the legitimacy of Russian reform. Although most of the shares in enterprises were distributed to their workers, managers ended up with controlling interests because they were able to buy up shares with cheap credits and repay the loans with deflated currency. Workers, on the other hand, had higher discount rates because they did not have access to subsidized credits, so they sold. While elites with political access make fortunes in inflationary times, ordinary citizens without access to arbitrage opportunities suffer from inflation because their savings are eroded and their wages and pensions fail to keep pace with rising prices.

In the post-Communist context, therefore, the first step toward establishing political legitimacy for reform is to slow inflation. The failure to restructure industry and attract foreign investment traps post-Communist countries in a spiral of economic decline, which poses severe challenges to the legitimacy of a democratic order. The corrosive influence of inequality is even more insidious. Economic reform always entails winners and losers, but at least rapid reform keeps the winnings and losses within bounds. An extended, inflationary transition transfers most of the dwindling wealth of society to a narrow and largely criminal elite that is closely linked to the government—a prospect profoundly disheartening to democrats.

1.2 WHAT WOULD WE LIKE THE IMF TO DO?

Inflation does not arise primarily because someone benefits from inflation per se; it arises primarily because politicians find it difficult to resist the short-term temptations that lead to inflation. The politicians who set monetary and fiscal policies face a commitment problem: *ex ante*, a policymaker prefers to be able to commit to an anti-inflationary policy for all future periods; yet, *ex post*, the policymaker prefers to renege.[10] Inflation rates depend on the expectations of private agents such as wage setters, investors, and currency traders, so the policymaker would like to be able to commit to an anti-inflationary strategy to reassure markets. The dilemma is that there are many temptations to renege on such commitments. Economic models often invoke the idea that "surprise" inflation has macroeconomic benefits, while political models point to imminent elections and the disproportionate power of narrow interests.[11] The temptation to pursue inflationary policies compels private agents to hedge their bets, driving the inflation rate higher than it would be were policymakers able to pursue a strategy of full commitment.

The consequence is that inconsistent authorities cast about for ways to tie their hands. The classic solution is to delegate monetary policy to an indepen-

[10]Kydland and Prescott 1977; Barro and Gordon 1983.
[11]Alesina and Perotti 1995; Alesina and Rosenthal 1995.

dent central bank, but this may not be feasible for countries still in the process of building democratic institutions. The same short-term considerations that drive politicians to promote inflationary policies will also compel them to undermine the independence of the central bank. In principle, however, the IMF can substitute for entrenched domestic institutions by monitoring compliance with stabilization programs and offering rewards and punishments that tip the balance of incentives in favor of the full-commitment equilibrium.[12]

International capital markets play a key role in enforcing the bargain. As the volume of international transactions increases, national governments become increasingly subject to the power of markets.[13] As barriers to capital flows fall, exit becomes less costly for private agents, and governments concerned about promoting welfare and productivity are compelled to provide more hospitable conditions for capital. The greater part of the IMF's leverage over borrowing countries arises, consequently, because it is able to coordinate the actions and expectations of the dispersed actors who comprise capital markets.[14] Investors can punish bad economic policies without coordination, simply by diving for cover. It is more difficult, however, for decentralized actors to reward good policies, because a sound investment climate is a state of mind that has to be painstakingly constructed. When the Fund negotiates a stabilization program with a government that imposes policy conditions, it creates a focal point for investors to coordinate their expectations. Investors benefit from following IMF signals, because the threat of IMF sanctions for noncompliance helps to protect the value of their investments. In return, the impact of the Fund's resources is vastly magnified by world capital markets, which are opened up by the IMF seal of approval. Under favorable circumstances, a virtuous circle can arise, in which IMF intervention, government policies, and international investment reinforce one another.

The picture becomes somewhat more complex, however, when we consider that the IMF's own credibility is in question. IMF lending decisions are not informative signals about the borrower's ability to repay, because they are not costly: The Fund does not have to worry about default.[15] Therefore, the IMF seal of approval is only valuable if conditionality is backed by rigorous enforcement. The IMF, however, is not an autonomous actor, analogous to an independent central bank. Rather, IMF policy is closely controlled by the Fund's board of directors, which is appointed by the donor countries. A coalition of a few large donors can set policy under the IMF system of weighted voting, and

---

[12]Dhonte 1997; Swoboda 1982; Jones 1987. Similarly, the European Monetary System (EMS) has been modeled as a means for low-credibility countries to borrow credibility for their macroeconomic policies from high-credibility countries. See Giavazzi and Pagano (1988).

[13]Cohen 1996; Keohane and Milner 1996.

[14]Lipson 1986.

[15]For a discussion of the complexity of official creditor seniority, see Bulow, Rogoff and Bevilaqua (1992).

all decisions about new agreements, loans and disbursements must be cleared by the board. Consequently, the autonomy of the IMF staff varies in inverse proportion to the international significance of the case at hand. The Fund has a relatively free hand in negotiating with small developing countries, but in important cases the interests of the donor governments dictate the negotiations.[16] International strategic concerns and trade policies frequently override the stabilization agenda.

A major objective of the research design described above is to address exactly this objection. Is it possible for an institution whose basic mission is compromised in this way to nevertheless exert a positive influence? How significant is the influence of noneconomic considerations on IMF lending decisions, and how strong are the effects of IMF intervention on government policies? Answers to each of these questions emerge from the formal model, the quantitative empirical analysis, and the detailed country studies and interviews with participants in the negotiations. The conclusions show that the IMF's credibility problem is indeed severe, and consequently the organization's effectiveness is compromised in some of the most important countries. At the same time, this study finds ample evidence that the IMF has exerted significant influence over the economic policies of post-Communist countries. This mixture of findings suggests a synthesis of perspectives on international relations that emphasize power and interests with those that emphasize the role of international institutions. The interests of powerful countries define the parameters within which the International Monetary Fund operates, and the limits of what it can achieve. The IMF is, after all, an international institution, not a supranational one. However, international institutions are not only instruments that powerful nations wield in order to obtain whatever objectives appear to be expedient; they are also strategic actors in their own right. Furthermore, even when the playing field is uneven and the rules are subject to manipulation, international institutions create incentives for countries to shape their national policies in accordance with international norms.

---

[16]I introduced a formal model based on this argument, and econometric tests using data from Russia, Poland, the Czech Republic, and Romania, in Stone (1997).

Part I

Models and Data

2

A Formal Model of Lending Credibility

THIS CHAPTER presents the main argument of the book in the form of a game-theoretic model. Game-theoretic modeling is a powerful tool, but it comes with a significant drawback: The predictions of a model are only as good as the assumptions that go into it. For example, the model can say nothing about whether the utility functions attributed to the players accurately reflect the values and priorities of real actors, or whether the parameters of the model accurately reflect the strategic situation they face. There are numerous, important questions about which game theory can tell us nothing at all. If its limitations are kept firmly in mind, however, game theory can help us to build more rigorous arguments than would otherwise be possible about a particular class of phenomena that play an important role in politics: strategic interactions. I develop a formal game-theoretic model because the strategic interaction between the IMF and borrowing countries is complex, and game theory is the most appropriate tool for analyzing the factors that are most important: credibility, market expectations, reputation, and information.

Formal theory must be empirically informed in order to be empirically relevant. While it is not technically feasible to model all the nuances of complex international interactions, I strive for a particular kind of realism: I seek to focus attention on the strategic variables that are empirically most important.[1] Consequently, my model is tested against extensive interviews with Russian, Ukrainian, Polish, and Bulgarian officials and their negotiating partners in the IMF. In a break with much work in formal theory, I consider it a valid criticism of my model if the strategies that it calls for do not seem realistic to the agents who would be required to implement them. Furthermore, I have worked

---

[1] Robert Powell describes this approach as a "modeling dialogue," in which the analyst uses contextual knowledge to improve models to better reflect empirical situations. The problem, of course, is circularity: If the data go into the model, they cannot be used to test it. The only solution is out-of-sample testing. In the case of this project, the key features of the model were derived from a case study of Russian relations with the IMF from 1992 to 1996 (Stone 1999). The portion of my Russian case study based on interviews conducted through 1997, therefore, can only be regarded as an illustration of the theory, not a test. The next four years in Russia, the other case studies and the quantitative tests, on the other hand, are out-of-sample tests of the model's predictions.

to build a realistic model in order to make possible more powerful empirical tests. For example, it is essential that the model capture the facts that cheating occurs under IMF programs, that IMF officials anticipate cheating when they design these programs, and that international capital markets anticipate cheating when they react to them. This makes it possible for the model to make empirically testable predictions about levels of inflation, international capital flows, and the conditions under which the IMF will suspend lending.

The following features of the strategic situation are built into the model:

1. *Dynamic inconsistency.* Economic policymakers in a variety of contexts suffer from commitment problems, or from dynamic inconsistency, as the phenomenon is called in the macroeconomic literature.[2] *Ex ante,* a policymaker would like to be able to commit to a goal of low inflation in order to attract foreign investment and forestall a spiral of self-fulfilling inflationary expectations; *ex post,* however, having reaped the benefits of noninflationary expectations, the policymaker prefers to exercise discretion. The basic problem in this model is that the government faces a temptation to throw sound economic policy to the winds for short-term political gain, and the IMF must somehow persuade it not to do so. If this temptation were a constant parameter, however, we would not observe both compliance and defection. Furthermore, the empirical stories we tell about particular countries generally dwell on the transient elements that intensified or relaxed political constraints at key junctures. Consequently, the model treats the temptation to defect as a random variable. This makes it possible for a government to negotiate a program in good faith that it subsequently proves to be unwilling to carry out. I found a few cases in my country studies in which governments negotiated with the IMF in bad faith, but it was much more common for countries to defect because political constraints had changed in ways they had not foreseen. Furthermore, I treat the realization of the countries' temptation parameters each period as private information. This reflects the fact that governments know their own assessments of how likely they are to fall, to win reelection, or to pass key pieces of legislation, whereas the IMF and the market can only guess.

2. *Partisanship.* The strategic literature in macroeconomics focuses attention on an exogenously given trade-off between inflation and output.[3]

---

[2] Kydland and Prescott 1977; Barro and Gordon 1983.

[3] Perfectly anticipated inflation cannot increase output, since wages and prices will be set to counteract its real effects. To get around this problem, these models incorporate an element of "surprise." If wages are inflexible in the short run, a surprise burst of inflation will depress real wages, increasing output. In the long run, wages adjust to the new equilibrium price level, and output gains evaporate. However, as Lord Meynard Keynes famously remarked, "In the long run, we're all dead." As long as the benefits are high enough in the short run, there is a temptation to pursue inflationary policies.

Thus, we have Rogoff's (1985) famous result that delegating macro-economic policy to a known conservative may have welfare-enhancing consequences, and Alesina's (1987) result that partisan competition can lead to political budget cycles, because left- and right-wing governments make these trade-offs differently. Partisanship is a natural way of interpreting this trade-off, since the immediate distributional costs of inflation and recession are borne disproportionately by different social groups, and these groups typically organize politically to defend their interests. Recent research has provided strong evidence that the partisan effect remains potent in advanced economies in spite of the forces of globalization and interdependence that were once expected to overwhelm it.[4] There is every reason to expect that partisan effects will be stronger in the post-Communist countries, since economic stabilization and reform are more salient issues there than in the stable polities and economies of the advanced industrial countries.

3. *The shadow of the market.* The countries that borrow from the IMF are already constrained by the reactions of market actors to their policies.[5] Indeed, to the extent that the Fund is able to exercise influence at all, it is by leveraging its own resources with the much greater economic impact of decentralized economic agents. Consequently, the game in which the Fund interacts with sovereign borrowers has to be nested in a game in which those borrowers interact with a market. However, I chose not to model the situation as a signaling game, where investors would follow IMF signals because the IMF had an information advantage over markets. First, I do not think it is empirically true that the IMF has an important information advantage. Market participants have stronger incentives and greater capacity than the IMF to gather the relevant information, and although governments provide the IMF with a great deal of privileged information, they have obvious incentives to distort it. Furthermore, the IMF reacts slowly to economic data, and market participants react much more rapidly. Second, there is a more important dynamic at work in the relationship between the Fund and the market that would be obscured by modeling it as a signaling game. Consequently, I build a model that shows that markets follow the IMF even under the pessimistic assumption that the Fund has no information advantage.

4. *The IMF's credibility problem.* The model assumes that the IMF bears a cost when it withdraws financial support from a country that has failed to fulfill the conditions of its program. This is intended to represent the influence over IMF decision making of the donor countries, which

---

[4] Alesina, Roubini and Cohen 1997; Garrett 1998; Franzese 2002.
[5] Cohen 1996.

frequently intervene to urge the Fund to be lenient toward their favored clients. As a result of this assumption, the Fund faces a political incentive to be lenient in the model, which makes it difficult to enforce conditionality agreements. A study of seventeen developing countries concludes that,

> In its worst forms, such political interference forces the Fund to provide essentially unconditional finance to governments with proven records of economic mismanagement. This undermines the legitimacy and credibility of the Fund, and was among the most important reasons for programme ineffectiveness.[6]

It may at first seem odd to model the IMF as a bank that prefers to lend to countries that are bad credit risks, but the reader must recall that the IMF does not face any of the incentives of a commercial bank. It need not show a profit, and the value of its loan portfolio is immaterial. The Fund has the functions and interests of a central bank: Its objectives are to manage global liquidity and prevent local financial instability, which in the global economy takes the form of inflation and exchange rate crises. Its resources are determined by its board of directors, and, in principle, they are as unlimited as those of any central bank: it can create international currency (special drawing rights, or SDRs), and it can borrow from the world's central banks whatever its members determine to be appropriate. Like any central bank, the IMF comes under continual pressure to bail out insolvent clients, and withholding financing during a crisis is analogous to a central bank allowing a commercial bank to fail. The difference is that the IMF's clients are national governments and central banks rather than commercial banks, so the pressure takes the form of high foreign policy.

5. *Reputation.* In spite of the incentive to relent, the IMF is able to build a reputation for punishing, because it values the future cooperation that it expects this strategy to elicit from borrowers. In order to capture this effect, I model the interaction as an infinitely repeated game.

6. *Precedent.* As a commitment device, the IMF attempts to assure that countries are treated according to standard procedures, which minimizes its discretion in particular cases. Fund negotiators frequently refer to the precedents that particular concessions would establish for their relations with third countries.[7] Consequently, I model the Fund's simultaneous in-

---

[6] Killick and Malik 1992, p. 629.

[7] Interviews with Ernesto Hernandez-Cata, February 17, 1999; Yosuke Horiguchi, November 8, 1999; Mark Allen, February 19, 1999; Mohammed Shadman-Valavi, May 4, 2000; Anne McGuirk, May 3, 2000; Marcus Rodlauer, June 23, 1997; and Peter Stella, May 12, 1999.

teraction with *n* borrowers, and I study an equilibrium in which a failure to maintain the Fund's reputation in a particular case causes a general breakdown of cooperation. The Fund's reputational strategy with any particular country is only sustainable because of the linkage to simultaneous games with all the others.

7. *All countries are not created equal.* Although standard procedures are desirable, it is not credible to apply them equally across the board. Countries that play a prominent role in U.S. foreign policy tend to escape the rigors of IMF enforcement. Examples include Russia under Yeltsin, Mexico after the North American Free Trade Agreement (NAFTA), and Zaire and the Philippines during the Cold War. I capture this in the model by attaching different weights to different countries, so that the IMF's comparison of present incentives for leniency and future benefits of stringent enforcement varies across countries. If a country has a large weight it is more costly to punish (i.e., withhold committed financing), so the strategy of defending the Fund's reputation may not be sustainable. I find an equilibrium in which countries of different sizes are subject to different enforcement schemes. "Russia gets a discount," a Ukrainian National Bank official assured me.[8] Bulgarian officials protested on several occasions, "Well, Bulgaria is not Russia!"[9]

Decision makers and analysts alike have often assumed that reputations depend on consistent treatment of dissimilar cases: For example, several U.S. administrations felt compelled to confront Communist guerrillas in Vietnam in order to signal U.S. resolve in Europe. Similarly, game-theoretic models typically assume that all players are treated equally, because this is an assumption that significantly simplifies the analysis. There is nothing inherent in game theory that requires equal treatment, however, so long as it is reasonable to assume that all the players know the rules for making distinctions. Reputations can be built around dissimilar treatment of dissimilar cases, and the strategies that result suffer from fewer credibility problems. As long as Bulgarians and Poles know that they cannot get away with behaving like Russians, they can be deterred regardless of what concessions the IMF makes to Russia.

8. *Macroeconomic policy is path-dependent.* IMF negotiators plan in terms of projected paths for macroeconomic aggregates, because the current level and velocity of those aggregates severely constrain the set of feasible policy scenarios. From an econometric perspective, there is autocorrelation in inflation and exchange rate data. From a strategic perspective, path dependence poses painful dilemmas. As a government deviates

---

[8] Interview with Oleg Rybachuk, July 3, 1998.
[9] Interview with Dimitar Popov, May 11, 1999; interview with Martin Zaimov, May 15, 1999.

from its targets, those targets become increasingly unrealistic because the future policy corrections required to reach them become more and more draconian. Should the Fund stay the course and insist on the fulfillment of increasingly irrelevant targets, thereby guaranteeing that the government will find its program too risky to adhere to? Or should it water down its program targets when they are not met, creating a perverse moral hazard? From a government's perspective, it becomes more difficult to meet future targets after the first deviation, so the balance of incentives shifts away from compliance. At the same time, since market participants are rational and anticipate the inertia that drives macroeconomic aggregates, increasingly higher levels of inflation are required to produce the same temporary rise in living standards. Thus, the first deviation is likely to lead to further deviations that fuel the inflationary spiral. Eventually, at the top of the spiral, the costs of hyperinflation become obvious to partisans of every stripe, and a period of restraint gradually brings inflation down. Lower levels of inflation, however, restore the incentives to surprise the market and bring renewed vulnerability to an inflationary spiral. In the model this roller coaster of surging and receding inflation is produced by a moving-average process that affects inflation, the assumption that the cost of inflation rises faster as inflation rises, and rational expectations. The roller coaster itself is an empirical observation: Many post-Communist countries have approached stabilization after several disastrous flirtations with hyperinflation, and it is rarely the first IMF program that succeeds in stabilizing an economy.

I capture these features in a game-theoretic model, which is presented formally in an appendix at the end of this chapter. The assumptions, logic, and results of the model are described here in more accessible terms. Readers who prefer a formal presentation, which is more precise, may prefer to read the appendix first. Other readers may question why a formal model is necessary at all, if it is possible to present the argument in plain English. There are two reasons. First, the plain English version does not give the reader any way to assess the truth of the claim that the conclusions follow from the assumptions. Convincing arguments are often false. If a formal argument is false, however, it can be disproved. Powell (1999) expresses this with an apt phrase: Formal modeling imposes "accounting standards" for arguments, making them more transparent and vulnerable to criticism.[10] Second, the process of solving a formal model often leads to insights and hypotheses that were not anticipated beforehand. This is certainly the case here, as I point out below.

---

[10]Mathematical symbols can obfuscate as well as clarify, however, which is why I chose to present the argument here in more straightforward terms.

2.1 THE MODEL

The players are the IMF, a number of borrowing countries that vary in size, and a large number of small foreign investors. The game is infinitely repeated. In each period the investors decide whether to invest, each government chooses an inflationary or anti-inflationary policy, and the IMF disburses or withholds an installment of a loan to each country, called a *tranche*. The funds become available in the next period.

Foreign Investors. Investors who choose to invest make profits when the government chooses an anti-inflationary policy and take losses when the government chooses an inflationary policy. I assume that the international market for capital is in equilibrium, so the rate of return to investment exactly compensates the investors for the risks they take in each market. Consequently, each foreign investor is indifferent as to where to invest, so long as the risks do not change. In equilibrium, the rate of return depends on the long-run probability that the government chooses inflationary policies. Events that increase the probability that the government defects in the short run cause investors to withdraw from the market.

The Governments. Each country's government has negotiated a macroeconomic stabilization program with the IMF, which commits it to abstain from a particular inflationary policy. The government is tempted to violate the agreement: It receives a lump-sum benefit each time it chooses to defect, and the size of this benefit varies from period to period. This reflects the fact that a government can never know, when it signs an agreement, exactly what political constraints it will face in the future. On the other hand, the inflation that results from these policies is costly, and the government benefits from foreign investment and IMF financing. The size of each government's benefit from inflationary policies in any given period—its temptation—is private information. Thus, the other actors can only make their strategies depend on the governments' policies, which they observe, and not on the governments' levels of temptation, which they do not.

The IMF. Two factors affect the IMF's utility in this model: The Fund dislikes inflation, and it finds it costly to punish countries by withholding financing. The IMF puts a weight on each country, which corresponds to its political influence and strategic importance. The intuition behind this is that it is more costly to deny financing to countries that figure prominently in the foreign policy priorities of the IMF's most important members. By the same token, however, financial instability is more costly when it occurs in very important countries. As a result, the IMF faces conflicting incentives in dealing with large countries, and I capture this by applying a country's weight to the IMF's disutility from inflation as well as to its utility of lending.

Figure 2.1 summarizes the sequence of events that occur in each period. This is a game of incomplete information, since governments know exactly

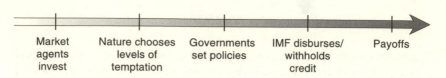

Figure 2.1: The Stage Game.

what political constraints they believe they face, whereas markets and the IMF can only guess (i.e., the realizations of the governments' variable temptation parameters in each period are private information). Foreign investors move first, deciding whether to invest in each country, so they cannot rely on any current-period signals from the IMF to build their strategies. The governments move next, after learning their levels of temptation, and thus are able to catch investors by surprise. This ability to surprise market agents who have already committed themselves is central to most stories about how governments can benefit from inflationary policies by seigniorage (revenue from creating money, which acts as an inflation tax on money balances and other nominal assets) or by using short-term labor market rigidity to exploit a Phillips curve (lowering real wages in order to expand employment and output). These strategies would not work if they were not surprises, because wages and assets would already be indexed and hedged. The IMF moves last, but its decisions do not take effect (money is not disbursed) until the following period. This reflects the fact that the IMF follows rather complex bureaucratic procedures and consequently does not react quickly to punish defection.[11]

2.2 THE EQUILIBRIUM

As is the case in infinitely repeated games generally, this model has multiple equilibria.[12] Thus, deciding which equilibrium to study is a modeling choice as important as setting the model's parameters and the sequence of actions. Since my objective is to design a theory that can be tested empirically, these choices are critical. The equilibrium that I study subsumes a large class of similar equilibria that would generate very similar predictions; nevertheless, important choices had to be made. My approach to this problem is to regard institutions as equilibria, and institutional details—standard operating procedures, norms, and rules—as the equilibrium expectations that support them. Since I am studying a concrete institution, the International Monetary Fund, the appropriate way to select an equilibrium for the game is to choose equilibrium expectations that conform closely to the Fund's own procedures. Viewed

---

[11]Interview with Shadman-Valavi, May 4, 2000. Mr. Shadman-Valavi was head of the IMF Mission to Ukraine 1997-2000.

[12]Fudenberg and Levine 1989; Fudenberg and Tirole 1991.

in this way, the "multiple-equilibria problem"multiple equilibria is not an obstacle that prevents the theory from generating testable hypotheses but, rather, an opportunity to incorporate some of our empirical knowledge into the theory to generate better hypotheses. For example, the IMF practice is not to impose punishment periods of any particular length on countries that violate their conditions; instead, its rule is to suspend financing until the country brings its policies back on track, ordinarily requiring them to meet the original conditions set forth in the memorandum of understanding that the government signed when it agreed to the program. When the IMF makes exceptions, it does so by allowing the country to resume borrowing after improving its policies and renegotiating its targets, without necessarily achieving the original ones. I incorporate this practice into the model not as a constraint but as an equilibrium expectation.

I find a perfect Bayesian Nash equilibrium (PBE), which means that in this equilibrium the actors are permitted to use only credible strategies and to hold only rational beliefs.[13] Credibility means that if the actors are ever called on to implement their strategies, they must find it in their interest to do so. Furthermore, they must not prefer to deviate from them under any possible circumstances, including circumstances that should never arise in equilibrium. In such an equilibrium, any incredible threats or promises that one of the actors might choose to make would simply be ignored; everyone assumes that everyone else will simply act in accordance with his or her own interests as they appear at the time. For example, in this model the IMF cannot credibly threaten to punish for eternity any country that fails to fulfill its commitments, because it would never be willing to implement such a threat if an important country defected. Consequently, no country would believe such a threat, so no one would be deterred by it. Similarly, in this model no country can credibly promise never to deviate from its program targets, since it might at any time draw such a high level of temptation that defection would be optimal regardless of the long-term consequences. In this equilibrium, therefore, governments defect whenever the temptation exceeds a critical value that depends on the IMF's strategy.

The critical value for defection depends on whether the government in question defected in the previous period. A government that defected last period knows that it will not receive capital inflows next period, irrespective of its policy choice this period, so the benefits of exercising restraint are deferred and therefore less valuable. Since its incentive to abide by its program commitments is lower, the threshold value is lower and the probability that the randomly drawn temptation parameter is high enough to lead it to defect is higher. On the other hand, defecting last period increases inflation next period. Since I assume that the cost of inflation rises more rapidly as the infla-

---

[13] Perfect Bayesian equilibrium requires that the players' strategies form a Nash equilibrium whenever they must make a decision, on or off the equilibrium path, and that their expectations and beliefs be consistent, using Bayes' Rule whenever it applies, on the equilibrium path. There are no restrictions on beliefs off the equilibrium path.

tion rate increases, this means that last period's inflationary policies make it more costly to choose inflationary policies in the future.[14] This effect mitigates the previous one to some degree. In a more general model the inflation rate could be generated by an autoregressive process rather than a one-period moving average. In other words, the effect of an inflationary policy in any given period would gradually die away, but the effects of inflationary policies chosen successively would accumulate indefinitely. In that case the mounting costs of inflation would eventually become so great that the balance of incentives would swing back toward macroeconomic restraint, and the government would be compelled to change course.[15]

Since governments cannot keep a promise not to defect, investors will never believe such a promise and will only invest if they are compensated for the risk of doing business in a country whose government may choose inflationary policies. I assume that, in the long run, real returns on investment adjust so that investors are indifferent as to where they invest. In practice, this means that the return is set precisely to offset the risk that a country that has not defected in the previous period defects in the current one. Investors observe each country's behavior in the prior two periods and invest in those that have not defected. If the country defected in the previous period, it is more likely to defect in the current period, and therefore the return to investment is no longer high enough to compensate for the risk. Therefore investors strictly prefer not to invest.[16] If the country defected in the period before last, but not in the last period, investors are indifferent. In this equilibrium, investors choose not to invest in this case. In effect, they require governments that have deviated from their programs to prove their dedication to sound macroeconomic policy

---

[14]To be precise, I assume that the cost of inflation is proportional to inflation squared. I chose a quadratic function because it is easy to work with, but any function that makes the cost of inflation rise more rapidly as inflation increases would generate the same results.

[15]I do not attempt to solve such a model. It is considerably more complex than the model I solve in the appendix, because there are many more possible states of the world. However, the model that I solve is a limiting case of such a model in the same sense that a one-period moving average is a limiting case of an autoregressive process: The effects of all lags of inflation except the first are assumed to be 0. A simple thought experiment suggests that in a more general model that allowed some of these lags to exert an influence on inflation, the incentive to defect would gradually decrease after successive defections. After the first defection, the inflationary cost of the next defection would be exactly as it is in the current model. After the second, the inflation rate would be somewhat higher, raising the cost. After three successive defections, it would be higher still. Provided that the effect of lagged inflation were great enough, the mounting cost of inflation would eventually overwhelm the incentives to defect.

[16]Note that this has the character of a self-fulfilling prophecy: Investors withdraw because governments are more likely to defect, and governments are more likely to defect because investors are expected to withdraw. In a sense, game theoretic arguments are circular because, in a Nash equilibrium, everyone's actions depend on everyone else's. One might wonder why the government and the investors cannot collude to break out of the vicious cycle. Since other equilibria exist, the best answer is that this is an empirical question. Investment climates and pyramid schemes are built on mutually reinforcing expectations, and those expectations can be very persistent.

by cooperating twice before they will take the risk of returning to the market. This is a realistic equilibrium expectation to adopt, since it reflects the fact that investors move into new markets cautiously, so a favorable investment climate takes time to produce investment. Furthermore, this additional delay is a substantively desirable feature of the model, since it simulates factors that were left out of the model in order to make it tractable. For example, if government policies were observed gradually, or were observed with uncertainty, delays of this sort would arise because investors would strictly prefer not to invest. Some delay is necessary in the model in order to support the equilibrium; I chose a one-period delay because it is the easiest to work with.

The IMF does not treat all borrowers consistently in this equilibrium: It uses two different punishment schedules. For less important countries it uses a regime that I call *hold the line*: It withholds financing if the government has defected from its program, and it does not resume financing until the country has achieved its original program target—that is, until the country has gotten itself back "on track" by its own efforts. In this model it is impossible for the government to achieve its original target this period if it defected last period, and the fact that it defected last period increases the incentive for the government to defect again. Consequently, when the Fund insists that a country achieve its original target before resuming financing, it consigns the country to a punishment interval that may be quite lengthy. Under the assumptions of the model, it lasts at least two periods and ends after the government has cooperated twice in succession.

It would not be credible to threaten to apply the *hold-the-line* regime to the most important countries. The reason is that the cost of punishment is all concentrated on the IMF's utility vis-à-vis the defecting country, but the cost of failing to punish affects the IMF's utility vis-à-vis all countries, because the IMF loses its reputation with all of them if it fails to carry out a punishment that its strategy requires. Thus, the cost of punishment is greater when the country in question is more important, while the cost of failing to punish remains constant. Beyond some threshold size, the cost of punishment multiplied by the importance of the country exceeds the total discounted benefits of maintaining a reputation. Consequently, the IMF applies a regime to important countries that is less exacting and is therefore possible to credibly enforce. I call this regime *tit for tat*. Instead of demanding that they return to their original targets by cooperating twice in succession, the Fund requires that they cooperate only once in order to become eligible to receive financing. In effect, it revises their short-term policy targets in return for a policy improvement. This regime also calls for indefinite periods in which countries may not be eligible for financing, since governments may defect repeatedly, but it imposes much lower expected costs on both the IMF and the government involved.

Since the punishment interval is shorter under *tit for tat* than under *hold the line,* governments are more tempted to defect, and as a result they defect more often. Thus, the model predicts that average inflation rates should be higher in countries that are more important, and foreign investment should be lower. In addition, the model predicts that since these countries defect from their agreements more often, all else being equal, they should be punished more often. However, they should be punished for shorter periods on average. Since the probability of defection is higher under the *tit-for-tat* regime, equilibrium interest rates will be higher in more important countries to compensate for the increased risk.

2.3 HYPOTHESES DERIVED FROM THE FORMAL MODEL

The model generates hypotheses about the behavior of three kinds of actors. The first set of hypotheses concerns the IMF's strategies. The Fund is expected to punish smaller, less important countries for longer periods than larger ones. On the other hand, larger countries should be subjected to punishment episodes more frequently, because they violate their agreements more often. For example, Russia has had its IMF loans suspended repeatedly but never for long, and the IMF has often had to scale back the conditions attached to its programs in order to reach an agreement to reestablish Russia's credit line.

The second set of hypotheses concerns the countries' strategies. First, IMF intervention should make a difference in countries' economic policies. Whenever the enforcement of an IMF conditionality program is at issue or the negotiation of such an agreement is possible and desirable—regardless of whether a program is currently in force—policies should be less inflationary on average. Second, the effect of IMF intervention should depend on the credibility of IMF threats to withhold financing in particular countries at particular times: The more credible, the greater the effect. Third, countries that have defected recently should be more prone to defect again, because capital markets and the IMF will only resume lending after some delay even if they exercise restraint. Countries in good standing with the Fund and the market are less likely to defect because they have more to lose. Fourth, the difference in policy between punishment periods and periods of good standing is greater for smaller, less influential countries. Smaller countries' policies deteriorate more when their programs are suspended because they have to wait longer for lending to resume, and consequently their incentives to comply are reduced more. Larger countries' policies improve less when their programs are in good standing, because they gain less credibility from good standing and therefore have less to lose when they defect.

The third set of hypotheses concerns the expectations of actors in capital markets. Capital markets are expected to respond to IMF signals. Thus, when a country becomes eligible to receive IMF financing, and therefore subject to the incentives the IMF provides to its members, the market should expect better policy, and this should be reflected in more stable exchange rates, capital inflows, and less capital flight. In addition, participants in capital markets are expected to form rational expectations about the probability that the IMF will suspend disbursements of loans, so these expectations should affect capital flows and the price of foreign currency. The more credible the IMF commitment to enforce conditionality, the stronger capital inflows and the national currency should be. Furthermore, capital markets are sophisticated about the incentives for repeat defection and the effects of the IMF's credibility on those incentives, so capital movements should anticipate them. Therefore, the capital account should deteriorate when a country's program is suspended; but this effect should be markedly less pronounced in the most influential countries.

2.4 CONCLUSIONS

In this model, governments are sometimes deterred from defecting, but still defect when the variable component of their temptation parameter is high enough. The IMF invests in its reputation by punishing countries that defect, but has different punishment schedules for different countries. The IMF does not have an information advantage over the market, and market agents are sophisticated about the Fund's credibility problems, but the market still responds to IMF strategies. Indeed, the fact that market participants condition their strategies on the IMF's behavior strengthens governments' incentives to cooperate with the Fund. The most striking findings of the model are that countries can indeed benefit from building a reputation for complying even though they often cheat, and that the IMF can indeed enforce cooperation without knowing anything that everyone else does not know, and despite the fact that it consistently favors some countries over others.

Several predictions of the model are quite counterintuitive. It is not surprising that countries that are more costly to punish are subject to shorter punishment periods. It is surprising, however, that the IMF is expected to punish more important countries more often than less important ones, *ceteris paribus*. Given the argument that the Fund finds it more costly to punish more important countries, one might naturally suppose the opposite, that it would punish more important countries less frequently. This is a case where formalizing the argument allows us to learn something important. I find that the constraint on punishment is not the average cost of withholding financing, but the credibility of threats to enforce long punishments on large countries. Thus, randomizing and punishing larger countries with a lower probability would not solve the problem, because whenever a costly punishment had to be meted out, the IMF would renege. Therefore, the IMF must resort to a shorter punishment regime for more important countries.[17] Given the shorter punishment regime, gov-

---

[17]Models of deterrence (Powell 1987) avoid this problem by assuming that the decision maker can credibly delegate its final decision to a random process, for example, by escalating a crisis in

ernments are more likely to defect, and be punished—for a short time—as a result.

Similarly, it is not obvious that the incentive to defect is greater for countries that have already defected in the recent past. Furthermore, although one might anticipate the model's expectation that countries that are difficult to punish are likely to have higher inflation, it is not obvious that small countries' policies will deteriorate more when their programs are suspended. Again, these expectations are plausible when they are explained, but they emerge from the complex strategic interaction in the model. Without the model, it is unlikely that it would have occurred to anyone to test them.

Several testable propositions emerge from the model, regarding the choices of the IMF, borrowing countries, and international investors. The chapters that follow test these hypotheses using quantitative analysis and detailed case studies.

---

a way that increases a risk that "things will get out of control." This would not be a reasonable assumption in the case of the IMF. If there were any way for the Fund to delegate its decision to an impartial process, it would not have a credibility problem.

Appendix
A Formal Model of Lending Credibility

THE MODEL

The players are the IMF, the governments of countries, i, $(i = 1, 2, \ldots, n)$, and a large number of small foreign investors. The game is an infinitely repeated game of incomplete information, and the private information in the game concerns one parameter of the governments' utility function. The actions available to the players are as follows: the IMF disburses or does not disburse a loan tranche to each country, $S_i = \{s, 0\}$, where $s \in (0, 1)$; the investors decide whether to invest, $K_i = \{k, 0\}$, where $k \in (0, 1)$; and each government chooses a macroeconomic policy, $X_i = \{x, 0\}$, where $x \in (0, 1)$.

The stage game is as follows. First, the investors choose whether to invest. Second, the countries observe their private information and simultaneously choose their policies. Third, the IMF observes the policies of the n countries in a randomized sequence, and decides whether to disburse funds. The funds become available in the next period.

The Investors

The international capital market is in equilibrium, so the return to investment exactly equals the risks in every market. Investors are risk neutral, so they are indifferent as to where to invest. If investors invest and there is no inflation, they receive r, the nominal interest rate. If investors choose to invest and there is inflation, they receive a payoff of -1, and if investors choose not to invest, they receive a payoff of 0. The condition that investors are indifferent implies that r is the market-clearing rate:

$$r = \frac{1 - b^*}{b^*}$$

where b^* is the equilibrium probability that the government chooses a noninflationary policy. I assume that r does not adjust in the short run in response to government policies, but adjusts instantaneously in response to a change in the IMF's strategy (i.e., assessments of individual country risks adjust slowly, but adjustment to systemic changes in the global economy is rapid).

The Governments

Each government has a policy instrument, X, which can create a spurt of inflation. In each period, t, it chooses $x_{i,t} \in X$. Inflation, π, is a first-order moving average process with $\rho \in [0, 1]$:

$$\pi_{i,t} = x_{i,t} + \rho x_{i,t-1}$$

Governments receive disutility from inflation but benefit by using their policy instrument. They also benefit from capital inflows and from receiving IMF funding. Each government's per-period payoff is

$$u_i = \begin{cases} -\alpha \pi_i^2 + k + s & \text{if } x_i = 0 \\ -\alpha \pi_i^2 + b_i + k + s & \text{if } x_i = x \end{cases}$$

The parameter b_i, which determines a government's temptation to inflate the economy, is an iid random variable drawn for each country each period from a uniform distribution on $[0, 1]$ and is private information to the government. The parameter $\alpha \in [0, 1]$ is the disutility from inflation multiplier. Each government maximizes its discounted stream of payoffs using a common discount factor $\delta \in (0, 1)$.

The IMF

The IMF can disburse or withhold a loan tranche. It receives disutility from inflation and utility from disbursing funds, ψ. For each country, $\psi_i = \omega$ if the IMF disburses funds, and 0 otherwise, where $\omega \in (0, 1]$. It assigns weight, $\lambda_i \in [0, 1]$, to each country, i, such that $\sum_{i=1}^{n} \lambda_i = 1$. The IMF's per-period payoff is

$$u_{\text{IMF}} = \sum_{i=1}^{n} \lambda_i (\psi_i - \pi_i^2) \tag{2.1}$$

and the IMF maximizes its intertemporal sum of payoffs using the common discount factor δ.

EQUILIBRIUM ANALYSIS

Consider three types of IMF punishment strategies: (i) *unconditional lending* (UNC), where it provides financing irrespective of the government's policy; (ii) *tit for tat* (TFT), where it withholds financing for one period after every deviation from the anti-inflationary policy; and (iii) *hold the line* (HTL), where it disburses financing to every government that has achieved zero inflation in the current period and withholds financing from any government with positive inflation.

Furthermore, assume $k - 2\alpha\rho x^2 > 0$. Recall that k is capital investment, and the other term is the interaction between the disutility of the inflation caused by current policy and that caused by last period's policy. The substantive significance of this assumption is that all the countries in the model are significantly dependent on foreign capital flows.[18]

Also, assume that the IMF's payoff from punishing defectors under the HTL regime is strictly lower than the payoff in the TFT regime, which itself is strictly lower than the payoff in the UNC regime.[19] If the condition did not hold, the IMF would never be tempted to be lenient. This assumption limits the rest of this discussion to cases in which the IMF has a credibility problem.

Proposition 2.1. *The following strategies form a perfect Bayesian equilibrium. Each country i plays according to three regimes, depending on λ_i. For every country i and any period t, investors invest k if $\pi_{i,t-1} = 0$, and 0 otherwise. The IMF disburses s if $\pi_{i,t} = 0$, and otherwise responds according to the three regimes:*

1. *If $\lambda_i > \lambda^*$, the IMF plays UNC. If the government complied in the previous period, it defects if $b_i \geq b^*_{UNC}$, and if it defected in the previous period, it defects if $b_i \geq b^{**}_{UNC}$;*

2. *If $\lambda^{**} \leq \lambda_i \leq \lambda^*$, the IMF plays TFT. If the government complied in the previous period, it defects if $b_i \geq b^*_{TFT}$, and if it defected in the previous period, it defects if $b_i \geq b^{**}_{TFT}$;*

3. *If $\lambda_i < \lambda^{**}$, the IMF plays HTL. If the government complied in the previous period, it defects if $b_i \geq b^*_{HTL}$, and if it defected in the previous period, it defects if $b_i \geq b^{**}_{HTL}$,*

where

$$b^*_{UNC} = E/F \qquad\qquad b^{**}_{UNC} = b^*_{UNC} + G$$
$$b^*_{TFT} = E/F + (2\delta s)/F \qquad\qquad b^{**}_{TFT} = b^*_{TFT} + G$$
$$b^*_{HTL} = E/F + \frac{2\delta s - 2\delta^3 k s - \delta^3 s^2}{F - 2\delta^2 s} \qquad\qquad b^{**}_{HTL} = b^*_{HTL} + G - \delta s$$

[18] In a richer model, where inflation was generated by an autoregressive process instead of a one-period moving average process, these interaction terms would accumulate as the government continued to defect in successive periods, until eventually the rising cost of inflation created incentives to exercise restraint that exceeded the incentives facing countries that had cooperated from the outset. In such a model, the probability of defection would initially increase after the first defection, and then gradually decrease as inflation rose. I use the moving-average assumption, however, because it simplifies the solution for an equilibrium.

[19] This assumption is formally stated in (2.9), and holds for sufficiently high values of s and sufficiently low values of δ. In other words, it is a restriction on the values of the exogenous variables. Substantively, it means that it is more costly to punish a country for a long period than for a short period, in spite of the fact that longer punishments imply lower inflation.

with

$$E = 2\alpha x^2 + 2\delta k - \delta^3 k^2 + 2\delta \alpha \rho x^2 (2 + \rho - G + \delta k)$$
$$F = 2(1 + \delta G)$$
$$G = 2\alpha \rho x^2 - \delta k$$

and where λ^*, λ^{**} are as defined in (2.12) and (2.13). If the IMF ever deviates from its equilibrium strategy, investors and governments expect it to stop defending its reputation and play UNC thereafter.

Proof. Note that, given the assumptions, $G \in (-1, 0)$, $F \in (0, 2)$, and $E \geq 1$. I shall prove the claim by construction. Consider first the government strategy at some arbitrary time t. Each country i falls into one of the three regimes, depending on λ_i. I shall examine the strategy for each regime in turn. Let $\iota \in \{\text{UNC,TFT,HTL}\}$ be an indicator of the regime for country i and define six value functions. Let V_ι be the present discounted value of i's payoffs given that it cooperated in the current period and inflation was zero; and let W_ι be the present discounted value of i's payoffs given that it defected in the current period. In the following text the subscripts i and t are omitted for clarity.

Case 1

$\lambda > \lambda^*$, in which case the IMF plays UNC. If the government has not defected in $t - 1$, then it defects in t if

$$-\alpha x^2 + b + k + s + \delta W_{\text{UNC}} > k + s + \delta V_{\text{UNC}}$$

or if

$$b > \alpha x^2 + \delta(V_{\text{UNC}} - W_{\text{UNC}}) \equiv b_{\text{UNC}}^* \tag{2.2}$$

On the other hand, if the government has defected in $t - 1$, then it defects in t if

$$-\alpha(\rho x + x)^2 + b + s + \delta W_{\text{UNC}} > -\alpha \rho^2 x^2 + s - \delta k + \delta V_{\text{UNC}}$$

or if

$$b > 2\alpha \rho x^2 + \alpha x^2 + \delta(V_{\text{UNC}} - W_{\text{UNC}}) - \delta k \equiv b_{\text{UNC}}^{**} \tag{2.3}$$

Since $k > 2\alpha \rho x^2$ by assumption, it follows that for sufficiently high δ, $\delta k > 2\alpha \rho x^2$ also, which implies $b_{\text{UNC}}^* > b_{\text{UNC}}^{**}$. We now have

$$V_{\text{UNC}} = k + s + b_{\text{UNC}}^* \delta V_{\text{UNC}} + (1 - b_{\text{UNC}}^*)\left(-\alpha x^2 + \frac{1 + b_{\text{UNC}}^*}{2} + \delta W_{\text{UNC}}\right)$$
$$= \frac{1}{1 - \delta b_{\text{UNC}}^*}\left[k + s + (1 - b_{\text{UNC}}^*)\left(-\alpha x^2 + \frac{1 + b_{\text{UNC}}^*}{2} + \delta W_{\text{UNC}}\right)\right] \tag{2.4}$$

Similarly, the value for the future conditional on current defection is

$$
\begin{aligned}
W_{\text{UNC}} &= s + b^{**}_{\text{UNC}}(-\alpha\rho^2 x^2 - \delta k + \delta V_{\text{UNC}}) \\
&\quad + (1 - b^{**}_{\text{UNC}})\left[-\alpha(\rho x + x)^2 + \frac{1 + b^{**}_{\text{UNC}}}{2} + \delta W_{\text{UNC}} \right] \\
&= \frac{1}{1 - \delta + \delta b^{**}_{\text{UNC}}}\Big[s - \alpha\rho^2 x^2 + b^{**}_{\text{UNC}}\delta(V_{\text{UNC}} - k) \\
&\quad + (1 - b^{**}_{\text{UNC}})\Big(-\alpha x^2 - 2\alpha\rho x^2 + \frac{1 + b^{**}_{\text{UNC}}}{2} \Big) \Big]
\end{aligned}
\tag{2.5}
$$

Substituting (2.5) in (2.4) and simplifying yields

$$
\begin{aligned}
V_{\text{UNC}} =& \left[(1 - \delta)(1 - \delta b^*_{\text{UNC}} + \delta b^{**}_{\text{UNC}}) \right]^{-1}\Big\{ (1 - \delta + \delta b^{**}_{\text{UNC}})(s + k) \\
&+ \frac{1}{2}(1 - b^*_{\text{UNC}})\Big[1 + \delta b^{**}_{\text{UNC}} - \delta(b^{**}_{\text{UNC}})^2 + 2\delta s - 2\delta^2 k b^{**}_{\text{UNC}} \\
&+ b^*_{\text{UNC}}(1 - \delta + \delta b^{**}_{\text{UNC}}) - 2\alpha x^2(1 + 2\delta\rho(1 - b^{**}_{\text{UNC}}) + \delta\rho^2) \Big] \Big\}
\end{aligned}
\tag{2.6}
$$

Substituting (2.6) in (2.5) and simplifying yields

$$
\begin{aligned}
W_{\text{UNC}} =& \left[2(1 - \delta)(1 - \delta b^*_{\text{UNC}} + \delta b^{**}_{\text{UNC}}) \right]^{-1}\Big\{ (1 - \delta b^*_{\text{UNC}})\Big[1 + 2s - (b^{**}_{\text{UNC}})^2 \\
&- 2\alpha x^2(1 + \rho)^2 \Big] + b^{**}_{\text{UNC}}\Big[\delta(1 - (b^*_{\text{UNC}})^2 + 2s + 2\delta k b^*_{\text{UNC}}) \\
&+ 2\alpha x^2(1 - \delta - 2\rho(1 - \delta b^*_{\text{UNC}})) \Big] \Big\}
\end{aligned}
\tag{2.7}
$$

Substituting (2.6) and (2.7) in (2.2) and (2.3), and simplifying the result, yields the values for b^*_{UNC} and b^{**}_{UNC} stated in the proposition.

Case 2

$\lambda^{**} \leq \lambda \leq \lambda^*$, in which case the IMF plays TFT. Using an argument analogous to the one used to establish the threshold values in the previous case, I find $b^*_{\text{TFT}} > b^{**}_{\text{TFT}}$. These are identical to expressions (2.2) and (2.3), respectively, up to the continuation values, which are now V_{TFT} and W_{TFT}. As before, I solve for the continuation values, simplify, and substitute the results into the expressions for the thresholds, which yields the values stated in the proposition.

Case 3

$\lambda < \lambda^{**}$, in which case the IMF plays HTL. Using the construction for the previous cases, *mutatis mutandis*, yields the thresholds $b^*_{\text{HTL}} > b^{**}_{\text{HTL}}$ in terms of the continuation values V_{HTL} and W_{HTL}. The condition for the inequality to hold is $\delta k + \delta s > 2\alpha\rho x^2$, which is satisfied. Solving for these values, substituting, and simplifying yields the values of the thresholds stated in the proposition.

These strategies are perfect, given the off-the-path beliefs stated in the proposition. In particular, if the IMF ever deviates from its equilibrium strategy, governments expect it to stop defending its reputation and to provide unconditional financing. In this case, the condition for defecting by the governments is given in (2.2) and (2.3). Therefore, the IMF has nothing to gain from punishing defections, so it reverts to unconditional finance. This establishes the optimality of the government strategy.

Consider now the investor strategy. Let $b_i^* \in \{b_{UNC}^*, b_{TFT}^*, b_{HTL}^*\}$ be the probability that the government defects, which depends on the punishment regime that applies to that country, and define b_i^{**} analogously. The interest rate is set to make the investor indifferent between investing in this market or elsewhere, so

$$r = \frac{1 - b_i^*}{b_i^*}$$

If the government has not defected in the prior period, $1 - b_i^*$ is the true probability that the government defects, so the investor will be indifferent. If inflation in the previous period was zero, some proportion of funds, k, is invested in the country. If the government has inflated in the previous period, however, the probability of defection is $1 - b_i^{**} > 1 - b_i^*$. Consequently, investors strictly prefer not to invest in the country.[20] If the government did not inflate in the previous period but did in the one before, the investors' equilibrium strategy requires them not to invest. This strategy is supportable in equilibrium because the probability of defection is $1 - b_i^*$, so the investors are indifferent.[21] Finally, suppose that the IMF deviates from its strategy. In this case, investors expect it to cease defending its reputation and play UNC thereafter. Consequently, governments are expected to choose inflationary policies with probabilities $1 - b_{UNC}^*$ if they have not defected in the previous period, and $1 - b_{UNC}^{**}$ if they have. Since interest rates adjust instantaneously to changes in

---

[20] Since by assumption interest rates do not respond to changes in government policy in the short run, any increase in the probability of an inflationary policy is fully reflected in a reduction of capital inflows.

[21] This modeling choice is arbitrary; since investors are indifferent, there exist multiple equilibria in which the investors take different amounts of time to resume investment, governments defect with different probabilities, and long-run interest rates and risks assume different values. Some delay is necessary to support the equilibrium, but any length of delay will serve. In effect, the capital market forces governments to prove their dedication to sound macroeconomic policy before renewing confidence. Delay is a substantively desirable feature of the equilibrium, since it represents effects of realistic factors that were left out of the model for the sake of tractability. For example, investors would strictly prefer to withhold investment in this model if they were uncertain about the government's policies, or only learned them with certainty after some time had passed. A one-period delay, which corresponds to waiting until inflation has returned to its original level, is the simplest to work with.

the IMF's reputation, interest rates rise to offset the increased risk of defection. This establishes the optimality of the investor strategy.

Consider now the IMF's strategy. The cost of failing to punish any country at any time, t, is constant over time: Starting immediately with t, all countries revert to the strategy for unconditional financing. The IMF's payoff depends on the proportion of countries to which each punishment regime applies, which depends on the exogenous distribution of country sizes. Let D_{TFT} and D_{HTL} be the proportions of countries subject to the TFT and HTL regimes, respectively. Also, let $\iota \in \{\text{UNC,TFT,HTL}\}$ be an indicator of the regime type that applies to some country i in equilibrium, and define two types of value functions. Let V_ι^{IMF} be the present discounted value of the IMF's payoffs given that it carries out strategy ι when i has cooperated; and let W_ι^{IMF} be the corresponding value when i has defected. Then, for each i:

$$V_\iota^{\text{IMF}} = \omega + b_\iota^* \delta V_\iota^{\text{IMF}} + (1 - b_\iota^*)(-x_i^2 + \delta W_\iota^{\text{IMF}}) \tag{2.8}$$

$$W_\iota^{\text{IMF}} = b_\iota^{**}\left[-\rho^2 x_i^2 + \delta(V_\iota^{\text{IMF}} - \omega)\right] + (1 - b_\iota^{**})\left[-(x_i + \rho x_i)^2 + \delta W_\iota^{\text{IMF}}\right]$$

Note that the following inequality is true by assumption:

$$W_{\text{HTL}}^{\text{IMF}} < W_{\text{TFT}}^{\text{IMF}} < W_{\text{UNC}}^{\text{IMF}} \tag{2.9}$$

Consider some arbitrary time, t, and suppose all countries have deviated in period $t - 1$. This is the worst situation the IMF could face because it has to punish deviations as called for by its equilibrium strategy, and such deviations are more likely given that the countries have defected in the previous period. Suppose now that the first country i the IMF has to deal with is subject to the HTL regime. If the IMF deviates and does not punish i, every government switches to the UNC strategy in the next period, and the IMF's payoff is

$$\lambda_i(\omega + \delta W_{\text{UNC}}^{\text{IMF}}) + D_{\text{TFT}}\left[\omega + \delta\left(b_{\text{TFT}}^{**} V_{\text{UNC}}^{\text{IMF}} + (1 - b_{\text{TFT}}^{**})W_{\text{UNC}}^{\text{IMF}}\right)\right]$$
$$+ (D_{\text{HTL}} - \lambda_i)\left[\omega + \delta\left(b_{\text{HTL}}^{**} V_{\text{UNC}}^{\text{IMF}} + (1 - b_{\text{HTL}}^{**})W_{\text{UNC}}^{\text{IMF}}\right)\right] \tag{2.10}$$
$$+ (1 - D_{\text{TFT}} - D_{\text{HTL}})\left[\omega + \delta\left(b_{\text{UNC}}^{**} V_{\text{UNC}}^{\text{IMF}} + (1 - b_{\text{UNC}}^{**})W_{\text{UNC}}^{\text{IMF}}\right)\right]$$

If the IMF follows its equilibrium strategy and punishes that government, the payoff then is

$$\delta\lambda_i W_{\text{HTL}}^{\text{IMF}} + D_{\text{TFT}}\left(b_{\text{TFT}}^{**}(\omega + \delta V_{\text{TFT}}^{\text{IMF}}) + (1 - b_{\text{TFT}}^{**})\delta W_{\text{TFT}}^{\text{IMF}}\right)$$
$$+ (D_{\text{HTL}} - \lambda_i)\left(b_{\text{HTL}}^{**}(\omega + \delta V_{\text{HTL}}^{\text{IMF}}) + (1 - b_{\text{HTL}}^{**})\delta W_{\text{HTL}}^{\text{IMF}}\right) \tag{2.11}$$
$$+ (1 - D_{\text{TFT}} - D_{\text{HTL}})\left(\omega + b_{\text{UNC}}^{**}\delta V_{\text{UNC}}^{\text{IMF}} + (1 - b_{\text{UNC}}^{**})\delta W_{\text{UNC}}^{\text{IMF}}\right)$$

The IMF will punish government i only when the payoff from doing so in (2.11) is at least as good as the payoff from deviating in (2.10). Note that the last term in each expression is identical. To simplify notation, let

$$A_\iota = W^{\text{IMF}}_{\text{UNC}} - W^{\text{IMF}}_\iota$$
$$B_\iota = A_\iota - (V^{\text{IMF}}_{\text{UNC}} - V^{\text{IMF}}_\iota)$$
$$C_\iota = (\omega + \delta B_\iota)b^{**}_\iota$$

After rearranging terms and using the simplified notation, the inequality becomes

$$\lambda_i C_{\text{HTL}} \leq D_{\text{TFT}}(C_{\text{TFT}} - \delta A_{\text{TFT}} - \omega) + D_{\text{HTL}}(C_{\text{HTL}} - \delta A_{\text{HTL}} - \omega)$$

which yields the country size threshold for the HTL regime:

$$\lambda^{**} = C^{-1}_{\text{HTL}}\Big[D_{\text{TFT}}(C_{\text{TFT}} - \delta A_{\text{TFT}} - \omega) + D_{\text{HTL}}(C_{\text{HTL}} - \delta A_{\text{HTL}} - \omega)\Big] \quad (2.12)$$

Thus, the IMF can credibly threaten to punish government i using the HTL regime if, and only if, $\lambda_i \leq \lambda^{**}$. By an analogous procedure we can find the corresponding value for TFT, which yields the necessary condition for punishment under that regime:

$$\lambda^* = C^{-1}_{\text{TFT}}\Big[D_{\text{TFT}}(C_{\text{TFT}} - \delta A_{\text{TFT}} - \omega) + D_{\text{HTL}}(C_{\text{HTL}} - \delta A_{\text{HTL}} - \omega)\Big] \quad (2.13)$$

Thus, the IMF can credibly threaten to punish government i using the TFT regime if, and only if, $\lambda_i \leq \lambda^*$. Although these threshold sizes are functions of exogenous variables, the expressions are very cumbersome and are omitted here. It remains to show that $\lambda^{**} < \lambda^*$, which is done in Lemma 2.2.

The IMF strategy is subgame perfect given the off-the-path beliefs of the governments and the players. This establishes the optimality of the IMF strategy. Therefore, the proposed strategies for the three players do indeed constitute a perfect Bayesian equilibrium of the game.   □

Before I present the result about the country size thresholds, I prove a useful lemma, which I then apply in the proof that follows.

Lemma 2.1. $b^*_{\text{HTL}} > b^*_{\text{TFT}} > b^*_{\text{UNC}}$ and $b^{**}_{\text{HTL}} > b^{**}_{\text{TFT}} > b^{**}_{\text{UNC}}$.

Proof. Consider the variable $F = 2 + 2\delta(2\alpha\rho x^2 - \delta k)$ as defined in the proposition and note that $1 > k - 2\alpha\rho x^2 \Rightarrow 2\alpha\rho x^2 - k > -1$, where the first inequality follows from $k < 1$. Since $\lim_{\delta \to 1} F = 2 + 2(2\alpha\rho x^2 - k) > 0$, it follows that for sufficiently high δ, $F > 0$. Since $b^*_{\text{TFT}} = b^*_{\text{UNC}} + 2\delta s/F$, this implies that $b^*_{\text{TFT}} > b^*_{\text{UNC}}$. Consider now the second term in the expression for b^*_{HTL}. For sufficiently high δ, the numerator lies in $(-1, 1)$. It can be verified that the smallest value of the numerator is obtained in the limit when $s, k \to 1$. In the limit, the largest value of the denominator in this case approaches 0 from the left (that it, it is negative because $F < 2$). This implies that the entire second term is positive and strictly greater than 1, which implies that it is larger than the second term in the expression for b^*_{TFT}. It can be verified that the same holds for the upper bound on the expression. Therefore $b^*_{\text{HTL}} > b^*_{\text{TFT}}$ for sufficiently high δ.

Since $b^{**}_{\text{UNC}} = b^*_{\text{UNC}} + G$ and $b^{**}_{\text{TFT}} = b^*_{\text{TFT}} + G$, we also have $b^{**}_{\text{UNC}} < b^{**}_{\text{TFT}}$. Since $b^{**}_{\text{HTL}} = b^*_{\text{HTL}} + G - \delta s$, and $b^*_{\text{HTL}} > b^*_{\text{TFT}}$, it follows that there exists some $\underline{s}$ such that for all $s \leq \underline{s}$, $b^{**}_{\text{HTL}} > b^{**}_{\text{TFT}}$. $\square$

Lemma 2.2. $\lambda_{HTL} < \lambda_{TFT}$.

Proof. Consider some country i and let Y_i be the IMF's stream of payoffs from maintaining reputation with all other countries, and let Z_i be the stream of payoffs from providing unconditional financing. The IMF will enforce its TFT strategy if

$$\lambda_i \delta W^{\text{IMF}}_{\text{TFT}} + (1 - \lambda_i)\delta Y_i \geq \lambda_i(\omega + \delta W^{\text{IMF}}_{\text{UNC}}) + (1 - \lambda_i)\delta Z_i$$

or

$$\lambda_i \leq \frac{\delta(Y_i - Z_i)}{\delta(Y_i - Z_i + W^{\text{IMF}}_{\text{UNC}}) + s - \delta W^{\text{IMF}}_{\text{TFT}}} \equiv \lambda_{\text{TFT}} \qquad (2.14)$$

Similarly, the IMF will enforce its HTL strategy if

$$\lambda_i \delta W^{\text{IMF}}_{\text{HTL}} + (1 - \lambda_i)\delta Y_i \geq \lambda_i(\omega + \delta W^{\text{IMF}}_{\text{UNC}}) + (1 - \lambda_i)\delta Z_i$$

or

$$\lambda_i \leq \frac{\delta(Y_i - Z_i)}{\delta(Y_i - Z_i + W^{\text{IMF}}_{\text{UNC}}) + s - \delta W^{\text{IMF}}_{\text{HTL}}} \equiv \lambda_{\text{HTL}} \qquad (2.15)$$

The expressions (2.14) and (2.15) are positive and differ only in the last term of the denominator, and since $W^{\text{IMF}}_{\text{HTL}} < W^{\text{IMF}}_{\text{TFT}}$, it follows that $\lambda_{\text{HTL}} < \lambda_{\text{TFT}}$, as required. $\square$

COMPARATIVE STATICS

The following comparative statics are derived from the model:

- The longer the punishment period, the lower the probability of defection (Lemma 2.1):

$$b^*_{\text{HTL}} > b^*_{\text{TFT}} > b^*_{\text{UNC}} \text{ and } b^{**}_{\text{HTL}} > b^{**}_{\text{TFT}} > b^{**}_{\text{UNC}}$$

- Larger countries are subject to shorter punishment regimes (Lemma 2.2):

$$\lambda_{\text{HTL}} < \lambda_{\text{TFT}}$$

- The probability of defection in period t increases after a defection in period $t - 1$ (Proposition 2.1):

$$b_\iota^{**} > b_\iota^* \text{ for all } \iota \in \{\text{UNC,TFT,HTL}\}$$

- The probability of defection in period t increases more after a defection in period $t - 1$ for countries subject to HTL than for countries subject to TFT. Formally,

$$(1 - b_{\text{HTL}}^{**}) - (1 - b_{\text{HTL}}^*) > (1 - b_{\text{TFT}}^{**}) - (1 - b_{\text{TFT}}^*)$$
$$\Rightarrow \qquad\qquad -G + \delta s > -G$$
$$\Rightarrow \qquad\qquad \delta s > 0$$

3

Studying IMF Effectiveness

CAN THE International Monetary Fund influence the economic policies of the countries to which it lends? Country experts and officials who represent borrowing nations contend that the IMF exerts tremendous influence, although they disagree about whether that influence is benign or harmful. Quantitative researchers, on the other hand, have tended to find little evidence that the IMF influences national economic policies. This chapter reviews the quantitative evidence published to date, as well as some unpublished studies, and suggests an explanation for the incongruity between the perceptions of those who know individual countries best and the findings of those who use quantitative data to study many countries. I contend that the vast majority of quantitative studies of IMF lending use data that are insufficiently precise, fail to control for variables that measure the political constraints that most often lead to program failure, and misspecify their statistical models because they do not treat the IMF's policies as endogenous. The chapter goes on to outline a series of political economy hypotheses that should be included in any statistical model of IMF effectiveness. It then describes the data set developed to test the formal model presented in Chapter 2, the Post-Communist Politics and Economics Database (PCPED).

3.1 PREVIOUS RESEARCH

There is a substantial econometric literature on the efficacy of IMF stabilization programs. Most of the empirical studies are inconclusive; although some studies show that the IMF's programs influence macroeconomic aggregates in the intended direction, others indicate that these programs are counterproductive in the same terms. Most of the findings reported in the literature are negative: they are unable to show any correlation between variables representing interactions with the IMF and variables representing national policies or economic outcomes. This rather impressive non-finding has attracted the sustained attention of reviewers of the literature and has led to pessimistic conclusions about the Fund's ability to influence the macroeconomic policies of its target countries.[1] The summary of the literature that follows suggests rather different conclusions. First, the results reported so far are quite mixed, suggesting the need for more research rather than a monolithic consensus. Second, the overwhelming majority of the studies in the existing literature are seriously flawed, so they do not form a solid basis for inferences about the effectiveness of the IMF. Third, the research conducted to date has failed to model the politics of stabilization or control for the credibility of IMF programs, so its conclusions have to be regarded as tentative.

Table 3.1 summarizes the findings in the literature on the effects of IMF programs on international accounts. The original purpose of the IMF was to serve as watchdog over the international exchange and payments system. Its mandate has broadened considerably, but it has continued to serve as lender of last resort to avert or contain currency crises and to promote policies to correct disequilibria in the balance of payments. Since the advent of flexible exchange rates in 1971, the Fund has typically promoted currency devaluations as part of a comprehensive adjustment program. If there is any set of variables that the IMF should be expected to influence consistently, it is the international accounts.

The results are mixed. The more recent studies, which tended to use larger samples and more sophisticated methods, usually found that IMF programs improved the balance of payments and the current account, and two found that they led to devaluations. This appears to contradict the wave of earlier research that had suggested no correlation. All the statistically significant results pointed in the expected direction. However, a number of earlier studies failed to find this pattern, and the results were not unanimous, even among the more recent studies.

Table 3.2 reviews the results of studies of the effect of IMF programs on inflation, which is a key target variable, and on policy variables that are typically included in conditionality programs: the government deficit, domestic credit, and the money supply. These are variables that the IMF must influence if it is to have any policy relevance. Moreover, whereas the balance of payments, the current account and the exchange rate may be subject to substantial exogenous shocks, these policy variables are more directly under the government's control. If governments implement IMF advice, IMF programs should influence these variables.

The results support the hypothesis that the IMF affects policy variables in the desired direction, but the evidence is mixed and rather weak. While all but two of the studies conducted in the 1990s concluded that IMF programs appear to reduce inflation rates, only one study found statistically significant results,

---

[1] Krueger 1998; Kahler 1992; Biersteker 1993; Bird 1996. A notable exception is Ul Haque and Khan (1998), which presents a more optimistic assessment of the literature's substantive findings and makes some of the same methodological points that I raise below.

Table 3.1: International Accounts.

	Balance of Payments	Current Account / GDP	Real Exchange Rate
Reichmann & Stillson (1978)	0		
Connors (1979)	0	0	
Donovan (1982)	+	+	
Killick (1984)	0	−	
Loxley (1984)	0		
Zulu & Nsouli (1985)	0	0	
Goldstein & Montiel (1986)	−	−	
Gylfasson (1987)	+		
Pastor (1987)	+*	0	
Edwards (1989)		+	
Khan (1990)	+*	+*	
Killick, Malik & Manuel (1992)	+*	+*	−*
Doroodian (1993)		−	
Edwards & Santaella (1993)[a]		+	
Schadler et al. (1993)	+	−	−
Conway (1994)		+*	0
Schadler et al. (1995)		−	
Bordo & Schwartz (2000)	+	+	
Lee & Rhee (2000)		0	

[a] Edwards & Santaella (1993) extensively discuss the behavior of real exchange rates, but because they focus exclusively on programs that call for deviations, their work is not based upon a representative sample of all IMF programs and their performance.

Notes: "0" indicates no apparent correlation between IMF programs and target variables; "+" indicates a positive correlation, and "−" a negative correlation. There is no entry if the variable was not included in a particular study. An asterisk indicates that the result is significant at the .05 level.

and earlier studies were all over the map on this issue. Two studies found significant evidence that the IMF decreases budget deficits. Only one study reported a statistically significant finding that the IMF succeeds in reducing the rate of growth of domestic credit. Four studies found statistically significant results, and all the significant results pointed in the expected direction.

Finally, many studies have been concerned with determining the effects of IMF programs on economic growth. Promoting economic growth is not an

Table 3.2: Policy Variables.

	Inflation	Budget Bal. / GDP	Gov't Cons. / GDP	Dom. Credit Growth
Reichmann & Stillson (1978)	0			−
Connors (1979)	0			
Donovan (1981)	−			
Khan & Knight (1981)	−, 0[a]			−
Donovan (1982)	−			
Killick (1984)	−*			0
Loxley (1984)	−*			
Zulu & Nsouli (1985)	0	+	0	
Kirkpatrick & Onis (1985)	+			
Goldstein & Montiel (1986)	+			
Remmer (1986)		−		
Gylfasson (1987)	−			−
Pastor (1987)	0			
Edwards (1989)	+			
Khan (1990)	−			
Haque & Wartenberg (1992)		−		
Killick et al. (1992)	−*	+*	−	−*
Doroodian (1993)	−			
Edwards & Santaella (1993)				−
Schadler et al. (1993)	−	+		
Conway (1994)	−	+*	−	+
Schadler et al. (1995)	−			
Bordo & Schwartz (2000)	0			
Dicks-Mireaux et al. (2000)	−			
Lee & Rhee (2000)	0			

[a] The two symbols indicate short-run and long-run effects, respectively.

IMF priority, although the IMF has long maintained that achieving its objectives of stabilizing currencies and prices promotes long-term growth by facilitating international investment. In the short run, however, we should expect IMF conditionality programs to be associated with recession rather than growth, since the Fund's conditions require governments to retrench and central banks to tighten the money supply. Table 3.3 reviews the evidence.

The results are again mixed. The studies differ in their time frames for evaluating the effects of programs, but this alone does not explain the variations in

Table 3.3: Growth, Savings, and Investment.

	Growth	Savings / GDP	Dom. Invest. / GDP
Reichmann & Stillson (1978)	+		
Connors (1979)	0		
Donovan (1981)	+		
Donovan (1982)	−		
Killick (1984)	+		
Loxley (1984)	0		
Khan & Knight (1985)	+		
Zulu & Nsouli (1985)	−	−	0
Goldstein & Montiel (1986)	−		
Gylfasson (1987)	−		
Pastor (1987)	0		
Edwards (1989)	+		
Khan (1990)	−*		
Haque & Wartenberg (1992)		−	
Killick et al. (1992)	+		
Doroodian (1993)	−		
Schadler et al. (1993)	+	−	0
Conway (1994)	−		−*
Schadler et al. (1995)	+	+	+
IMF Staff (1997)	+		
Bordo & Schwartz (2000)	−		
Dicks-Mireaux et al. (2000)	+*		
Lee & Rhee (2000)	+		
Przeworski & Vreeland (2000)	−*		

the results. There is no consensus on the long-term effects of IMF programs on growth. A few studies find that IMF programs reduce domestic savings, one finds that they reduce domestic investment, and a number find that IMF programs cause recessions. However, the studies are about evenly split about whether IMF programs increase or decrease countries' long-term growth prospects. Only three of the studies claim that their results are statistically significant.

To summarize, the existing quantitative literature provides evidence that the IMF affects policy variables and international accounts in the expected direction, although the evidence is surprisingly weak and somewhat mixed. The evidence about growth, savings, and investment is quite mixed and inconclu-

Table 3.4: Quantitative Studies of Conditionality Programs.

	Programs	Span	Countries	Cases	Freq[a]	Method[b]
Reichmann & Stillson (1978)	79	1963-72	NA		Q	B
Connors (1979)	NA	1973-77	31		A	B
Khan & Knight (1981)	NA	1967-75	29	232	NA	S
Donovan (1981)	12	NA	12		A	B,W
Donovan (1982)	78	1971-80	NA		A	B,W
Killick (1984)	38	1974-79	24		A	B
Loxley (1984)	38 *70-90*	NA	62		A	B,W
Khan & Knight (1985)	NA	1971-80	29-34[c]	232-340	A	S
Kirkpatric & Onis (1985)	29	1971-76	29		A	B
McCauley (1985)	99	1976-81	56		Q	B
Zulu & Nsouli (1985)	35	1980-81	22		A	B
Goldstein & Montiel (1986)	68	1974-81	NA	397	A	GEE
Remmer (1986)	114	1954-84	9		A	B
Gylfasson (1987)	32	NA	37		A	B,W
Pastor (1987)	NA	1965-81	18		A	B,W
Edwards (1989)	34	1983	34		A	B
Khan (1990)	259 *315*	1973-88	NA	1104	A	B,W, GEE
Killick et al. (1992)	NA	1979-85	16		A	B[d]
Haque et al. (1992)	NA	NA	15		A	GEE
Doroodian (1993)	27	1977-83	43	301	A	W
Edwards & Santaella (1993)	26	1948-71	48	NA	A	B,W
Schadler et al. (1993)	55	1983-93	19	NA	A	B
Conway (1994)	217	1976-86	74	584	A	GEE
Schadler et al. (1995)	45	1988-91	36	NA	A	B

Table 3.4 continued from previous page

	Programs	Span	Countries	Cases	Freq	Method
Rowlands (1996)	NA	1973-89	99	1500	A	GLS
Franklin (1997)	NA	1980-82	47-56	47-56	A	OLS
IMF Staff (1997)	68	1986-96	36-84	NA	A	B,W
Conway (2000)	NA	1974-92	90	3721-7120	Q	O[e]
Bordo & Schwartz (2000)		1973-98	24		A, Q	W, GEE
Dicks-Mireaux et al. (2000)	88	1986-91	61	271	A	GEE
Garuda (2000)	58	1975-91	39	370	A	O[f]
Lee & Rhee (2000)	159	1968-94	NA	2352	A	B
Przeworksi & Vreeland (2000)	NA	1951-90	135	1024	A	O[g]

[a] Q refers to quarterly frequency and A refers to annual.
[b] "B" refers to before-after studies, those that compare the values before and after IMF program. "W" refers to with-without studies, those that compare the macroeconomic aggregates of program countries to those of non-program countries. "S" refers to simulations. "O" refers to other, see note.
[c] Many of the results programmed into the simulation were taken from Khan & Knight (1981), which uses a sample of 29 countries; however, the import demand and export supply equations were estimated from data on 34 countries covering 1971-80.
[d] Completed and uncompleted programs.
[e] Pooled probit and duration analysis.
[f] Selection model, comparison of means.
[g] Dynamic bivariate probit and simulations.

sive. However, limitations in the research methods used in this literature, summarized above in Table 3.4, render this verdict far from final. The first thing to note is that the empirical basis for the generalizations cited above is much weaker than the sheer volume of the literature might suggest. The majority of these studies used a small number of observations to reach their conclusions, and this in itself must explain many of the insignificant results and much of the inconsistency reported in the literature. In addition, almost all existing studies rely on annual data. Although many of the studies cited above note the coding and measurement problems involved in using annual data, only three use quarterly data, and none of the existing studies uses monthly data. Tests using annual data are less sensitive than tests using monthly data, because economic and political events that destabilize the economy may fall in the same year as IMF intervention and therefore cancel out its effects. Monthly data make it possible to draw inferences about causation that would be inaccessible in studies using annual data, because it is difficult to determine with annual data whether the policies or the programs came first. In addition, many of these studies suffer from serious methodological shortcomings, which are discussed below.

3.2 CRITIQUES RAISED IN THE LITERATURE

The early studies relied on simple methods: They compared groups of countries that participated in IMF programs to groups that did not (With-Without), or compared the same countries over time before and after programs were in place (Before-After), and drew inferences about the effect of IMF programs on policy and outcome variables from differences in the means of the samples. In some cases difference-of-means tests were used to show statistical significance, but in many of the early studies they were not, and often the data were not described precisely enough to make it possible to determine whether the results are meaningful. As the subsequent literature emphasized, the With-Without and Before-After studies were not particularly informative, since they failed to control for the possibility that the groups being compared were inherently different. Twenty of the thirty-three studies of IMF effectiveness relied on these methods, and they continue to be the primary approach used in IMF Occasional Papers on the subject.

Studies that employed multiple regression were an improvement, because that made it possible to control for some of the exogenous variables that might influence the outcome of programs. However, these studies still failed to control for selection bias: If countries that are in danger of suffering economic crises are more likely to turn to the IMF for support, for example, countries in the "treatment" group will be systematically more likely to suffer economic downturns than countries in the control group. More generally, whenever the outcome variables of interest influence the propensity of countries to participate in IMF programs, estimates of the effect of programs that do not take this into account will be biased.

Goldstein and Montiel (1986) argued this case convincingly and proposed the Generalized Evaluation Estimator (GEE) as a way of getting around two particular kinds of bias that may arise.[2] First, if randomly distributed exogenous shocks—such as changes in the terms of trade—cause recessions and simultaneously make it necessary for countries to approach the Fund for help, there should be a tendency for programs to be associated with economic recoveries simply because of regression to the mean. "Bad" shocks might generally

---

[2]Goldstein and Montiel 1986.

precede programs; if they were not repeated, there would be an economic improvement even if the IMF exerted no influence. Second, if national authorities autonomously react to prior-period economic outcomes (such as inflation or exchange rate movements) and the likelihood of being involved in a Fund program depends on the same economic outcomes, then there will be a correlation between the governments' reactions and the presence of an IMF program, even if the program had no effect. Both problems lead to bias, and other hypotheses leading to selection bias are not difficult to imagine. Depending on how economic outcomes affect the likelihood of participating in a program, the bias may overstate or understate the program's effects.[3] For example, suppose that severe external demand shocks cause recessions and reduce government revenue, compelling the government to rely on deficit financing. If these shocks are long-lasting and lead countries to turn to the IMF for support, studies of IMF programs that fail to account for selection effects will be biased in favor of the null hypothesis, because the very countries that will have the most difficulty implementing IMF conditions—because they have been subjected to severe shocks—are most likely to turn to the IMF for assistance. The fiscal imbalances and unsustainable levels of foreign debt that typically cause countries to turn to the Fund for support are long in the making and take a long time to overcome. In the meantime they damage economic performance and create political instability, producing highly unfavorable conditions for macroeconomic stabilization.[4]

The GEE adjusts for these problems by estimating a "policy reaction function" —a formula that captures the reaction of national policies to prior-period economic data in the absence of an IMF-supported program—from data for non-program countries or periods, and then using this function to generate a control variable for a subsequent regression. Seven of the studies in Table 3.4 use this method. The GEE has two serious limitations, however. First, in order for the GEE to generate unbiased results, it must be the case that the policy reaction functions are stable over time and comparable across countries. Unfortunately, recent empirical work shows that the results are very sensitive to the specification of the reaction function and are unstable as observations are excluded or included.[5] Second, the GEE does not address a more fundamental problem: Unobserved factors may influence both participation in Fund programs and policy performance.[6] Some scholars argue that the bias problems

---

[3] Ibid., 317.

[4] Nelson 1990; Stallings 1992; Santaella 1995; Knight and Santaella 1994. In the post-Communist cases, this source of bias was reversed early in the transition, since it was the countries with the most advanced reform programs that received early access to Fund credits. More recently, however, this bias has been replaced by the one familiar in studies of developing countries, as almost all the slow reformers have begun drawing on Fund credits, and a few of the most advanced reformers have stopped doing so.

[5] Dicks-Mireaux, Mecagni and Schadler 2000.

[6] Goldstein and Montiel (1986) acknowledge this problem. Heckman (1979) identified this

inherent in a With-Without or Before-After comparison are so intractable that the research agenda should shift to simulations based on the effects of adopting fund-like policies; this, however, sidesteps the central question of this study, which is whether the Fund succeeds in influencing government policies.[7] On the other hand, some of the most recent studies have attempted to control for selection bias in innovative ways.[8] Nevertheless, it is fair to say that in spite of the prodigious volume of scholarship accumulated on the issue of IMF program effectiveness over the last twenty years, scholars are just beginning to apply appropriate methods to investigate it. The question is by no means closed.

3.3 NEW CRITIQUES

This study introduces two new avenues of research. First, the formal model presented in chapter 2 concludes that the effects of IMF intervention should vary across countries, depending on the credibility of the IMF's threat to enforce its conditions by withholding funding. Credibility should be reflected in the length of punishment intervals, and lax enforcement of conditions for more influential countries should lead to less effective program implementation. If this is true, a cross-national study that fails to control for the country-specific differences in the IMF strategy could erroneously conclude that the IMF had no effect across the board. Previous research has allowed large countries like Russia and Brazil to convince us that the IMF is ineffective, when it may in fact be quite effective in countries like Poland and Uruguay. This is the first quantitative study to investigate the consistency of IMF responses to countries that deviate from their programs or to use the credibility of the IMF as an instrument for assessing its influence.[9]

Second, although previous studies have controlled for a host of economic variables that make compliance with Fund programs more difficult, such as debt-service ratios and terms-of-trade shocks, none has attempted to model the *politics* of stabilization. This is a glaring gap in the literature, since there is a consensus among qualitative researchers that domestic politics is the most important place to look for explanations when stabilization fails. Indeed, a growing case-study literature argues that the effectiveness of international intervention may be very limited because of the overwhelming importance of domestic politics in determining the outcome of stabilization programs.[10] The

---

problem as a source of selection bias and proposed a widely used solution that involves estimating a probability that an observation belongs to a particular state (in this case, a post-program period) and using a variable derived from that probability in the second stage of estimation.

[7] Khan and Knight 1981, 1985.

[8] Conway 2000; Przeworski and Vreeland 2000; Garuda 2000.

[9] The politics behind the initiation of IMF programs has recently begun to be studied systematically (Thacker 1999).

[10] Haggard 1986; Nelson 1990; Kahler 1992; Biersteker 1993; Williamson 1994; Haggard and

authors of recent quantitative studies, too, have acknowledged that politics plays an important role in stabilization, and that their analysis suffers because of excluding political variables.[11] Econometric studies that fail to model the politics of stabilization suffer from omitted variable bias, which distorts their results in unpredictable ways.[12] My solution is to use a statistical model that captures the political variables that influence macroeconomic policy.

3.4 RESEARCH DESIGN

The previous discussion highlighted the limitations of traditional control-group studies of the effects of IMF programs, suggesting that it would be more fruitful to develop new approaches. Accordingly, this study relies on a different method, one that makes it possible to test the theoretical model presented in Chapter 2 more directly. In contrast to the assumption underlying the traditional ways of testing for the effects of IMF intervention, the game-theoretic model does not predict that the IMF exercises influence only when a program is in place; rather, governments also respond to the incentives the Fund creates before they are involved in programs and after programs have been suspended. According to the model, the most important "moving part" that provides leverage for testing the effect of IMF programs is not whether countries have IMF programs in place, but rather the credibility of IMF programs in particular countries. If we can measure the credibility of IMF enforcement of conditionality in particular countries at particular times, and if that credibility varies enough that it accounts for a significant diversity in policy outcomes, then we can infer that the IMF influences policy outcomes. Note that this is a very demanding test of the hypothesis that the IMF influences policies, since it is quite possible that the IMF does influence policies but that the credibility of its enforcement does not vary enough to affect outcomes significantly. However, this is a very natural way to go about testing the formal model developed in Chapter 2 because it allows me to ask the question, does the credibility of the IMF's policy enter into the equation as an intervening variable between IMF intervention and policy outcomes?

Variables and Data

The analysis in this book uses the Post-Communist Politics and Economics Database (PCPED), an original time-series cross-section data set with monthly data from January 1990 through December 1999 for twenty-six post-Com-

---

Kaufman 1995.

[11] Conway 2000; Przeworski and Vreeland 2000.

[12] Omitted variable bias arises when a statistically significant variable is omitted from an equation. It makes estimators biased and inconsistent, so it can lead to false inferences about the direction and magnitude of coefficients and to false conclusions about statistical significance.

munist countries, for a theoretical maximum of 2,760 observations.[13] Because of missing data, my empirical analyses make use of up to 2,629 observations.[14] Appendix A contains detailed descriptions of the variables.

Endogenous (Dependent) Variables

Each of the dependent variables in my statistical model represents the decisions of one of the actors in my formal model: IMF status (controlled by the IMF), inflation and domestic credit (controlled, albeit imperfectly, by the government), and the exchange rate (controlled by participants in the markets for foreign exchange and capital).

The formal model assumes a very simple macroeconomic policy environment, but a small amount of complexity has to be added in order to test it empirically. The model assumes that governments have only one policy lever, when in fact they have numerous policy levers that affect prices and real outcomes, and it also assumes that governments have no ability to directly influence capital flows, when in fact they have significant leverage here as well. In order to take advantage of the economic variables with the most comprehensive coverage of countries and time periods, I limit myself to three economic dependent variables: inflation, central bank domestic credit, and exchange rates. Some discussion of how these variables are theoretically related is necessary.

Central banks issue credits either to finance government deficits, to finance economic activity, or to rescue failing commercial banks. In each case, these are activities that directly increase the money supply and consequently create upward pressure on prices, but they may result from a variety of policies initiated by the government directly or by the central bank at the government's behest. Consequently, this is a variable that captures a broad range of direct and indirect government policies that affect the macroeconomy. Inflation is an even broader gauge of the relevant policies, with even broader data availability, but it also incorporates more exogenous shocks, such as increases in international oil prices, and is more directly related to exchange rates because they determine the relative price of imports. Unlike domestic credit, which is clearly a policy variable, inflation is an outcome that depends significantly on expectations

---

[13]The data were gathered at the University of Rochester by a team of research assistants including Kalina Popova, Timothy Carter, and Branislav L. Slantchev. The project was made possible by NSF grant # SES-9974663. The replication data set for this study and accompanying documentation are publicly available on the author's website. The countries included in the sample are Albania, Armenia, Azerbaijan, Belorus, Bulgaria, Croatia, the Czech Republic, Estonia, Georgia, Hungary, Kazakhstan, Kyrgyzia, Latvia, Lithuania, the Former Yugoslavian Republic of Macedonia, Moldova, Mongolia, Poland, Romania, Russia, Slovakia, Slovenia, Tadzhikistan, Turkmenistan, Ukraine, and Uzbekistan. Some of the countries were not in existence for portions of the time period covered.

[14]Gaps in the data were filled using a multiple-imputation method developed by Honaker et al. (1999) and described in King et al. (2001), using software available from Gary King's website: http://Gking.Harvard.edu. For a detailed discussion of this approach, see Appendix B.

and on the decisions of large numbers of market actors. Exchange rates are included in the analysis in order to capture the decisions of foreign investors. A direct measure of capital flows would be preferable in some respects, but no such variable exists with wide coverage for the countries in the sample. The objective of stabilizing the nominal exchange rate played an important role in the macroeconomic strategies charted by most post-Communist countries, so exchange rate devaluations were a clear sign of deteriorating investor confidence. The series for the economic policy and outcome variables, inflation, exchange rate, and central bank domestic credit, come from the IMF's main statistical publication, *International Financial Statistics (IFS)*.[15]

IMF Status

A more difficult variable to measure, and consequently one that contains a greater element of error, is IMF status. At any point in time, some countries have good relations with the IMF and are either officially authorized to draw on IMF resources or could be so authorized if they wished to be. Other countries are either not yet members or are members in poor standing, because they (1) have failed to implement the conditions attached to an IMF program or (2) have failed to meet the prior conditions required to begin a program. Unfortunately, the IMF does not publish lists of countries in each category; instead, it leaves to the analyst and the capital markets the task of inferring its relations with particular countries from its lending decisions. Nor does the IMF publish the complete lists of conditions attached to particular programs, so the analyst must often infer that conditions have not been met when disbursements of funds are suspended or agreement is delayed.

My procedure in coding this variable was to compare the patterns of disbursements of IMF loans with the publicly available information about agreements that had been reached. The information about agreements sometimes specifies the schedule of planned disbursements, so departures from the schedule could be taken as evidence that a program had gone off track. In other cases the schedule could be inferred from the size of the tranches, the type and duration of the agreement, and the IMF's general operating procedures. In some cases—Russia, Ukraine, Poland, and Bulgaria—I have specific information about the timing of IMF decisions, because I have carried out extensive interviews with country officials and IMF officials responsible for those relations. In other cases press reports or public statements by the IMF making positive assessments of a country's policies helped to clarify the situation. (Negative public assessments of a country's policies are almost never made, except in the context of later statements congratulating a country on how much its policies have subsequently improved.) Still, a considerable amount of uncertainty re-

---

[15] *IFS* is the most complete source available, and is the one to which IMF and national officials alike refer, so it is the natural one to use for this analysis.

mains in the measurement of this variable, so I expect to see large standard errors.

Exogenous (Independent) Variables

The literature in comparative political economy focuses on three main categories of variables that influence macroeconomic policies in democratic systems: the *timing* of elections, the *fragmentation* of governments and legislatures, and the *partisanship* of governments' preferences and constituencies. Particular authors stress one or another of these factors, and some have argued that some of them are overemphasized, but the research agenda clearly includes all three. Negative findings on any of the three are deemed noteworthy. Almost all this research has been conducted on the history of advanced industrialized countries—members of the Organization for Economic Cooperation and Development (OECD), for which quality time-series data are plentiful—and these data have been so thoroughly combed for correlations that new data sets are needed to test the received wisdom. Since some of the countries in this study are not democracies, it will also be possible to investigate the relationship between democratic politics and economic policy. In addition, I introduce the hypothesis that changes in government *discount factors*—the degree to which they take a long-term rather than a short-term view of their interests—affect macroeconomic policy.

Timing of Announced Elections

The timing of elections has long been believed to influence macroeconomic policy. Following Nordhaus (1975) and Tufte (1978), it may be the case that voters are not fully informed about the costs of expansive macroeconomic policies and naïvely reward policymakers who use inflationary policies to boost incomes and employment shortly before elections. As macroeconomists came to insist on arguments that were consistent with the assumption of rational expectations, however, this argument appeared to be increasingly suspect. Why do voters not learn that inflationary policies are costly and punish the politicians who attempt to manipulate them? Why, indeed, do these policies continue to boost income and employment, if they are fully anticipated by market agents who have every reason to adjust their nominal contracts in ways that would cancel out their real effects? Formal models have been devised that produce this behavior in a rational-expectations equilibrium where more "competent" incumbents use inflationary policies to signal their superior qualities, but these models seem rather unrealistic.[16] It would not be difficult to produce a simi-

---

[16]Ferejohn 1986. Other similar models are Rogoff and Sibert (1988), and Lohmann (1998). Shi and Svensson (2000), avoid some of the undesirable strategic calculations in a model using competence and uninformed voters. They test the model using a data set including developed and developing countries, conduct extensive robustness checks, and find strong evidence of political

lar result, however, using a model similar to the one introduced in Chapter 2. Since the temptation in that model varies over time, rational agents cannot perfectly anticipate when a government will deviate from its targets; as a result, surprise inflation is possible. If elections were explicitly included in the model as a factor that influences the distribution of the temptation parameter, it could lead both to more inflationary policies and higher anticipated levels of inflation around elections. The evidence in favor of the electoral timing hypothesis has been mixed.[17] Recent work has shown that electoral timing has a strong effect on government transfers and budget deficits in the OECD countries.[18]

I tested for the effect of parliamentary and presidential elections on macroeconomic variables; I subsequently dropped the presidential election variable, because it was not significant. These variables were coded as the number of months to the next scheduled election. In cases where early elections were announced, the variable is coded according to the previously announced election date until the announcement is made. The variable is coded zero in parliamentary systems for the months immediately following an election until a coalition has received a vote of confidence. This reflects the fact that the constitutions of parliamentary countries require imminent new elections if a coalition is not successfully formed.

Fragmentation

Fragmentation in decision-making processes—in parliaments, in coalition governments, and in the division of powers between branches of government—is a key variable in the qualitative literature on structural adjustment in developing countries.[19] It has also been shown to have significant effects on deficits in OECD countries.[20] The intuition behind these correlations comes from two sources. First, if macroeconomic policymaking is a social choice problem involving a series of actors with opposing interests, it may be the case that increasing the number of actors with veto power makes it more difficult to move away from the status quo.[21] Since structural adjustment requires policy change, the proliferation of veto players blocks adjustment. This argument assumes that the inflationary status quo is superior to all proposed reforms from the perspective of some relevant veto player. Alternatively, we could conceptualize the process of reform as the apportioning of costs, and policymaking as

---

budget cycles. Indeed, they find that the phenomenon is much stronger in Sub-Saharan Africa and Latin America than in high-income countries.

[17] A good survey and some provocative results are in Alesina, Roubini and Cohen (1997). Clark and Hallerberg (2000) argue that the occurrence of preelectoral monetary and fiscal expansions depends on whether the exchange rate is flexible or fixed.

[18] Franzese 2002.

[19] Haggard and Kaufman 1995.

[20] Franzese 2002.

[21] Romer and Rosenthal 1978; Tsebelis 1995; Bawn 1999.

a process of bargaining over the distribution of those costs. If the actors have incomplete information—and in the real world, they surely do—reform will be delayed while the bargaining takes place.[22] To the extent that fragmented legislatures and governing coalitions increase the number of veto players, they cause the number of bargaining games and the potential sources of delay to proliferate.

An alternative hypothesis suggests that fragmentation may have precisely the opposite effect, because political competition and an active opposition are necessary conditions for maintaining the behavioral independence of a central bank.[23] Independent central banks, meanwhile, have been shown to exercise significant restraint on macroeconomic policy and investor expectations.[24]

I use two measures of fragmentation in my analysis: the strength in parliament of the largest party supporting the government and the number of parties in the governing coalition.

Partisanship

Partisanship—the ideological space that governments occupy along a left-right dimension—is the third hypothesis inherited from the literature in comparative political economy. There is a significant literature in comparative politics that suggests that ideological differentiation along a left-right economic-policy dimension is meaningful, intelligible to voters, and comparable over time and across countries.[25] Furthermore, the comparative political economy literature has found that the left-right composition of governments has significant effects on economic policies in the advanced industrial democracies.[26] This is not surprising: Officials representing left- and right-wing parties have different policy preferences, and, to the extent that they have discretion to implement their own preferences, policies will differ. Indeed, party politics, in most democracies, is driven by the distribution of costs and benefits between sectors of society that benefit from active government policies (the poor, the working class) and sectors that prefer financial stability, limited government, and low levels of transfers (holders of capital). A social choice theorist may ask why officials who implement policies that differ from the interests of the median voter stay in office.[27] It is reasonable to suppose, however, that parties pursue policies

[22] Alesina and Drazen 1991.

[23] Bernhard 1998.

[24] Alesina, Roubini and Cohen 1997; Iversen 1999, Franzese 2002.

[25] Powell 2000, Chapters 7-9; Gabel and Huber 2000; Huber and Inglehart 1995; Huber and Powell 1994; Huber 1989; Budge, Robertson and Hearl 1987; Inglehart 1990.

[26] The classic article is Hibbs (1977). More recent treatments include Alvarez, Garrett and Lange (1991); Alesina, Roubini and Cohen (1997); Alesina and Rosenthal (1995); Simmons (1994); Garrett (1995); Garrett and Lange (1995); Garrett (1998); Iversen (1999); Oatley (1999); Franzese (2002). Clark and Hallerberg (2000) present a negative finding.

[27] The answer could be simply that median voter theorems do not apply because voters have preferences along multiple dimensions or because of differences in electoral rules and institutions

skewed away from the median because the probability of election depends on support from political contributors or party activists as well as from the public.[28] In terms of the model presented in Chapter 2, the trade-off between inflation and output is assumed to be a function of partisanship.

I code all governments of post-Communist countries on a left-right scale, ranging from -10 (far left) to 10 (far right). This is an enterprise fraught with difficulties, since standard data sets covering these countries have not yet been produced.[29] I have relied on press accounts, interviews for some countries, a wide range of published sources, and the advice of country specialists to compile these rankings.[30] The overriding concern has been to base the rankings on the perceived or announced policy preferences of the governments, before taking office where possible, rather than on the governments' subsequent economic policies. To the extent that subsequent economic policies have crept into the assessments, of course, there is circularity, since I am trying to use partisanship to explain economic policies. Thus, for example, the careful reader will notice that the post-Communist coalition of the Alliance of the Democratic Left (SLD) and the Polish Peasant Party (PSL) in Poland in 1993 is coded as being much farther to the left than its subsequent economic policies might lead one to expect, because its electoral program was much farther to the left than the policies it actually pursued. Similarly, there are marked differences in the codings given to the governments of Chernomyrdin, Kiriyenko, and Primakov in Russia, in spite of significant continuity in economic policies. The reason, again, is that very significant rhetorical differences existed among these governments, and they were perceived to hold very different policy preferences.

Another difficulty in coding governments according to partisanship is that the rules for forming governments vary across countries. It is straightforward to determine which parties support a government in the parliamentary democracies of Eastern Europe, which makes it uncomplicated to infer the government's partisanship from the stands taken by the parties that compose it. For simplicity, I take the partisanship of the prime minister's party as the partisan-

---

across countries. However, this fails to account for the emergence of stable patterns of ideological differentiation of parties in democracies with single-member district electoral systems, which suggests that a more general factor is at work. For the argument about multiple equilibria, see Riker 1980, 1982.

[28]Grossman and Helpman 1994.

[29]The one published study with wide coverage is Huber and Inglehart (1995), which includes forty-two countries, including some of the ones in this study. The authors relied on rankings by country experts. However, the number of responses to their questionnaire was small, some of the experts' judgments were idiosyncratic, and they had to rely on different experts for different countries, so the coding is not consistent. Where possible, I used secondary literature. For example, Kitschelt et al. (1999) conducted a sophisticated analysis based on survey data for four countries, and I adopted many of their judgments.

[30]I particularly want to thank Doug Blum, Arkadii Moshes, and other participants in conferences sponsored by the Program on New Approaches to Russian Security for their help coding governments in countries of the former Soviet Union.

ship of the government; for nonparty coalitions and caretaker governments, I use the largest party voting in favor of the government to determine the government's partisanship. In the presidential regimes that prevail across most of the former Soviet Union, however, it is much more difficult to determine the partisanship of the government. If the prime minister belongs to a parliamentary party, I use that party's position to determine the government's partisanship. Otherwise, I use public statements by the president and prime minister at the time the government was appointed, votes of confidence in the government, public perceptions and expectations gleaned from the press, and cabinet reshufflings that increase or decrease the influence of ministers with known reformist or antireformist policy agendas. I paid a great deal of attention to assuring the consistency of the rankings within each country over time and across countries, and made scrupulous efforts to avoid inferring preferences from the actual policies pursued; nevertheless, I recognize the inevitability of these problems. When there are strong reasons to believe that a control variable is important, however, it is better to use an imperfect measure than to omit the variable from the analysis.

Discount Factors

Discount factor is the term game theorists use to represent the degree to which actors value future payoffs relative to current payoffs. Discount factors close to 1 indicate patience (future payoffs are valued almost as much as current ones), and discount factors close to 0 indicate impatience (future payoffs are valued very little). Discount factors play an important role in any repeated-game model, because the point of repeating the game is to allow players to consider how their future welfare affects their current choice of strategies. Game-theoretic models of macroeconomic policymaking that rely on long-term incentives to restrain governments from using inflationary policies lead to the conclusion that higher discount factors—more patient governments— are associated with lower inflation.[31] The model developed in this book is no exception. The difficulty of measuring governments' preferences has prevented this hypothesis from being systematically tested. However, if it were possible to measure governments' expectations about how much longer they will last, that would be a natural proxy for discount factors. This is not directly measurable, either; however, it is possible to estimate a government's expected duration using statistical techniques. My approach is to calculate expected durations of governments using a hazard model, and use the vector of predicted durations as a proxy for discount factors.

---

[31] The seminal article in this vein is Barro and Gordon (1983).

International Influence

The international influence of particular countries plays an important role in the formal model, because it determines the cost to the IMF of enforcing conditionality when countries defect from their commitments. This is not directly observable, so I use several proxies. First, I use the country's quota in the IMF, which is a measure of a country's economic size. Countries have quotas of different sizes, which determine the size of the drawings they are permitted to make on IMF resources and the number of votes that they get on the board. These quotas are roughly proportional to real gross domestic product (GDP) and trade volume, but they are revised infrequently, so they do not capture the trend in GDP over a short time series.[32] Consequently, their errors are not correlated with errors in the economic variables. Best of all, from the perspective of this study, the IMF quota is the natural way for IMF officials to weight the importance of particular countries.

IMF quotas, however, do not capture the quality of a country's relations with the advanced industrial countries, nor do they capture changes in those relations over time. To do this, I use another measure: foreign aid. Measuring political significance in terms of foreign aid flows allows me to ask more penetrating questions about which dimensions of political influence determine the credibility of IMF programs. For example, how significant is the role of U.S. policy, compared to European Union policy? Interviews at the IMF confirm that the United States continues to exercise an influence out of proportion to its voting share on the board (currently about 18%).[33] Quantitative analysis measures this influence with much greater precision. The most comprehensive data on U.S. foreign aid are from the American Statistics Index (ASI), which measures aid appropriations on a fiscal-year basis. In addition, the OECD publishes calendar-year time series for bilateral official aid (OA) and official

---

[32]The original quotas were determined by a formula established at Bretton Woods and have been adjusted eleven times since. The original formula was the following:

$$\text{Quota} = (.02Y + .05R + .1M + .1V) \times (1 + X/Y)$$

Where Y is national income, R is gold and dollar balances, M is average imports, V is the maximum variation in imports and X is average exports. In the 1960s a system of five formulas was introduced, using broader data coverage, redefining some of the variables, and increasing the weight of foreign trade and variability of exports. The formulas were further revised in 1982. Quotas are currently awarded as the larger of (1) the Reduced Bretton Woods Formula, or (2) the average of the two lowest results from the other four formulas. The Reduced Bretton Woods Formula is:

$$\text{Quota} = (.01Y + .025R + .05P + .2276VC) \times (1 + C/Y)$$

Where Y is GDP, R is average monthly reserves, P and C are annual average current payments and receipts, respectively, and VC is variability of current receipts. The four alternate formulas use different weights for the same variables, and two omit the nonlinear element (International Monetary Fund 1998, pp. 20-7).

[33]Interview with Yuriy G. Yakusha, December 2, 1998; interview with Wieslaw Szczuka, December 2, 1998.

development aid (ODA) by donor, recipient, and category, which makes it possible to distinguish the effects of close U.S. ties with borrowing countries from those of close European or Japanese ties. The World Bank also publishes aggregated aid data by recipient country, relying on the same data source but using a somewhat different methodology. The correlation between the aggregate aid flows using the OECD methodology and the aggregate aid flows using the World Bank methodology is .94. Since each database uses its own methodology, some use calendar years and others use fiscal years, and each excludes some categories of flows, the correlations among the various other sources are low. Consequently, I have replicated all the analyses presented in the next chapter using each of these alternative measures to test for robustness.

3.5 CONCLUSIONS

There is a contradiction between the consensus among area specialists and practitioners, on the one hand, that IMF intervention is a powerful (if blunt) instrument and the results of quantitative research, on the other, which have so far been unable to show convincingly that IMF intervention has an effective influence over macroeconomic management. However, it is only recently that studies of IMF effectiveness have begun to apply appropriate statistical methods. The analysis presented here uses new data and addresses several criticisms of past studies: (1) it takes into consideration the endogeneity of IMF policies when testing for their effects; (2) it incorporates variation in the credibility of IMF programs into a test of their effectiveness; and (3) it explicitly models the politics of stabilization. The next chapter summarizes the results of the analysis.

4

An Empirical Test of the Model

THE PREVIOUS chapter summarized the existing literature on the effectiveness of the IMF and outlined a series of objections to the current state of the art. It concluded that there are no clean solutions to the problems inherent in control-group approaches that use IMF programs as the unit of analysis, and it would therefore be more fruitful to develop an alternative approach. Furthermore, the formal model presented in chapter 2 is not amenable to testing in the traditional way, using before-after or control-group comparisons, since it does not share the prediction implicit in such studies that IMF intervention exerts its influence only during periods when programs are active. Rather, it predicts that the IMF exerts an effect on countries' policies both when they have programs, because countries want to avoid program suspensions, and when they do not, because countries without active programs may hope to take advantage of IMF financing in the future.

The model offers novel testable hypotheses about the pattern of IMF lending—when programs are suspended and when they are resumed—and about the effect of interaction with the IMF on government policies and investors' responses. These hypotheses follow from the logic of strategic interaction and, in some cases, are quite counterintuitive. The tests of the hypotheses reported in this chapter make it possible to assess indirectly both the effectiveness of IMF intervention and the variation in that effectiveness across countries and over time. The hypotheses are as follows:

1. Countries with substantial international influence will be subject to shorter punishment intervals, because the threat of longer punishments is not credible;

2. Influential countries will deviate from their programs more often and consequently will be subject to more frequent program suspensions;

3. Countries eligible to participate in IMF programs should have less inflationary policies than countries that are ineligible, regardless of whether they have active programs in place;

4. More influential countries—those subject to shorter punishment durations—will choose more inflationary policies, because they cannot be deterred by the prospect of lengthy program suspensions;

5. Countries will pursue more inflationary policies during punishment periods, because they have less to lose when their programs are already suspended;

6. The policies of more influential countries will deteriorate less than those of smaller countries when programs are suspended, because suspensions are not as costly (lengthy) for them. Since active programs are less valuable, incentives do not change as much when a program is suspended;

7. Capital will flow into countries with active IMF programs and out of countries whose programs are suspended;

8. Influential countries will experience less capital inflow and more capital outflow;

9. Influential countries will experience smaller shifts in capital flows as a result of program suspensions.

Hypotheses 1, 3, 4, and 8 are straightforward and follow intuitively from the assumptions that interaction with the IMF deters inflationary policies and that more influential countries are more costly to punish. The other hypotheses are not obvious, however. They emerge from the complex strategic interaction among the IMF, several borrowing countries, and international investors, and demonstrate that a formal model can generate new hypotheses that follow in a non-obvious way from common assumptions. This chapter tests each of these hypotheses.

4.1 MODELS OF IMF LENDING DECISIONS

The formal model focuses attention on the conditions for program suspension and program resumption: when the IMF punishes violations of conditionality agreements, how long it suspends lapsed programs, and when it relents and renews support for countries' economic policies. Consequently, the method that is appropriate to test hypotheses about the IMF's lending decisions is duration analysis, which explicitly treats the length of the punishment interval and the length of the interval between punishments as dependent variables. The analysis is conducted as follows. A variable called *IMF Status* is coded 0 when an IMF program is in good standing (disbursements are being made on schedule) and 1 when the program is off track (there has been a delay or suspension of disbursements and no new program has been initiated). The dependent variable for the analysis is coded as the number of months until the next change of IMF status from good to bad or back again. Independent variables are correlated with the dependent variable using a Weibull duration model, and each independent variable is interacted with IMF status so that it is possible to retrieve the effects of the correlates on the durations of good and bad status episodes.[1] Since the results of duration models are not easy to interpret, I summarize the results here using charts and graphs rather than by presenting tables of coefficients. The tables are in Appendix B.

The primary hypotheses about IMF lending decisions are that the most strategically important countries (1) will be subject to shorter punishment intervals and (2) will be punished more often. For the purposes of testing these hypotheses, I use four variables as indirect measures of strategic importance: IMF quota, two measures of U.S. foreign aid, and aid from OECD members other than the United States.

4.2 COVARIATES OF THE DURATION OF PUNISHMENT INTERVALS

Table 4.1 summarizes the direction and significance of results of four models of the duration of program suspensions—that is, the length of punishment episodes. The most restricted model includes the four strategic influence variables, several control variables that capture dimensions of economic policy that figure prominently in the conditions attached to IMF programs, and a dummy variable for IMF status; subsequent models add additional political control variables. Political covariates were included in the model because there were two alternative hypotheses about how they might affect IMF lending decisions. First, it might be the case that compliance with the conditions of IMF programs is correlated with political variables. In that case, variables that represent political constraints on economic policymaking would be expected to lead to more frequent interruptions of programs and longer punishment intervals. Alternatively, it could be the case that the IMF conditions its decisions on political considerations by showing leniency toward countries that face severe domestic constraints, such as lack of parliamentary support or fragmented coalitions. This would lead to the opposite expectation: Political constraints would be associated with leniency, rather than with enforcement. Finally, it may be the case that the IMF forgoes actions that might destabilize particularly favored governments, such as those that rank highly on the left-right scale, which is coded 10 for extreme right-wing governments and -10 for extreme left-wing governments.

---

[1] I conducted this analysis using a variety of alternative duration models, including Cox (nonparametric), Weibull (parametric), and exponential (parametric). The results are substantially the same in each case. The parametric models seem preferable, since there is a strong theoretical reason to expect the hazard rate to be increasing—that is, I expect punishment durations to become more likely to end over time and countries to become more likely to deviate from their targets over time. The results support the hypothesis that the hazard rate is monotonically increasing.

Table 4.1: Durations of Punishment Intervals.

	Model 1	Model 2	Model 3	Model 4
IMF Quota	+	+	−	−
U.S. Aid (appropriations)	−**	−**	−**	−
U.S. Aid (disbursements)	−	−	−	−
Non-U.S. OECD Aid	−	−	+	+
Inflation ($t - 1$)	−	−	−	−
Inflation ($t - 6$)	−*	−**	−**	−**
% Ch Domestic Credit ($t - 1$)	+	+	−	−
% Ch Reserves ($t - 1$)	−	−	−	−
IMF Status	+	+**	+**	+
Authoritarian		+*	+	+
Months to Parliamentary Election		−**	−**	−
No. of Coalition Partners			−	−
Left-right Scale			+	+
Parliamentary Support				+
Pr(Gov't Fall)				−
Left-Right × Pr(Gov't Fall)				+

$^*p < .1$; $^{**}p < .05$, two-tailed tests

The table codes the positive or negative direction of the effect of each variable on the duration of punishment intervals. The results support the hypothesis that strategic importance is associated with shorter interruptions of IMF financing, confirming a key prediction of the formal model. Influential countries receive the equivalent of a slap on the wrist when they violate their program targets: predictable program suspensions or delays that are short in duration. U.S. foreign aid appropriations are strongly significant in three of the four models.[2] These results hold even when controlling for the sheer size of countries (IMF quota) and aid from other countries (non-U.S. OECD aid). Indeed, a striking pattern emerges: Whereas U.S. foreign aid exerts a strong influence over IMF lending, aid from other countries does not. This finding has two possible interpretations: first, that although the United States holds a minority of votes, it does indeed call the shots at the IMF, as critics allege; second, that other OECD countries do not target their aid as consistently to strategically

[2]Log likelihood ratio tests support Models 2 and 3 rather than 1 or 4.

important countries, so their aid is a poor measure of the targets' international influence. The present data do not make it possible to distinguish between these hypotheses. However, the pattern, which will be repeated throughout the analyses in this chapter, is strongly consistent with the interpretation that U.S. aid appropriations are a good measure of international influence and that international influence results in shorter punishment intervals.

This analysis uses two different measures of U.S. foreign aid, which makes possible a more precise test. The first, U.S. aid (appropriations), includes the categories of aid listed in the United States Agency for International Development (USAID) appropriations request to Congress. It measures aid appropriated by fiscal year, so it is the best measure of a country's current political standing in Washington. U.S. aid (disbursements) totals U.S. development aid reported by the Development Assistance Committee of the Organization for Economic Cooperation and Development (OECD), and U.S. military aid reported by the Federation of American Scientists. The overlap in categories with USAID requests is substantial, but these figures are for disbursements by calendar year, so they are more closely related to a country's influence in the previous budget cycle. Since the two series are reported for different periods, the correlation between them is small (.42), so it is possible to include both in the model.[3] If the effect on IMF lending is driven by countries' political influence, the measure of appropriations should be more significant; if it is driven by a correlation between aid and country behavior, then the disbursement measure should be more significant. Appropriations rather than disbursement of aid exercises influence in the model, which supports the interpretation that political influence affects IMF lending decisions.

The evidence about political variables is mixed, some coefficients pointing in favor of the hypothesis that governments with severe domestic constraints are more likely to suffer lengthy program interruptions, and others suggesting the opposite. Authoritarian government—using the Freedom House scale of political rights and freedoms—is strongly associated with longer punishment episodes, which suggests that the IMF may be more lenient toward liberal democracies than toward authoritarian countries. On the other hand, this may indicate that it is simply not true that democracies find it more difficult to adjust their policies than authoritarian countries do. To the contrary, once we control for political constraints that are only meaningful under democracy—notably the timing of elections—democratic systems may be more inclined to pursue economic reforms of the type favored by the IMF. The timing of elections, on the other hand, clearly supports the political constraints hypothesis. Program interruptions are likely to be significantly shorter if elections are far off,

[3] The correlation is low primarily because the appropriations data are for fiscal years and the disbursement data are for calendar years, but also in part because of different coding choices made by the U.S. government and the OECD, which include different categories of spending in foreign aid.

presumably because governments have more latitude to take painful measures when they do not have to face the polls immediately afterward.[4]

One economic covariate that plays an important role in explaining the duration of punishment episodes is the six-month lag of inflation. The six-month lag was included in the model because high-inflation countries have higher inflation targets built into their programs. Consequently, for any given level of current inflation, higher levels of inflation in the past should predict compliance with targets, rather than deviation from them, and therefore shorter punishment periods. The results confirm this expectation. Inflation one month in the past was included in the models as well, as an indicator the IMF frequently uses to determine whether a country is currently in compliance. (Current inflation, and current values of economic variables generally, cannot affect IMF lending decisions, because the IMF does not have the technical capacity to react to economic data that are less than a month old.)[5] This effect is not statistically significant, controlling for policy instruments (domestic credit and reserves), past values of inflation, and political variables. The negative sign of the coefficient, however, suggests the reverse causation predicted by the formal model: Shorter expected punishment periods lead to higher levels of inflation.

Substantive Significance

Figure 4.1 summarizes the substantive effects that relate to the primary hypotheses. The model used for the comparison is Model 4, which includes all the variables, so the estimate of the effect of the aid variables is conservative. The estimates represent the positive or negative contribution of IMF Quota, U.S. aid appropriations, and U.S. aid disbursements to the expected duration of punishment intervals for each country.[6] The effects are dramatic: The mean punishment interval is 3.3 months shorter for Russia and 3.2 months shorter for Ukraine than for the median country. Using the extreme values for Russia and Ukraine instead of their means yields 6.5 months for Russia and 5.1 for Ukraine, confirming that variation in influence over time makes a significant difference even in the treatment of important countries.[7]

---

[4]It is puzzling, given this finding, that I find such weak correlations between election timing and macroeconomic policy later in this chapter. One possible explanation for the divergent findings is that election timing accounts for performance on other targets of IMF programs, such as structural adjustment.

[5]Interview with Shadman-Valavi, May 4, 2000.

[6]I calculate the expected duration based on each country's mean for each of the three influence variables, holding all other variables at the sample mean, and then calculate the difference between this and the expectation when all variables are held at the sample mean. I then compare the results for each country with the results for the country with the median result.

[7]As significant as these differences are, the estimates understate the variation in the dependent variable. The average duration of a punishment interval for participating countries is 8.6 months. The average for Russia is 3.6 months, and the average for Ukraine is 2.5. The three influence variables account for two-thirds of Russia's deviation from the average and 52 percent of Ukraine's.

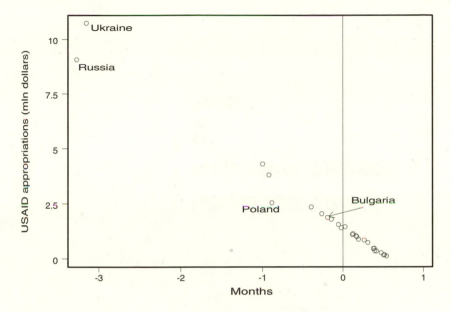

Figure 4.1: Country Variations in Expected Duration of Punishment
Intervals.

Figure 4.2 summarizes the substantive effects of each of the independent
variables. The bars show the (positive or negative) effect on the duration of
punishment intervals in months of increasing the value of each variable by
one standard deviation above its mean while holding all other variables at their
means. The strongest substantive results are for inflation. Holding last month's
inflation constant, having inflation one standard deviation above the mean six
months ago reduces the length of program suspensions by eleven weeks—
presumably because high inflation in the recent past implies more generous
targets in the present. Similarly, however, high inflation one month ago is correlated with shorter punishment intervals. It is only reasonable to assume that
this correlation is a case of reverse causation, since it cannot be the case that
the IMF systematically rewards countries for increasing inflation by resuming
suspended programs. Rather, it must be the case that the expectation of short
punishment periods leads to high levels of inflation. Indeed, this is consistent
with a central prediction of the formal model. If short punishment periods are
anticipated—as the formal model argues they should be—then it is reasonable
to assume that this anticipation can lead countries to make more inflationary
policy choices. Because of the large standard error, however, this result cannot
be considered confirming evidence.

The substantively most important political covariates are autocratic government, elections, and parliamentary support. Autocratic government is mea-

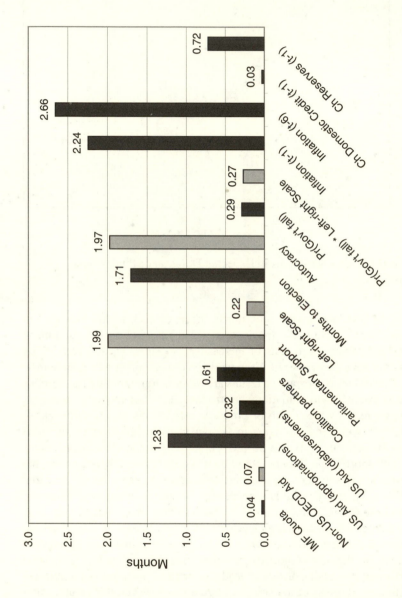

Figure 4.2: Effects of Variables on Expected Duration of Punishment Intervals. Dark bars represent negative effects, light bars positive effects.

sured on a fourteen-point scale, with the sample mean at 7 and a standard deviation of 3.3. Since one standard deviation increased the punishment interval by almost two months, the range in effects between the most authoritarian and most democratic states is substantial. In Belarus, for example, the Freedom House score was 7 before President Lukashenka took office and 12 after he suppressed parliament and established authoritarian rule. The predicted effect of this change is to increase punishment durations by three months. To take another example, democratic Poland has an average Freedom House score of 3.5, and authoritarian Uzbekistan has an average score of 13.25. The effect of this difference in political regimes is to make the average predicted length of punishments almost six months longer in Uzbekistan. The scale of effects for the timing of parliamentary elections is less dramatic but still quite important. The average punishment is almost one month shorter when elections are six months off than when they are imminent and almost two months shorter when elections are a year away, suggesting that election timing has a lot to do with how long it takes countries to get their lapsed programs back on track. The effect of parliamentary support is less substantial, and it is unwise to put much interpretation on the effect because this variable is not statistically significant. The results indicate that increasing parliamentary support from 45 to 55 percent increases punishment durations by three weeks, and going from a simple parliamentary majority to a two-thirds majority increases them by five weeks.

4.3 COVARIATES OF PROGRAM SUSPENSIONS

Table 4.2 summarizes the results of the same four models for the duration of episodes in which programs are in good standing. Again, the symbols indicate a positive or negative correlation with the length of periods of good standing, so negative signs indicate variables that increase the probability of program interruptions. As the model predicts, influence does not buy a waiver; to the contrary, the most influential countries are the ones whose programs are most frequently suspended. U.S. aid appropriations and U.S. aid disbursements are both significant, and both point in the predicted direction. This confirms my second hypothesis, that influential countries will be punished more often, because they deviate from their programs more frequently. This is an important result, because the hypothesis is counterintuitive. The confirmation of counterintuitive hypotheses not only shows that the model is on track, but also demonstrates the value of formalizing an argument. Again, aid from countries other than the United States does not have a significant effect, suggesting either that U.S. influence is decisive or that U.S. aid is the best measure of international influence more generally.

Most of the political variables point in the direction of the first hypothesis: Variables that represent political constraints are correlated with unmeasured dimensions of program failure and consequently explain the frequency of pro-

Table 4.2: Durations of Programs in Good Standing.

	Model 1	Model 2	Model 3	Model 4
IMF Quota	+	+	−	−
U.S. Aid (appropriations)	−***	−***	−*	−**
U.S. Aid (disbursements)	−**	−**	−**	−
Non-U.S. OECD Aid	+	+	+	−
Inflation $(t-1)$	−	−	−	−
Inflation $(t-6)$	+	+	+	+
% Ch Domestic Credit $(t-1)$	−**	−*	−*	−*
% Ch Reserves $(t-1)$	+	+	+	+
IMF Status	−	−**	−**	−
Authoritarian		−**	−***	−**
Months to Parliamentary Election		+	+	+
No. of Coalition Partners			−*	−**
Left-right Scale			+	−
Parliamentary Support				−
Pr(Gov't Fall)				−
Left-Right × Pr(Gov't Fall)				+**

$^*p < .1;\ ^{**}p < .05;\ ^{***}p < .01$, two-tailed tests

gram suspensions. The number of parties in a governing coalition significantly increases the probability that a program will be interrupted, suggesting that fragmented coalitions are less able to implement IMF programs. Other variables are insignificant but point in the same direction: Programs fare better when elections are far off and when governments are less likely to collapse. The IMF may be tougher on countries with more backing in parliament, but that result is not statistically significant.

There are two important exceptions. First, authoritarian government is highly significant: The IMF is considerably more likely to punish authoritarian states (which have high scores) than democracies, all other things being equal. Furthermore, the effect is substantial enough to create the appearance that the IMF makes fine distinctions between countries based on the quality of their democratic systems. It is possible that the causation takes a different path: More democratic countries are more likely, not less, to pursue policies the IMF recommends, at least when one controls for a variety of political constraints that are only meaningful under democracy.[8] However, the results here also support the hypothesis that the IMF is more lenient toward more democratic post-Communist countries, which have warmer relations with the major donor countries. The present analysis does not provide grounds for choosing between these alternative interpretations.

Second, the IMF is less likely to suspend financing for right-wing governments when they are close to collapse. There is a strong interaction between the probability that a government will fall and its position on a left-right scale. The independent effects of government instability and right-wing partisanship are to reduce the duration of IMF programs in good standing. When the probability that a government will fall is high enough, however, programs of right-wing governments last longer than those of left-wing governments, and when the government is right-wing, increasing the probability that the government will fall extends the life of IMF programs. The turning points are close to the mean of each variable. Thus, when the probability that a government will fall is above .04 (mean is .05), right-wing governments are less likely than left-wing governments to have their programs suspended. This condition was met in Poland for most of 1993; in Russia, for most of the Chernomyrdin governments, including the last two months before the presidential elections in 1996, and in 1998 up through the August crash; and in Ukraine, almost continuously from 1992 to 2000. The turning point for left-right partisanship is .95, on a scale that ranges from -10 to 10. Thus, in general, for right-leaning governments, increased instability leads to more long-lasting programs, and for left-leaning governments, the opposite is the case.

This effect is strong, significant, and intuitive: It is much more costly to suspend support to a favored government if it is on the brink of collapse, since program interruptions often cause severe economic difficulties that could push a fragile government over the edge, bringing a less accommodating partner to power. Conversely, the same result means that the IMF is more likely to suspend financing when a left-wing government is close to collapse, since that would be likely to bring about a favorable change of government.

IMF officials vigorously reject the claim that they play politics with their lending decisions this way.[9] Indeed, they are at pains to show that they have been even-handed, and in Bulgaria, for example, they appear to have been remarkably so.[10] Similarly, the Fund never hesitated to suspend a program under a series of fragile reformist governments in Poland. However, there remain prominent cases where the Fund has suspended its better judgment instead of suspending a program: A case in point was Russia during the 1996 presiden-

---

[8] This is consistent with Hellman's (1998) conjecture that contestation breaks down political deadlocks that favor special interests opposed to reform.

[9] Interview with McGuirk, May 3, 2000.

[10] Chapter 8 discusses the Bulgarian case in detail.

tial election, which was a time of profound instability when the right-leaning government appeared to be at risk. The result found here, that right-wing governments are systematically treated differently than left-wing governments in a way that depends on their degree of political vulnerability, is difficult to explain except as the result of political calculations in the IMF's decision making.

The economic covariates were generally insignificant but had effects running in the expected direction: inflation and expanding central bank credit make programs more likely to be suspended, and increasing central bank reserves makes them less likely to be suspended. This is heartening, since these are the formal criteria that are most important in invoking program suspensions. The long lag of inflation appeared to decrease the probability of program suspensions, which is consistent with the earlier argument that high-inflation countries have higher inflation targets.

Substantive Significance

The substantive effects of measures of international influence on program suspensions are striking; indeed, the aid variables have even stronger effects on program suspensions than on punishment interval durations. Receiving a level of U.S. aid appropriations one standard deviation above the mean cuts four months off the average duration of IMF programs in good standing. A one standard deviation increase in either IMF Quota or U.S. aid disbursements cuts more than another month off the life of a program. Once again, aid from countries other than the United States does not play an important role in explaining IMF decisions to suspend lending. Combining the effects of IMF quota, U.S. aid appropriations, and U.S. aid disbursements predicts that the average length of an IMF program in Russia will be more than a year shorter than in the median country in the sample, and ten months shorter in Ukraine. At their maximum values, these variables predict that Russian programs will be sixteen months shorter and Ukrainian programs almost fourteen months shorter than in the median country. Figure 4.3 shows the combined substantive effects of these three variables on the duration of programs in each country in the sample.[11]

Figure 4.4 presents the substantive significance of each independent variable on the suspension of IMF programs across the sample.[12] The economic policy variables have short-lived effects, which is not surprising: Monthly fluctuations in policy should not have long-term effects. The effect of inflation is

---

[11] In this case the predicted effects overstate the variation in the dependent variable. The average duration of a program in good standing was 14.3 months. The average for Russia was 5.4 months, and the average for Ukraine was 3.2.

[12] I use the same procedure as before, varying each independent variable by 1 standard deviation while holding everything else at its mean. The results are for Model 4, which includes all of the variables.

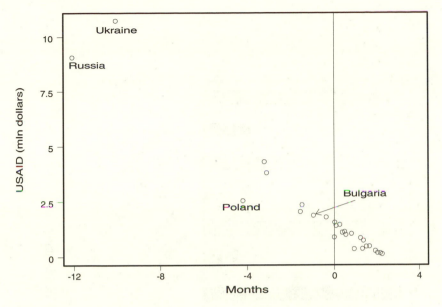

Figure 4.3: Country Variations in Expected Duration of Programs in Good Standing.

very small, perhaps because inflation is not consistently targeted as a performance criterion: An increase of one standard deviation cuts only a few days off a program's duration. The variables that are more commonly used as program criteria, however, have stronger effects: domestic credit (one month) and reserves (almost four months). The effect of a shift in reserves may be more long-lasting because it is difficult to reverse.

Some of the political variables have very substantial effects. Less democratic countries, other things being equal, are much more likely to have their programs suspended. Returning to the example of Belarus, the consolidation of authoritarian rule under Lukashenka cut more than six months off the predicted length of IMF programs in good standing. Programs in democratic Poland are predicted to be in good standing for fifteen months longer than in authoritarian Uzbekistan.

Some variables measuring political constraints account for substantial decreases in program durations, presumably because they influence the speed of economic adjustment. Adding a coalition partner to a one-party government cuts ten weeks from the average program's life, and adding a second partner to the coalition cuts off another two months. This is consistent with the conventional wisdom about the effects of political fragmentation on economic reform. However, the effect of election timing is substantively small, as well as statistically insignificant. Holding elections in six months rather than next month

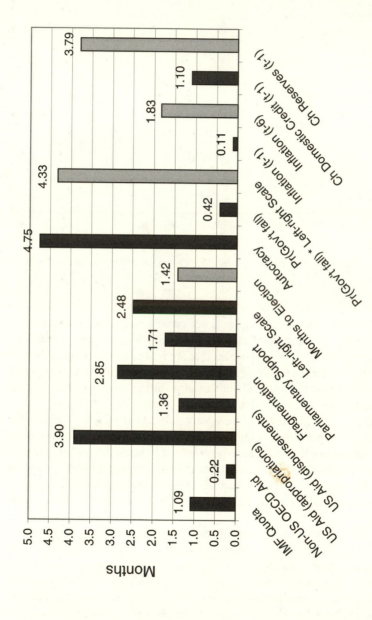

Figure 4.4: Effects of Variables on Expected Duration of Programs in Good Standing. Dark bars represent negative effects, light bars positive effects.

extends the life of a program by less than two weeks, and putting elections off for a year extends it by less than a month. These effects are smaller than the effects on the duration of punishment intervals, suggesting that imminent elections play a larger role in delaying the adjustments needed to bring a program back on track than in boosting the incentive to deviate from a program in good standing. This is consistent with the model's expectation that governments are more willing to pay a political price to sustain the current program than to negotiate a new one, because they have more to lose when their program is in good standing. On the other hand, increasing parliamentary support for the government from a bare majority to 75 percent *decreases* the average length of a program in good status by seven weeks. This may suggest that the IMF does make allowances for countries that face parliamentary opposition by giving them more time to implement their conditions. However, as we will see below, substantial parliamentary support is surprisingly associated with worse economic policy, so the causation may run in the other direction: Secure majorities fail to promote reform, and therefore lead to suspensions of IMF programs.

The political variables with the most striking substantive effects are the probability that a government will fall, left-right partisanship, and their interaction. The IMF is more likely to punish secure right-wing governments than secure left-wing governments and less likely to punish vulnerable right-wing governments than vulnerable left-wing governments. This is difficult to interpret otherwise than as evidence of political calculations in the IMF. The substantive effects are dramatic: When the probability of collapse is one standard deviation below the mean, the average program of an extreme left-wing government lasts almost eight months longer than the average program of an extreme right-wing government. This is consistent with a pragmatic political calculus: Right-wing governments can generally be pushed farther along the path of reform, and the Fund is tough with them; left-wing governments are more intransigent, so the Fund sets lower standards that are easier to meet. On the other hand, when the probability of collapse is one standard deviation above the mean, a program lasts an average of ten months longer under an extreme right-wing government than under an extreme left-wing government. This is consistent with a pragmatic calculus as well: There is no point in suspending a program if the result will be to bring down a favored government and bring the opposition to power.

4.4 MODELS OF POLICY VARIABLES

The theoretical model also generates testable hypotheses about policy variables and capital flows. The most primitive hypothesis is that being a participant in IMF programs—regardless of whether these programs are active or suspended—should make policies less inflationary and stabilize the macroeconomy. Furthermore, if the model is correct, the credibility of IMF programs should have an effect on macroeconomic policy and international capital flows. Consequently, less influential countries should have lower inflation rates and more stable macroeconomic environments than more important countries. This hypothesis suggests that the aid variables that were shown to influence IMF lending decisions should also be associated with poor macroeconomic performance. Furthermore, it is possible to test the model more directly. The model predicts that it is the expected duration of program suspensions that influences governments' policy choices, so longer expected durations should be associated with more conservative economic policies and more stable financial markets. This hypothesis suggests that the predicted duration of punishment intervals derived from the previous analysis should explain economic outcomes. The model generates additional hypotheses that are more counterintuitive. First, countries should choose more inflationary policies when their IMF programs have been suspended. The model shows that countries deviate from their targets with a higher probability when they are in punishment status, because they have "less to lose"—they anticipate being punished for the immediate future regardless of their current policy, so the benefits of exercising restraint are delayed. Second, this effect should be most pronounced for the least influential countries. Small countries gain more credibility than large countries from a program in good standing, because it is known that they have stronger incentives to comply; thus, they are the ones whose policies deteriorate the most when they revert to noncooperative behavior. This hypothesis implies that, when possible, the model should be specified with an interaction term between measures of influence and the indicator variable for program suspensions, and that the coefficient of the interaction term and of the basic effects of those variables should have opposite signs.

Effects of International Influence

The first cut at testing these hypotheses is to regress the variables that represent a country's international stature and influence on policy and outcome variables. The dependent variables most relevant to IMF program conditions and with the broadest data coverage for these countries are inflation and change in central bank domestic credit. The ideal data for testing the hypothesis about capital flows would be monthly data on the flows themselves or on interest rates on bonds. Unfortunately, the first are unavailable, and the second are only available for part of the time series and for the countries sufficiently advanced to have developed effective domestic bond markets. Consequently, I use a proxy with much broader data coverage: change in the nominal exchange rate. Devaluation is not necessarily a symptom of deviation from an IMF program; indeed, many programs mandate devaluation in order to improve the current account. However, devaluation is the inevitable consequence of the loss of investor confidence. Many of the post-Communist countries have used the nominal exchange rate as an anchor for their macroeconomic policies and a symbol of political resolve, so devaluation became visible evidence that the market had delivered a negative verdict on government policies.

The variables of primary interest are those that represent national stature and influence, and that were previously shown to influence IMF lending decisions: U.S. aid appropriations and disbursements. The model predicts that these variables should be associated with poor compliance with IMF conditions (increased rates of inflation and domestic credit growth) and with devaluation (increasing exchange rates). Since the theoretical model predicts that the incentive to abide by IMF conditions deteriorates after a defection, IMF status—which indicates whether a country is currently in a punishment stage, 1, or not, 0—is included in the model, with the same expectation: that it will be associated with poor performance on all three variables. Since the incentive to comply is expected to deteriorate more for smaller countries than for larger ones after a defection, IMF status is interacted with each of the measures of national status, with the expectation that the interaction term should be negative. In addition, an indicator variable for participants in IMF programs (active or suspended) is included as a rough test of the hypothesis that interaction with the IMF leads to less inflationary policies.

Table 4.3 summarizes the results of this analysis for each of the three dependent variables. The first block of variables consists of economic time series controls. The lag and the lag squared of the dependent variable are included in the equation for each policy variable, because the theoretical model predicts that past states of each policy variable should affect the incentive to deviate from current program targets. Deviation in the immediate past should make current deviation more likely, but, as the scale of accumulated deviations grows, the incentive to defect should gradually decline. The expectation, therefore, is that the lagged dependent variable should have a positive correlation and the squared term a negative correlation. Since the estimation is performed on pooled time-series data, I use panel-corrected standard errors (PCSEs), which account for correlation in the errors within countries and autocorrelation of errors over time.[13]

The most straightforward hypothesis drawn from the model was that being an actual or potential participant in an IMF program should lead to lower inflation and a more stable policy environment. In this analysis the variable *Participant* is a dummy variable coded 0 if a country has not yet joined the IMF or has graduated from active participation in IMF programs, and coded 1 if it is a member actively participating or negotiating to participate in a stabilization program. The variable is highly significant in the models for infla-

---

[13]The estimation assumes correlated panels and a common AR(1) process. The PCSE approach, proposed by Beck and Katz (1995), has small-sample properties that are superior to those of other common methods of analyzing panel data.

Table 4.3: Effects of Foreign Aid on Policy Variables.
Panel-corrected standard errors in parentheses.

	Inflation	*Credit*	*Exchange Rate*
Lagged Depend. Var. (LDV)	.3177*** (.0503)	.1374*** (.0397)	.3739*** (.0639)
LDV^2	$-.0003$*** (2.71×10^{-5})	-3.79×10^{-5} (.0006)	3.61×10^{-5}*** (6.16×10^{-6})
Average Inflation	.7387*** (.0369)		.1580 (.3278)
Average Change Exchange Rate	$-.0470^{\dagger}$ (.0181)	$-.0101^{\dagger}$ (.0035)	.8958*** (.0536)
Average Change Domest. Credit		.7119*** (.0409)	
IMF Quota	$-.0005$ (.0008)	.0001 (.0003)	$-.0026$ (.0045)
IMF Quota × IMF Status	.0011 (.0024)	$-.0005$ (.0005)	$-.0024$ (.0086)
U.S. aid (appropriations)	.3312** (.1674)	.2216*** (.0802)	1.0664 (1.0150)
U.S. aid × IMF Status	$-.6398$ (.5795)	$-.1727$* (.1086)	$-.0870$ (3.4500)
U.S. ODA (disbursements)	.0109 (.0177)	$-.0020$ (.0085)	$-.0028$ (.0842)
U.S. ODA × IMF Status	.0004 (.0555)	.0337† (.0157)	.0245 (.2286)
U.S. military (disbursements)	.1053 (.3012)	$-.1826$ (.1326)	.2884 (.9007)
U.S. military × IMF Status	-3.0012 (9.2856)	.3043 (.9186)	-6.8785 (40.7631)
Participant	-3.0528*** (.7282)	-2.6276*** (.5111)	-7.4284* (4.7868)
IMF Status	4.2098* (2.6886)	2.7895*** (.5536)	8.4440 (14.4007)

Table 4.3 continued

	Inflation	Credit	Exchange Rate
Months to Election	−.0097 (.0295)	−2.36x10^{-5} (.0159)	.1595 (.1064)
Support in Parliament	9.6939† (2.6261)	2.7264†† (1.4822)	17.0759 (13.8567)
No. Coalition Parties	.8472** (.3684)	−.3170†† (.1676)	−1.2903 (2.2821)
Left-Right Scale	−.0409 (.0702)	−.0722** (.0351)	−.1489 (.2648)
War	12.9318*** (4.9058)	4.2035*** (.9317)	39.9171* (26.6167)
Pr(Gov't Fall)	18.1716** (10.0166)	1.9441 (4.6360)	91.3500*** (35.3217)
Constant	−7.9519† (2.0879)	−.0163 (1.0329)	−12.8633 (8.7898)
Adjusted R^2	.18	.42	.13
No. Observations	2629	2629	2629
No. Countries	26	26	26

$^{*}p < .1$; $^{**}p < .05$; $^{***}p < .01$ in the predicted direction (one-tailed test)
$^{†}p < .05$; $^{††}p < .1$ in an unanticipated direction (two-tailed test)

tion and change in domestic credit, and marginally significant in the model for exchange rates. Its substantive effects are impressive: Participants have 3 percent per month lower rates of inflation, 2.6 percent per month lower rates of credit growth, and 7.4 per month percent lower rates of devaluation than non-participants. These results have to be interpreted with some caution, since there is clearly a selection mechanism at work here. For example, Ukraine became an active participant two years after Russia, in large part because its macroeconomic management was so poor. On the other hand, there is also a selection mechanism at work at the other end: Poland graduated from active participation in IMF programs in 1995, because its strong macroeconomic performance made further conditionality programs unnecessary. One can say with confidence at least that these results are consistent with what we expect to observe if it is true that the IMF exercises important influence over national policies.[14]

[14]Ideally, I would like to estimate these effects using a selection model, but two difficulties interfere with doing so here. First, there are no good instruments. Second, this is a variable that

A deeper cut at the problem tests the impact of variables that measure nations' international influence, which the model and the previous duration analysis suggest determines the credibility of IMF enforcement of conditionality. Of the measures of international status, only U.S. aid appropriations were a statistically significant predictor of punishment durations, and only U.S. aid appropriations are statistically significant in this analysis. U.S. aid appropriations are associated with a sharp increase in inflation, far beyond what could be ascribed to the demand-stimulating effects of foreign aid flows; indeed, the fact that it is appropriations rather than disbursements of aid that is significant points to a political interpretation rather than an economic one. The difference between the average level of U.S. aid appropriations in Russia and the sample mean contributes 2.4 percent per month to Russian inflation, and raising aid appropriations to their maximum value in Russia accounts for an increment of 7.7 percent of monthly inflation. The comparable figures for Ukraine are 2.9 percent and 5.7 percent. U.S. foreign aid appropriations are similarly associated with more rapid expansion of domestic credit. At the average level of appropriations, the effect contributes 1.6 percent to the monthly rate of credit growth in Russia and 2 percent in Ukraine; at the maximum level, the effect adds 5.2 percent in Russia and 3.8 percent in Ukraine. Aid appropriations are only marginally significant in the model for exchange rates ($p < .15$), but have a marked substantive effect in the direction predicted by the model. At the average level for Russia, U.S. aid appropriations account for an 8 percent monthly devaluation; at the maximum value, they account for a devaluation of 25 percent. Taken together, these results strongly support the model's prediction that influential countries suffer from greater credibility problems.

The model makes the secondary prediction that economic policy should deteriorate when a country is in punishment status, so the model incorporates a dummy variable coded 1 when a program has been suspended. IMF Status has the expected sign in each of the three models and is substantively quite significant: When IMF programs are suspended, monthly growth rates are 4.2 percent higher for inflation, 2.8 percent higher for domestic credit, and 8.4 percent higher for exchange rate (i.e., devaluation). The result for domestic credit is significant at $p < .05$, and the result for inflation is significant at $p < .06$, but the result for exchange rate is not ($p < .28$). These results are consistent with the model's expectation that policy should deteriorate when a program is suspended but, again, are not decisive, because there is a selection effect at work. The duration analysis in the previous section showed that high rates of change of domestic credit were associated with high probabilities that IMF programs would be suspended, so it is possible that expanding central bank credit causes IMF program suspensions rather than the reverse. Indeed,

---

can have very little variation by definition, because each country can transition only once from applicant to participant, and only once more from participant to graduate.

this is a natural interpretation, since the central bank's domestic assets are a standard component of conditionality. However, the duration analysis in the previous section found that short-term inflation did not significantly increase the probability of program suspensions. This suggests that the best interpretation of the finding about inflation is that program suspensions cause inflation to deteriorate, as the model predicts.

In addition, the model generates a secondary hypothesis that the effect of a program suspension is ameliorated for influential countries, because they have less to lose. (Their policies are not particularly credible when they are in good standing, so they should not change very much when they are not.) The results provide support for this hypothesis, but the evidence is uneven. The interaction effect between IMF Status and U.S. aid appropriations is in the predicted direction. They are insignificant for change of exchange rate and marginally significant for inflation ($p < .14$) but stronger for change in domestic credit ($p < .06$). Substantively, the effects on inflation and domestic credit are almost exactly what the model predicts. For Russia, the negative effect of the interaction term on inflation averages 4.6 percent, which erases the 4.2 percent increase occasioned by having a program suspended, so inflation does not change significantly when Russia loses good standing with the IMF. For Ukraine, the interaction effect is even stronger. Turning to domestic credit expansion, in both Russia and Ukraine the interaction term blocks, on average, about half the effect of having a program suspended. When each country is receiving its maximum levels of aid, the effect disappears completely.

Most of the domestic political control variables are not significant in these models, although almost all are significant and have the conventionally expected effects in more restricted models. In particular, both election timing and left-right partisanship have much weaker effects in these models than the comparative political economy literature would lead one to expect. Election timing is insignificant in all three models. Left-right partisanship has only modest effects on inflation and domestic credit, which run in the expected direction: Right-wing governments pursue more restrictive policies. Only the coefficient for change in domestic credit is significant. The largest substantive effect of left-right partisanship occurs in exchange rates, where there is a maximum spread of 3 percent in the monthly movement of a currency, with left-wing governments presiding over the most rapid devaluations. The large standard error, however, makes this result insignificant ($p < .29$).

A few of the political variables point to interesting developments in the politics of macroeconomic policymaking in post-Communist countries. Support in parliament was expected to depress inflation and central bank credit, because it would facilitate the passage of austere budgets; IMF officials typically assume that the impact of parliamentary opposition is felt in higher budget deficits. On the contrary, this variable has a surprising effect: It leads to more rapid inflation ($p < .001$) and higher rates of domestic credit expansion ($p < .07$). This may lend support to Bernhard's hypothesis that parliamentary opposition increases the autonomy of the central bank.[15] The number of coalition partners in the government has the anticipated effect of increasing inflation, because the proliferation of veto players blocks reforms—each member added to the coalition adds .85 percent to the monthly inflation rate ($p < .02$). However, the number of coalition partners also has the surprising effect of decreasing the rate of domestic credit expansion ($p < .06$). This supports an interpretation that party competition within a governing coalition has a different impact in the central bank than in the legislative arena, and while it may postpone legislation necessary for adjustment, it also prevents the government from manipulating the central bank.

The probability that a government will fall, which is an expectation derived from a Weibull duration model, was expected to increase inflation, inflationary policies, and the rate of devaluation. The discount factor plays a critical role in the formal model—governments with higher discount factors are less inclined to violate their agreements with the IMF—and it seems reasonable that a government that expects to fall imminently has a low discount factor (i.e., discounts the future heavily). The empirical results confirm this expectation. The effects of government instability on inflation and the exchange rate—causing both to deteriorate—are substantively impressive and statistically very significant. An increase in the probability that a government will fall in a given month by one standard deviation (.05) causes an increase in the monthly inflation rate of almost 1 point, and a monthly devaluation of 4.6 percent; increasing that probability to its maximum value (.52) increases inflation by 8.4 percent and causes a devaluation of 42 percent. Reverse causation can be ruled out fairly confidently, because short-term inflation and exchange rate movements did not have a significant effect on government durations.

Finally, it comes as no surprise that involvement in an international or civil war is associated with higher inflation, more rapid expansion of central bank credit, and a dramatic depreciation. Countries involved in violent conflict suffered monthly inflation rates 13 percent higher than average, increased central bank credit 4.2 percent faster, and devalued their exchange rates at a monthly pace 91 percentage points higher than their more stable or pacific neighbors.[16]

Effects of Credibility

A deeper cut at the hypothesis that the IMF's credibility affects government policies uses the duration of punishment intervals—the consequence of underlying political influence and the intervening variable between influence and

---

[15]Bernhard 1998.

[16]The data do not include observations for the Republic of Yugoslavia (Serbia) or Bosnia. The wars and civil wars coded included observations for Croatia, Slovenia (one month), Russia (the first and second Chechen wars), Moldova, Georgia, Armenia, Azerbaijan, and Tadzhikistan.

policy decisions—as a measure of credibility. This specification should be a better test of the model, because it is more direct: in the model, it is the expected punishment interval that drives differences in countries' policies. The analysis would be biased, however, if the length of actual punishment intervals were used, since punishment intervals are endogenous to economic policymaking. Consequently, I use a measure derived from the predicted length of punishment intervals, which is the hazard rate. The hazard rate is the probability that the interval ends, so it is proportional to the inverse of the duration, and I refer to it below as Pr(punishment ends). In order to interpret the results, it is important to note that the hazard rates are calculated from the coefficients that predict the duration of punishment intervals, not program suspensions, because the theoretical model predicts that the IMF's credibility problem manifests itself in the duration of punishment intervals, not in the probability of punishment. These hazard rates are calculated for every observation after a country becomes a participant in IMF programs, regardless of whether the current program has been suspended.[17] For observations in which the current program is in good standing, therefore, this hazard represents a hypothetical: the expected duration of punishment at time t if the program were currently suspended. This reflects the model's prediction that expected punishment durations influence policy both when a program has been suspended and when it has not. Although theoretically the hazard rate represents a probability, the estimated rate ranges as high as 1.2 because the hazard rate is calculated outside the sample in which the coefficients were estimated. Unlike the previous analysis, this series of models is estimated without an interaction term between Pr(punishment ends) and IMF status, because the interaction term and the hazard rate itself are too highly correlated to make the results meaningful.

This analysis is performed using the same block of control variables for economic policy and domestic political conditions employed in the previous models. Thus, the interpretation of the coefficient of the hazard rate in this model is the effect of the probability that the punishment period ends in a given month, *holding observed economic policy and the political factors that influence unobserved measures of economic policy constant.* This is precisely what is meant by a measure of the effect of variation in the IMF's credibility. In principle, if the credibility of the IMF's threat to withhold financing until the original program targets are met does not vary across countries or over time, only past policy and the factors that influence current policy should be signif-

---

[17] Pr(punishment ends) is coded 1 for periods before a particular country joined the IMF, since the probability of being punished in the following month without being an IMF member is 0. An alternative specification of the model would be to exclude data from the analysis for nonparticipant countries. This eliminates almost five hundred observations and depresses the statistical significance of the results I report below, but does not change the results qualitatively. In the restricted sample, the coefficients of the hazard rate are substantially larger than in the full sample. I report the results for the full sample because they are more efficient and the smaller standard errors make them the most reliable estimates.

Table 4.4: Effects of Punishment Duration on Policy Variables. Panel-corrected standard errors in parentheses.

	Inflation	Credit	Exchange Rate
Lagged Depend. Var. (LDV)	.3416*** (.0642)	.1281*** (.0422)	−.3622*** (.0413)
LDV^2	−.0003*** (3.79x10^{-5})	3.46x10^{-5} (.0007)	3.89x10^{-5}*** (5.99x10^{-6})
Average Inflation	.7309*** (.0274)		−.0238 (.1119)
Average Change Exchange Rate	−.0536† (.0172)	−.0127† (.0046)	.9495*** (.0236)
Average Change Domest. Credit		.6149*** (.0486)	
Pr(Punish. Ends)	3.9140** (1.8914)	5.0416*** (1.2515)	18.4552** (8.1547)
IMF Status	1.7499** (.7600)	1.8693*** (.5009)	2.1092 (1.9699)
Participant	−1.1959** (.6386)	−.1121 (.4539)	1.9211 (3.0627)
Months to Election	−.0146 (.0321)	−.0163 (.0159)	.1206 (.1192)
Support in Parliament	9.0353† (1.7932)	1.3884 (1.3629)	15.7922 (10.0707)
No. Coalition Parties	.8265*** (.3439)	−.3660† (.1509)	−1.0694 (1.1196)
Left-Right Scale	−.0376 (.0500)	−.0572** (.0324)	−.1019 (.2271)
War	12.7423*** (2.1254)	3.7326*** (.7774)	39.7910*** (6.6138)
Pr(Gov't Fall)	16.3533* (11.2195)	−.6553 (4.5904)	83.7621** (39.8134)
Constant	−8.8528† (1.5708)	−.6647 (.9685)	−19.5313† (6.2990)

$^*p < .1$; $^{**}p < .05$; $^{***}p < .01$ in the predicted direction (one-tailed test)
$^†p < .05$ in an unanticipated direction (two-tailed test)

Table 4.4 continued from previous page

	Inflation	*Credit*	*Exchange Rate*
Adjusted R^2	.17	.43	.10
No. Observations	2599	2599	2599
No. Countries	26	26	26

icant; punishment intervals should not exercise any independent effect. To the extent that punishment intervals depend on economic policies, this should be captured by the economic and political controls. Any remaining effect of the expected duration of punishment intervals must be attributable to variation in the IMF's credibility.

The results of the analysis are presented in Table 4.4. Again, the results confirm the expectations of the theoretical model. The key variable for this analysis is Pr(punishment ends). A large value for the predicted hazard rate means that the country is less likely to be subject to a lengthy punishment, so the expectation is that this variable should be correlated with higher levels of inflation. The effect of the hazard rate is in the correct direction and is significant in each of the three models. To illustrate the substantive significance of these results, consider the case of Russia in 1996, when U.S.-Russian cooperation was at a high point and both countries were in the midst of competitive presidential elections that dramatically raised the stakes in Russia's interactions with the IMF. The average estimated probability that a punishment ends in a particular month in 1996 was .24, or about .20 above the mean. This translates into an average increase in monthly rates of inflation of .8 percent, growth of central bank credit of 1 percent, and devaluation of 3.7 percent. Calculating the cumulative effects of the predicted monthly hazard rates yields a 10 percent increase in annual inflation, a 13 percent increase in the rate of credit growth, and a 55 percent devaluation. The actual rate of inflation in Russia in 1996 was 22 percent, credit grew by 48 percent, and the ruble declined 16 percent. The hazard rate, then, accounted for 46 percent of Russia's inflation, 27 percent of the rate of credit growth, and significantly overpredicted ruble devaluation. To put this overprediction in perspective, one should keep in mind that there was tremendous pressure on the ruble in 1996. The federal budget's voracious appetite, increasing skepticism about the Russian bond market, and declining confidence in the ruble required the Central Bank of Russia to run down its foreign reserves to prevent the ruble from declining farther. Indeed, I argue in chapter 6 that the IMF was extraordinarily tolerant of Russia's poor performance during its presidential campaign and the failure to carry out fiscal adjustment in 1996 set the stage for the financial crisis of 1998.

As in the previous analysis, the results show that economic policy deteriorates during the punishment phase, because the coefficients of IMF Status are positive and significant. When a program is suspended, inflation is 1.7 percent higher per month ($p < .02$), domestic credit expands 1.9 percent faster ($p < .001$), and the currency is devalued 2.1 percent faster ($p < .15$). The caveat bears repeating that some of this may be the result of selection effects. However, since inflation does not appear to contribute to the suspension of IMF programs in this sample significantly, we can infer that program suspensions increase inflation.

The effects of the domestic political control variables are all substantially the same as in the models that included measures of national influence rather than punishment durations, which is reassuring; this suggests that expected punishment durations and the measures chosen as proxies for national influence are, in fact, getting at the same underlying phenomenon. Again, election timing has the expected sign in two of three models but is not significant. Right-wing governments pursue more restrictive policies, but the effect is very small and only significant in the model for central bank credit. The number of government coalition partners has the anticipated effect of increasing inflation, presumably because there are more veto players to reconcile. Two effects lend support to the hypothesis that fragmented governments provide the best support for independent central bankers: Support for the government in parliament increases inflation, suggesting that parliamentary opposition reinforces the independence of the central bank, and the number of coalition partners restrains central bank credit. The probability that the government will fall exacerbates inflation and devaluation, with an increase of one standard deviation in the probability leading to .8 percentage points of inflation ($p < .075$) and a 4.2 percent devaluation ($p < .02$). Wars, internal or external, cause a significant jump in inflation and credit policy and lead to a significant devaluation.

4.5 CONCLUSIONS

It is difficult to isolate the effects of IMF intervention, particularly if we acknowledge that those effects may not be strictly limited in time to the duration of IMF programs or in space to the countries that choose, or are allowed, to adopt them. This analysis, consequently, has taken a different tack: It has attempted to explain the variation in the success of IMF programs across countries in terms of the varying credibility of enforcing conditionality. I hypothesize that credibility is negatively correlated with several dimensions of a target country's international stature, notably economic size and receipt of foreign aid. I test this hypothesis by modeling the duration of IMF punishment intervals and the decision to suspend programs, and find that measures of U.S. foreign aid are the best predictors of decisions to suspend and resume programs. This confirms the hypothesis of the formal model that countries that are "advantaged" by their influence in the international system will suffer shorter program interruptions—because it would not be credible for the IMF to impose longer ones—but also more frequent interruptions, since they deviate from their agreements more often. I then turn to the effects of credibility on policy variables. The results of the analysis demonstrate directly and indirectly that the credibility of IMF intervention has a dramatic effect on levels of inflation, the policies that cause inflation, and the stability of financial markets. Both the expected durations of punishment intervals and the variables that explain punishment duration, notably U.S. foreign aid appropriations, play a statistically significant and substantively critical role in explaining economic policy. The analysis goes on to find evidence to support the hypothesis that macroeconomic policy should deteriorate during punishment phases. Furthermore, it confirms the prediction that this effect should itself be mitigated in the most influential countries. Since their policies are not very credible at the best of times, they do not deteriorate much when the weak constraints provided by a program in good standing are removed.

The model also predicts that the same considerations should apply to international capital flows. Lacking direct measures of capital flows that are comparable across the countries in my study and with sufficiently wide and precise data coverage, I had to settle for an indirect measure, exchange rate movements. I argue that this is a good proxy, because stabilizing the nominal exchange rate was a prominent policy goal in most of these countries and therefore became the bellwether of investor confidence in government policy. The analysis using predicted punishment duration strongly supports the primary hypothesis of the model about capital flows: countries with shorter punishment durations had dramatically greater rates of devaluation. Measures of international influence had dramatic substantive effects in the expected direction but were not statistically significant.

Of the nine hypotheses listed at the beginning of this chapter, the analysis confirmed all but two. The two hypotheses that were not supported were number 7, that program suspensions are associated with capital outflows, and number 9, that influential countries experience smaller capital outflows when programs are suspended. In both cases the regression coefficients took the appropriate signs and magnitudes but were not significant.

This analysis is a direct test of several counterintuitive expectations derived from the formal model, and strong evidence is found to support them across several dependent variables, several ways of operationalizing the independent variables, and several different statistical methods. The results have implications, furthermore, that go well beyond a test of a single model. This analysis demonstrates the breadth of outcomes that are possible from IMF intervention, showing that its effectiveness can vary dramatically depending on the credibility of enforcement—ultimately, on the size and influence of the target state. One necessary conclusion to draw is that the Fund's influence is greatly circumscribed in the most important cases. Detailed discussion of the Russian and Ukrainian cases will follow. However, because statistical analysis is the analysis of variation, this pessimistic conclusion implies an optimistic one: It is impossible for the Fund's intervention to be vastly less effective in some countries without also being vastly more effective elsewhere. The very failures of the IMF in some post-Communist countries are what make it possible to detect the successes in others. This chapter, therefore, serves as an indirect proof that IMF intervention itself can have significant effects-but only when IMF commitments are credible.

The previous chapter summarized the existing literature on IMF effectiveness, showing that it was far from conclusive, and outlined a series of objections to the methods and data employed in previous studies. The present study is the first to control explicitly for a variety of political variables that are believed to influence the success of stabilization, to estimate a model to explain the variation in punishment for noncompliance with program conditions, and to estimate the impact of the credibility of IMF programs on their effectiveness. The results presented here demonstrate that the previous literature has omitted key variables and misspecified its models. Looking for a uniform effect across countries, researchers often found none. Looking for an effect that varies as a function of the IMF's credibility, however, I find that the Fund plays a role that is every bit as important as practitioners and area specialists believe.

Part II

History

5

Poland

LOOKING BACK from the end of a decade of reform in Eastern Europe and Eurasia, Poland stands out as an example of successful transition. Poland was one of the first countries to tame inflation; it was the first country to begin growing again; and, by 2000, it was one of a handful of countries that had higher levels of GDP after the transition than before it began. In 1990, however, Poland did not look like a likely success story. Poland began the decade in the throes of an economic crisis, with long lines for basic products, a crushing debt burden, soaring inflation, a vibrant black market, and collapsing demand for its exports. Polish industry was hopelessly addicted to cheap energy subsidized by the Soviet Union, and its products were so poor in quality that they were in demand nowhere else. In the early years of the transition the bold Polish reform program appeared likely to be derailed by a fractious parliament, a disgruntled populace, and a series of fragile coalition governments.

Poland owes its success to the remarkably consistent pursuit of a set of economic policies that accelerated economic reform, imposed tight budget constraints on firms, and tamed inflation. In one respect, Poland's historical legacy was advantageous: Poland entered the decade with a broad popular consensus that everything associated with central planning and Soviet-style socialism was anathema. After years of martial law, the Poles were prepared to suffer in order to break away from Soviet imperialism, and they were grimly determined to make their way to the West, whatever the cost. In another sense, however, Poland was disadvantaged by the need to break new ground for democracy in Eastern Europe, because it was saddled with dysfunctional political institutions. The roundtable agreement that ultimately brought the first Solidarity government to power in August 1989 also left it with a Communist president and a parliament that was only partially elected under democratic procedures. This parliament, in turn, wrote the election law used in 1991, and the result was a fragmented legislature. Polish governments were compelled to cobble together improbable coalitions and lurch from crisis to crisis. Meanwhile, the famous Polish consensus on economic reform barely outlasted the first year of transition. It is a remarkable achievement, under the circumstances, that a succession of heterogeneous coalitions managed to follow a basically consistent policy.

The role of the IMF in Poland was also remarkably consistent; if anything, in Poland the Fund erred on the side of being too consistent, rather than too forgiving. Poland suffered from a series of exogenous shocks that made its IMF targets too strict, but, instead of adjusting the targets pragmatically, Fund officials suspended Poland's first two agreements. As a result, the Fund played a role in Poland that it never succeeded in duplicating in Russia or Ukraine: It established a credible set of incentives to which the most diverse political coalitions found it necessary to accommodate themselves.

5.1 THE BALCEROWICZ PLAN

Communism collapsed first in Poland. The reform-Communist government of Rakowski sought to legitimize itself by holding roundtable talks with the leaders of the outlawed Solidarity movement and agreed to hold elections under tightly stage-managed conditions that guaranteed the Communist Party (Polish United Workers' Party, or PUWP) and their allies a majority in the critical lower house of parliament, the Sejm. To everyone's surprise, Solidarity overcame its organizational disadvantages to win every contested seat, and many prominent Communists were defeated in uncontested races.[1] For a while in the summer of 1989 it appeared that Rakowski would succeed in forming a governing coalition by relying on the Communists' satellite parties and the threat of Soviet intervention, but by August his efforts fell through. The first Solidarity government of Poland—and the first non-Communist government in Eastern Europe since 1948—came to power largely on the votes of the Communist satellite parties, and under a pragmatic political compromise pithily described by Adam Michnik: "Your President, our Premier."

The new prime minister, Tadeusz Mazowiecki, quickly surrounded himself with liberal economists who were committed to rapid economic reform.[2] Indeed, it was a group of Polish economists led by Finance Minister Leszek Balcerowicz, not foreign advisers or the IMF, that was the driving force behind the ambitious reform project that came to be known as the Balcerowicz Plan, or "shock therapy." As Stefan Kawalec, one of Balcerowicz's top advisers, put it,

> In 1989, the program proposed by the Mazowiecki government went much further than anything that the IMF could dare to suggest to

---

[1] This was possible because the election law allowed voters to vote "against all."

[2] Balcerowicz recalls that he was initially an unwilling recruit, who had planned to have a pleasant academic leave in England. Mazowiecki urged him to take the job, saying that he needed him to be "his Erhard," a reference to Ludwig Erhard, the no-nonsense monetarist Finance Minister of the FRG who presided over the German *Wirtschaftswunder* after World War II (Balcerowicz 1992, p. 10).

the Polish authorities. In the fall of '89 we discussed the technical details with the IMF, and we benefited from their expertise, particularly in terms of assuring the consistency of the assumptions in the program, but the basic policies went much further than the IMF recommendations.[3]

Polish officials and their IMF counterparts agree that the Poles insisted on writing more ambitious targets into their program than IMF experts thought achievable.[4]

The members of the economic team that Balcerowicz gathered had spent the last ten years arguing that institutional transformation was essential to economic reform, and they placed the highest priority on privatization in their theoretical writings. However, they believed that the galloping inflation that emerged in the second half of 1989 threatened to make the transition much more protracted and costly, and they quickly became convinced that their first task was to tame inflation. As Balcerowicz puts it in his memoirs of the period:

> Inflation was like a spreading inferno, which had to be quenched, or at least contained, in order to make it possible to change the economic system.
>
> We started by putting the question to ourselves: Is it possible to emerge from hyperinflation by means of gradual changes in macroeconomic policy?
>
> The experience of other countries, the opinion of international authorities, and the diagnosis of the international financial institutions showed that this road is condemned to failure. The method of gradually reducing the tempo of inflation can be successful if inflation is between ten and twenty percent per year. At this point in Poland prices were rising by ten to twenty percent per month. A much more radical anti-inflationary strategy was necessary to stop such galloping price increases—one that some call "shock therapy."[5]

He goes on to explain that he and his advisers felt that any delay in fighting inflation would make inflation ultimately more difficult to overcome, would impose serious economic costs in the meantime, and would frustrate attempts to introduce reform in other elements of economic policy.

> Serious arguments spoke against such a [gradual] approach, and at the same time for the variant of introducing a radical anti-inflationary program. Tolerating rampaging inflation for a longer time would lead to an entrenchment of inflationary expectations, which—with the passage of time—would become all the harder to overcome.

[3] Interview with Stefan Kawalec, June 13, 1997.
[4] Interview with Mark Allen, February 19, 1999.
[5] Balcerowicz 1992, p. 40. All translations from Polish are by the present author.

Maintaining galloping inflation must at the same time disorganize and lower production. It was also most doubtful whether it would be realistic to introduce rapid changes in the economic system in the presence of such inflation. The experience of countries that delayed the undertaking of comprehensive systemic reforms (for example, Russia and the republics of the former USSR) confirmed the basis for these concerns.[6]

Balcerowicz's calculations were not only economic, however, and even home-grown reformers would have been remiss had they failed to take international politics into account. He makes it quite clear that he believed that anything short of shock therapy would have jeopardized Western support for the Polish reforms.

My advisers and I were also certain that a strategy of tolerating galloping inflation would be interpreted—correctly—by the international financial institutions and the governments of Western countries as a fundamental error in economic policy and an expression of our lack of political determination in our approach to the economy. It would have been difficult under those circumstances to expect to conclude the agreements necessary to open access for Poland to international credits or to reduce the burden of our foreign debt.[7]

This is a remarkable admission, since the Polish reformers have been at pains to emphasize their independence from the IMF. The Fund did not compel Poland to adopt a more ambitious plan than its authorities preferred, rather the contrary. However, the Polish reformers worked the international financial institutions into their calculations as constraints on their freedom of action and considered them an important argument in favor of a radical reform program. Balcerowicz believed that Polish inflation represented a serious threat to economic reform in any case and that the best chance of overcoming it lay in a radical, dramatic program; however, it was an important consideration that there was a brief window of opportunity during which to gain the Western support that might make the difference between success and failure. This, more than anything else, dictated the rapid pace of preparations to launch the Balcerowicz Plan on January 1, 1990.

Political support for the Balcerowicz Plan was based on a fleeting conjunction of circumstances and some very adroit maneuvering and lobbying. By all accounts, the unity of the government around the reform program, the grimness of the economic crisis in which Poland found itself, and the political momentum generated by Solidarity's victory at the polls and the collapse of interna-

---

[6] Ibid., 41.
[7] Ibid., 41-42.

tional Communism combined to provide a brief period of consensus.[8] A very effective public relations campaign was led by Balcerowicz at the elite level and by Labor Minister Jacek Kuron in the public media. Above all, however, it was the crisis atmosphere that convinced the Sejm to push the necessary legislation through with minimal debate. "January 1, 1990 was a magic day; we built up to it, and everyone worked at a feverish pitch," recalls Balcerowicz. "We had the parliament working day and night on draft legislation. I met with each of the factions in the parliament, and argued with them about why we needed rapid reform."[9] Indeed, it was not until December 17—two weeks before the deadline for implementation—that the government was prepared to present the packet of eleven draft laws to the parliament. Time was too tight to leave the printing of the draft laws to the parliament printing press, so the military press was drafted into service. Balcerowicz recalls that someone joked that the best way to distribute the materials would be to send the military to the deputies' homes early on the morning of December 13. When asked by the marshall of the Sejm how to justify calling the parliament on Sunday, Balcerowicz replied, "So that the deputies understand how important the issue is."[10] After forming an Emergency Committee to study and finalize the drafts, the Sejm passed ten of the eleven laws on December 27 with only minor amendments, and the Senate immediately followed suit.

The program's progress through the Sejm was not entirely smooth, but for a fleeting moment the government exercised a degree of influence that it was never able to regain subsequently. For example, the Agriculture Commission was working simultaneously on a draft law to guarantee minimum prices for agricultural goods, cheap agricultural credits, and a guaranteed relationship between the prices of agricultural and manufactured goods, all propositions that Balcerowicz strongly opposed. He regarded them as inconsistent with the market liberalization that was the heart of his program, and he believed that they would require budget subsidies that would unbalance the macroeconomic program. He was able to get the bill changed, however, to a resolution that simply called on the government to pay particular attention to agricultural issues.[11]

The most unpopular element of Balcerowicz's program was the *popiwek*, a special tax imposed on wage increases.[12] This was a controversial measure

---

[8]Consensus within the government was assured by the fact that Balcerowicz, who served simultaneously as Deputy Prime Minister, was allowed to nominate the entire economic policy team; all of them were well known to him or to his close associates. The single exception was Wladislaw Baka, whom President Jaruzelski appointed as Chairman of the National Bank of Poland. There was some concern in 1990 that Baka and Balcerowicz might come into conflict, but it proved to be unfounded (Balcerowicz 1992, p. 18-21).

[9]Interview with Leszek Balcerowicz, June 23, 1997.

[10]Balcerowicz 1992, p. 59.

[11]Ibid., 61.

[12]*Popiwek* was the popular abbreviation; the title of the tax was "podatek od ponadnormatywnych wynagrodzen," or "tax on wages above the norm."

even within the group of economic advisers, where some members argued that wages should be freed from government regulation immediately so that labor markets could clear rapidly. Among Solidarity supporters, the new tax sounded like an echo of the old regime; after all, was it not for wage increases that they had mobilized to overthrow the Communists in the first place? The effect of imposing wage controls (albeit indirect ones) during a phase of high inflation was to impose most of the costs of controlling inflation on the working class, whose wages fell in real terms and in comparison to pensions and social benefits. However, Balcerowicz argued for the *popiwek* on the grounds that state-owned enterprises lacked owners who had an interest in enforcing wage discipline, and that the immature credit and banking system was not yet ready to bear the full brunt of applying the brakes to aggregate demand. Furthermore, the credibility of the government's macroeconomic program would be strained if it depended entirely on the threat of wholesale bankruptcies. By forcing wages to rise more slowly than prices, the *popiwek* would turn inflation into a self-restraining process, because price rises would undermine the basis for demand.[13] The remaining issue was how high to set the normative wage increase. The initial draft of the program suggested a norm of 70 percent of monthly inflation; any wage increases above that level would be subject to punitive taxation. In November 1989, when the best available estimates suggested that it would be very difficult to defend the exchange rate if inflation were excessive, Balcerowicz decided to reduce the norm to 20-30 percent. He subsequently learned that the members of the cabinet had received a draft containing the 70 percent figure, and negotiations were already under way with the unions on that basis. He faced a dilemma: whether to lower the threshold and risk a political upheaval that might block the entire program or allow wages to rise so rapidly as to make it impossible to stabilize the economy. "I recognized that the lower risk was to lower the figure, even if that might set off a political storm. That is what I did, and under the generally positive climate of the time, the storm turned out to be weaker than I had anticipated."[14]

The assumptions of the first IMF program for Poland were mistaken in several respects.[15] First, the program assumed that the initial burst of inflation from liberalizing prices would be much lower than actually turned out to be the case, and consequently the money supply targets turned out to be more conservative than originally intended. Second, the fiscal assumptions of the program were initially too conservative, largely because the program did not anticipate the large windfall profits that state enterprises made because of high inflation as they liquidated their inventories and sold products for high prices that had been produced with low-priced inputs. The result was a strong budget

[13]Balcerowicz 1992, p. 45-6.
[14]Ibid., 47.
[15]Gomulka 1995.

surplus for the first quarter of the year. Third, the program was too pessimistic about the current account, because it had not anticipated the dramatic surge of exports that immediately followed the devaluation in January 1990. The reformers and the IMF had expected the most severe test of the program to come from the balance of payments, and since Poland started its program with virtually no foreign reserves, this was expected to put pressure on the exchange rate. The exchange rate was fixed at 9,500 zloty to the dollar on January 1, a devaluation of 46 percent, and was intended to play a key role in the stabilization of the economy as a nominal anchor—a fixed point that would exert a drag on inflation. Thus, the credibility of the whole program depended on the sustainability of the pegged exchange rate. There had been extensive debates about where to peg the zloty. The minister of foreign economic relations, Marcin Swiecicki, argued that it could not be stronger than 12,000 to the dollar without bringing exports to a halt—even then his experts expected a negative trade balance for 1990—and the whole program was believed to depend on the $1 billion zloty stabilization fund provided by the West.[16] In fact, however, the zloty soon turned out to be undervalued at 9,500. The current account surged, and the National Bank of Poland filled its foreign reserve coffers as firms and households liquidated their foreign currency holdings to pay their expenses. This experience was subsequently repeated in other transition economies, as current accounts and budget revenues surged in the early months, but it was a surprise in Poland because Poland was the first post-Communist country to attempt the transition.

The Balcerowicz Plan has been roundly criticized for overshooting the initial stabilization and consequently sacrificing too much of the output and wealth of the country during the devaluation and credit crunch of 1990.[17] In retrospect, it is fairly clear that the devaluation of the zloty need not have been quite so severe and that the budget need not have been cut quite so drastically in the first quarter. However, whether it was a mistake to overshoot these targets is much harder to determine. It took several years for inflation to come down to single digits even with the policy package that was chosen, and the budget deficit

---

[16]Interview with Kawalec, June 13, 1997; Balcerowicz 1992, p. 50. The Zloty Stabilization Fund was considered so critical to the reform effort, in fact, that a panic was set off in Warsaw when some of the countries' contributions were delayed in December. Balcerowicz recalls "dramatic telephone conversations" with the IMF Managing Director, Michel Camdessus. Finally, just before Christmas, he tracked Deputy U.S. Treasury Secretary David Mulford to a hotel in Brussels, and the latter made a flurry of telephone calls that succeeded in collecting the outstanding contributions. When *Gazeta Wyborcza* ran a story on the delayed contributions, Balcerowicz had to scurry to the Sejm to answer questions about why Poland had to hurry so much to meet the January 1 deadline, if its international partners were not holding up their side of the bargain (Balcerowicz 1992, p. 62-3). Ironically, the need to draw on the fund never arose. Indeed, it was so thoroughly hedged in with bureaucratic obstacles that it probably could not have been drawn on had it been needed. Interview with Michael Mussa, former IMF senior staff member, November 15, 2001.

[17]Rosati 1993; Kolodko 2000a, 2000b.

Table 5.1: 1990 Targets and Results.

	Targets	*Results*
Gross Domestic Product (GDP)	−3.1%	−11.6%
Inflation		
First Quarter	75.0%	132.0%
1990	95.0%	249.0%
Unemployment	2.0%	6.3%
Industrial Output	−5.0%	−23.4%
Budget Balance (% of GDP)	−0.5%	0.5%
Trade Balance ($US bn)	−0.8	3.8
Change in International Reserves	—	2.4

reemerged as a problem before the end of the year. Meanwhile, the main risk to the program appeared to be that it would not be perceived as credible and consequently would not deliver results quickly; it might therefore prove impossible to sustain the coalition to keep it on track. Something like this scenario was, in fact, played out in many of the other post-Communist countries, which experimented with half-hearted stabilization efforts and quickly retreated from them when they did not lead to rapid improvements. It is hard to estimate the psychological impact of overshooting the program targets, but it is clear that the Polish program established its credibility early and stayed on track.

As Table 5.1 makes clear, the program overachieved its objectives for the primary policy variable, the budget balance. In addition, the devaluation of the zloty was indeed greater than the program required, which was reflected in a surprise trade surplus and consequent capital inflows, which bolstered the reserves of the National Bank of Poland. On the other hand, the recession provoked by these policies was much steeper than expected (and longer lasting; the IMF projections expected growth to resume in 1991, which turned out to be another year of deep recession). Meanwhile, in spite of the recession, inflation proceeded at a much faster tempo than anyone had anticipated.[18]

[18]The inflation estimates used to develop the budget had been based upon an expected exchange rate of 11,000 zloty to the dollar, so when the Polish authorities decided to peg the zloty at 9,500 to the dollar instead, the IMF insisted that this meant that the budget had to be revised. "Because, of course, they understood it logically: if you are going to adopt a lower exchange rate now, then there must also be lower inflation. And if there will be lower inflation, then the quantities in the budget must be changed, both on the income and the expenditure sides. They were right, but there was no longer time for a correction, because the draft of the budget law had been delivered to the Sejm. Later it turned out that inflation was higher than had been projected in the budget" (Balcerowicz 1992, p. 54).

The reservoir of Polish patience with the pain and disruption of reform was not bottomless; indeed, it began to run dry before the end of the first year. Sensing the new mood, Lech Walesa became restive and began to criticize the Mazowiecki government. Meanwhile, the rapid collapse of Communism in Eastern Europe in 1989 and the dismantling of the Council for Mutual Economic Assistance (CMEA) and the Warsaw Pact negotiated in 1990 removed the rationale for retaining Jaruzelski as president in order to appease the Soviet Union. Walesa began a campaign for holding early presidential elections, which he intended to win. In order to position himself to prevail, he took up the cry of labor and agriculture against the crash liberalization undertaken under Mazowiecki. Mazowiecki, in turn, was convinced by Walesa's populist rhetoric that the only hope to sustain the reform program was to defeat his drive for the presidency. Therefore, when it became clear that Jaruzelski would step down to permit early elections in the fall, he threw his hat into the ring.

The presidential election in 1990 completed the process of dismantling the Solidarity coalition and the political consensus it represented.[19] Walesa attacked Mazowiecki as out of touch with the common person and indifferent to the suffering caused by his economic policies. In the process, he drove a wedge between the intellectual wing of Solidarity, which supported Mazowiecki's program, and the labor union that had been the backbone of the mass movement for independence. It was not difficult to convince working people that the intellectuals were out of touch; for their part, the intellectual elite that had supported Solidarity against Communism found the former electrician Walesa a gauche spokesperson, ill-suited to the task of governing a republic. Walesa failed to win the election outright in the first round, but Mazowiecki was kept out of the second round run-off by an unknown Canadian émigré businessman named Stanislaw Tyminski.

Mazowiecki resigned as prime minister following this ignominious defeat, and for a brief time uncertainty reigned as to the future of Poland's economic strategy. In spite of his preelection rhetoric, however, President Walesa proved to be a solid supporter of Mazowiecki's policies. His camp had made overtures to Balcerowicz during the campaign, but Balcerowicz had carefully maintained neutrality. Indeed, as the personification of the successful effort to tame inflation, the guarantor of economic stability, and the chief contact with Western financial institutions, Balcerowicz had become a figure with tremendous influence. Walesa apparently made retaining Balcerowicz as minister of finance his condition for supporting any new government, and at least one potential coalition failed to form because of this. Balcerowicz reports that Walesa asked him, "If you do not want to be premier yourself, would you make your own proposal?"[20] Finally, Walesa supported Jan Bielecki's effort to form a pro-reform

[19]Zubek 1991.
[20]Balcerowicz 1992, p. 84.

government. Balcerowicz remained as deputy prime minister and minister of finance, and worked closely with Bielecki to choose the new ministers in the economic field. Although they represented several parties, the new ministers were all people whom he knew and with whom he expected to work well. The new cabinet was overwhelmingly approved at the beginning of January, and the position of the economic liberals was consolidated rather than compromised. Walesa was even convinced to support the hated *popiwek*, which was the target of the labor unions; when asked about it on a radio show, he responded that before the tax could be abolished, it was necessary to lower costs and prices, "by fifty, or even by one hundred percent."[21]

In spite of the initial overachievement of program targets, a more chilling reality soon came crashing in. By the third quarter of 1990, unemployment was higher than originally forecast and production had fallen further, leading to rising transfer payments and falling revenues. The result was a growing gap in the state budget that could only be financed by central bank credit, which automatically led to an expansion of the central bank's net domestic assets. Since the level of net domestic assets was a performance criterion for the 1990 Stand-by Arrangement (SBA), the IMF suspended the fourth tranche.[22]

This first program suspension was a telling signal. Unlike later program interruptions in Russia, Bulgaria, and Ukraine, this one was not the result of any political decision by Polish authorities to deviate from their program targets. Poland followed a program that the IMF had agreed on, implemented a budget law that the IMF had approved, and continued to exceed several IMF targets. It missed only one performance criterion and only because the prognoses on which the IMF program had been based turned out to be too optimistic in some respects. Furthermore, Poland took immediate steps to restrain the money supply.[23] It was clear to IMF officials at the time that the Poles had not made any substantive deviation from their program, that they were imple-

---

[21]Balcerowicz credits himself with convincing Walesa to support the *popiwek*. He visited him shortly before the radio show in the presidential residence, and argued that Walesa should not follow the example of Raul Alfonsin, former President of Argentina, who came to office with great popularity and lost it because he allowed hyperinflation to ravage the Argentine economy (Balcerowicz 1992, p. 89).

[22]Interview with Kawalec, June 13, 1997. For the conditions of the first Stand-By, see International Monetary Fund (1990). Bjork (1995, p. 99) incorrectly attributes the suspension of the program to the level of inflation. It is true that the level of inflation in the third quarter exceeded the indicator in the program; however, the inflation rate was not a performance criterion, so it was not in itself a reason to suspend disbursements. This followed the standard IMF practice in the 1980s, which was to target only policy variables, and not outcome variables. The IMF began to target inflation as a performance criterion in transition countries in part because of its experience in Poland, where inflation turned out to be more stubborn than had been expected.

[23]The National Bank of Poland, working in close consultation with the minister of finance, raised the interest rate that banks pay for credit in November, increased the level of required bank reserves against assets, and froze market-rate credits for state-owned enterprises (Balcerowicz 1992, p. 79).

menting their program in good faith, and that they remained as committed as anyone in Eastern Europe to the kind of reform the IMF supports. "The Poles were totally committed to their program," said Mark Allen, the IMF resident representative in Poland at the time. "There was no doubt that they wanted to transform Poland into a West European economy, and the people around Balcerowicz wanted reform to proceed as quickly as possible."[24] Indeed, the IMF learned from the Polish experience, and programs for other countries consequently made more generous allowances for inflation and expected greater falls in output. Why, then, should Poland be punished for technical errors for which it was no more responsible than the IMF, particularly when these errors arose because the transition from central planning to a market economy was essentially uncharted territory when the Poles set out?

The first reason, of course, was the need to defend the Fund's credibility.[25] Although some analysts have pointed to the unusual international support for Poland in the early years of reform and the unprecedented—and unrepeated—success of Poland in attracting substantial foreign aid and debt relief because of its acknowledged strategic role as the first chink in the armor of the Warsaw Pact, Poland's trailblazing role also meant that precedents set here would be widely repeated. All the transition countries were watching, and the IMF felt compelled to follow its procedures to the letter. On the other hand, by the end of 1990 it was possible to suspend Poland's program without seriously jeopardizing the reform program, because the current account's surprisingly strong performance in the first half of the year had left the National Bank with strong reserves. Meanwhile, it was useful to the reformers to be able to lean on the IMF as they negotiated with the parliament over the budget for 1991. According to Mark Allen,

> What they didn't need was for us to say that they were good guys and give them a check. They didn't need our money. The balance of payments was in good shape, the exchange rate peg was working marvelously. The program was off track, but it didn't really matter. We were providing a useful countervailing force to the spending side because it was important to the good guys to be in the process of reaching an agreement with the IMF.[26]

5.2 THE EXTENDED FUND FACILITY

The new Bielecki government immediately set to work negotiating a new agreement with the Fund. The term of the first SBA was almost at an end by the time the tranche was withheld, the next disbursement would have to depend

---

[24] Interview with Allen, February 19, 1999.
[25] Interviews with Kawalec, June 13, 1997, and with Jerzy Osiatynski, June 14, 1997.
[26] Interview with Allen, February 19, 1999.

on the budget for 1991 in any case, and it was clear that there would have to be a significant adjustment of the targets, so Poland and the IMF dropped the SBA by mutual agreement and moved directly to negotiating a three-year Extended Fund Facility (EFF) to replace it. This was itself an acknowledgment that the first program had been successfully completed and that the groundwork had been set for a structural adjustment program to cement the gains already made in stabilizing the economy. The government and the IMF agreed that a significant fiscal adjustment was necessary to reduce the budget deficit that had emerged in the last quarter of 1990, and the budget for 1991 was designed accordingly, with most of the adjustment on the expenditure side. There were no fundamental disagreements as to what had to be done.[27] Meanwhile, the government was nearing completion of negotiations with the Paris Club of government creditors on a substantial reduction of Poland's bilateral debts in two stages: a first tranche of 30 percent after signing an agreement with the IMF and a second tranche of 20 percent after successful implementation of that agreement. This was seen as a precondition for Poland's reentry onto global capital markets, because it would dramatically reduce the cost of servicing Poland's debts and reduce the risks of investing. Consequently, concluding the 1991 agreement with the IMF took on special significance. However, the agreement on the EFF was delayed because Poland, which had originally sought a debt reduction of 80 percent, refused to accept optimistic IMF projections as the basis for the EFF because such projections would undermine its case for drastic debt relief.[28]

The performance criteria for the 1991 agreement were based on budget projections made in the fall of 1990. As the negotiations with the Paris Club dragged on, these projections became increasingly unrealistic. Firms had exhausted the surplus inventories and hard-currency reserves that had allowed them to make paper profits during the first year of transition, and now the hard budget constraint began to be felt more clearly. The currency had remained pegged to the dollar as inflation continued at a high rate, so the zloty had appreciated in real terms, making exports less profitable. Revenues to the state budget fell precipitously. Meanwhile, inflation had fallen enough that seigniorage no longer made a significant contribution to financing the budget (for example, by raising each month's nominal revenue and deflating the value of unpaid bills left over from the previous month).[29] In addition, many firms became unprofitable because the CMEA market had collapsed at the beginning of 1991. The result was a widening budget deficit, as revenues came in 20 percent under the target level in spite of the drastic corrections made in the fall.

[27]Interviews with Kawalec, June 13, 1997, and with Allen, February 19, 1999.

[28]Interview with Kawalec, June 13, 1997.

[29]Interviews with Kawalec, June 13, 1997, and with Lidia Wilk, head of the Department of Macroeconomic Analysis, Ministry of Finance, June 12, 1997.

Balcerowicz argues that it was this series of unforeseen circumstances that led to the budget shortfall:

> There were economic forecasting mistakes, especially in the 1991 budget. We did not anticipate the size of the external shock, especially the importance of the collapse of trade in the CMEA.... We prepared the 1991 budget in November 1990, and the budgetary situation was very different four months later.... We got information about the budgetary situation gradually. There was a lot of uncertainty, and we made gradual adjustments.... It was not that the IMF insisted on conditions that we did not think we could meet; in fact, the differences between our proposal and the IMF's proposal were marginal compared to the shortfall in the second quarter of 1991.[30]

By the time the EFF agreement was approved in April, the budget situation had become dramatic, and both sides anticipated that the program targets would have to be revised as a result. However, the program was the key to the Paris Club negotiations, so neither side wanted to delay enough to renegotiate the program. An IMF official acknowledged that the program's prospects were bleak from the outset.

> We realized soon after the program had gone to the Board that it would not be implemented. Still, it was not in the interest of the Paris Club to withhold the debt reduction that we had agreed upon.... We had a program, and it suited all of our purposes to pretend that we were in the process of bringing it back on track.[31]

It quickly became clear that the program targets were not being met. There was a dramatic shortfall on the revenue side, and, although the Ministry of Finance introduced weekly monitoring of the budget and drastically slashed cash expenditures, the budget deficit continued to soar on a commitments basis. In the end, the ministry covered only two-thirds of the shortfall by cutting spending, and since Poland did not yet have an operational bond market, the rest of the government deficit had to be financed by credits from the National Bank of Poland (NBP). This violated the Fund's criterion for net domestic assets (NDA), and the Fund suspended disbursements again in September. Years later, Balcerowicz recalled the events of 1991 without rancor:

> In 1991, we decided to leave the negotiation of a revised IMF program to the incoming government. By the time the program was suspended in the summer, it was clear that the elections in the fall would lead to a change in government. That is why we didn't have

[30] Interview with Balcerowicz, June 23, 1997.
[31] Interview with Allen, February 19, 1999.

an immediate agreement.... We never bargained for softer conditions from the IMF. We had an economic problem to be solved, and we took the steps needed to solve it. My recollection is that we were partners with the IMF.[32]

As Gomulka writes, the program did have one concrete accomplishment: It paved the way for the Paris Club agreement.[33]

When the program was suspended, both sides assumed that it would be renegotiated to incorporate new measures to reduce the budget deficit, and the program would be renewed. The government revised the budget in August, using a provision that had been written into the legislation allowing it to adjust expenditures if there were a shortfall in revenues, and it accepted the IMF recommendations.[34] However, the budget situation continued to deteriorate rapidly, and political instability and fragmentation in Poland made it impossible to agree on a new package of policies. As president, Walesa had quickly begun to struggle with the Sejm over a wide spectrum of issues. Walesa was determined to assert civilian control over the military and secret police, dismantle the formal and informal structures that allowed the former Communist elite to exert influence, and strengthen the presidency vis-à-viz the parliament, and he repeatedly clashed on all fronts with the Sejm—packed by the former Communist Party as part of the roundtable agreement. Walesa called for early elections to produce a new, democratically elected parliament, and it was difficult for the deputies to resist because of the broad popular consensus that the existing parliament was illegitimate. However, the parliament did succeed in delaying the elections from spring until October. The shadow of impending elections gradually sapped parliamentary support for the government, which found itself under intensifying criticism for the lingering recession. The government announced an "anti-recession" program, which was focused on supply-side measures such as accelerating the pace of privatization, but its program became bogged down in parliamentary debate. The Sejm rejected Bielecki's resignation in August but refused to grant the government special powers to push through reforms, and the parliament itself was paralyzed until the October elections.

Poland's first democratic parliamentary elections, in October 1991, nearly succeeded in derailing the reform effort (Table 5.2). Fearful that they would be completely shut out of the new Sejm if the elections were held at large and parties were required to surpass a threshold percentage of the vote to enter the parliament, the former Communists and representatives of the satellite Peasants' Party crafted an election law that was very nearly pure proportional representation and passed the election law over Walesa's veto. The election law

[32] Interview with Balcerowicz, June 23, 1997.

[33] Gomulka 1995.

[34] Interview with Balcerowicz, June 23, 1997. It was compelled to resort to this measure, however, because it was unable to get parliamentary approval to revise the budget (Balcerowicz 1992, p. 106).

Table 5.2: Sejm Election of October 27, 1991.

	Vote (%)	Total Seats
Democratic Union (UD)	12.31	62
Alliance of the Democratic Left	11.98	60
Catholic Electoral Alliance (WAK, also ZChN)	9.84	53
Polish Peasant Party (PSL)	8.67	48
Confederation for an Independent Poland (KPN)	8.58	46
Center Alliance (PC)	8.71	44
Liberal Democratic Congress (KLD)	7.48	37
Peasant Alliance (PL)	5.50	28
NZSS Solidarity	5.05	27
Polish Beer Lovers' Party (PPPP)	3.27	13
German Minority	1.17	7
Christian Democracy	2.36	5
Christian Democratic Party	1.11	4
Labor Solidarity (later Union of Labor)	2.05	4
Polish Western Union	0.23	4
Union of Real Politics (UPR)	2.25	3
Party 'X'	0.47	0
11 other parties won one seat each		

Sources: Sanford (1999, pp. 36-7), Kitschelt et al. (1999, pp. 112-3).

created little incentive for parties to coalesce or for voters to vote strategically: 391 seats were elected in thirty-seven districts by pure proportional representation with no threshold, and 69 were drawn from a National List apportioned to parties that exceeded a 5 percent threshold and national minorities. The result was a parliament with twenty-nine parties.

For the next two months the weak factions of the new, fragmented parliament struggled to put together a viable coalition. The minimum winning coalition included five parties, and none of the post-Solidarity parties were willing to consider a coalition with the post-Communist Alliance of the Democratic Left. Walesa's first choice for prime minister was Bronislaw Geremek (Democratic Union, or UD), a medieval historian who had played an important role in

Solidarity under Communist rule and had served as chairman of the Solidarity faction in the previous parliament; when he proved unable to form a coalition, Walesa turned again to Jan Bielecki (Liberal Democratic Congress, or KLD), but he, too, was unable to create a new government. Finally, a shaky coalition of small right-wing parties united primarily by their conservative preferences on social policy formed under Jan Olszewski (Center Alliance, or PC), and Walesa reluctantly acquiesced. Economic policy remained the most salient issue on the political agenda, however, and Olszewski's would-be coalition partners had no consensus there. Olszewski had campaigned as a vocal opponent of shock therapy and was hoping to deliver on his promise to relax the pace of reform and bring the country out of recession. Several of Olszewski's other potential coalition members also favored reflation, lower interest rates, renegotiating Poland's agreements with the IMF, and increasing government aid to state-owned industries and farmers. However, it was impossible to form a majority without either Bielecki's KLD or Mazowiecki's UD, which steadfastly refused to support any government that moved away from their commitment to rapid economic reform. The KLD finally withdrew from the coalition, calling its economic program "unrealistic and irresponsible."[35] It was replaced by the Polish Peasant Party (PSL), which, although a post-Communist party itself, had won some respectability by supporting the previous Solidarity-led governments.

During the extended negotiations, the IMF waited for a new government to emerge with which it could negotiate a new reform package. Negotiations began again after the Sejm approved the Olszewski government, but they were delayed because of conflict within the coalition about the economic program. In a signal that the commitment to fighting inflation was slipping, the new chairman of the Central Planning Agency (CUP), Jerzy Eysymontt, announced that recession would replace inflation as the number-one enemy; however, the message was mixed, since he also suggested Balcerowicz to head the National Bank of Poland.[36] The central obstacle to a new agreement was the fiscal deficit. The IMF insisted on a package that would make a significant reduction in the deficit, and the government was unable to get such a package through the Sejm.[37]

Ironically, the Olszewski government failed to make a sharp break with the reform program not because it was strong, but because it was weak. Olszewski's government was unable to command a majority in the Sejm, so to stay in power it needed the tacit support of the UD and the KLD, both of which

[35] "Polish Premier Wins Vote of Confidence," *Facts on File*, December 19, 1991.

[36] "New Polish Cabinet OK'd by Parliament," *Chicago Tribune*, December 24, 1991. The Central Planning Office (CUP) was the successor to the central planning agency that had managed the economy under Communism, but had been stripped by this time of all prerogatives except preparing forecasts and strategy papers.

[37] Interview with Allen, February 19, 1999.

insisted on maintaining the priority of economic reform. Meanwhile, the room to experiment with fiscal policy was very narrow: By early 1992 the government faced a projected budget deficit of 10-13 percent of GDP, and an agreement with the IMF depended on reaching a level of 5 percent.[38] Olszewski accepted Karol Lutkowski, a former Balcerowicz adviser, as acting minister of finance, and the interim budget he presented to the Sejm for the first quarter of 1992 was the one Balcerowicz had prepared.[39] This was a tough budget, dubbed "the poverty bill" by the left-leaning newspaper *Trybuna Ludu*, which kept the projected budget deficit to 18 trillion zloty (1.6 billion U.S. dollars) in the first quarter. Lutkowski warned the deputies against giving in to pressure to increase spending, saying, "There are no grounds to expect that pumping money into the economy will bring relief to our present troubles."[40]

Olszewski presented a rather different budget for the rest of the year, which was intended to stimulate the economy by increasing the budget deficit; however, the Sejm defeated it on March 5. Olszewski's coalition at this point teetered on the edge of dissolution, because it controlled a minority in the parliament and consisted of seven factions: his own PC, the Christian National Union (ZChN), three small peasant parties, and two small Christian Democratic parties. Walesa called on Olszewski to broaden the coalition, and the coalition began negotiations with the UD and the Confederation for an Independent Poland (KPN). The UD, the largest faction in the parliament, insisted that it would only join the cabinet if the government passed an appropriately conservative budget. Negotiations over the budget and the coalition continued throughout March and April. Meanwhile, the IMF insisted on a restrictive budget as a condition for resuming lending under the EFF. Western donors began to put significant pressure on Olszewski to appoint a stronger finance minister; when he chose Andrzej Olechowski in March, it was widely viewed as a sign that the government's economic strategy was moving back to the hardline reform posture of the Mazowiecki and Bielecki governments. Olechowski told the IMF representative in Warsaw that his condition for accepting the job had been that he would have control over economic policy: He would be the first to speak on economic matters in the cabinet, and the prime minister's role would be to support him.[41] However, the Sejm passed a bill in May authorizing $2.2 billion in salary and pension increases, which expanded the budget deficit by 50 percent. Olechowski, who had bitterly opposed the bill, resigned

[38] Gomulka 1993, p. 206.

[39] Government ministers remained in office as acting ministers until they were replaced, and Olszewski asked Balcerowicz to chair meetings of the provisional government while he formed a new one. Consequently, the ministers of the former Bielecki government prepared the "provisional" draft budget for the first quarter of 1992, along with necessary drafts of implementing legislation. The budget increased certain taxes and payments for housing services, and cut the rate of indexation of pensions (Balcerowicz 1992, p. 115-17).

[40] Reuters, "New Polish Government Passes Interim Budget Test," January 25, 1992.

[41] Interview with Allen, February 19, 1999.

in protest. Asked afterward what he would say to the IMF about the budget deficit, Olechowski replied, "I haven't the slightest idea."[42]

Only one month later, the weak Olszewski government collapsed. The interior minister was a long-time Solidarity activist who was determined to prosecute Poles who had cooperated with the security forces in persecuting Solidarity under Communism, and he publicized a list of alleged former agents of the secret police. Included on the list were many prominent politicians, including Lech Walesa. Subsequently it became clear that the list was unreliable, since secret police agents, anxious to advance their careers under the Communist regime, had fabricated contacts with opposition members. Furthermore, many people had been listed as collaborators simply because they had answered innocuous questions when they were arrested. This appears to have been what happened in Walesa's case. The uproar that followed was predictable, and the fragile Olszewski government was swept aside.

Walesa nominated as prime minister the young leader of the PSL, Waldemar Pawlak, and the Sejm approved him by a strong majority; however, he never succeeded in forming a government that the Sejm could approve. He did succeed in passing a tough budget that had been approved by the IMF, which limited the deficit to 5 percent of estimated GDP, fulfilling a precondition for resuming IMF aid. After a month of fruitless struggling, however, Pawlak concluded that he would not be able to form a government; the UD and KLD were suspicious of his economics, and the ZChN and PC were suspicious of his party's Communist past. Walesa was becoming very critical of the Sejm, and deputies began to fear that he would dissolve parliament or name himself prime minister if they failed to compromise. In this climate, they arrived at a surprising solution, nominating a relatively unknown professor, Hanna Suchocka (UD), to be prime minister. Suchocka was as surprised as anyone; she learned of her nomination by reading a newspaper while traveling in London.[43] Walesa quickly agreed, and, after several weeks of negotiating cabinet portfolios, the Sejm approved her government by a vote of 286 to 10, with 107 abstentions. For the first time since the elections the previous fall, the Sejm had managed to form a government that commanded a slim majority. However, the new government's 6-vote majority in the Sejm gave it little margin for error, particularly with a coalition of seven quite heterogeneous parties.

5.3 THE SECOND STAND-BY AGREEMENT

Suchocka, who immediately drew comparisons to Margaret Thatcher for her steely personality and commitment to free markets, insisted that she would not be daunted by her government's shaky foundations. She would compromise

---

[42] "Polish Minister Quits to Protest Spending Bill," *The Washington Post*, May 7, 1992.

[43] "Poland Puts its Faith in a Firm Female Hand," *The Independent* (London), July 15, 1992.

when possible, but not on the economy. Her cabinet was strongly committed to reform, including Janusz Lewandowski, who returned as head of the
privatization agency; the former prime minister Jan Bielecki, who returned to
take over relations with the EU; and Jerzy Osiatynski, who, as finance minister,
continued Balcerowicz's program. In August the government proposed a series
of extraordinary measures to reduce the budget deficit, including the introduction of indirect taxes, reducing the indexation rate of pensions to wages, and
imposing an import surcharge of 6 percent in 1993 and 3 percent in 1994.[44]
The Polish government had relied heavily on corporate taxes for revenue in the
early years of reform, but these sources were drying up as state-owned enterprises contracted their operations, and corporate taxes were difficult to collect
from the new private sector. The introduction of the value-added tax (VAT) put
Polish finances on a much more stable basis, and, as economic activity picked
up steam in the private sector, it became the basis for solving the chronic fiscal
problems that had fueled Polish inflation.[45] Osiatynski emphasizes that the
new government was committed to an austerity program independent of the
IMF: "I didn't need to be pushed."

> In mid-1992 I had to revise the budget and introduce extra austerity
> measures, because the targets for inflation and so on built into the
> budget were not achievable. The package reduced the deficit by
> 3 percent of GDP over two years, from 1992 to 1993. When the
> Fund realized that we were serious about accomplishing what one
> thought was proper, they reached an agreement with us.[46]

By November the government was able to submit a budget to the Sejm that
incorporated these proposals and envisaged a deficit of 5 percent of GDP. This
made it possible to reach an agreement with IMF negotiators. In December
Poland and the Fund agreed on a Letter of Intent, and in March the executive
board approved it. The import surcharge was a measure that the IMF discouraged, and it required a special waiver from the OECD; however, since it
was needed as a stopgap fiscal measure and was intended to be temporary, the
Fund agreed to make an exception.[47] The Paris Club, in turn, agreed that if
this agreement with the Fund were fully implemented, the second tranche of
debt reduction negotiated in 1991 would finally be released.

Polish politics had been marked since the presidential election in 1990 by
jousting between parliamentary governments and the president, which destabilized cabinets and often paralyzed policymaking. A fundamental question
that had never been resolved was how much authority the president actually
had to appoint and dismiss prime ministers and other cabinet members. One

[44]Gomulka 1993, p. 206.
[45]Interview with Wilk, June 12, 1997.
[46]Interview with Osiatynski, June 14, 1997.
[47]Ibid.

of Suchocka's major accomplishments was to reassure Walesa sufficiently to allow him to accept an interim constitutional arrangement that resolved much of this uncertainty. The "Small Constitution," adopted in December 1992, took away the president's right to dismiss the prime minister or dissolve parliament, unless certain conditions were met. Nevertheless, the progress of reform was significantly delayed by political uncertainty. The much-hailed and oft-delayed mass privatization program was blocked in the Sejm for months, defeated once in March 1993, revised, and then defeated again in April.

As privatization stagnated it became impractical to enforce bankruptcy, and the power of workers' councils and unions prevented dramatic administrative reforms to downsize unprofitable state-owned enterprises. By 1993 it was clear that macroeconomic stabilization had been successful and that the new private sector was rapidly growing; it was unclear, however, whether the slow pace of structural reform might jeopardize the Polish reform effort. At the outset of the transition it had been regarded as an article of faith that a successful transition required rapid privatization, and the Polish reformers had been no less committed to it than to their macroeconomic objectives.[48] However, a series of administrative difficulties in 1990, followed by the onset of political uncertainty in 1991 and stalemate in 1992 and 1993, had delayed large-scale privatization for the foreseeable future.[49] Fortunately, as gradually became clear, widespread privatization was not a necessary condition for a successful transition, provided that a stable macroeconomic and regulatory environment was in place.[50] In Poland the industrial dinosaurs of the Communist era gradually shrank in terms of output, employment, and economic significance, and a new, smaller-scale economy grew up around them. Industrial wages in state-owned enterprises fell in real terms and relative to both the private sector and pensions and social services, so industrial employment became less attractive, and the most productive employees of state-owned enterprises left. Meanwhile, the growing private sector provided tax revenue that balanced the fiscal drain from loss-making state enterprises, so they never destabilized the macroeconomic environment.

The Suchocka coalition was in tatters by the spring of 1993, and many of its legislative initiatives, including the budget, could only pass the Sejm with the quiet support of the post-Communist Social Democracy of the Republic of Poland (SdRP). In mid-April the Peasant Alliance (PL) agriculture minister,

---

[48] Balcerowicz's failure to push through mass privatization was what pained him most about his time in office. Reforming the structure of ownership in the economy in favor of entrepreneurs was, indeed, the step that he believed to be most essential to making a successful economic transition. He held out for mass voucher privatization instead of some form of insider privatization that might have attracted the support of organized labor, and in his 1992 memoirs he wonders whether that was an important tactical mistake, notwithstanding the risks that he believed would have followed from worker ownership (Balcerowicz 1992, p. 91).

[49] Interview with Balcerowicz, June 23, 1997.

[50] Berg 1994.

Gabriel Janowski, withdrew from the cabinet after it refused to increase aid to Poland's depressed agricultural sector. Ten days later the PL withdrew its nineteen votes from the coalition because it had refused to accept guaranteed crop prices and import restrictions, making Suchocka the prime minister of a minority government. A few weeks later Suchocka found herself personally negotiating with Solidarity trade union leaders who threatened to topple the government and declare a general strike if their demands to raise the salaries of teachers, doctors and scientists by 600,000 zloty per month were not met. Acquiescing to the demands would have violated IMF conditions by increasing the state budget deficit. "It would be an unforgivable mistake to let Poland abandon its chosen course now," Suchocka argued in a last-ditch televised address. "A general strike overthrowing the government and dissolving parliament would not solve anybody's problems, but would undermine everything we have been building for the past three years."[51] On May 28 the delegates of the Solidarity trade union brought a vote of no confidence, which passed by one vote. Walesa dissolved the Sejm on the following day.

5.4 POLAND'S TURN TO THE LEFT

The elections of September 1993 were contested under a new electoral law, which had been designed to avoid the disastrous fragmentation of the previous parliament. The new electoral law awarded seats according to the d'Honte formula, instead of the Hare-Niemeyer formula, and divided the country into fifty-two constituencies instead of thirty-seven, both changes calculated to benefit large parties and make the electoral results less proportional.[52] The most decisive reform was that the new law established that parties must surpass a threshold of 5 percent of the vote, and multiparty electoral alliances a threshold of 8 percent, in order to enter parliament. The result of these changes—combined with a gradual shift of public opinion in favor of left-leaning parties as a result of the painful transition—was to produce a parliament with only seven parties. The small, fractious parties that had occupied the center-right part of the political spectrum in the last parliament and had participated in all its governments—the PC, KLD, ZChN and PL—disappeared from the political landscape. Ironically, these were parties that had strongly supported the new election law after their experience with a fragmented parliament under the previous formula. Meanwhile, the disproportionality of the electoral system and the large number of votes that went to parties that failed to meet the threshold allowed the SLD and the PSL to form a majority coalition with 66 percent of the seats in the Sejm after winning only 36 percent of the vote. After only three years out of power, the heirs of Poland's Communist Party swept back into office (Table 5.3).

[51]"Polish PM struggles to stay in power," *The Independent* (London), May 19, 1993, 12.
[52]Taagepera and Shugart 1989, Chpts. 7,11.

Table 5.3: Sejm Election of September 19, 1993.

	Vote (%)	Total Seats
Alliance of the Democratic Left (SLD)	20.41	171
Polish Peasant Party (PSL)	15.40	132
Democratic Alliance (UD)	10.59	74
Union of Labor (UP)	7.28	41
Confederation for an Independent Poland (KPN)	5.77	22
Non-Party Bloc for Reform (BBWR)	5.41	16
German Minority	.41	4[a]
Fatherland (Ojczyzna)	6.38	0
Solidarity	4.90	0
Center Alliance (PC)	4.42	0
Liberal Democratic Congress (KLD)	3.99	0
Others	15.04	0

Sources: Sanford (1999, p. 41), Kitschelt et al. (1999, pp. 112-3).

[a] The law contained an exception to the 5% threshold for parties representing ethnic minorities.

"We are going to be a good partner for the West," assured Alexander Kwasniewski, the SLD leader. "We are going to continue the reforms."[53] If the first miracle of the Polish transition was the ability of a fragmented parliament without popular support to sustain coalitions that advanced a consistent macroeconomic stabilization agenda, the second was the decision of the post-Communist government that was elected by campaigning against shock therapy to follow an economic strategy that was essentially a continuation of the one it had nominally opposed. Indeed, in some respects the post-Communist coalition of SLD and PSL was better poised to carry out reforms, because it commanded a fairly unproblematic parliamentary majority. Now that it was once again shackled with the responsibility for governing, and facing the prospect of doing so for four years, the new government dropped its extreme rhetoric and moved to implement a responsible budget. In his first address to the Sejm as prime minister, Waldemar Pawlak assured the body, "The government does not intend to hastily look for new concepts for reforming the country. We want to calmly carry out reforms beneficial to society."[54]

[53]"Post-communists win Polish parliamentary elections," BBC, September 19, 1993.
[54]"New Polish Government Adopts Low-Risk Policy," Reuters, November 9, 1993.

In retrospect, this seems less surprising than it did in the wake of the hard-fought electoral campaign. After all, the last Communist government of Poland had already been trying to implement fairly radical economic reforms in 1989, and a broad consensus had emerged in the Polish economics profession supporting some kind of market-oriented reform as early as the 1960s. In Russia the reformers faced committed advocates of central planning, but in Poland the opposition to the monetarists consisted mainly of Keynesians and supporters of industrial policy. The room for respectable debate was narrower, and the terms of the debate were much more familiar to Western-trained economists. In addition, during its long period in the political wilderness, the SdRP (the direct successor of the PUWP, or Communist Party) had been compelled to reinvent itself as a moderate, responsible party of the Left in order to regain respectability, and had enjoyed the luxury of very little electoral competition from more extreme leftist groups that might have pulled it away from the center. Furthermore, since 1990 the SdRP and the SLD, the broader electoral coalition it sponsored, had been assiduously soliciting the support of the new entrepreneurs who had emerged from the *nomenklatura* privatizations under the last Communist government. Both came to be led and supported largely by these well-placed officials, industrialists, and bankers, whose interests as businessmen in the new Poland led them to support continuity with the policies of the post-Solidarity governments, rather than radical change.[55] The redefinition of the interests of the former *nomenklatura* occurred in Poland because of the rapidity and inexorability of market reform; in countries where reform proceeded more slowly, such as Bulgaria, Ukraine, and Russia, the interests of the former Communist elites were very different in 1993. Consequently, the first post-Communist government in Poland turned for economic advice to mainstream economists who criticized the implementation of the Balcerowicz program but agreed with its basic objectives. The new minister of finance, Marek Borowski, indeed continued the policies of his predecessor and submitted a budget to the Sejm for 1994 that was a slightly modified version of the one Osiatynski had prepared. The budget foresaw a deficit of 4.2 percent of GDP, which met the IMF's main performance criterion for the critical program review that would unlock the second 20 percent reduction in Poland's $30 billion debt to official creditors.

Nevertheless, in February the government's economic program appeared to vacillate. Polls showed that the PSL/SLD coalition's popularity had plummeted since the election, and the Solidarity trade union began organizing strikes and street demonstrations. Pawlak announced that the budget would be altered, and he dismissed one of Borowski's aides. When Borowski demanded that the lines of authority on economic matters be clarified in the government, Pawlak refused, and Borowski resigned. To replace Borowski, the SLD nominated

---

[55]Zubek 1995.

Dariusz Rosati, a prominent economist who had published articles critical of the Balcerowicz program. However, Walesa blocked Rosati's nomination, apparently perceiving him to be far more unfriendly to the reform agenda than he actually was. The coalition settled on Grzegorz Kolodko as a compromise candidate. Kolodko had been more critical of the Balcerowicz program than Rosati had, but since he was not directly associated with the SLD, he was acceptable to Walesa. He came into office without any political backing; he controlled no votes in the Sejm, had no union to mobilize, and enjoyed no public image.

Kolodko came into office promising a sharp break with the policies of the first three post-independence governments, but the break he had in mind was rhetorical rather than substantive. He argued that he was in favor of a policy of growth rather than a policy of recession. The centerpiece of his program was his *Strategy for Poland*, a booklet that outlined macroeconomic targets and priorities for the next five years. The *Strategy* was vague on the details of fiscal policy, but, where it contained details, they tended toward policy continuity rather than sharp change. The *Strategy* did not really represent a blueprint for government policy for five years, or even for the budget priorities for 1995. However, it did serve a valuable rhetorical purpose, and Kolodko used it to masterful effect. He insisted that the cabinet adopt the *Strategy for Poland*; thereafter he leaned on it at cabinet meetings, whenever proposals were made that would have broken the budget, by pointing out that they were not foreseen in the program. Since no one was quite sure what was in the program, the argument was unassailable; meanwhile, he managed to set an agenda of budgetary restraint.[56]

By the time the first post-Communist government took over in Poland, all that was necessary to consolidate the macroeconomic stabilization was to hold on long enough for the country to grow itself out of the crisis. It was not too late in 1994 to restart the inflationary spiral by spending irresponsibly; however, the incentive not to do that in order to receive the debt reduction offered by the Paris Club was tangible. As the country continued to grow and attract foreign investment in successive years, the temptation to run large budget deficits declined because tax receipts were growing.[57] Meanwhile, cash privatization picked up steam as the Polish economy became perceived as a safe place to invest, and this allowed the government to use privatization receipts to offset spending on pensions and social services. The post-Communist govern-

[56]Interviews with Allen, February 19, 1999, and with Grzegorz Kolodko, March 20, 1999. Kolodko did not originate this account, but he confirms the broad outlines of the way he used the document strategically. He takes issue with the assessment that the *Strategy for Poland* was too general to be used as an operational program, which was a case that his opponents in the Sejm made at the time. He lays out his arguments in Kolodko and Nuti (1997). The *Strategy for Poland* is available in an English translation, Kolodko (1996).

[57]Interview with Kolodko, March 20, 1999.

ments of Pawlak, Oleksy, and Cimoszewicz were able to cut tax rates, remove the punitive excessive wage tax, the *popiwek*, and expand government programs, primarily because the growing private sector filled government coffers and relaxed the budget constraint. They also extended numerous informal tax breaks to political allies; however, in the general economic upswing, the scale of these favors was too small to seriously jeopardize macroeconomic stability.

By the end of 1994, the era of Poland's active participation in IMF conditionality programs was coming to an end. The last drawing in 1995 was needed in order to facilitate a debt-restructuring agreement with the London Club of private creditors. Thereafter Poland found itself with ample foreign reserves and a confident investment climate, and it was no longer dependent on the Fund's financing or its seal of approval. Poland might suffer again from a crisis of confidence and need support, but the transition was essentially over in Poland. Poland asked the IMF to reduce its line of credit—since a commitment fee must be paid on the line of credit even if the funds are not drawn—but requested that the Fund continue its biannual audits of the Polish economy.[58] The Polish authorities shifted their attention to World Bank projects in a variety of areas intended to promote structural adjustment, clean up the environment, and strengthen domestic institutions. Meanwhile, the overwhelming incentive to be a good international citizen became the suddenly very real prospect of joining the European Union. Poland initiated a wide variety of legal reforms in order to harmonize its legislation with EU requirements, and Poland, in fact, met the Maastricht budget requirements that Germany found so onerous.

This is not to say that Poland's economic management by the 1997 elections that brought a coalition of Solidarity and Balcerowicz's Union of Freedom (UW) into office—or by the 2001 elections, which returned power to the SLD—was not in some ways highly inefficient and distorted by political incentives. Polish governments maintained high levels of subsidization for Poland's inefficient agricultural sector, which was dominated by farms too small to be economically viable even in the EU, and farming methods that were technologically primitive and labor intensive. This was gradually beginning to change, and the pressure on the small family farm was one of the major factors in the PSL's poor showing in the 1997 elections. In addition, the heavily subsidized, inefficient, and dirty Polish mining industry, which produces low-grade coal at a cost well above its price, proved very difficult to reform because reform would have to mean closure. Furthermore, the restructuring of the economy was delayed by granting tax favors to large, inefficient, and often state-owned enterprises in a way that suggests patronage rather than industrial policy. As a result, the tax burden remained too high on small business—the dynamic, innovative sector of the economy—and too low on large enterprises that should

[58]Interview with Jerzy Hylewski, director, International Department, National Bank of Poland, June 11, 1997.

have been downsized or liquidated. After a decade of transition, the Polish economy remains full of structural problems, and privatization is an unfinished project. However, the Polish case is a clear example of the benefits of rapid macroeconomic stabilization. In spite of numerous failures in structural policy, the private sector grew up around the ruins of the old economy and eventually replaced it. Although structural reform lagged, confidence in the economy was high enough by the middle of the decade that the failure to privatize industry and rapidly restructure the banking system was unable to jeopardize macroeconomic stability as it did in many other post-Communist countries. Meanwhile, the stable macroeconomic climate laid the groundwork for a recovery that was more rapid and dramatic than anywhere else in the post-Communist world.

5.5 CONCLUSIONS

Poland's transition was among the most successful in the post-Communist world, but one cannot say that Poland succeeded because of unusually fortuitous political circumstances. The euphoria of the early months of reform rapidly gave way to a grimmer reality, and the broad consensus in favor of the Balcerowicz strategy rapidly evaporated. The first parliament to be elected under democratic rules was hopelessly fragmented, produced three fragile governments in the space of two years, and had to be dissolved. The second parliamentary elections brought the post-Communist parties back into power. Here, finally, one could say that Poland was fortunate, as Poland has always been very fortunate in its choice of Communists. The Polish Left turned out to be a very responsible actor, which continued along the reform path. This pattern was repeated in Hungary and the Baltic states, but was in marked contrast to the role of the Left in Russia, Ukraine, and Bulgaria.

The strongest impetus for reform in Poland seems to have come from the external environment. It was the Poles, not the IMF, who designed the initial stabilization program; however, they were operating under extremely constrained circumstances. Poland was in a state of economic collapse in 1989, and it was clear that nothing but a radical program could have rescued it. Furthermore, Poland had a desperate need to restructure its foreign government-held and commercial debt in order to stabilize its investment climate and attract foreign capital, which the reformers saw as an essential ingredient for modernizing the Polish economy. Three times, in 1991, 1993 and 1994, international institutions used the opportunity to restructure Polish debt to create an incentive to carry out painful reforms. More than one governing coalition swallowed its policy preferences in order to implement a budget that was perceived as objectively necessary because the external environment that Poland faced was highly constraining.

The most telling contrast between the Polish case and the others that will be related in this volume is the role the IMF played. When Poland departed from its program targets, it was almost always an accident or the result of a serious miscalculation. A series of heterogeneous and fragile governments backed by divisive and suspicious parliamentary deputies nevertheless hewed to an orthodox conception of macroeconomic stabilization, and, against the odds, they eventually carried it out. In spite of these exceptional circumstances, the IMF did not budge from its role as the enforcer of programmatic details. In 1990 and 1991 it suspended programs immediately when Poland missed its targets and insisted that the programs be brought back on track before new lending could begin. In 1992, while Poland did the hard work of finishing the macroeconomic stabilization begun two years before, the Fund waited for positive proof that the budget was on track before restarting a program. The result was that, in Poland, the IMF bolstered the position of the reformers. The reformers always insisted that they were carrying out Polish reforms, not IMF agendas; but they were able to argue that the IMF seal of approval carried weight with international capital markets as well as with the Paris and London creditors' clubs, and was essential to establishing the credibility of the Polish programs. Unlike their colleagues in Russia and Ukraine, the Poles had no doubt that the IMF had the determination to suspend their programs when that was what the situation warranted.

6

Russia

RUSSIA IS often cited as an example of the folly of following the advice of Western economists, who called loudly for Russia to undergo "shock therapy." To characterize the policies that Russia actually followed as "shock therapy" is grossly inaccurate, however, since the initial effort to control inflation lasted only four months. In the early years of the transition (1992-94), the Russian government imposed discipline on monetary and fiscal policy for short periods, and repeatedly pulled back from the precipice of hyperinflation; yet, as quickly as they took hold, efforts to restrain demand evaporated and inflation surged forward. In comparison with the East European countries, Russia has been very unsuccessful in controlling inflation and stabilizing its currency; in comparison with the abysmal records of most of the other countries of the former Soviet Union, Russia's performance has been about average. The effect of delaying stabilization in Russia was a roller coaster of inflation and contraction, which combined the worst effects of both: a precipitous decline of production, living standards, and government services, combined with monumental levels of capital flight and without substantial restructuring of industry. These lost years had lasting impact on the health of the Russian economy, the legitimacy of Russian democracy, and Russia's status as a great power.

From 1995 to 1998 Russia used a tight money policy to stabilize the ruble and bring inflation down, but failed to reduce its budget deficit. Consequently, large capital inflows were used to finance the deficit, and high interest rates squeezed out investment in the private sector. This was not a sustainable policy, because the need to finance the deficit required ever greater inflows of capital, and mounting government debt made the investment increasingly dubious. Finally, on August 17, 1998, the game was up and the ruble collapsed, sweeping away the government of the reformers. Again an opportunity had been missed, and the cost in terms of Russia's purchasing power and the real wages of its citizens was staggering: Russia's per capita real income in 2000 was 46 percent of its level in 1998. The third stage of the transition, which was inaugurated by the ruble's collapse, has been a period of improvised monetarism. A surprising consensus has finally emerged among Russia's political parties and elites that should make the early reformers feel vindicated: Even the Communist Party of the Russian Federation (KPRF) removed the plank calling for rapid monetary expansion from its election platform.

Some critics blame the IMF for Russia's economic woes, either pointing to particular tactical mistakes or blaming the Fund's monetarist orientation for Russia's wholesale economic decline. I discuss the first set of criticisms in the detailed historical reconstruction below. Some are well taken; for example, I conclude that the IMF's insistence on dismantling capital controls in 1996 was misguided. However, the disasters of Russian economic policy are attributable to failure to follow sound advice, rather than to faulty advice. In the most spectacular case, the huge budget deficits that were run up in 1995-98 led to the crash in August; but it was the politics of tax collection that created the ruble's vulnerability, and urging the government to improve tax collection was the IMF's primary preoccupation throughout that period. The tactical decision to peg the ruble in 1995 can be questioned—this is discussed extensively below— but, right or wrong, this was a Russian decision, not something imposed by the Fund. If the Russian case speaks to the issue of whether the Fund's basic monetarist orientation is appropriate, it points to the extreme dangers of an accommodating monetary policy (1992-94) or a profligate fiscal policy (1995-98) rather than to the costs of implementing policies that the IMF supports. A more serious critique of the IMF is that it failed to enforce the conditions attached to its programs for Russia. This is clearly true. However, it is a criticism more aptly leveled at the Western governments, and above all the United States, which undermined the IMF's credibility by pressing for special treatment of Russia.

One could never conclude from the Russian case in isolation whether the disastrous course of economic policy described above could have been avoided had the IMF been a more credible constraint; perhaps politics would have had its way with economic policy in any case. There simply is not enough variation in one country on the independent variable of interest—the IMF's credibility— to draw firm conclusions. However, one can conclude that the IMF was a much less effective constraint on Russia than on other post-Communist countries, and that Russian and IMF negotiators were aware of the IMF's lack of credibility and took it into account when they planned their strategies. Although the IMF exerted some influence over particular Russian policies, it was unable to deter flagrant violations of its stabilization programs, in large part because the Russian government had too much influence in Washington.

Russian influence, however, was not a fixed asset. An important part of the story of Russian economic reform is the evolution of U.S.-Russian relations, since this is what set the stage for all of Russia's interactions with the IMF. In 1992, U.S.-Russian relations were at a high point from which they would gradually decline. The United States had declared the end of the Cold War, and both the Bush and Clinton administrations were determined to support the Russian reformers, symbolized by the image of Boris Yeltsin astride a tank during the abortive 1991 coup attempt. In 1992-94 this led to pressure on the IMF to support programs that its officials considered too weak and to disburse funds after the conditions of previous programs had not been met. This policy of benign neglect reached a high point during the Russian presidential election campaign of 1996, when the Fund was compelled to tolerate wholesale violations of the program. By the end of the U.S. electoral season in 1996, however, American policy toward Russia was undergoing significant changes. The Clinton administration was gradually moving away from the cautious liberal internationalism of Anthony Lake and Warren Christopher to embrace a more realist perspective articulated by Madeleine Albright. In the first Clinton administration, Strobe Talbott had been able to block policy initiatives that would harm relations with Moscow, such as expanding NATO and intervening in the Bosnian civil war. In the second, the argument of Russian security interests carried less weight, as Russia came to be viewed less as a potential superpower than as a regional nuisance.[1] Numerous regional issues of the day came to trump considerations of the long-term U.S.-Russian relationship: sanctions on Iraq, sales of sensitive equipment to Iran, and finally intervention in Kosovo. In the long run, this may have the beneficial consequence of making the IMF a more credible constraint for Russia. In the short run, however, it seems to have made the second Clinton administration even more willing to use whatever leverage the IMF provided as a bargaining chip to achieve short-term foreign-policy objectives.

6.1 THE WINDOW OF OPPORTUNITY CLOSES: 1992

Russia's understanding with the IMF upon joining the organization in 1992 promised a decisive plunge into shock therapy.[2] Real money balances declined sharply, inflation fell rapidly from a monthly rate of 245 percent in January to 12 percent in May, and enterprises began to feel the pressure of scarcity. The budget showed a small surplus for the first quarter, and the ruble appreciated against the dollar. Had the policies of the first few months been continued, Russian inflation might have been under control by year's end. The opportunity was missed, however. Opposition gathered quickly, and one should not underestimate the political constraints or the uncertainty of the early days of reform, but never again would the political risks involved in stabilizing the economy be so low.

The Russian Congress of Peoples' Deputies initially granted Yeltsin broad authority to rule by decree and initiate reform, but the logic of institutional incentives gradually asserted itself. Powerful lobbies coalesced around agri-

---

[1] Goldgeier 1999.

[2] Russia was negotiating to join the IMF when it launched its reform program in January 1992, so it was unable to receive funding or sign a formal Stand-by agreement. As a condition of the negotiations over membership, however, the government cleared its reform program with the Fund.

culture, industrial interests, and the military. Concentrated interests demanded more spending for their constituencies, and the diffuse interest of economic stabilization was poorly represented. Furthermore, the Soviet-era constitution left legislative institutions that lent themselves to the centralization of power. An unworkably large Congress of Peoples' Deputies was the supreme legislative authority, but it delegated its powers between sessions to the Supreme Soviet, which it elected from its own membership. Speaker Ruslan Khasbulatov soon found that the best way to win support in the Congress was to appeal to economic populism, and he stepped up the pressure on the government to change its course. Yeltsin's economic convictions wavered, and he began to distance himself from his own government in April.[3] Policy shifted dramatically in May, with a jump in the money supply of 27.5 percent. The Russian inflation rate spiked upward in June, and the ruble resumed its long slide against the dollar, as the market responded to signs that Russian commitment to restraining demand was flagging.

Meanwhile, in the midst of an election campaign, the Bush administration sought to deflect criticism of its policy toward Russia by cobbling together a $24 billion relief package from the Group of Seven (G-7) leading industrialized countries. Since new direct government aid was scarce, however, the G-7 turned to the IMF as the one source of aid unconstrained by the need for legislative ratification.[4] The package included a $4 billion Stand-by Arrangement with the IMF, a $6 billion fund from the IMF to stabilize the ruble, and a $500 million loan from the World Bank. Yeltsin, however, struck a hard bargaining posture, asking for a two-year moratorium on Russian debt service and demanding that IMF conditionality be waived because "Russia is unique and its reform is unique."[5]

IMF negotiators refused to agree to a loan unless Russia rededicated itself to financial stabilization. They demanded a monthly inflation target no higher than 3 percent, with strict limits on the money supply and federal spending. Negotiations broke down, and the IMF decided to postpone a Stand-by Arrangement ten days before the G-7 meeting. The Bush administration intensified its lobbying campaign, however, urging the IMF to soften its usual requirements. An agreement with Russia was the only promising item on the G-7 agenda, since the United States and the European Union remained far apart on the Uruguay Trade Round, and macroeconomic coordination was as inaccessible as ever because of the respective domestic preoccupations of Germany,

---

[3]"All the people that he regarded as authorities on economic matters—heads of enterprises, ministers, and so on, his old colleagues—were all telling him that we were carrying out a terrible policy that would lead to the ruin of the country. He kept supporting us, but his internal certainty declined" (interview with Yegor Gaidar, June 20, 1997).

[4]Most of the package consisted of debt relief on obligations that could not have been met in any case and of export credits from budgets for agricultural programs.

[5]*New York Times,* July 5, 1992, A1, A6; July 6, 1992, A1, A7.

the United States and Japan. Finally, on the weekend before the summit was to begin, the IMF Managing Director, Michel Camdessus, flew to Moscow to smooth over differences. The commitments that Russia undertook under the new agreement were predictably watered down. Russia consented to cut its budget deficit and control inflation, but its goal for monthly inflation remained a generous 10 percent. Limits were set for monetary policy including the expansion of the base money supply (M0), credit issued by the Central Bank of Russia (CBR), and the CBR's net domestic assets (NDA). In addition, the fiscal deficit was not to exceed 5 percent of GDP.[6] Discussion of reducing subsidies and liberalizing energy prices was put off indefinitely. The IMF's bargaining position was dramatically weaker than had it been able to wait to disburse the first tranche on its own preferred terms. The Fund lent Russia a first tranche of $1 billion immediately, reserving the remaining tranches of the loan and other elements of the $24 billion package pending the results of further negotiations.[7]

6.2 THE FIRST STAND-BY AGREEMENT, JULY 1992

No sooner was the ink dry on the agreement than Russia took steps to undermine it. The first step was Yeltsin's appointment of Viktor Gerashchenko—with the reluctant acquiescence of his acting premier, Yegor Gaidar—as Chairman of the Central Bank of Russia.[8] Boris Fedorov, a leading Russian reformer, jokes that his entry in the English-Russian financial encyclopedia should read, "Geraschenko, Viktor: Chairman of the State Bank of the USSR in 1989-91 and of the Central Bank of Russia in 1992-94; in the words of specialists, the worst central banker in the world."[9] An official with long experience in the Soviet international banking system, Gerashchenko argued that it was his responsibility to assure adequate liquidity in the money market and protect industry from the rigors of reform; in short, to abort stabilization.[10] One of his

[6]Smyslov 1999, p. 54.

[7]*The New York Times,* July 6, 1992, A1, A7. The line of credit was available immediately. It was not actually drawn until November and December, in two installments, but by then the program had been declared off-track.

[8]Gaidar explains that Gerashchenko appeared at the time to be the best candidate who could be confirmed by the Supreme Soviet, but, in retrospect, he recognizes that this was a misjudgment (interview with Gaidar, June 20, 1997).

[9]Fedorov 1999, p. 105.

[10]Gerashchenko was born in 1937, the son of a professor of economics who went on to be deputy chairman of the State Bank of the USSR. In the 1960s he worked as an accountant in the State Bank of the USSR and the Foreign Trade Bank of the USSR, and then as a representative of the Moscow National Bank in London and Libya. In 1972 he became deputy managing director of the USSR Foreign Trade Bank, and then represented the Soviet Bank in West Germany and the Moscow National Bank in Singapore. In 1982 he became a deputy chairman of the USSR Bank for Foreign Economic Operations, and in 1989 he became chairman of the USSR State Bank and a member of the Central Committee of the Communist Party of the Soviet Union (CPSU).

first official acts was to resolve the problem of interenterprise arrears by flooding the market with subsidized credits. Interenterprise arrears—uncollectable debts between industrial enterprises—had proliferated as the immediate consequence of Gaidar's policy of tightening the money supply and liberalizing domestic trade. State orders continued to be the major source of demand for industrial products, but they were drastically cut back in the first half of 1992, so most of industry found itself with no final consumer for its products. In a market economy that would bring production crashing to a halt, but in the chaotic conditions that prevailed in 1992, it did not seem credible to enterprise managers that the government would really carry out a policy that promised the ruin of the Soviet industrial structure. The same problem had arisen in Poland, and the initial period of reform was critical because it was then that industrial managers had tested the credibility of the government's commitment to reform. In Russia managers bet that the reformers would lose, so they extended credits to one another to maintain some demand for their products. The only way to eliminate this practice and establish the sovereignty of money over the economy was to make it costly to extend uncollectable credits by liquidating enterprises with weak balance sheets. This, however, turned out to be politically unpalatable. In essence, the managers won their wager. The policy of extending Central Bank credits to liquidate these arrears proved that they had been right to bet against the reformers in the first place and set the stage for the widespread nonpayment and barter problems that emerged a few years later.

This was the decision that closed the window of opportunity, but it would be incorrect to lay the full blame for it at Gerashchenko's feet. His position, after all, represented the consensus view at the Central Bank; on the board of directors, only Sergei Ignatiev opposed it.[11] Furthermore, it was a joint decision by the government and the Central Bank, so Yegor Gaidar also reluctantly acquiesced. A mid-level Central Bank official recalls briefing Gaidar on the disastrous effects of the decision in November 1992. Gaidar said that he agreed, but this was a case where political realities had forced him to choose between standing on principle and losing his office. When pushed whether this compromise had not given away the essence of the reform program, Gaidar had to acknowledge in retrospect that it had.[12] As deputy finance minister at the time, Andrei Vavilov saw this as a case of the government caving in to pres-

---

[11] Interview with Aleksandr Khandruev, November 12, 1999. I have been guilty of blaming Gerashchenko for more than his due; see Stone (1999), which was written in 1997. After more extensive research I have come to the conclusion that this was excessively personalized. Although Gerashchenko supported the decisions I criticize here, he never had the power to make decisions of this magnitude, because the CBR never had any of the characteristics of an independent central bank. For a contrary view, see Johnson (2000).

[12] Interview with Aleksandr Potemkin, November 14, 1999. Potemkin was Director of the Department for International Operations, which was responsible for managing the ruble exchange market, from early 1992 until September 1998, and a member of the Board of Directors of the Central Bank from March 1996 to September 1998.

sure from the Supreme Soviet. He doubted that Georgii Matyukin, the previous CBR chairman, would have pursued a more rigorous monetary policy than Gerashchenko did in 1992; the political constraints were simply too binding.[13]

Furthermore, as part of the policy of sustaining an international ruble zone, the Central Bank of Russia granted large credits to the former Soviet republics. The IMF has been widely criticized for pressuring Russia to support the ruble zone, and there is some truth to this, but both the Fund's role in promoting this policy and its negative consequences have been greatly exaggerated.[14] Maintaining the ruble zone was a question of high foreign policy. It was a basic part of Yeltsin's strategy of using the as a forum to salvage some of Russia's influence in the Near Abroad, as Russia designated the non-Russian former Soviet republics, and the decision had been ratified at an international conference under Matyukin's leadership. The IMF's part in developing the strategy was to attempt to build a high degree of coordination among the central banks of the CIS countries in order to impose a uniform, austere monetary policy on all of them.[15] It quickly became clear, however, that it was impossible to maintain control over the money supply with twelve independent countries and twelve central banks creating money. This arrangement transformed the macroeconomic stability of the whole region into a public good, which could only be maintained if all the CIS countries refrained from issuing unilateral credits to support their own enterprises. Consequently, the CBR quickly moved to create a system of correspondence accounts for the other central banks and required that any noncash payments or interbank transfers be conducted through these accounts. The IMF initially resisted this decision, and this was clearly a mistake; however, Russia paid no attention to the IMF's objections.[16] The system of correspondence accounts effectively insulated the Russian economy from the noncash monetary emissions of the other former Soviet republics. The real source of inflationary pressure in Russia, therefore, was not the existence of the ruble zone per se but the decision to extend huge credits to cover transactions on the CIS countries' correspondence accounts. Again, it is probably unreasonable to blame Gerashchenko for this, since this

---

[13]Interview with Andrei Vavilov, June 26, 1998.

[14]Åslund 1995, Chap. 4.

[15]Trying to maintain an international currency zone is a terribly ambitious undertaking, as the European Union's recent experience has shown, and trying to launch such a high degree of international cooperation in the midst of the chaotic transition from central planning showed a degree of unfounded optimism. To be fair, however, the Fund was counting on being able to enforce an austere credit policy in Russia, which would have given it leverage to push for strict credit limits in the other Soviet successor states, and the CBR's rapid expansion of credit and policy of rolling the printing presses at full tilt destroyed the basis for such an approach.

[16]Interview with Sergei Dubinin, November 17, 1999. Dubinin was a member of the Russian presidential staff and deputy chairman of the State Committee for Economic Cooperation with CIS member states from 1992 through March 1993, and served as chairman of the Central Bank of Russia from 1994 to 1998.

was not a decision he was free to make; it was a cornerstone of Yeltsin's foreign policy in 1992.

The third major factor driving the expansion of the money supply in 1992 was the federal budget deficit, which rose rapidly. Commitments to the IMF to rein in the budget deficit notwithstanding, government spending steadily rose from 25 percent of GDP in the first quarter of 1992 to 39 percent in the second, 42 percent in the third, and 46 percent in the fourth, driven primarily by subsidies to enterprises and price supports. This, again, was the government's decision, not the central bank's, and the CBR was legally obligated to provide whatever credit the government required to finance its deficit. When combined with the decision to bail out insolvent enterprises and extend credits to the other CIS countries, the effect of covering the Russian budget deficit was to increase the total level of central bank credit by more than 50 percent per month in June, July, and August. The money supply tripled by September.[17] Capital markets quickly moved to punish the prodigal government by fleeing the ruble, whose value tumbled. The nominal exchange rate rose from 135 rubles to the dollar in June to 241 in September, 338 in October, and 419 in November. Figures for capital flight are unreliable for 1992, but the gross capital drain from Russia, including legitimate and illegitimate transfers and unremitted earnings from foreign trade, has been estimated at nearly $2 billion per month.[18] After stabilizing in May, the demand for dollars on the Russian market surged 31 percent in June and 38 percent in July. Private savings were rapidly "dollarized," since foreign currency represented the most effective hedge against inflation: Dollar deposits in Russian banks rose from 34 percent of M2 in April to 119 percent of M2 in November.[19] Investment continued to fall, and enterprises accumulated vast stocks as a hedge against inflation. The inflation rate jumped from a low of 9 percent in August to a roaring 23-26 percent per month that was sustained from October through February. As the Russian stabilization program collapsed, the IMF froze the additional tranches of its loan under the Stand-by Arrangement. Since much of the $24 billion international aid package had been linked to agreement with the IMF, this meant that half the package cobbled together by the Bush administration was suspended. Circumstances conspired, however, to bring Russia back to the top of the U.S. agenda and to compel the IMF to extend further loans in spite of this experience.

The Congress of Peoples' Deputies ousted Yegor Gaidar as acting premier in December 1992, but the new government, headed by Viktor Chernomyrdin, proved to be surprisingly friendly to the stabilization agenda. Reform might be an issue without a political constituency, but it possessed two strong, silent allies: galloping inflation and a retreating ruble. Russia flirted with hyperin-

[17] Government of the Russian Federation, *Russian Economic Trends* 2, no. 1 (1993): 12, 2, no. 3 (1993): 9-10.

[18] ASIDA-Moskva, courtesy of Kent Moors.

[19] Åslund 1995, p. 192-93.

flation in December, when the weekly inflation rate reached 10 percent. The ruble fell almost 40 percent in January on the news of Gaidar's departure, and capital streamed into Western investments at a rate of $1.5 billion per month. The domestic demand for dollars doubled each month in January, February, and March. Events on the capital markets tipped the political balance back in favor of the reformers, and Yeltsin appointed a vigorous, young economist named Boris Fedorov as finance minister. Fedorov launched a systematic assault on commodity subsidies, import controls, the lax credit policies of the CBR, and the federal budget deficit.

As winter gave way to a frosty spring, however, the opponents of reform began to regain momentum. Khasbulatov launched a noisy campaign to "impeach" Yeltsin, which, in Russian usage, meant a two-thirds vote of the Congress to remove him from office. The government's allies narrowly defeated the measure in March, but only by agreeing to hold a politically risky national referendum on the president and his economic reform program. The drama in Moscow sent Western leaders scrambling to show their support for Yeltsin before the referendum on April 25, particularly in view of the imminent summit meeting between Clinton and Yeltsin in Vancouver. In advance of the summit, President Clinton publicly called on the IMF to forgo its tough conditionality and lend Russia $13.5 billion per year.[20] He further signaled the seriousness of his intentions by launching an effort to rally the Western allies behind a new $30 billion package of aid.[21] The Paris Club of official creditors responded by granting Russia a ten-year deferment on $15 billion of former Soviet debt, and when Clinton met with Yeltsin over the next two days, he offered $1.6 billion in new direct aid.[22] Clinton used personal calls to the Japanese prime minister, Kiichi Miyazawa, to press Japan to drop its refusal to aid Russia because of the Kurile Islands dispute, and Miyazawa surprised Japanese opinion by giving in, opening the way for Yeltsin to come to the G-7 summit in Tokyo.[23] After strenuous U.S. lobbying, the G-7 countries announced a $28 billion package that relied heavily on contributions from the international financial institutions.[24]

The impact of Clinton's lobbying campaign was felt most directly in the halls of the IMF. Under severe pressure from the United States and other governments, the Fund announced on April 10 that it would change its approach to Russia and offer up to $4.5 billion without the usual conditions concerning inflation and the budget deficit.[25] On the eve of the Russian referendum, the Fund announced a new program for the former Soviet-bloc countries called the Systemic Transformation Facility (STF), designed to help ease the pain of eco-

---

[20]*New York Times,* March 27, 1993, I, 1.

[21]Ibid., April 1, 1993, A1.

[22]Ibid., April 3, 1993, I, 4; April 5, 1993, A1.

[23]Ibid., April 14, 1993, A1; April 15, 1993, A1.

[24]Ibid., April 16, 1993, A1.

[25]Ibid., April 10, 1993, I, 5.

nomic transition without imposing strict conditions. A total of $4 to $6 billion would be available, of which $3 billion was allocated for Russia. At the same time, Michel Camdessus announced that the Fund intended to lend Russia up to $30 billion over the next four to five years.[26]

Yeltsin won the referendum resoundingly, but by then the Fund had committed itself to a much softer bargaining position. In fact, Fedorov complained afterward that the IMF was too soft on Russia. As IMF negotiators acknowledge, it was Fedorov, not they, who proposed the toughest conditions in the package. According to Hernandez-Cata, "Fedorov always said, 'I don't need your money, I just want a tough program that I can impose on these bastards.' " He remembered his negotiations with Fedorov as the easiest he ever conducted. The only difficulty was that Fedorov insisted on keeping the program to two pages, so that Chernomyrdin would actually read it; this required some difficult negotiations within the Fund.[27] Final agreement on the terms of the STF came in May, and the Fund promised to try to reach a Stand-by Arrangement in the fall with stricter conditions if the stabilization program remained on track. This additional agreement would provide up to another $10 billion, including the $6 billion fund discussed the previous year to stabilize the ruble.

The Fund made a determined effort to enforce its 1992 agreement with Russia: it suspended the Stand-by Arrangement, triggering clauses in several other international agreements, and withheld financing for at least six months. The outcome, on the other hand, did little to reinforce the Fund's credibility. Faced with an intransigent Fund—and armed with a convenient domestic emergency—Yeltsin appealed to Clinton and had the rules changed. In effect, the Fund was compelled to overlook Russian behavior in the previous year and finally agreed to provide the remaining $3 billion promised under the original 1992 agreement under revised terms. This reinforced Russian confidence that the Fund's conditions could be flouted in the future. Fund officials hoped that the fact that the next round of financing would be provided under the STF would help to insulate the damage to the IMF's reputation, since exceptions made for post-Communist countries under the new STF would not be expected automatically to extend to the more rigorous standards used for Stand-by and Extended Fund Facilities.[28] However, at least in Russia, such fine distinctions were rarely made. According to Andrei Vavilov, a top official at the Ministry of Finance, only a handful of people in the Russian government understood the technical distinctions the IMF made between the STF, SBA and EFF programs, and Chernomyrdin was not one of them.[29]

[26] Ibid., April 21, 1993, A1.
[27] Interview with Ernesto Hernandez-Cata, February 17, 1999.
[28] Ibid.
[29] Interview with Vavilov, June 25, 1998.

6.3 THE SYSTEMIC TRANSFORMATION FACILITY: MAY 1993

The IMF offered Russia terms that were much gentler than those under the Stand-by Arrangement of the previous year. The target for inflation fell to 7-9 percent per month, but the limit for the budget deficit rose to 10 percent of GDP, and the limits on Central Bank credits were significantly relaxed. Nevertheless, after only four months, the Fund was compelled to declare Russia off track and suspend the agreement. On the other hand, offering a new loan in 1993 gave the Fund leverage to bargain for a reform of the regime covering the CBR's credit ceilings and interest rates, and for a fiscal policy down payment. As with previous agreements, the provisions that could be carried out before the money changed hands were implemented, but the long-range provisions were not. The most significant achievement of the 1993 agreement was the nudge it gave to the balance of power between the CBR and Boris Fedorov's Ministry of Finance. Fedorov's objectives of reaching an agreement with the IMF and restraining the CBR coincided, and his strategy demonstrates what a wily negotiator can achieve in the midst of a two-level game.[30] As a condition for disbursing the first tranche of $1.5 billion, the IMF insisted that CBR credit come under a more restrictive set of rules (a condition Fedorov was struggling to impose on the CBR), and Fedorov convinced key Gerashchenko allies to accept this deal. Premier Chernomyrdin and Gerashchenko signed an agreement in May committing the CBR to credit ceilings and tying the CBR refinance rate to the interbank market rate.[31] Fedorov and the IMF negotiators considered this a major victory, and it is certainly the case that Gerashchenko opposed it, but Central Bank officials claim that they did not really regard it as an important concession because, at the time, the CBR had already drastically reduced its lending to banks.[32] At the same time, Russia agreed with the IMF to reduce money and credit growth to 4-5 percent per month by the end of the year. IMF and Ministry of Finance officials considered this a major victory, because it reduced the flexibility of the policy instruments available to the CBR.[33] It became clear several years later that the CBR retained a significant capacity to extend credit to the government and to commercial banks covertly through its network of offshore banks and that, ironically, it did so primarily by using funds transferred from the IMF in 1992 and 1993.[34] Nevertheless, forcing the CBR to rely on such indirect methods constrained the scale of these operations.

Fiscal policy had tightened significantly by the time of the agreement. Fedorov had aggressively sequestered funds that had been appropriated by the

[30]Putnam 1988.

[31]Fedorov 1999; *Russian Economic Trends,* 2, No. 3 (1993), 5.

[32]Interview with Khandruev, November 12, 1999.

[33]Interviews with Hernandez-Cata, February 17, 1999, and with Vavilov, June 26, 1998.

[34]PricewaterhouseCoopers 1999.

Supreme Soviet for the military industries, investments, and social services—a policy for which he was widely vilified and occasionally praised.[35] He had engineered an impressive contraction of government spending from 42.5 percent of GDP in 1992 to only 27 percent of GDP in the second quarter of 1993 and briefly brought the budget back into surplus. As soon as the agreement with the IMF had been signed, however, the Chernomyrdin government moved to relax budget discipline and soon found itself in a bidding war with the Congress of Peoples' Deputies for the allegiance of strategic lobbies and regional leaders.[36] "After we received the first part of the IMF 'Systemic Credit' at the beginning of July," Fedorov writes, "the greater part of our government immediately forgot about reforms and the systemic transformation of the economy. Everything fell apart." Fedorov himself wrote a letter to Camdessus in August urging that the second tranche be suspended.[37] Subsidies to industry doubled in the third quarter, and total government spending expanded by 120 percent. In nominal terms, federal spending on subsidies and price supports in the fourth quarter of 1993 exceeded Russia's gross domestic product for all of 1992.[38] Meanwhile, the confrontation with the Supreme Soviet had been building to a climax. Its appetite for government spending unsatiated, the Supreme Soviet passed 432 amendments to the budget for 1994, amassing a projected deficit of 25 percent of GDP.[39] Yeltsin vetoed the budget, and the impasse lasted through the summer.

In the fall of 1993, Yeltsin executed a fateful about-face in his economic policy, which turned his conflict with the Supreme Soviet into a constitutional crisis. Swelling government spending created a surge of inflation, which reached 26 percent in August. For Yeltsin, this appears to have been a telling argument: Two years of experience confirmed his ministers' arguments that inflation really could not be controlled without cutting government spending.[40] Currency traders responded to the desperate state of Russian finances by fleeing the ruble: demand for dollars surged 165 percent in August. Meanwhile, legitimate and illegitimate forms of capital flight reached new heights, as Russia exported nearly $12 billion of capital during the summer. Capital flight in August reached 60 percent of Russia's international reserves, and 15 percent of the month's GDP. Yeltsin felt compelled to change course.

---

[35]"New Target for the Deputies: Minfin. Strengthening the Ruble is Considered Criminal," *Segodnia* 37, July 27, 1993, 3.

[36]Spending jumped to 40.5 percent of GDP in the third quarter, with a deficit of 7.5 percent of GDP. *Russian Economic Trends,* 3, No. 1, (1994): 9.

[37]Fedorov 1999, p. 126.

[38]Ibid., 2, no. 3 (1993): 9-10, 3, no. 1, (1994): 9-11.

[39]"Supreme Soviet Has Planned a Budget with a Record Deficit: Popular 'Dirt Scratchers' Tear a Hole for the Government," *Segodnia,* 37, July 27, 1993, 3.

[40]Interview with Gaidar, June 20, 1997.

On September 21 Yeltsin set aside the constitution, dissolved the Supreme Soviet, and called new elections for December, which would also serve as a referendum on a new constitution. The parliament resisted; Yeltsin besieged the building and finally, on October 5, stormed it with shock troops and artillery. After the defeat of the Supreme Soviet, the way was cleared for new parliamentary elections and a sharp turn toward stabilization, but at grievous cost to Russian democracy. The legitimacy of the new state had been founded on the Supreme Soviet's brave defiance of the military coup against Gorbachev in 1991, and now Yeltsin had turned the same military on the parliament he had once led against it. If consolidating democracy means, above all, establishing routine, institutionalized means of resolving conflicts, building confidence that such means will be used rather than force, and linking the reputation of leaders to their adherence to democratic norms, the fall of 1993 represented a severe setback for Russian democracy.

The clash in 1993 had another important consequence for Russian political institutions: It allowed Yeltsin to consolidate his power by writing a new and much more authoritarian constitution. The constitution inherited from the Soviet period had many failings, but it provided for a separation of powers between the legislative, executive and judicial branches of government. The Supreme Soviet had to confirm cabinet appointments, pass the budget, and approve major pieces of legislation. Yeltsin ruled by using numerous extraconstitutional expedients, but the Supreme Soviet was a real alternative center of power, and it imposed serious constraints on his policies. The 1993 Constitution, on the other hand, provided for a form of government that has been called "superpresidentialism."[41] It allows the president to issue legislation by decree, requiring a two-thirds majority of the new Duma to override presidential orders, and allows the president to dissolve the Duma if it fails to pass a major piece of legislation or rejects a government appointment three times. After 1993, this allowed Yeltsin to rule with vastly reduced legislative restraints, giving him more extensive formal powers than any other democratically elected president.[42]

6.4 THE STF RENEWAL, APRIL 1994

On September 20 the IMF delayed disbursing the second tranche of the STF ($1.5 billion) because of Russia's failure to meet its inflation target. This was a step with serious consequences, because it froze negotiations for up to $10 billion of additional loans. Fund officials hinted that the money could be dis-

---

[41]Holmes 1993.

[42]The Russian president has more formal power, according to the Shugart and Carey scale, than any currently elected president in their study (Shugart and Carey 1992, pp. 150-55). Most of the countries that have approached this concentration of formal power in the president have been authoritarian.

bursed by the end of the year if Russian policy improved. Yegor Gaidar, who had recently returned to the government, abolished subsidized credits, deregulated agricultural prices, and slashed expenditures by refusing to disburse funds. Interest rates finally became positive in November, and M2 grew by an average of less than 9 percent per month from October through January. Inflation fell to 13 percent in December, the lowest figure since the summer of 1992. In spite of the reformist consolidation in the Russian government, however, the budget deficit swelled alarmingly in the last quarter of 1993. Federal budget revenues fell from 33 percent of GDP in the third quarter to only 19.3 percent in the last, opening up a deficit of 16 percent of GDP. Since this had to be financed by the central bank, the result was a flagrant violation of IMF targets for CBR credit. This became seen as a test of the IMF's resolve to enforce the budget agreement, and the IMF again suspended the second tranche of the Systemic Transformation Facility, which had been due to be disbursed in November.

Once again, however, Russia provided a crisis to test the Fund's resolve. The electorate decisively rejected reform in the December 1993 parliamentary elections. Gaidar's Russia's Choice collected only 15.4 percent of the vote for its party list in the new State Duma. The ultranationalist Liberal-Democratic Party (LDPR) of Vladimir Zhirinovskii received the highest vote count (22.8 percent), followed by an alliance between the Communist Party (KPRF, 12.4 percent) and the Agrarian Party (7.9 percent). The results of the election on policy were indirect, because the new constitution dramatically reduced the Duma's role, and Chernomyrdin remained at the head of the government. However, the election represented a stark rejection of economic reform by the electorate; more troubling, it demonstrated disillusion with democracy as well, as voters deserted the center and embraced extreme right- and left-wing alternatives. Gaidar, Fedorov and most of the other reformers left the government in January. The reaction of the market was swift. In one week, in January 1994, the ruble dropped 18.5 percent against the dollar. Inflation jumped from 13 percent per month to 21 percent.

The Clinton administration signaled almost immediately that it was time for the IMF to relent. Vice President Gore, in St. Petersburg, called the IMF "insensitive" and argued that the West should help the Russian government to subsidize Russian workers. In Germany he suggested to Helmut Kohl that the IMF should relax its inflation targets and accelerate aid to Russia. On December 21 Warren Christopher and Strobe Talbott seemed to abandon the stabilization agenda, criticizing the Russian reformers for callousness toward the pain of the transition.[43] The next day the IMF announced that it would consider relaxing its conditions. Ernesto Hernandez-Cata, the head of the Fund's Mission to Russia, said that he would push for a monthly inflation target of 3-5 percent for 1994, instead of the 2 percent he had been seeking.[44]

---

[43] *New York Times,* December 18, 1993, I1; December 19, 1993, I19; December 21, 1993, A1.
[44] Ibid., December 22, 1993, A1.

There was a gradual shift in the Fund in 1993 and 1994 from a strategy of enforcing conditionality to a short-term bargaining posture, as the emphasis shifted away from past performance and toward bargaining over the minimum conditions Russia must meet to receive the next loan installment. The Clinton administration intensified its criticism of the Fund on February 1, suggesting that the IMF had been slow to engage Russia in dialogue, and proposed that the G-7 take a more active role in monitoring negotiations between the IMF and Russia to resolve the continuing loan impasse. The pressure was intense enough that Camdessus felt compelled to respond publicly. He spelled out a number of points that were under discussion, including industrial subsidies, price controls, privatization, and the budget deficit. His statement seemed to suggest, however, that the one irreducible IMF condition was that the Russian inflation rate fall back to the promised 10 percent per month before the second tranche could be disbursed.[45] Hernandez-Cata took a tougher position. He felt that the Russian government had shown a flagrant disregard for IMF conditions in 1993, and he was firmly opposed to renewing the STF in 1994. He argued the point with Michel Camdessus, pointing out that renewing the agreement after Russia's poor performance the previous year would severely damage the IMF's credibility with other countries. His position was that Russia should adopt a program, which the IMF would monitor, but that no funds should be disbursed until the results of the program were in.[46] According to Dubinin,

> The disagreement with the IMF in February 1994 was the following. Camdessus's position was that Russia should take on the obligations of a program, but for the duration of one year it would receive no funds from the IMF. The Fund would monitor the situation in Russia, and then draw conclusions about what to do about credits for Russia in the following year. For us, speaking openly, it was not so much a question of money—but of course that wouldn't hurt the budget, and would help service our debts and provide a non-inflationary means of financing the deficit—but we understood that for Chernomyrdin and those around him, it was an important argument that we would only get the IMF credits if we fulfilled the conditions. It was very hard to carry out economic policy without the help of money. We were in agreement with the IMF about the steps we had to take, but without connecting the program to credits, it would be a much less convincing argument for the president and our colleagues in the cabinet and in the Duma that we had to carry out the conditions.[47]

[45] Ibid., February 1, 1994, A6; February 2, 1994, A1.

[46] Interview with Hernandez-Cata, February 17, 1999.

[47] Interview with Dubinin, November 17, 1999. Dubinin was not aware of differences between the positions of Hernandez-Cata and Camdessus.

Meanwhile, the Russian government was continuing the efforts begun in the fall to reduce inflation. Although Chernomyrdin called for a more pragmatic approach to managing the economy and surrounded himself with industrialists, his policy in early 1994 was, in fact, designed to placate the market and the Fund. Real interest rates rose steadily, to a peak of 10 percent per month in March and April. After the budget-tightening measures introduced in the fall, demand for dollars stabilized at a manageable level, and capital flight declined from a high of $4.5 billion per month in October to $1.5 billion in April. In the first quarter of 1994, M2 grew at a modest rate of 7 percent per month, and inflation finally dipped under 10 percent per month in March. Camdessus took this as his cue, flying to Moscow to meet with Chernomyrdin. Apparently, Chernomyrdin took him on a hunt for wild pigs, which provoked Gerashchenko to quip that someone should slap a tax on wild pigs. In the end, renewing the STF was Camdessus's call to make, and he agreed in return for promises of unspecified new taxes and spending cuts, a budget deficit for 1994 of no more than 10 percent of GDP and a target for inflation of 7 percent per month by year's end. He announced that Russia was eligible to apply for a Stand-by Arrangement worth $4 billion of additional financing. In addition, the agreement made Russia eligible for up to $2 billion in loans from the World Bank that had been put on hold.

The Fund had taken a firm stand for the second time, but had been forced to fight a rear-guard action against its principals that reduced its room for maneuver and strained its credibility. The Fund imposed a cost on the Russian government by delaying the disbursement from September until April. This sent a signal that the IMF would not sign a Stand-by agreement or release additional funds to stabilize the ruble until Russia had made progress in controlling inflation. It became increasingly apparent, however, that Russia was able to bring substantial diplomatic pressure to bear on the Fund and that the Fund had to modify its bargaining positions when Russia flexed its muscles. The Fund gradually started looking for an excuse to disburse the second tranche in spite of the violations of the 1993 agreement, and the bargaining came to revolve around the short-term measures that Russia could take to bring its policies back on track. The consequence was greater flexibility in the spring of 1994, which gave the Fund greater leverage over short-term Russian policy but also undermined Russia's long-term incentives to abide by the next agreement.

The disbursement of the second tranche of the STF seems to have removed the pressure for fiscal and monetary restraint. A new complacency crept into public statements about economic policy, as leading officials suggested that Russia's economic woes were largely a thing of the past.[48] The acting minister of finance, Sergei Dubinin, asserted "without excessive optimism," that hyper-

---

[48]"The Government Prepares for an Investment Boom, Investors Seek Guarantees," *Segodnia*, June 29, 1994, 2.

inflation had been avoided and that "financial stabilization has taken place."[49] Both fiscal and monetary restraint quickly fell victim to the new mood.

For the first half of 1994 most of the difficulty with the budget continued to be on the revenue side. Revenues declined to 8 percent of GDP in the first quarter and only recovered gradually.[50] This had a variety of causes, including local fraud, the difficulty the government experienced in collecting taxes from the new private sector, and the conflicts between the center and the regions. The most important problem, however, was that the Russian government relied heavily on tax favors as a way of building patronage. Sergei Aleksashenko cites a memo he wrote to Dubinin in August:

> In any country, the collection of taxes is an indicator of the political will of the government. The nominal tax rates in Russia at present were supposed to yield much more significant income to the budget than they do. However, with a series of decisions the leadership of the country has made it impossible to achieve even the modest goals for increasing the level of tax income included in the budget. Consider a few examples:
>
> - The massive liberation of enterprises and organizations from paying import tariffs on goods imported into Russia;
> - Lowering taxes on light automobiles for each individual factory under pressure from their directors;
> - The adoption of the directive on the special procedure for calculating expenses in the gas industry (whose cost to the budget has been equal to approximately 500 billion rubles);
> - The expansion of off-budget funds for branches of industry, which are formed as a percentage of the cost of production, i.e., on the basis of reducing profit. It has been impossible to impose any kind of control on the collection or expenditure of these resources, and the implementation of Decree 1004 on limiting the size of these funds and consolidating them into the budget was very quickly blocked;
> - The extension of tax holidays (*otsrochek*) and tax credits to "influential" directors for hundreds of billions of rubles by decisions of the President and the Government.
>
> It would be possible to continue with more examples....[51]

---

[49] Dubinin predicted that inflation would run at 7-8 percent per month by the end of 1994 and fall to 3-5 percent by the end of 1995. "Minfin Announces That Financial Stabilization Is Near," *Segodnia,* July 5, 1994, 1.

[50] *Russian Economic Trends* 3, no. 1 (1994): 9; 4, no. 1 (1995): 10.

[51] "From an internal memorandum of the author to the Minister of Finance, 8.18.1994," reprinted in Aleksashenko (1999, p. 17-18).

The revenue picture gradually improved during the year, but government spending also resurged, increasing by almost 50 percent in each of the last two quarters. The federal budget deficit rose to 12 percent of GDP in the third quarter of 1994.[52] Meanwhile, monetary policy returned to an expansionary course, because the Central Bank was compelled to extend direct credits to the Ministry of Finance to cover the budget shortfall.[53] The watchword in the Central Bank was the self-contradictory phrase, *umerennaya zhestkost'*, or "moderate firmness," which turned out to be no more moderate than it was firm.

In a series of meetings over the summer, Dubinin's group at the Ministry of Finance managed to convince key players in the government that the current course was unsustainable and would sooner or later lead to a collapse of the exchange rate and a return to the high levels of inflation that had prevailed in 1992-93. Events in the summer and early fall finally lent their arguments weight. Capital flight had slowed but remained a steady drain of $1 billion per month. Demand for dollars surged 265 percent during the summer, and the ruble steadily declined, indicating a deep lack of confidence in the government's policy. The CBR intervened furiously in September, spending $4 billion in futile efforts to staunch the hemorrhage of rubles. Finally, a meeting of the government was convened in Sochi on October 9 to discuss the proposals of the Ministry of Finance. Chernomyrdin presided, and the other participants included the four deputy chairmen of the government, Zaveriukha, Chubais, Shakrai, and Shokhin; Gerashchenko; Dubinin; and other representatives of the CBR, Ministry of Finance, and Ministry of the Economy. The Ministry of Finance proposed adopting a monetarist strategy based on an exchange rate pegged to the dollar. Further, the Central Bank should be prohibited from extending credit to the government and should take defending the exchange rate as its primary objective. Given the gravity of the situation on the exchange market, consensus prevailed. After a brief, two-hour discussion, at which no one raised strong objections, the government adopted the proposals of the Ministry of Finance. The protocol of the meeting makes it clear that the major points of the 1995 program had already been determined: a drastic reduction of CBR credit to the budget, increasing reliance on domestic and international borrowing to replace monetary financing, and basing the 1995 budget on the assumption of a greatly reduced deficit.[54]

---

[52] *Russian Economic Trends* 4, no. 1 (1995): 10.

[53] From a base of 7.5 trillion rubles, the CBR's holdings of Russian domestic assets increased by 7 trillion rubles ($3.4 billion) in July; by 8 trillion rubles in August; and by 8 trillion rubles in September. Furthermore, M2 jumped by 17 percent in April, and it continued to grow by an average monthly rate of 13 percent through August. Monthly inflation had been brought down to single digits by the policies in place in the fall and spring, so this amounted to a real expansion of the money supply of almost 50 percent over five months. In addition, the CBR gradually lowered interest rates, which again became negative in real terms in October.

[54] Aleksashenko 1999, 29-36. The document is consistent with interviews with other participants: Dubinin, November 17, 1999; Yasin, November 17, 1999; Potemkin, November 14, 1999.

Only two days after the Sochi conference, the markets exacted their bitter revenge. The head of the international operations department at the Central Bank, Aleksandr Potemkin, realized there was no way to avoid a serious depreciation of the ruble, but the Central Bank was under strict orders from the government and the president to avoid a devaluation at all costs. The Central Bank had managed to accumulate significant foreign reserves in the spring and had received the latest IMF tranche, so government officials argued that it was time to return part of the windfall to the market.[55] Finally, when international reserves fell to only two weeks' worth of imports, the CBR withdrew from the market. The result was quickly dubbed "Black Tuesday" in the Russian press. The ruble fell 40 percent against the dollar on October 11 and then rebounded for a two-day devaluation of 27 percent. Potemkin subsequently argued that since the CBR had found itself unable to manage the ruble by ordinary means, it had made a virtue of necessity by withdrawing all support from the ruble suddenly, thereby creating a panic. The Central Bank counted on the fact that the panic would severely overshoot the necessary correction in the value of the ruble, and, when the ruble rebounded, as it did the next day, numerous speculators would find themselves with heavy losses. CBR officials believed that the moderate, predictable behavior of the Central Bank had made it relatively safe to bet against the ruble and hoped that allowing the market to gyrate would punish the speculators enough to force them to be more cautious in the future. The stratagem appeared to work, since the demand for rubles rebounded a few days after Black Tuesday, and the Central Bank began buying dollars again.[56] The psychological effect of Black Tuesday, however, went far beyond anything the central bankers had predicted. Inflation jumped to 15 percent per month and remained at 1993 levels until February. The flow of foreign investment into Russia, which had reached a peak of $500 million in August, fell to $100 million in November.[57]

The financial crisis provoked a full-scale secret police investigation directed at alleged profiteers and speculators, headed by Yeltsin's old friend, Oleg Lobov.[58] Potemkin and many others found themselves dragged before the secret police, questioned, and charged with *vreditel'stvo*—"wrecking," or economic sabotage—which is a term from the Stalinist lexicon of the 1930s. In the process, the Russian government underwent a wholesale reshuffling, which brought in new hardline elements sympathetic to the military and police agencies. As Potemkin later put it, with some deliberate exaggeration, "our hoax unleashed the war in Chechnya."[59] The immediate impact of the panic turned

[55]Interview with Potemkin, November 14, 1999.

[56]Ibid.

[57]Åslund 1995, p. 206.

[58]"Read Off the List, Please, and Seek Out Methods of Punishment," *Segodnia,* November 4, 1994, 1.

[59]Interview with Potemkin, November 14, 1999.

out to be positive for economic reform, however. Overruling Chernomyrdin, Yeltsin promoted the liberal Anatolii Chubais to the position of first deputy premier and granted him control over the entire range of economic policy. Tatyana Paramonova, who subsequently proved her dedication to a sound currency, replaced Gerashchenko at the CBR. Although this was a gain for economic reform, the ease with which Yeltsin fired Gerashchenko did not bode well for the independence of the Central Bank. Ironically, Dubinin, who had done more than any other member of the government to warn about the impending crisis, was also one of its victims and was sent into temporary retirement in the private sector. Chubais announced a new policy course, which he dubbed the "second stage of the Russian reforms."[60] For the first time, the foreign exchange market had toppled a Russian government—something that neither the Russian electorate nor the State Duma had been able to do.

The concept for the new Russian policy was in place before the crash, but Black Tuesday was a key event in the education of the Russian central bankers, which was not lost even on Gerashchenko.[61] Nor was it lost on Yeltsin, who saw that repeating the events of October 1994 could pose a severe threat to his authority. A constituency was in place to introduce a new policy, and the groundwork had been laid for basing that policy on a pegged ruble and a tough monetary policy. Alternative versions of the policy proliferated in the government. Chubais, who expected another imminent crash, kept a secret decree in his personal computer ready for the president to sign on short notice declaring an administrative devaluation. On the other hand, Tatyana Paramonova turned out to be the strongest proponent of defending the ruble.[62] Both positions were presented in a meeting with Yeltsin in early January. The CBR had calculated that after the crash in October and the inflation that followed, the money supply was close to its estimates of the minimum level of supply needed to support basic economic transactions. At the same time, however, reserves had fallen below $1 billion, so there was very little room for maneuver. Moreover, given that January was a month in which exports traditionally fell and imports rose and that military operations had just begun in Chechnya, this appeared to be a very risky time to launch a policy based on a strong currency. For Yeltsin, however, the risks appeared to be high on both sides. The overwhelming political need to avoid another major devaluation led him to accept a whole series of tough new measures proposed by the Central Bank to staunch the flow of rubles onto the foreign exchange market: increased reserve requirements for banks, including the first (albeit low) reserve requirements for deposits in for-

[60]"Anatolii Chubais Has Introduced 'the Team for the Second Stage of Reforms,' " *Segodnia*, November 12, 1994, 1.

[61]Interviews with Khandruev, November 12, 1999, and Potemkin, November 14, 1999.

[62]Interview with Potemkin, November 14, 1999. This account was confirmed by Yevgenyi Yasin (interview, November 17, 1999). Yasin was Minister of the Economy from September 1994 to March 1998, and Minister without portfolio until September 1998.

eign currency; higher interest rates; and cutting off all direct CBR credits to the federal government.

In April 1995 the Russian government signed its most ambitious agreement with the IMF. The Russian government had been clamoring for a new loan from the IMF since October to help cover a projected 1995 budget deficit of $26 billion.[63] In return, the IMF demanded a substantial policy down payment. Russia agreed to finally implement a 1994 decree to liberalize the oil sector, where prices remained 30 percent below world levels.[64] Instead of downgrading Russia's credit as a result of its dismal performance in 1994, the Fund offered a loan of $6.4 billion, at the time the second largest in its history following the bailout of Mexico earlier in the year. The new agreement set an inflation goal of no more than 3 percent per month by the end of the year and a budget deficit limit of 73 trillion rubles, or 5.1 percent of estimated GDP. The Russian Duma, furthermore, agreed to prohibit the CBR from financing the federal budget, compelling the Ministry of Finance to seek outside funding and to rely increasingly on the domestic bond market. In addition, CBR net domestic credit was not to increase by more than 35 trillion rubles.[65] After the experience of 1994 the Fund insisted on monthly disbursement in order to retain some leverage after the agreement was signed.

6.5 THE SECOND STAND-BY ARRANGEMENT, APRIL 1995

The new economic policy was a tremendous gamble from the outset. It promised a stable currency and a sharp reduction of inflation. However, by pegging the ruble and relying on borrowing to finance the budget, the government created a situation that would inevitably lead to a financial collapse unless the fiscal deficit were swiftly brought under control. Mounting debt payments would only cause the fiscal situation to deteriorate. Meanwhile, in the event of a deterioration of market confidence, the central bank would face two contradictory objectives: supporting the market for state bonds or supporting the exchange rate. By buying bonds to support the government's ability to finance the deficit, the central bank would increase the money supply and put downward pressure on the ruble. If it failed to support the bond market, however, fear that bond prices were about to crash could cause bond holders to sell off and bolt for the exchange market, which would have the same effect. The only way to square the circle in the long term was to reduce the government's need to borrow. In fact, financing stability by issuing domestic debt could only be a reasonable

[63] *New York Times,* October 24, 1994, A5.

[64] Ibid., January 6, 1995, A3. Chernomyrdin resisted this, especially the IMF demand to abolish export taxes on oil and gas, which were a major source of government revenue. When Camdessus flew to Moscow in March, he convinced Chernomyrdin to concede on this point, against Chernomyrdin's judgment (interview with Yasin, November 17, 1999).

[65] *Russian Economic Trends* 4, no. 1 (1995): 3.

strategy for one year; following it any longer would create a dangerous debt overhang and a fiscal burden that would compromise any efforts to balance the budget. The hope of the reformers was that somehow the government would avoid this and that the danger of an impending financial crisis would be the one argument that might be able to trump special interests and short-term political considerations.

In spite of the war in Chechnya, the federal budget deficit remained below the ceilings in the IMF program for the first year.[66] Monetary policy was conservative, IMF targets for CBR credits and M2 were maintained, and the CBR's policy of substantially increasing its foreign reserves as confidence in the ruble returned became the basic source of liquidity in the economy.[67] As a result, the currency stabilized within an official exchange rate corridor, and inflation fell steadily, from a monthly rate of 17.9 percent in January (an annual rate of 600 percent) to 3.2 percent in December (an annual rate of 40 percent). The budget adopted for 1996, furthermore, called for even greater austerity, with a projected deficit of 3.9 percent of GDP. Capital markets responded favorably: Capital outflows fell to record lows of $500 million per month in the summer.

The campaign for the parliamentary elections in December led to a modest expansion of government spending in October and November.[68] The government resisted the temptation to override the IMF spending targets, however, even as the election campaign became increasingly desperate. In part, the government was complacent because the Russian Constitution vests so little power in the parliament; it is apparent, however, that Chernomyrdin overestimated his party's popular appeal. The party-list voting was a disaster: The government party, Our Home Is Russia, polled only 10.1 percent of the party-list vote, putting it in third place behind its undemocratic opponents of the Left and the Right: Gennadyi Zyuganov's Communist Party (22 percent) and Vladimir Zhirinovskii's Liberal-Democratic Party (11.2 percent). Grigorii Yavlinskii's liberal Yabloko Party polled 6.9 percent, and the rest of the vote went to small parties that failed to meet the 5 percent threshold for representation in the Duma. Half the seats were elected from single-member constituencies, however, which diluted the results. Although the government was left controlling only 12 percent of the total seats, no stable coalition emerged to oppose it. Since the Duma requires a two-thirds majority to pass legislation

[66] *Russian Economic Trends, Monthly Update* (November 14, 1995): 3, 8.

[67] Brigitte Granville, *Monetary Report* 75 (September 7, 1995): 12; *Russian Economic Trends, Monthly Update* (November 14, 1995): 7; interview with Yusuke Horiguchi, November 8, 1999.

[68] The government requested budget increases in several sensitive categories: 4.7 trillion rubles ($1.1 billion) to settle accounts with pensioners, 6.2 trillion ($1.4 billion) to rebuild Chechnya's economy, 10 trillion ($2.3 billion) to increase army wages and 2.3 trillion ($500 million) to provide the army with food. (*Izvestiia,* September 29, 1995, 2). In addition, it financed grain imports to prevent an increase in the price of bread because of the poor 1995 harvest (OMRI [Open Media Research Institute] Daily Digest I, No. 205, (October 20, 1995): 4). However, the budget deficit fell below 1.5 percent of GDP in October and November.

over a presidential veto or to block a presidential decree, even the disastrous defeat of the reformist parties in December did not prevent Yeltsin from governing. However, it did make it extremely difficult to pass the budget or other major pieces of legislation in the future. Furthermore, it indicated the country's deep disillusionment with economic reform and the willingness of substantial portions of the electorate to flirt with totalitarian alternatives. Some form of dictatorship was endorsed by 84 percent of Communist voters and 67 percent of Liberal-Democratic voters; only 45 percent of the electorate was unwilling to support either a return to Communism, dictatorship, or military rule.[69] The long, painful transition had severely eroded the legitimacy of Russian democracy.

6.6 THE EXTENDED FUND FACILITY, FEBRUARY, 1996

The next IMF program was negotiated against the backdrop of a desperate presidential election campaign in which the Communist candidate, Gennadyi Zyuganov, seemed almost certain to prevail over an incumbent Yeltsin with an approval rating of 6 percent. A Communist victory in Russia—unlike in Poland or Hungary—was very threatening to reform everywhere in Eastern Europe, and an ability to deliver Western assistance seemed to be one of Yeltsin's few electoral assets. Yeltsin was in a strong position at least in bargaining with the IMF, if in no other respect. As the head of the IMF Mission to Russia put it in an interview several years later, this was "the most important—well, one of the most important—political campaigns in modern history." Toward the end of the interview, he put the Fund's relations with Russia in context:

> They say that Indonesia is too big to fail, but Russia is something totally different. Think of the nuclear weapons! I never made the programs easier because of this, but it is just realism that we have to integrate them into the modern world economy, or we will have a nightmare. It would only take five or six crazy people in Russia, and just imagine what might happen.[70]

As a signal about the upcoming presidential election in June, the parliamentary elections in December were clear enough: The population was dissatisfied with Yeltsin's government. The sense of crisis that mobilized the reformers and major financial interests around Yeltsin's campaign is difficult to recreate. Anatolii Chubais took the first steps toward consolidating that alliance in the fall of 1995 by convincing the government to go ahead with a tremendously lucrative series of privatization deals. Mass privatization had stopped short of offering some of the choicest industrial properties, and now the government

[69]White, Rose and McAllister 1997, p. 245.
[70]Interview with Horiguchi, November 8, 1999.

agreed to offer shares in these enterprises to commercial banks at very low prices as collateral for loans. The government retained the right to repurchase the shares by repaying the loans at the end of 1996. The political significance of the deal was that it created a strong common interest in Yeltsin's reelection between the government and the banks, since the banks would have to expect the deal to be repudiated if Yeltsin lost. The low price of the shares, under the circumstances, can be considered a hefty risk premium. As one of the government's key economic advisers explained,

> It was a forward contract. If Yeltsin wins, you get the property; if he loses, you lose your money. Loans were made in December 1995, on the condition that if the loan is not repaid, then you get the property after one year. Everyone understood that if Yeltsin lost, they wouldn't get the property and they would lose their money. In effect, they bought forward contracts based on the outcome of the election.[71]

Chubais stepped down from his government posts in January and took charge of Yeltsin's reelection campaign. His impressive organizational skills were more than equal to the task, but perhaps more important, he was able to use his ties to the commercial banking sector to attract huge campaign contributions and to coordinate an informal advertising campaign through the media. Yeltsin replaced the head of the All-Russian State TV and Radio Company with a loyalist and appointed the head of Russia's only independent television station to his campaign. A study of the three national television stations' coverage of the campaign from May to July by the European Institute for the Media found that positive references to Yeltsin outnumbered negative ones by 492, whereas negative references to Zyuganov outnumbered positive ones by 313.[72] Furthermore, the liberal press, which was usually quite critical of Yeltsin, rallied to his side once it became clear that it faced a choice between Yeltsin and Zyuganov. This might have happened in any case, but common interests were reinforced by the purchase of all the major newspapers by the financiers who supported the Yeltsin campaign. Throughout the campaign, media coverage remained extraordinarily one-sided, and Yeltsin's share of the projected vote gradually increased.

Yeltsin gave his economic policies a more populist cast in January, promising to pay wage arrears and reschedule $6.7 billion in taxes owed by enterprises. In order to end a nationwide miners' strike, the government allocated an additional $2.2 billion for the coal industry. Meanwhile, the Duma raised the ante by pressing ahead with plans to raise the minimum wage by 20 percent. Apparently signaling a change of course, Yeltsin replaced Chubais with

[71] Interview with Vladimir Mau, November 19, 1999.
[72] Cited in White, Rose and McAllister (1997), pp. 251-2.

Vladimir Kadannikov, an industrialist and advocate of increased subsidies to industry.[73] Markets reacted swiftly. After more than six months of stability, the ruble fell almost 8 percent in one week.

Meanwhile, the IMF came under public pressure from the Clinton administration to reach agreement with Russia quickly. When Chernomyrdin came to Washington to lobby for a new loan, Clinton stated, "I believe the loan will go through, and I believe that it should." U.S. officials downplayed the importance of personnel changes in Moscow and expressed understanding for Yeltsin's need to maneuver in advance of the elections. In a telling statement, Chernomyrdin observed that both countries were having presidential elections this year, lending "a special tone" to their relationship.[74] The IMF was solicitous of the new Russian course, and Michel Camdessus again visited Moscow to smooth the way to an agreement. In negotiations for a new three-year, $10.2 billion loan under the Extended Fund Facility, the IMF pushed for a number of institutional changes, including lifting controls on capital flows, liberalizing foreign trade, resuming privatization, and revising the tax code to abolish preferences for some of Russia's most influential lobbies. However, in a concession to election-year pressures, the Fund agreed to accommodate high levels of spending in the first half of the year.[75] The IMF head of Mission to Russia argues that some of the concessions on fiscal policy were made for technical reasons rather than political ones; for example, a number of indicators were revised when Germany and France agreed to provide a significant amount of aid to allow Yeltsin to pay off wage and pension arrears in the run-up to the election, because in cash terms, paying off these arrears increased the deficit. In addition, the high degree of political uncertainty brought about by the impending election pushed up risk premiums, driving up interest rates and increasing the cost of government debt service. The IMF regarded this as an exogenous shock and agreed to accommodate half the increase by raising the deficit ceiling. Nevertheless, there was a clear sense in the IMF that expectations had to be lowered during a presidential campaign, particularly in Russia.

> We were in a holding operation during 1996. We knew that we couldn't improve the situation. Russia was very explosive. If we had not been there, applying pressure to contain spending, I don't know what would have happened. People don't realize what power it takes—what persuasive power—to prevent chaos from breaking out. We held back the explosion. We felt that we were successful. If you compare Russia to other countries, there should have been

---

[73] In his first public interview, Kadannikov stated, "We had to live under this strict regime for some time, but this time is over.... It is all leading to the death of all national industry" (*New York Times,* January 26, 1996, 1).

[74] Ibid., January 31, 1996, A8.

[75] *Financial Times,* February 5, 1996, 1.

either hyperinflation or price controls in the midst of such an election campaign. It didn't happen. We even liberalized some energy prices.[76]

In fact, however, Russia was far from implementing the conditions of the IMF program in 1996. As the election drew closer, the government exerted all its efforts to buoy the economy by increasing spending over budgeted levels and extending tax benefits to key enterprises and regions. Meanwhile, the uncertainty of the election campaign expressed itself in accelerating capital flight, which amounted to $16 billion from January through June. Consequently, the demand for rubles was too low to allow the government to finance its deficit by issuing bonds. The effort to do so pushed up interest rates, which further undermined the budget by increasing debt-service costs, requiring still more borrowing. A memorandum from the CBR to Chernomyrdin in May summed up the problem:

> As a result, in the last months Minfin [the Ministry of Finance] has found itself in a position to receive tax revenue in the form of money covering not more than 40 percent of federal budget expenditures. From January through March it was possible to find various sources for financing the budget deficit: resources from realizing GKO-OFZ [short-term state obligations (Russian treasury bonds) and official federal loans] on the basis of the temporary drop in yields in January and February, the last two tranches of IMF credit in the beginning of February, the French and German credits and the first tranche of the new IMF credit in March and the beginning of April, and the flow of nonresident capital in February and March.
>
> Nevertheless, Minfin's revenue sources were already insufficient by the end of March.... In the auctions on April 17th and 30th, Minfin was unable to cover the principal of the maturing debt, as a result of which the Bank of Russia bought state obligations in the sum of 1.5 trillion rubles in April in order to make it possible for Minfin to fulfill its obligations. In addition, the Bank of Russia in fact financed more than 2.5 trillion rubles of budget expenditures in April by buying that sum in state notes itself or through non-resident firms. In the beginning of May the Bank of Russia organized the transfer of more than $300 million (1.5 trillion rubles) of Minfin's foreign currency obligations to Russian banks abroad, and in the second half of May, under an understanding with Minfin, the Bank of Russia obtained GKO-OFZ for the sum of 2.2 trillion rubles, which went to finance budget expenditures. In this way, the total "support" of the budget by the Bank of Russia in the last two

---

[76]Interview with Horiguchi, November 8, 1999.

months alone has exceeded 8 trillion rubles, a sum comparable to the budget's monthly income.[77]

This, however, was not enough to cover the government's expanded needs during the campaign season. On May 22 Yeltsin plunged the staff of the CBR into a panic by signing a decree "recommending" the transfer of 5 trillion rubles of CBR profit to the state budget. The CBR's official reserves had dropped to $16.6 billion, but this vastly overestimated its resources because only about $7.5 billion of this was in a liquid form that could be used to intervene on the currency market. The CBR had sold $1.8 billion to support the ruble in April, and $870 million more in the first two weeks of May. CBR experts estimated that they would need to spend another $.8-$1 billion by the end of the month, $1.5-$2 billion in the first two weeks of June, and another $2-3 billion between the two rounds of the presidential election. Meanwhile, if anything happened to destabilize the GKO market, a sell-off of 10 percent of its value would flood the market with 10 trillion rubles (which would cost $2 billion to sterilize), and a rush to withdraw bank deposits could lead to withdrawals of 2-3 trillion rubles per day.[78] The CBR board was convinced that acceding to Yeltsin's demands ran a high risk of provoking a currency crisis. Meeting at Dubinin's bedside, the board of directors decided to reject the president's decree, arguing that it conflicted with the 1995 federal law on the Bank of Russia.[79] Not to be blocked, however, Yeltsin turned to the Duma, and found that even in an election season he could find allies if he turned on the central bank. On June 6 a law confiscating 5 trillion rubles from the CBR was rushed through the Duma in three readings and signed by the president.

This series of events made it impossible for the CBR to meet its portion of the IMF's conditions under the EFF. The conditions of the 1995 and 1996 agreements set minimum levels for foreign reserves and maximum levels for net domestic assets, which include Central Bank credits to the government and private sector. Using foreign reserves to buy government bonds, therefore, caused the reserve level to fall below the minimum and the net domestic assets level to rise above the maximum allowable. In May, just weeks before the

---

[77]"Iz pis'ma Banka Rossii Predsedateliu Pravitel'stva Rossiiskoi Federatsii (27.05.96)," reprinted in Aleksashenko (1999, p. 78-9). The term *non-resident firms* refers to FIMACO, a wholly owned subsidiary of the CBR. Between March 27 and May 28, the CBR directed Eurobank, another subsidiary, to invest in six GKO contracts on behalf of FIMACO for a total of $705 million (PricewaterhouseCoopers 1999, p. 14). Members of the board of the CBR at the time confirm this interpretation of what occurred (interviews with Aleksandr Khandruev, November 12, 1999, and with Potemkin, November 14, 1999). Potemkin directed the department in the Central Bank that oversaw these transactions.

[78]"Iz pis'ma Predsedatelia Banka Rossii Prezidentu Rossiiskoi Federatsii (21.05.96)," reprinted in Aleksashenko (1999, p. 73-4).

[79]Dubinin was hospitalized at the time, so the meeting took place in the hospital. Inevitably, rumors circulated in Moscow that Dubinin was hiding or was about to be replaced, but he was simply ill.

election, an IMF mission arrived in Moscow to find that Russia was far from implementing its program according to almost every indicator. The extent to which the CBR accommodated the political pressure of the election campaign can be read from the figures for CBR net domestic assets, which rose by 16 trillion rubles in April, 9 trillion rubles in May, and 10 trillion rubles in June. It was clear to the Russian negotiators that the IMF officials desperately wanted to approve the next tranche; above all, they wanted to avoid being the reason for a Zyuganov victory. There was no way, however, that they could overlook the stunning discrepancy between the targets and the actual numbers for foreign reserves and net domestic assets; after all, these indicators were the heart and soul of a program based on a fixed exchange rate. Meanwhile, it was essential to the Central Bank that the fragile market not suffer the shock of a suspension of IMF credit before the election. To avoid this outcome, the CBR engaged in some creative accounting that took advantage of the fact that it held a portion of its reserves in untraceable, numbered accounts owned by the Foreign Investment Management Company (FIMACO), one of its foreign subsidiaries, and located in a French bank, Eurobank, which was another of its subsidiaries. The Central Bank sold a portfolio of Russian government debt to FIMACO for $1.178 billion, reducing its holdings of government debt by that amount and increasing its holdings of foreign reserves. The IMF was informed of the transaction but was not informed that the transaction had been carried out with a subsidiary. In effect, the CBR was "selling" government notes to itself, which allowed it to double-count more than $1 billion of foreign assets and not count at all $1 billion of Russian government debt.[80] This allowed the IMF to approve the next tranche under the EFF.

This chicanery came to light after Gerashchenko took over as chairman of the Central Bank in 1998, when he used it to discredit his erstwhile political foes. Stanley Fischer stated in 1999 that it was ironic that Russia had gone to such lengths to conceal the true state of its reserves in 1996, since, under the circumstances, the IMF probably would have granted a waiver on its condition for international reserves (NIR) anyway. It did not appear so at the time, however. Sergei Dubinin said years later, "I am sorry, if Fischer wanted to send us a

---

[80]Figures from PricewaterhouseCoopers (1999, p. 14-5), referring to "tranche M." The report claims that these transactions were not recorded by FIMACO or Eurobank, so their balance sheets continued to reflect the prior level of foreign currency holdings. If so, that would represent a violation of French banking law, but it would have no bearing on the IMF since FIMACO and Eurobank balance sheets were not part of Russian reporting obligations. Indeed, there were no conditions on how Russia managed its foreign reserves until September 1999, when the IMF imposed such conditions after the FIMACO affair came to light. The Western press made a great deal of the fact that the money invested in FIMACO originally came from the IMF in 1992 and 1993, but this was not the issue that concerned the Fund. Those funds were intended to be used as international reserves, and how the CBR chose to manage its reserves was not the issue. The problem was that by using them to buy government securities, the CBR was misrepresenting its balance sheet to the IMF.

signal that he would give us the tranche in any case, regardless of what we did, we did not get it."[81] An interview with Sergei Aleksashenko, the first deputy chairman of the Central Bank who authorized these transactions, is revealing of the mood at the time.

Q: What was the purpose of this transaction?

The purpose was to meet the monetary program. The mid-year targets had to be met. We were under a regime of monthly reporting to the IMF. This was at the time of the presidential elections. There was enormous pressure on the CBR to finance the government. A special law was passed in June requiring the CBR to give a billion dollars to the government for nothing, and this simply destroyed the program. The IMF stated officially that if Russia does not meet its targets, we will withhold the tranche in July, and meet again in the autumn. This was an operation in which FIMACO purchased securities, paying dollars to the Central Bank. If we're talking about arithmetical reporting, the reporting was correct. The transaction was real, not fictional; it really took place. The IMF was aware of the operation, but it did not know the name of the company. At that time, they received information on our program every five days, and they identified a significant decline in net domestic assets, and a corresponding increase in NIR. They asked, "why?" We told them that we had sold securities. They asked, "What were the terms?" We told them that the Central Bank had to repurchase them in two months. They decided that that was good enough, and they approved the program.

Q: Do you think they would have approved the tranche if they had known the details of the transaction?

You see, approving the tranche in 1996 was a political question for the Fund and for the Central Bank. No one was interested in knowing the details about the operations. The program was tight enough in spite of our allowances for pressure during the elections, there was no real softening of the program, so we knew that if Yeltsin wins, we can restore the program in 2 months. If Zyuganov wins, it does not really matter what the balance sheet of the Central Bank looks like, anyway.

Q: What do you think of Stanley Fischer's statement that they would probably have given Russia the tranche anyway, if they... had known that the CBR's reserves were below the target level?

[81] Interview with Dubinin, November 17, 1999.

It's not true, it's not true. Russia had not met many targets: the target for budget revenue, the target for the budget deficit. If we had informed the IMF that we could not meet the NIR targets, that would have been the end. You have to meet the NIR targets. There is a special term in the Fund: a waiver. Fischer's statement was that we could have been granted a waiver on NIR, but that is not true. We had already received waivers on two other targets, for budget revenue and the budget deficit; a third waiver was impossible.

Q: Really? Even in a presidential election year, when the whole world was holding its breath to see who would win? Could the IMF really have refused to disburse the funds?

It was a clear statement of the Fund in June 1996 that if we do not meet the target for NIR, we will be considered off track. I think we should take it seriously.[82]

This is a particularly illuminating statement of Russian expectations regarding the IMF. Credibility is not an all-or-nothing proposition. The Russian negotiators were fully aware of the political constraints under which the IMF had to operate, and they played them to the hilt in an election year, when the stakes were as high as they would ever get. At the same time, however, they recognized real limits to how far the IMF could be pushed in the name of political necessity, and they were willing to take some personal risks in order to avoid pushing beyond those limits. Aleksashenko was later investigated by the Russian Prosecutor's Office for his part in this operation. It is rare to get such a precise estimate from a political negotiator of an opponent's reservation price. Aleksashenko thought that the IMF was sufficiently constrained to be willing to overlook what he thought of as transparent window dressing, but not sufficiently constrained to be willing to openly waive a third key condition after already waiving two others.

The Yeltsin campaign surged back from the brink of defeat by convincing voters that a Communist victory would be even worse than another term for Yeltsin. It was aided by Zyuganov's own mistakes, which allowed Yeltsin to portray him as an extreme Communist who would restore all the horror of the former Soviet Union. Faced with such a grim choice, a slim plurality of the electorate (35 percent) chose Yeltsin in the first round of voting, and a short-lived alliance with the right-wing military officer Aleksandr Lebed' gave

---

[82]Interview with Sergei Aleksashenko, November 16, 1999. The other two CBR officials who knew about the decision confirmed Aleksashenko's account of the reasoning behind it and agreed that the IMF must have known what was happening (interviews with Potemkin, November 14, 1999, and with Dubinin, November 17, 1999). One of the other directors emphasized that these decisions were not shared with the board of directors (interview with Khandruev, November 12, 1999).

Yeltsin a majority (54 percent) in the run-off election. Skillfully managed by the Yeltsin campaign, the election became a referendum on Communism rather than on Yeltsin's policies: respondents' attitudes toward the former Soviet regime, rather than their economic fortunes during the transition, were the best predictor of votes for Yeltsin or Zyuganov.[83]

It was not until immediately after Yeltsin had won the run-off election on July 3 and secured a second term that the IMF began seriously to scrutinize the Russian fiscal position, which had deteriorated considerably in the interim. Previous rounds of reform had restricted the use of direct subsidies and loans as instruments of patronage, so the government had turned to selective collection of taxes in order to cobble together a coalition and prevent lay-offs just before the election. The government had granted so many favors to influential firms that tax collections were 12 percent below projected levels by July. The Fund responded by delaying the monthly installment of $330 million of its loan that month but signaled leniency by declaring that the disbursement could be made within weeks if Russia took action to increase tax collection.[84] The Fund again accepted the reality of Russian pork-barrel politics and agreed to forgive the indiscretions of the election season, provided that policy improved afterward.

A reformist coalition consolidated its position in Yeltsin's cabinet in the aftermath of the election, and Anatolii Chubais became the president's chief of staff. Yeltsin appointed Aleksandr Livshits, a relatively unknown member of his presidential staff, but one committed to economic reform, as minister of finance and deputy premier responsible for relations with the IMF. However, the problem of tax collection was never solved. The IMF suspended the disbursement of two more loan tranches because tax collection was inadequate, but its reaction was very gentle. The Central Bank complained that "the 'liberal' posture of the IMF toward the implementation of the program at the end of 1996" was reducing the pressure on the Ministry of Finance to increase tax collection and to cut spending.[85]

Inflation fell, and foreign investment surged—driven, in large part, by low interest rates in the United States and extraordinarily low interest rates in Japan, but also by a growing conviction among investors that Russia was recovering and that its assets represented the most attractive high-yield gamble on the market. Capital outflows returned to the low level reached in 1995 as soon as the election results were announced. In the next year the Russian government floated Eurobonds successfully, as did major cities and even large enterprises. Interviewed in his office in 1999, Livshits proudly displayed a framed copy of the first Russian Eurobond, "The first since the tsar," he pointed out. For the time being, Russia's isolation from international capital markets

---

[83] Colton 2000.

[84] *New York Times,* July 23, 1996, A1, A4.

[85] "Iz pis'ma Banka Rossii Predsedateliu Pravitel'stva Rossiiskoi Federatsii v sviazi s podgotovkoi zasedaniia VCh (26.12.96)," reprinted in Aleksashenko (1999, p. 86).

seemed to be a thing of the past. As a result, the pressure on the Ministry of Finance to step up efforts to collect taxes and cut spending was drastically reduced.

The first few months of 1997 marked a high point of Russian confidence and Western optimism about the course of Russian reforms. After months of high-stakes, behind-the-scenes jousting with Aleksandr Lebed', Anatolii Chubais prevailed and replaced Livshits as deputy premier and minister of finance; Lebed' left office in disgrace. The Chechen war had been reduced to an uneasy truce. Boris Nemtsov, the charismatic young governor of Nizhny Novgorod who had carried out far-reaching local reforms, was brought in as deputy premier. The head of the IMF Mission called the new Russian government a "dream team," and stepped down in 1997, convinced that his job in Russia was finished.[86]

In what was clearly the IMF's biggest tactical mistake in Russia, this was the point at which the IMF chose to press Russia to liberalize its bond market. Liberalizing world capital flows had become a key foreign policy objective of the Clinton administration under the leadership of Robert Rubin and Lawrence Summers at the Treasury Department.[87] The first step was a major effort by the IMF to get its members to adhere to Article VIII of the Fund's charter, which called on them to abolish restrictions on current payments.[88] The next was a campaign of steadily increasing bilateral and multilateral pressure to dismantle capital controls, and in the mid-1990s this became a standard condition inserted into IMF stabilization programs. Russia had formally agreed to be bound by Article VIII in 1996 but was permitted to retain a few existing capital controls during a transition period. The Russian Central Bank, however, considered capital controls to be central to its strategy of sustaining a pegged ruble under conditions of high government borrowing. The CBR's strategy for limiting the volatility of the GKO market was to limit foreign participants on the market to making long-term investments that were brokered by the Central Bank. This was intended to prevent foreign investors from fleeing GKOs in the event of a fluctuation in the exchange rate—exactly what triggered the crash of 1998. Key Russian negotiators felt certain that it would have been possible to insist on maintaining capital controls in 1997 had Russia not been pressing simultaneously for lax targets across the board on fiscal policy and restructuring. According to Aleksashenko:

> Negotiations with the IMF are traditionally based on the principle
> of compromise: it is possible to defend your position on virtually

[86] Interview with Horiguchi, November 8, 1999.

[87] Aleksandr Khandruev recalls a meeting in 1996 in which Larry Summers, then deputy treasury secretary, urged Sergei Dubinin to abolish capital controls (interview with Khandruev, November 12, 1999).

[88] This was also a precondition for Russia's accession to the World Trade Organization (WTO). Negotiations began in 1993, and remain unfinished as of this writing. For the details of the negotiations, see Naray (2001).

> any question, if you compromise on others. In the spring of 1997 it
> was much more important for the government to get an agreement
> on a low level of planned tax collection and on less decisive actions
> in the area of reform of natural monopolies, than to build defensive
> barriers against a possible threat in the future.[89]

The government negotiators overrode CBR objections to making concessions
on capital controls and agreed to the IMF demand that all controls be abolished
by the beginning of 1998. This left no institutional cushion to dampen the
market's volatility when a crisis of confidence struck.

It became clear in early 1997 that the looming budget deficit was leading to
an extremely dangerous situation. The interest on government debt increased
as a percentage of the portion of government income collected in money from
33 percent in 1995 to 65 percent in 1996. It fell in 1997 as capital inflows
lowered interest rates and the proportion of barter income to the budget fell,
but at 46 percent it remained alarming. Meanwhile, the stock of government
debt in GKOs swelled to the point that it represented a significant reservoir of
money that could bolt for the exchange market at the first sign of trouble. The
year 1997 represented Russia's best chance to bring the budget deficit under
control. Instead of a dramatic departure from the patterns of the past, however,
Russia's fiscal policy in 1997 could best be described as muddling through.
Expenditures increased slightly over 1996 in constant December 1997 rubles
(1.5 percent), and revenues improved modestly (7.3 percent), for a decrease in
the budget deficit of 9.4 percent. However, the apparent stability in the annual
figures masks the underlying volatility: The monthly budget deficit in 1997
oscillated between 4.6 and 23.5 trillion constant rubles, as the government
lurched from one political crisis to the next.

The most visible cause of the failure to bring the budget deficit under control in 1997 was the Duma, which remained dominated by its largest party,
Zyuganov's Communist Party of the Russian Federation. A large segment
of the parliament was composed of independents elected in single-member
districts, and the combination of Russian electoral law and the Duma's own
rules made it impossible to assert party discipline even over the 50 percent of
members elected on party lists.[90] The only votes Chernomyrdin could count
on were those of his small loyalist party, Our Home Is Russia. Yabloko—
Yavlinskii's liberal party—supported economic reform but often voted against
the government because its reforms did not go far enough. The Communists
were divided. On one side, a hard-line faction wanted to force Yeltsin to call
new parliamentary elections by stalling all major pieces of legislation and, on

[89] Aleksashenko 1999, p. 104-5.

[90] Smith and Remington 2000. Russian electoral law allots 50 percent of the seats to single-
member districts, with election by plurality with no runoffs, and 50 percent to party lists with a 5
percent cutoff. This fragments the party caucuses. In addition, the Duma's rules concentrate power
in a number of committees, undermining the efforts of Party leaderships to impose discipline.

the other, the leadership wanted to use brinkmanship and periodic cooperation with the government to blunt the sharp edges of reform. Under the circumstances, passing an austere budget was extremely difficult, and the result was a great deal of delay and numerous compromises. Livshits acknowledges that it would have been possible to govern Russia without a budget approved by parliament but claims that he argued against this strategy in conversations with Yeltsin, Chubais, and Dubinin because it would have done irreparable damage to the weak fabric of Russian democracy. Looking back after the financial crisis of 1998, he wondered whether perhaps he had been wrong.[91]

Chernomyrdin managed to cobble together opportunistic alliances, often relying on Zhirinovskii's LDPR, whose support could be purchased with bribes, to form the core of his parliamentary support. No major piece of economic legislation could be passed without resorting to brinkmanship, however, so Yeltsin threatened to dissolve parliament unless the budget were passed. The bargaining power of each side depended on how many votes it controlled and on the polls that projected the Communists' fortunes in upcoming elections. The government had to make enough concessions to secure a victory, but the concessions that had to be made were reduced by the fact that many members would be swayed by the threat of early elections.

The effect of the Duma was most heavily felt in the fate of Russian tax reform. By the summer of 1997 Yegor Gaidar's Institute for the Economy of the Transition Period had prepared for the government a draft of a new tax code, whose purpose was to vastly simplify the tax system and lower tax rates so that it would be feasible to collect the taxes that were nominally due.[92] This was a necessary first step toward increasing tax collection, since the sheer complexity of Russian federal and regional tax laws made it impossible to design a transparent, efficient, or even reasonably fair tax-collection regime, on the one hand, and made it possible to avoid taxes easily, on the other. The informational requirements of administering the existing system exceeded the capacity of the bureaucracy, making it safe for tax inspectors to demand bribes and for taxpayers to offer them. However, the tax code became mired in distributional politics in the Duma, as particular regions and interests opposed eliminating special provisions. Some of the lobbyists opposed the objective of simplification per se, since that would eliminate the advantages that a complex system allowed them to squeeze from their influential connections. The Duma debate raged on for more than two years, and the original purpose of the reform—simplification—became unrecognizable in successive versions of the draft law. In 1997 Yeltsin could probably have pushed the original draft through by threatening to dissolve the Duma, but at the time the political risks seemed excessive and government officials underestimated the risks of delay.

---

[91] Interview with Aleksandr Livshits, November 12, 1999.

[92] Interviews with Gaidar, June 20, 1997, and with Mau, November 19, 1999. Gubina and Rubchenko 1997, p. 18-23.

Unfortunately for the reformers, the favorable international economic climate in 1997 made it impossible to convince Yeltsin to carry out painful measures. Meanwhile, the 1996 election had allowed a new social force to consolidate its influence over the government and the Central Bank. Privatization under conditions of high inflation and extensive government intervention had allowed well-connected managers to gain control of industrial empires all over Russia. The astronomical yields on GKOs—pushed higher because of the Russian state's enormous need to borrow after 1995—allowed banks that had made their initial capital by speculating on the currency market to amass tremendous fortunes by investing in government securities. By 1997 a number of prominent Russians were counted among the world's wealthiest elite. These people owed their wealth to Yeltsin's policies, and they had supported his campaign generously in 1996, but in a number of instances they opposed changes, such as abolishing tax preferences, that were essential to consolidating financial stabilization.[93]

Furthermore, the Russian policy of economic stabilization ran head on into the cornerstone of Russian industrial policy. It was not simply that the heads of large enterprises were politically influential or that they could control politics at the local level, although both were true. More fundamentally, there was never a consensus in the Yeltsin government that reform should ultimately mean dismantling the structure of Soviet industry. It was widely recognized that little of Russian industry was efficient enough to compete, even on the domestic market, and even that much of it produced negative net value. However, Minister of the Economy Yevgenyi Yasin argues that it was simply unthinkable to close it down.[94] Instead, the Russian government used informal pressure to impose a policy of low energy prices that subsidized heavy industry at the cost of the most productive exporting sector. Furthermore, it tolerated and even encouraged a byzantine proliferation of barter arrangements, monetary surrogates, and payment arrears whose purpose was to protect the inefficient sector of the economy from the rigors of reform. Under these circumstances it became increasingly difficult to collect taxes.

In August 1997 the first tremors of the Asian financial crisis of 1997 struck home in Thailand and Hong Kong, and the Russian reformers realized that

---

[93]This confirms Hellman's (1998) hypothesis that partial reforms can foster new elites with interests opposed to further reform, leading to what he calls a "partial reform equilibrium." This is not the same claim as the argument that the beneficiaries of the partial reform were the ones who designed it in the first place. Treisman (1998), for example, argues that since the large banks benefited from the arbitrage opportunities provided by high levels of inflation, they were the political force behind the policies that led to inflation. Similarly, it is now popular in Moscow to claim that the bubble economy of 1995-98, and even the crash in 1998, were deliberately manipulated by unidentified sinister forces. In fact, these events were unintended consequences of policies that were never fully implemented because of a variety of pressing, short-term political objections that never added up to any sort of grand design.

[94]Interview with Yasin, November 17, 1999.

they would have less time than they had hoped to get their fiscal house in order. Chubais and other leading government officials became embroiled in the "Writers' Crisis" in the fall and found themselves fighting for their political lives when it came to light that they had received enormous advances for a book they had not written from a publishing house controlled by one of Russia's leading financiers. This was particularly damaging, coming as it did after numerous allegations that Chubais—always pragmatic to the point of cynicism—had helped his political allies to make tremendous profits by privatizing some of Russia's most attractive enterprises in rigged auctions. The political struggle surrounding the crisis, which became extremely personal between Chubais and the media and banking magnate Boris Berezovsky, helped to paralyze the government at the very time that the 1998 budget was being debated in the Duma.

The Central Bank took the message of the Asian crisis seriously but decided that moving away from its publicly announced policy of pegging the ruble to the dollar would be more dangerous than continuing to bluff a confidence its officials did not really feel. As Dubinin later explained in an interview,

> In the summer of 1997, the Asian crisis made it clear to us that we were in a very difficult situation. The question is whether we needed to devalue quickly, or try, in the period in which we could create political and economic stability, to solve the problem of tax collection. That was the basic problem leading to the budget crisis. We and the government of Chernomyrdin, along with Chubais, decided to try to solve that problem and not devalue. There was a wide range for devaluation within the ruble corridor, so we decided not to make an official announcement, but to keep it [the policy of the ruble corridor] for a basis and to allow the ruble to fall. But any change in the exchange rate led to such a crisis in the market for GKOs.... In January 1998, I think, there was an effort to devalue the ruble a bit, but this led to such a panic on the GKO market that we had to intervene pretty heavily to stop it. Our resources were very limited. If we even began to mention exchange rate devaluation, that would lead to a panic.[95]

Dubinin's immediate subordinates with responsibility for exchange rate policy, Sergei Aleksashenko and Aleksandr Potemkin, took the same view.[96]

This view will seem self-serving to critics of the CBR, who point to the overconfident public statements by Dubinin and Aleksashenko and the general impression that the monetary policy of the Central Bank of Russia was

[95] Interview with Dubinin, November 17, 1999.
[96] Interviews with Aleksashenko, November 17, 1999; and with Potemkin, November 14, 1999. Sergei Aleksashenko discusses this dilemma and provides documents that shed light on the thinking in the CBR in the fall of 1997 (Aleksashenko 1999, p. 107-31).

predicated on the assumption that the international environment would remain favorable. CBR interest rates had steadily dropped since 1995, reserve requirements on ruble deposits were steadily lowered, and the CBR had steadily expanded the money supply by accumulating reserves.[97] A prominent sign of confidence was the decision to peg the ruble for a year at a time beginning in September 1997, and another was the decision to introduce new ruble notes in January 1998 and strike three zeros from their denominations. Of course, public confidence is exactly what a central bank tries to project when times become dangerous. Furthermore, the bankers' account is supported by the testimony of one of their chief critics within the government, Yevgenyi Yasin:

> At the end of 1997 I told Dubinin that we needed to devalue to avoid a crisis, that we should make a change to a floating exchange rate. He said that they were planning to allow a significant devaluation to happen without changing their official policy, since they had a corridor of 15 percent. Actually, they ended up keeping a very tight corridor in order to save the banking system. I think that policy was not correct.[98]

This account confirms the details of the strategy that Dubinin and his aides outlined in the fall of 1997.

In fact, it would have been hard for anyone inside the Central Bank or Ministry of Finance to miss the signs of crisis in the fall of 1997. Nonresidents began withdrawing from the GKO market in October, and the Ministry of Finance was unable to find buyers to refinance its bonds. The Central Bank's intervention to support the bond market cost $5.25 billion from the beginning of the crisis on October 27 to the end of November, and Central Bank reserves declined by more than $6 billion, or one-third, as the money withdrawn from the bond market flowed into the exchange market. The CBR described the situation as a "crisis" in a letter to President Yeltsin on November 30, declaring that it had reached the point where it must either stop trying to support the bond market and allow interest rates to rise, or stop trying to maintain the ruble corridor. The policy of "chasing two rabbits" would simply allow both of them to escape.[99] A renewed influx of foreign capital stabilized the situation in the

[97] On the other hand, the CBR had gradually increased reserve requirements on foreign currency deposits to match the level imposed on ruble deposits, which eliminated the incentive for banks to take deposits in foreign currency. Also, accumulating foreign reserves was a prudent precaution if a crisis was seen as imminent.

[98] Interview with Yasin, November 17, 1999.

[99] The letter is excerpted as "Iz pisma Banka Rossii Prezidentu Rossiiskoi Federatsii (30.11.97)," in Aleksashenko (1999, p. 127-29). The exact amount of Russian intervention was subsequently difficult to establish, since it was deliberately concealed at the time. The most reliable estimate is probably Aleksashenko's, since he oversaw these operations at the CBR. The $6 billion decline in reserves and the fact that this represented one-third come from the CBR letter to Yeltsin, which suggests that the official figure of almost $23 billion for gross reserves in October,

first week of December, but the vulnerability of the Russian financial pyramid to the mood swings of foreign investors had become clear.

6.7 THE THIRD STAND-BY, JULY 1998

In early 1998 the government had one last chance to avoid the impending economic meltdown by making a significant improvement in the fiscal deficit. As foreign investors became jittery, rumors flashed around the world at the speed of the Internet about the state of the CBR's foreign reserves. At this worst of all possible times, Yeltsin chose to reenter the political stage by firing his prime minister, Viktor Chernomyrdin. Yeltsin had been incapacitated by health concerns for most of the fall and winter, and was poorly informed. According to one of his advisers, he dismissed the Chernomyrdin government not because he recognized the impending danger but because he was confident that stabilization had been achieved and it was now time to introduce a new cast to meet new challenges.[100] When Yeltsin nominated a relatively unknown junior minister, Sergei Kiriyenko, to be his new prime minister, he ignited a firestorm of criticism and resistance in the Duma. He finally prevailed in a test of wills by threatening to use his constitutional power to dissolve the Duma if it failed to confirm Kiriyenko in its third vote, but, in the process, he wasted the political capital that should have been used to push through an austere budget and a significant tax reform. The new government had none of the experience that Chernomyrdin had accumulated over five years, which had allowed him to govern without a Duma majority by cobbling together alliances of convenience. In addition, since Kiriyenko was identified with the extreme reformers, the new government could never play Chernomyrdin's trump card with the Communists, that if they failed to make an arrangement with him, Yeltsin might replace him with someone more liberal.

In addition to facing implacable opposition in the Duma, the new government lost several months trying to get itself organized. This was terribly frustrating for the leadership of the Central Bank, which watched the crisis looming ever closer on the horizon. According to Dubinin:

> The crisis could have occurred under Chernomyrdin, but there might have been a possibility of delaying it until the price of oil went back up, and then we might have avoided it altogether. What had to be done wasn't done.... Let me just tell you something to indicate the level of disorientation of our government. At the end of May Mr. Summers came to Moscow, and Kiriyenko and his deputy prime ministers didn't even know who he was or why he had come. Kiriyenko's advisers told him he was the deputy finance minister

---

reported by *Russian Economic Trends*, was exaggerated.

[100]Interview with Livshits, November 12, 1999.

of the United States, and so they thought he should meet with the
deputy finance minister of Russia! This kind of foolishness shows
how the situation was in the government at that time. No one asked
me who Mr. Summers was. Chubais understood who Mr. Summers
was and what he represented, of course, but it was already too late
for that when he joined the government.[101]

In May 1998 it became painfully clear that the international environment had
taken a turn for the worse. Russia had borrowed extensively, and most of its
bonds had short maturities, so it faced the need to refinance approximately
$1 billion of debt every week. When the GKO market turned down sharply,
the CBR raised interest rates from 45 percent to 150 percent. Even as the
case began to look increasingly grim, it was clear to high-ranking officials
of the Central Bank that there was no practical alternative to attempting to
defend the ruble. As the ruble's chief defender later explained, "We became
prisoners of our own policy."[102] The government's anti-inflationary strategy
was predicated on a stable ruble, as was the surge of foreign investment Russia
had received between 1996 and 1998. Devaluing preemptively would simply
have brought on the crisis it was intended to avert by destroying the value
of the GKO market, which was denominated in rubles. This, in turn, would
wipe out the liquidity of the Russian banking system, make it impossible for
the government to attract noninflationary finance, and lead to capital outflows.
Even a small movement in this direction would shake the confidence of the
market, frighten away foreign investors, and very likely bring about a collapse.
Having come to this pass in the summer of 1998, there was nowhere to go but
forward. On the Eastern front, the government began a frantic assault on the
natural gas monopoly, Gazprom, to attempt to demonstrate its determination
to collect overdue taxes.[103] On the Western front, it launched an invasion
of Washington to bring pressure to bear on the IMF to provide preemptive
support.

The Clinton administration obliged with a barrage of public statements supporting the Russian case. Treasury Secretary Robert Rubin stated the case in
a letter to Speaker Newt Gingrich. "Our interest in successful political and
economic reform in Russia is compelling," he wrote. "A collapse of the ruble would undoubtedly strengthen Russian opponents of reform, who include
ultra-nationalists and Communists." Furthermore, the financial crisis created

---

[101] Interview with Dubinin, November 17, 1999. At the time, Lawrence Summers was deputy
treasury secretary, and had special responsibility for international finance.

[102] Interview with Potemkin, November 14, 1999.

[103] The government's change of tactics was made possible by the dismissal of Gazprom's chief
defender in the government and former chairman, Viktor Chernomyrdin. Gazprom made some
concessions but, in the end, weathered the storm and emerged as influential as ever. Chernomyrdin
himself reassumed the chairmanship of Gazprom in 1998, and, after the currency crisis in August,
he recruited Sergei Dubinin to serve as deputy chairman.

an opportunity for the IMF to exercise leverage that might not come again. In the treasury secretary's words, "We have a significant opportunity to use the leverage of IMF financing to help the Russian government finally take the myriad steps needed to put its finances on a sustainable path."[104] The IMF had withheld the tranches of the EFF that were due in May and June because Russia had failed to meet its conditions, primarily those regarding tax collection. Nevertheless, the IMF announced that it would lend up to $11.2 billion to Russia in 1998 and another $2.6 billion in 1999. A total of $4.4 billion was disbursed in July, and the remainder was to be disbursed in tranches through the first quarter of 1999.[105] Together with the World Bank and the Japanese government, the IMF extended an offer of $17.1 billion in new loans to Russia over the next two years. Coming on the heels of the huge rescue packages to South Korea and Indonesia, this threatened to reduce the IMF's reserves to a dangerous level, compelling it to draw on its General Arrangements to Borrow for additional liquidity from major donor countries and requiring the U.S. Congress to act on the Clinton administration's request to extend more credit to the Fund.

In retrospect, the Fund has been severely criticized for supporting the Russian government's efforts to support the overvalued ruble in the summer of 1998; indeed, that was the purpose of the program signed in July.[106] Fund officials certainly recognized the gravity of the risks the program faced, and some quietly lobbied against it. There were powerful arguments in favor, however, and it is likely that the IMF would have moved ahead with the rescue plan even if the U.S. administration had stayed on the sidelines. First, the Russian financial crisis was not inevitable, even as late as the beginning of August. Financial crises are stochastic events that are impossible to forecast with certainty; if this were not the case, large numbers of well-informed Western investors would not have suffered staggering losses because they were caught unprepared. By 1998 all the necessary ingredients for a crisis were in place, and all that was necessary to cause a meltdown was a deterioration of market confidence. Had the bull market lasted, however, Russia could have continued to refinance its debt; given time, perhaps it might have solved its fiscal problems without suffering the damage the crisis caused. Had the IMF refused to support Russia, on the other hand, that would have been the event that precipitated the crisis, and IMF officials feared that this would deal a severe setback to economic reform and even to Russian democracy. Second, the extremity of the Russian financial situation in 1998 presented a rare opportunity for the

[104]*Reuters,* August 4, 1998. Cited in Rogov (1998), p. 25-6.

[105]The IMF originally agreed with Russia on an initial tranche of $6.5 billion, but its executive board cut the first tranche to $4.4 billion to indicate its dissatisfaction that some of the agreement's prior conditions had not been met.

[106]Rogov 1998. Hills, Peterson and Goldstein (1999) argues that the IMF should "Just say no" to pegged exchange rates, citing the example of Russia along with several East Asian cases.

IMF finally to achieve some of the fiscal reforms that it had advocated for years. The Kiriyenko government was prepared to accept almost every condition the Fund recommended, and, for the moment, it appeared to have all the presidential support it needed to implement them.

The summer of 1998 was the high-water mark of IMF influence in Moscow, as an impending economic meltdown made the Fund's financial support and confidence more important than ever. The urgency of the fiscal crisis lent credibility to Yeltsin's threats to dissolve the Duma, and that body became remarkably compliant. It passed some of the major elements of the government's tax reform program and revised the budget for 1998 downward. The government draft foresaw cutting financial support to Russia's regions by 50 percent, which was significant because aid to the regions had amounted to 17 percent of federal spending in 1997. However, the Duma blocked numerous important points. The government requested changes in the tax laws aimed at generating 102 billion rubles, and the Duma approved changes worth only 28 billion.[107] As a result, on July 18 President Yeltsin resorted to implementing key conditions by issuing decrees (*ukazy*), including new taxes on real property, increased import tariffs, and a 10 percent VAT on a wide range of goods.[108]

The policy was sequentially rational given the uncertainty about how the fiscal drama would play itself out. From the vantage point of 1999, it looks like Russia should have devalued in 1998; from the vantage point of 1998, devaluation in 1997 looks like a good idea. In retrospect, the decision to rely on debt to finance the deficit looks suspect from the outset, since it was clearly unsustainable in the long run if government deficits failed to shrink. On the other hand, the only way to break the inflationary spiral was to commit the government to anti-inflationary policies by making the consequences painful if they were not carried out. In this sense, a pegged exchange rate is an ideal instrument precisely because the failure to adjust fiscal policy will lead to a disastrous collapse of the policy. The reformers saw no politically feasible way to impose fiscal discipline except to give the economy's stability as a hostage to achieving it. The first step along the fatal path was the decision to throw fiscal discipline to the winds during the 1996 presidential campaign, instead of finishing the job of stabilizing the economy begun the previous year. By 1997 the amount of debt accumulated in the previous two years was a crushing burden, which made fiscal stabilization much more painful and difficult to achieve. Like players at Russian roulette, the reformers saw the stakes become

[107] Rogov 1998, p. 41.

[108] Ibid., 42. This was criticized in Russia and abroad as a violation of the separation of powers in the Russian constitution. Aleksandr Livshits denied that any budget matters had been covered in the decrees (interview, November 12, 1999), but this requires a very strict definition of what constitutes a budget matter. The decrees increased taxes, and they provided for increased spending, for example, by transferring resources to the Pension Fund.

more dangerous with each turn of the wheel, but at each step it appeared more dangerous to retreat than to advance. Eventually they had to lose their wager.

As investor confidence slipped, the CBR dug deeply into its foreign reserves to support the ruble, buying rubles for $9 billion in July and August. In the second week of August uncertainty on the GKO market led to the collapse of foreign demand, and on August 17 the government's financial arrangements collapsed. Suddenly, the government was unable to refinance its debts or cover its current expenses. Panic spread to the exchange market, and the frantic intervention of the CBR was overwhelmed by the sheer size of the capital flows involved. The Russian government and CBR suspended all payments by Russian banks to foreign creditors and gradually unveiled a unilateral restructuring of government ruble-denominated debt. Capital fled the country, and the exchange rate fell. The collapse of the ruble in August 1998 spurred Yeltsin, once again, to dismiss his government. Yeltsin had become increasingly feeble, capable of no more than a few hours of work per day, and had become more and more detached from the day-to-day realities of government. Almost the only lever that remained to him to affect policy was the threat to dismiss the government, and the quality of his information about the government's performance had deteriorated to the point that he could no longer evaluate the alternative arguments about why the ruble had crashed. In his view, he had given the liberals a chance to prove they were right, and they had failed; consequently, he fired them and turned to Chernomyrdin as a respected figure who could lead the country out of the mess they had made. The Duma refused to accept Chernomyrdin, however. Zyuganov's Communists were buoyed by opinion polls that showed they might gain from early parliamentary elections, so they refused to be intimidated by Yeltsin's threats. As a result, the balance of power that had favored the president in the summer now favored the Duma. When Chernomyrdin was rebuffed twice, Yeltsin withdrew his name and agreed to nominate Yevgenyi Primakov as prime minister.

Primakov had been a reform Communist under Gorbachev and had played a significant role as Director of the Institute of the USA and Canada in articulating his policy of New Thinking in foreign policy. Subsequently he had headed the Federal Security Service (FSB), the organ that took over the task of foreign intelligence from the Committee for State Security (KGB), and then served as Foreign Minister at the time when Russia's relations with the West cooled. Primakov brought with him a new economic team, led by Yurii Masliukov as first deputy prime minister. Masliukov had served Gorbachev as chairman of Gosplan, the state planning agency that managed the entire economy, and had subsequently emerged as the chief economic spokesman for the Communist Party of the Russian Federation. Meanwhile, Yeltsin compelled Sergei Dubinin to resign as chairman of the Central Bank of Russia, and then restored the post to Viktor Gerashchenko. Yeltsin had no constitutional power to compel the chairman of the CBR to resign, but Dubinin complied when asked to step down. If any doubts remained as to whether the Central Bank of Russia was independent, this should put them to rest.

6.8 THE FOURTH STAND-BY, JULY 1999

The return of Gerashchenko and Masliukov was widely hailed as the end of reform and the return of the disastrous policy of financing the budget deficit by printing money. I made this prediction myself; it appeared that the financial markets had finally deserted the cause of reform and now had helped to consolidate a government that would dismantle its accomplishments. In fact, however, the political impact of the August 1998 crash was more profound: It transformed the political landscape by converting even the radical Left to the basic tenets of monetarist orthodoxy. Whereas in 1995 the KPRF platform called for printing money to finance the deficit and fuel growth, the crash of the ruble demonstrated the tangible political costs of an expansionary monetary policy. Masliukov engineered an impressive fiscal contraction, which led to a primary budget surplus—that is, a surplus before counting expenditures for debt service—for the first time in 1999. A leading reformer argued that, in fact, only the Communists could have accomplished this, because they were the first government that enjoyed the support of the Duma.[109] Meanwhile, Gerashchenko followed a tight monetary policy. To those who knew him well, this was not surprising; he had changed his views since 1994, and, in any case, his policies in the early 1990s had been as much the product of political constraints as of personal preferences.[110]

By January 1999 the Clinton administration had completed the transition from treating Russia as a potential superpower to treating Russia as a regional power. The proven weakness of the Russian military in Chechnya surely played a role in this. After Russia experts lost the internal debate about NATO expansion in 1996, the administration steadily downgraded Russia's priority.[111] Whereas Russian opposition had once represented a serious obstacle to the development of administration policy on Bosnia, it could now be trumped by urgent regional considerations in Iraq, Iran, and North Korea, and even by the commercial interests of American arms exporters. The United States Commerce Department became actively involved in trying to develop a pipeline to Caspian Sea oil reserves through Turkey in order to bypass Russia, a move that would have been unthinkably aggressive a few years before. The fall of the Russian reformers in 1998 further undermined the argument for appeasing Russia. Consequently, when Madeleine Albright pushed for a military response to Serbian violations of human rights in Kosovo in January

---

[109] Interview with Yevgenyi Yasin, November 17, 1999.

[110] Interviews with Aleksandr Khandruev, November 12, 1999; and with Igor' Bubnov, November 16, 1999.

[111] Goldgeier 1999.

1999, the argument that this would anger Russia because of its traditional ties to the Serbs fell on deaf ears.

Primakov launched an intense campaign of shuttle diplomacy to head off NATO action in Kosovo. Meanwhile, Russia was lobbying the IMF to launch a new program. In a remarkably high-handed piece of diplomacy, the Clinton administration chose the moment Primakov's airplane was over the Atlantic, headed for a series of meetings at the IMF, to announce the beginning of a NATO bombing campaign against Serbia.[112] Primakov turned his plane around and flew back to Moscow, announcing that Russia could do without IMF aid, but not without calling Michel Camdessus and inviting him to come to Moscow to complete the deal the following week. He did so, and, although the evidence is not conclusive, the timing strongly suggests that an agreement with the IMF was the price of Russia's relatively moderate opposition to the NATO campaign. If so, this indicates that U.S. policy had evolved from seeing Russia as so important that the IMF's rules should be flouted to ensure the survival of reformist governments to a very different posture. Now Russia was seen largely as an influential nuisance, and the IMF became an instrument that was available to reward it for compliant behavior.

One sign of the change in Russia's status was that the 1999 agreement was the first that was neither essentially crafted by the Russian side nor substantially changed during the negotiations.[113] The conditions in 1999 were the same ones that the Kiriyenko government had accepted, and the IMF simply insisted that they be adopted as the condition for resuming financial support. Nevertheless, mid-level Fund officials opposed the agreement, insisting that a country that effectively defaults on its obligations should be required to demonstrate its credibility before being rewarded by further support. By the time the agreement was approved in July 1999, however, the Fund was able to point to a significant improvement in macroeconomic indicators. In part, this was because the unilateral restructuring of Russia's debt in 1998 reduced the fiscal burden of paying interest and the substantial devaluation that began in August and continued throughout the following year increased the competitiveness of Russian industry—in short, because of the crisis itself. In part, it was a consequence of the recovery of international oil prices, which increased export earnings and tax receipts. More fundamentally, however, it was because of the remarkable restraint practiced by the Primakov government and its immediate successors. By the time of the Duma elections in 1999, Russia had seen two

---

[112] The administration saw the timing as unfortunate, but dictated by the weather in Yugoslavia, which had an important impact on the tactical situation because the NATO strategy relied on air strikes. Only a few years before, however, the fact that the Russian prime minister was on his way to Washington would have been more important than the weather.

[113] Interview with Mau, November 19, 1999.

more governments—Stepashin's and Putin's—but the trajectory of economic policy remained steady. The party platforms deployed in 1999 were a startling contrast to those of 1995: All were pro-market, and all eschewed the policy of rapid monetary expansion.[114]

By the end of 1999 two coincidental events conspired to create the appearance of a linkage between IMF aid and the Russian renewal of the Chechen war. The first was the revelation by the CBR of its covert transactions during the 1996 election campaign, which was calculated to damage the credibility of the former leadership of the central bank. This became linked in U.S. public opinion with allegations that IMF funds had been embezzled and that the Bank of New York had engaged in money laundering for Russia's elite. In the fall the U.S. Congress began debates about the wisdom of extending IMF credits to Russia and of increasing the IMF's resources in general, so the IMF felt compelled to respond to the revelation that it had been deceived in 1996.[115] Stepping outside established procedure, the IMF imposed four new conditions on the 1999 Stand-by in September, after the board had already approved it: (1) a quarterly audit of CBR reserves; (2) an accounting of all CBR foreign operations, (3) progress reports on reform of the system of bank auditing, and (4) adoption of a code of best practices regarding international capital flows. Aleksandr Livshits, at the time an adviser to the prime minister, reported that his contacts at the IMF informed him that this was intended as retaliation for Russia's irregularities regarding FIMACO.[116]

The second development was the renewal of the Chechen War. The Russian side had failed to implement its side of the 1996 ceasefire agreement, and radical Chechen leaders had launched a series of terrorist raids in surrounding provinces. In the fall, several grisly terrorist explosions in Moscow escalated the stakes and united Russian public opinion for the first time around the need to crush the Chechen insurgents. In addition, the newly appointed prime minister, Vladimir Putin, a relatively unknown Minister of Federal Security whom Yeltsin had elevated in August and declared his successor, saw the renewed war in Chechnya as an opportunity to establish a public persona that might

[114]Mikhail Dimitriev, "Party Economic Programs and Implications," in McFaul, Petrov and Ryabov (1999), p. 37.

[115]In November Michel Camdessus announced his surprise decision to resign as managing director of the IMF in January, and although it is unclear whether he was forced out by the United States, and to what extent this may have reflected dissatisfaction with his handling of Russia, that is a likely explanation. It clearly was not because of any broad disagreement with the Clinton administration, but his resignation was useful because it would help to deflect criticism of the administration's handling of Russia and weaken opposition to the IMF in Congress. Larry Summers took the opportunity to distance himself from the IMF's policies and call for reforms, calling on the Fund to focus on its "core competencies," meaning that it should concentrate on preventing and responding to crises rather than providing long-term financing. (*Financial Times,* December 15, 1999, 1).

[116]Interview with Livshits, November 12, 1999.

carry him through the presidential election scheduled for June.[117] The military saw renewed operations as an opportunity to recoup their humiliating losses in 1995 and perhaps expand their claim on financial resources. Russia launched a renewed offensive, making extensive use of artillery and rocket attacks on civilian areas.

One of the costs of the politicization of IMF lending in the earlier stages of the Clinton-Yeltsin relationship was that Russians naturally assumed that their difficulties with the IMF in the fall represented a tacit linkage to the Chechen war. Russian opinion leaders argued that if NATO could intervene with impunity in Kosovo, so could Russia in Chechnya; the real fear, however, was that NATO's intervention in the Balkans would establish a precedent for intervention in Russia's internal ethnic disputes. There was no such direct political linkage; in fact, the Clinton administration was careful to disavow any intention of becoming involved in an "internal Russian affair," even as it hastened to criticize Russia's methods. The real sticking points in negotiations to disburse the next tranche of the Stand-by were more mundane: the IMF's objections to the government's optimistic forecasts for economic activity in the 2000 budget and difficulties implementing the four new IMF conditions.[118] There was an indirect linkage in operation, however. For the first time, the combination of the war in Chechnya, the deterioration in U.S.-Russian relations, the absence of an identifiable "reformer" in the government to support, and pressure from Congress made the U.S. administration unwilling to intervene with the IMF on Russia's behalf. As a result, the IMF Mission was able to strike a tougher posture than had formerly been the case.

Agreement between Russia and the IMF proved illusive throughout the next year, in part because high petroleum prices had so improved Russia's balance of payments that it did not require IMF support, but, in larger part, because no one in Washington particularly wanted the embarrassment of another agreement with Russia during an election year. Indeed, the period from July 1999 has stretched into the longest interruption in IMF financing for Russia since Yeltsin launched his reforms. Early in 2000 Putin found it advantageous to strike an obstinate pose toward the IMF as part of his populist election campaign. Once he was elected president, he quickly moved to adopt a package of economic reforms promoted by his economic adviser, German Gref; to consolidate the powers of the federal government; and to push Russia's first balanced budget through the Duma. After four years of languishing in the Duma under Yeltsin, a comprehensive tax-reform package was passed almost at once under Putin. The new rules vastly simplified the tax code, removed numerous

---

[117] The elections were actually held in March, after Yeltsin resigned on New Year's Eve.

[118] At the time it appeared that these projections had been doctored to get the budget through the Duma without violating the Fund's target for the projected deficit. In fact, however, the estimate turned out to be reasonable because the rapid increase in oil prices powered an economic expansion of approximately 7 percent of GDP in 2000.

exceptions, and transferred revenues from the regions to the center. This significantly improved central tax collection and represented important progress in restoring a healthy fiscal posture. Indeed, it was the necessary first step toward Putin's avowed primary goal of rebuilding the Russian state. Other objectives of the reform program to be introduced in 2001 included improving accounting standards and protection of property rights, reforming and increasing transparency in the banking system, accelerating privatization, reforming the energy monopolies Unified Energy System (UES) and Gazprom, reforming the labor code to increase the powers of employers, and refocusing spending on education, health care, and targeted social assistance. In the event, a remarkable quantity of legislation intended to address these issues was passed in 2001, but in 2002 it remained unclear what its impact would be.

In previous years this would have been more than sufficient progress to guarantee an agreement with the IMF, but in 2000 Russia and the IMF continued to agree to disagree. An IMF Mission to Moscow ended inconclusively in November in the midst of uncertainty over the outcome of the U.S. presidential election. The Fund pushed Russia to hold the line on spending in order to use its budget surplus to retire its debt, to reform the corrupt banking sector, and to allow the ruble to appreciate against the dollar.[119] The significant depreciation of the ruble in 1998 had created a surge in Russian production of consumer goods, which led the initial recovery after the crash. The CBR attempted to depreciate the ruble against the dollar at a steady pace in order to sustain these conditions and compensate for the fact that inflation—86 percent in 1999—was rapidly eroding this competitive advantage. However, the high price of oil caused Russia's current account surplus to surge and put tremendous upward pressure on the ruble, so the CBR was compelled to intervene heavily in the foreign exchange market, selling rubles for dollars. These foreign exchange purchases caused a substantial expansion of the money supply, which threatened to accelerate inflation.[120] The CBR contained these inflationary pressures—consumer inflation was estimated at 18.6 percent for 2000—by accepting large deposits of government funds made possible by the budget surplus, which sterilized most of the inflows of foreign currency. However, the IMF did not regard this as a sustainable long-term strategy and consequently urged the authorities to allow the ruble to appreciate gradually in real terms.

Some progress was made on the budget and bank reform in the following months, as Putin pushed through a more aggressive budget plan and vetoed a parliament draft of bank-reform legislation that did not go far enough.

---

[119]"IMF, Moscow Unlikely to Reach Deal," *Financial Times,* January 31, 2001, 2.

[120]The IMF estimated the 1999 current account surplus at $26.7 billion. Of this, the Fund estimated that between $9 billion and $22 billion was covered by capital flight; methods of estimating capital flight vary, but IMF experts leaned toward the higher figure. Another $5.2 billion was absorbed by the expansion of Net International Reserves (International Monetary Fund 2000c, p. 18-9).

However, after George W. Bush's victory in the U.S. presidential election, the mood in Washington turned even colder toward Russia. The U.S. president announced that new aid to Russia should be limited to the purpose of dismantling nuclear weapons, proposing cuts even in that popular aid program, and appointed a foreign policy team—Condoleeza Rice at the National Security Council, Colin Powell at the State Department, and Donald Rumsfeld at Defense—that was firmly opposed to the Clinton policy of engagement with Russia and grimly determined to proceed with a strategic missile defense regardless of Russian objections. A spy scandal and expulsions of diplomats by both sides did nothing to improve relations. Russia, for its part, continued to oppose Fund proposals to allow the ruble to appreciate as discussions continued for a $1-$1.5 billion Stand-by agreement. Russia had no immediate need for the funds but required Fund endorsement in order to proceed with negotiations to restructure its Paris Club debt. The latter was not particularly urgent, however, because Russia's strong payments position made the Paris Club unlikely to be forthcoming.[121] Putin shifted his attention to efforts to accelerate Russia's accession to the WTO, which had been the subject of negotiations since 1993, and had been delayed by the 1998 crisis. For most of 2001 he seemed unlikely to make much progress on this front as well, because WTO members raised concerns about the lack of transparency of the Russian economy and the weak protection of investors' rights that would be difficult to address quickly, and the economic interests of concentrated interest groups in Western countries were directly engaged in the trade issue area in a way that they never were in macroeconomic policy. This changed dramatically as a result of the September 11, 2001 terrorist attacks on the United States. In return for Putin's support in the war in Afghanistan, the United States reevaluated its strategic relationship with Russia and agreed to push for rapid Russian accession to the WTO.

Putin's overwhelming victory in the snap presidential election that followed Yeltsin's surprise New Year's resignation marked a new phase in Russian pol-

---

[121] "IMF, Moscow Unlikely to Reach Deal," *Financial Times,* January 31, 2001, 2. Russia reached an agreement with the London Club of commercial creditors in February 2000, shortly before the presidential election, which reduced interest payments and cut the principal of the $31.8 billion of Soviet-era debt that Russia owed to banks by $10.6 billion. Finance Minister Kasyanov estimated the value of the agreement to Russia at more than $16 billion. It is an interesting observation in this case that the London Club was so much more flexible than the Paris Club. This is presumably because the London Club cares a great deal about the value of debt on the secondary market, which had been depressed since Russia suspended servicing the Soviet-era debt in 1998. In return for their consent to rescheduling, the banks won the transfer of the obligation from Vneshekonombank to the Russian government, which increased the ultimate likelihood of repayment, and consequently the value of the debt. These considerations are much less important to official creditors. Putin evidently believed that he could win agreement by Gerhard Schroeder to push for a comparable deal on official debt, but the German chancellor made it clear when they met, in April 2001, that the size of the Russian current account surplus fatally undermined his case for relief.

itics, and its long-term implications for economic policy and the consolidation of democracy in Russia remain unclear as of this writing. The fact that the identity of the president remains such a critical factor in Russia after nine years of democratic politics, however, is a disheartening legacy of the Yeltsin era. Russia seems no closer to consolidating political institutions capable of resisting efforts by the new president to overthrow them than it was a decade ago. Putin's agenda will be shaped by other legacies of Yeltsin's failed policies: the collapse of the Russian state, the rise of organized crime, the quagmire in Chechnya, the huge disparities between Russia's new rich and new poor, and the dramatic economic decline. Whatever Putin achieves, for good or ill, will be severely constrained by the consequences of the eight years of economic mismanagement that went before.

6.9 CONCLUSIONS

The IMF's advice to Russia to defuse inflation rapidly was sound. Russia is an example of the economic and political price that is ultimately paid for tolerating high levels of inflation—and substitutes for hyperinflation, such as barter, monetary surrogates, and payment arrears—in post-Communist countries. Russia's GDP fell 38 percent between 1992 and 1996, grew slightly in 1997, and then fell again by 5.5 percent. The Fund, however, had limited influence over Russian policy. It can be blamed for failing to do more to constrain Russian policy, but this could probably have been done only if the United States were prepared to allow the Fund to function as an independent actor. Instead, Russian policy was constrained only by the decentralized decisions of capital markets, and the result was a dangerous and damaging delay in the stabilization of the Russian economy. Unfortunately, capital markets can only enforce discipline by proving that policies are disastrous, and democracy does not always survive the evidence. In the Russian case, years were lost in which the foundations of a competitive economy and a consolidated democracy could have been built. Russia is left with corrupt and unreformed industrial, agricultural, and service sectors. Interenterprise arrears and the reemergence of widespread barter are symptoms of the failure to restructure Russian industry, which occurred because of the ready availability of government favors. Furthermore, Russia, although one of the poorest industrialized nations, has exported $150 billion of capital since it launched its reform in 1992 and has attracted less foreign direct investment per capita than its more advanced neighbors. This represents a tremendous drain of resources from the Russian economy, which, if reversed, would have financed much faster growth. Finally, the combination of high inflation, corruption, and privatization has lent credibility to Communist propaganda: After ten years of reform, Russia has a more unequal distribution of income than its former archnemesis, the United States. Income inequality jumped in 1992 and again in 1993, during the years with the highest levels of inflation, and increased markedly again in 1998 when the ruble crashed. In 1991 the richest decile of the population received twice the income of the average citizen and approximately four times as much as the poorest decile. By 1997 the wealthiest 10 percent received three times the average income and more than ten times the income of the poorest 10 percent.[122]

A basic assumption of the formal model is that governments' choices about inflation are opportunistic: There are short-run benefits to be had from inflationary policies that sometimes outweigh the long-term costs. An alternative view would be that inflation, per se, is in someone's interest. The Russian case, again, seems to support the assumption of the model. The cyclical expansion and contraction of Russian macroeconomic policy is explained by the political incentives generated by inflation rates, with their three- to four-month lags behind policy, and the capital flows that respond to them. When inflation is in a tolerable range, the argument for restraint is drowned by a chorus of demands for industrial subsidies and price controls. Injecting money into the economy at such times is tempting, because it generates a short-lived demand boom that raises the fortunes of sinking enterprises and allows the government to distribute favors to loyal banks and firms. The consequences can be put off for at least several months, which is often long enough to get the government out of a crisis or through an election. When inflation rates are much higher, however, the threats of uncontrollable hyperinflation, capital flight, and the collapse of the ruble become more hazardous than resisting political pressures. At such times, high inflation and a weak ruble become the strongest allies of reform. The burst of inflation that followed price liberalization in 1992 strengthened the hand of the reformers, but the temptation to use monetary and fiscal policy to ease the pain of adjustment became overpowering as soon as inflation came under control in late spring. The ruble crashed, and inflation soared. The new minister of finance, Boris Fedorov, was isolated in 1993 in a government of industrialists, but inflation was the wild card that allowed him to bid on a weak hand. Once inflation declined again, however, fiscal discipline was quickly abandoned. High inflation and growing budget deficits by the end of 1993 called for austerity again in early 1994, but caution was thrown to the wind once again when lower inflation rates in the summer ushered in a new round of complacency. It took extraordinary inflation and the dramatic collapse of the ruble in 1994 to convince Yeltsin to delegate economic policy to a group of committed reformers, who carried out the temporary stabilization of 1995-98. Their very success, however, undermined the political leverage necessary to address Russia's fiscal weakness, which was the necessary condition for a long-term stabilization. The stage was set for the crisis of 1998. This crisis, in turn, ushered in a new period of improbable stabilization, as Communists came into the government and proceeded to use their parliamentary muscle to

---

[122]International Monetary Fund 2000c, Table 16, p. 51.

produce a streamlined budget.

Another key assumption of the model is that international capital markets can impose meaningful costs on governments that pursue inflationary policies, and this is certainly borne out by the Russian case. In spite of Russia's low levels of foreign investment and tenuous integration into the world economy, capital markets displayed a striking capacity to discipline Russian policy through capital flight and by exerting pressure on the exchange rate. Markets were very sensitive to changes in government policies and even to changes in the composition of the Russian government. The departure of prominent reformers from the government invariably shook the ruble and unleashed further capital flight. In turn, the four crashes of the ruble in the autumn of 1992, winter of 1993, autumn of 1994, and summer of 1998 had severe consequences for the governments in office, leading, in the last two cases, to the reshuffling or dismissal of the government. The government opposed devaluation because the nominal exchange rate was a very visible symbol of its commitment to reform; when that commitment came into question, capital flowed into foreign investments, and the ruble fell. One expectation of the model that fails is that governments will anticipate the costs of potential currency crises and moderate their policies as a result. In the Russian case, governments generally ignored the warning signs, and tighter fiscal and monetary policies were not imposed until after dramatic exchange rate movements proved how necessary they were. The problem was not that Russian officials failed to anticipate the market's response to their policies, however, but that Russian prime ministers were typically unwilling to take the painful medicine that their advisers prescribed. This is what the model predicts when governments are very insecure and heavily discount the future.

The formal model predicts that important countries will have greater credibility problems than their smaller neighbors, because the IMF will not be able to credibly deter them from violating its conditions. The Russian case strongly supports this expectation. It is very costly for the Fund to enforce the conditions attached to its loans to Russia, so these agreements are not constraining and global capital markets have discounted them. Bargaining with the IMF has constrained Russian policy in the short term. In the long run, however, agreement with the IMF guarantees little, which accounts for the slow pace of foreign investment in Russia during the first four years of the transition. Russia has met the fiscal and monetary targets set forth in only one of its six completed programs. In three others, inflation rose and the ruble fell in the months following the announcement of a stabilization program, and, in every case but one, macroeconomic policy deteriorated immediately after a program was announced. Interviews with Russian and IMF negotiators make it clear that both sides were aware that the IMF's credibility was severely strained where Russia was concerned. The IMF's ability to enforce conditionality was circumscribed by its major shareholders, because Russia is simply too important to the international system for the ordinary rules to apply. The Fund repeatedly attempted to enforce conditionality by suspending loan tranches, but in the face of insistent criticism from donor countries—in particular, from the United States—it was compelled to compromise. In each case the Fund adopted a bargaining strategy, trading additional credits for short-term improvements in policy rather than investing in a reputation for enforcing conditionality. A limitation of the formal model is the assumption that a country's relative importance does not change over time. In the case study we are able to take a more fine-grained view, and we see that Russian leverage depended on factors like the timing of U.S. presidential elections and the evolution of perceptions within the State Department of Russia's potential for global leadership. Meanwhile, the most sensitive quantitative indicator of international influence, U.S. foreign aid appropriations, was increasing while Russian influence was falling, so it fails to pick up the trend. As a result, the case study provides some variation on the independent variable that is not measured in the statistical data, and we find that, indeed, the IMF's strategy responds to these variations. The IMF quickly abandoned its attempt in 1992 to enforce rigorous conditionality on Russia and made a series of compromises that culminated in the spectacular violations of conditions during the Russian presidential elections in the spring of 1996. After the U.S. presidential election season closed in the fall, however, Russia's weight in U.S. policy steadily dropped. After the crash of the ruble in 1998, U.S. policymakers again revised their expectations about Russia's role as a great power and gave the Fund unprecedented discretion in its approach. The Fund insisted on more concessions and withheld funding for longer periods.

The consequences of the Fund's accommodating strategy toward Russia came home to roost in 1998. Between 1996 and 1998 there was a window of opportunity when the ruble was stable, inflation was falling, and production was slowly beginning to rebound. There were ample incentives to reform fiscal policy. The looming financial crisis that emerged in Asia in 1997 and finally struck Russia in August 1998 was visible on the horizon. Even without this sea change in expectations on global capital markets, it was inevitable that the ruble would eventually collapse if Russia continued to cover a huge government deficit by borrowing. This inexorable logic should have driven the Russian government to close the gaping hole in its budget, and the very fragility of the Russian financial pyramid should have lent the IMF tremendous bargaining power. However, this was not the case. Russian governments remained convinced, and rightly so, that international leverage would allow them to evade the rigors of IMF programs to which their less powerful neighbors were exposed; consequently, short-term political imperatives overrode long-term considerations, and the opportunity was lost. When Russia finally negotiated a serious program of reform in 1998 and the IMF stepped forward with a rescue package, neither actor had much credibility. In many other countries, such dramatic intervention had stabilized markets; but in Russia the market discounted all promises and collapsed, sweeping away the government and delaying the onset of serious reform efforts for two more years.

7

Ukraine

UKRAINE belongs to the ranks of the late reformers. Ukraine's first president, Leonid Kravchuk, failed to make a decisive break with the past, instead combining Soviet-style economic micromanagement with the introduction of elements of a market economy. For the first three years of the transition, Ukraine trailed the pack of former Soviet republics in terms of every major indicator: Inflation was high, reaching a 10,200 percent annual rate late in 1993; privatization was nonexistent; GDP was falling steadily; and corruption was ubiquitous. Ukraine's second president, Leonid Kuchma, has followed a policy of stop-and-go reform that delayed macroeconomic stabilization and prevented structural adjustment in the agricultural, energy, and industrial sectors. Although Ukraine eventually achieved a shaky macroeconomic stabilization, political instability and an ill-defined division of powers blocked the government's efforts to liberalize and deregulate the economy until after the third presidential election at the end of 1999. The result of this delay was rampant economic mismanagement. "Among the post-socialist countries that have avoided military conflicts," wrote Viktor Yushchenko and Viktor Lysytskyi, "independent and democratic Ukraine is the undeniable leader in the rate of price increases, the decline in the scope of production, and in the population's standard of living."[1] The cumulative decline of GDP from 1991 to the end of 1998 was more than 60 percent. Ukraine is the best argument against the gradualist approach to economic reform in former Communist countries.

The IMF required the former Soviet republics to provide some evidence of their readiness to launch market reforms before agreeing to finance their programs, and it was not until 1994, after three years of high inflation and declining production, that Ukraine first qualified for an IMF program. Ukraine managed to impose a provisional stability on financial markets in 1996, but stabilization remained a hostage to microeconomic reforms. Like Russia, Ukraine developed a vibrant barter economy that concealed the profits of enterprises that kept their export earnings offshore as well as the losses of enterprises

---

[1] Viktor Yushchenko and Viktor Lysytskyi, "Nadmirne derzhavne spozhivannia iak golovnyi faktor finansovoi nestabil'nosti Ukraini," unpublished manuscript, July 1998.

that received substantial subsidies from the state. Remonitizing the economy became a necessary condition for macroeconomic stabilization, therefore, because the barter economy eroded the tax base and inflated government consumption and quasi-fiscal deficits. However, the enterprises and their accomplices in the government found numerous ways to extract rents, and the Fund's programs became increasingly Byzantine and nontransparent as they sought to adapt to the moving target of structural adjustment. Fund programs continued to apply pressure for reform, but progress slowed and became more difficult to measure.

At first, the Fund was less constrained by the political priorities of its donor countries in its relations with Ukraine than in its vastly more important relations with Russia. However, relations with Ukraine became increasingly politicized as Ukraine began to play a larger role in U.S. strategic thinking, and the credibility of IMF threats to withhold financing deteriorated as a result. According to Victor Lysytskyi, a close adviser to Yushchenko both as chairman of the National Bank of Ukraine and as prime minister, the Fund came to treat Ukraine "like an indulgent nanny with a disobedient child."[2] Within a few months, whatever the indiscretion, a new program was approved with a new set of indicators. In 1997-98, as the looming crisis in Russia threatened to swallow up the Ukrainian financial markets, the National Bank resorted to committing a large share of its reserves to supporting the bond market; some of these transactions were approved by the Fund, and others were concealed from it. As a result the 1998 Extended Fund Facility was a case in which the Fund bent the rules substantially in order to approve financing for Ukraine, and yet it probably would not have approved financing had Ukraine not withheld critical information.

As a result of Ukraine's extended transition, the task of reform has become vastly more complex, and the political interests that clash with particular reform measures have become deeply entrenched. The political system has become unstable, nontransparent, and deeply penetrated by corruption. Consequently, expectations for what the Fund can achieve should be modest. However, in spite of all the unfulfilled commitments, shady offshore transactions, and blatant corruption, and in spite of the IMF's own credibility problems and some notable mistakes, the IMF has played a positive role in Ukraine.

7.1 FROM HYPERINFLATION TO MARKET REFORM, 1992-1994

Ukraine's starting point in 1992 was considerably less favorable than Poland's in 1990, or even than Russia's in 1992. Whereas Poland was able to carry out the first year of its transition under the umbrella of the CMEA system of subsidized trade, the former Soviet republics were compelled to reform their

[2] Interview with Viktor Lysytskyi, June 30, 1998.

economies while simultaneously coping with the collapse of the highly specialized Soviet internal market. For a country like Russia, which comprised three-fifths of the former Soviet Union and was self-sufficient in almost every kind of product, the impact was much more modest than for the smaller republics. For Ukraine, it was devastating. Ukraine was disadvantaged in another important respect; whereas Poland had substantial ties to the West and numerous Western-trained economists, and Russia had, in Moscow, the heart of the former Soviet Union, which had attracted the best minds of the empire and contained all the ministries that once had administered it, Ukraine was a provincial backwater. Ukraine's economic elite was used to taking its orders from Moscow, not from Kiev, and there was no effective group of managers prepared to take charge, no team of zealous reformers comparable to the group around Leszek Balcerowicz in Warsaw or Yegor Gaidar in Moscow. Nor were there even the personnel to staff a ministry of finance or a central bank.

The most serious obstacle to thoroughgoing reform, however, was the absence of a clear division of powers that allocated both responsibility and capacity to formulate economic policy. The most powerful figure in the constellation of Ukrainian government organs was the president, but until the division of powers was revised in 1995, the president had only indirect influence over economic policy. The president had the power to nominate and dismiss the prime minister and members of the cabinet, and was therefore able to exercise influence over policy; however, both powers were shared with the parliament (Verkhovna Rada, or Supreme Soviet), which could dismiss the government or remove cabinet members in detail and had to approve all nominations. The effect of this arrangement was that the government served two principals, and neither very well. Since it was not formed by the parliament and could not call new elections, the government never enjoyed the loyalty of a parliamentary majority; on the other hand, it could not afford to offend powerful interests in the parliament. Meanwhile, the government served at the sufferance of the president, but the president had to choose nominees that were acceptable to the parliament and was unable to shield the government from the parliament's wrath. This was a recipe for weak, ineffectual governments that took half steps instead of making bold decisions. To complicate the picture, this set of institutional arrangements created an incentive for the president to distance himself from the government, particularly when it made unpopular decisions such as advancing economic reforms.[3]

The first parliament of Ukraine was elected in March 1990 under Soviet electoral rules that gave the overwhelming majority of seats to Communist Party officials. Similarly, the first president of independent Ukraine was a holdover from the Soviet period, who became president of Ukraine through

---

[3] Charles R. Wise and Volodymyr Pigenko, "The Separation of Powers Puzzle in Ukraine: Sorting Out Responsibilities and Relationships between President, Parliament, and the Prime Minister," in Kuzio, Kravchuk and D'Anieri (1999).

a series of accidents. Leonid Kravchuk had been second secretary of the Communist Party of the Ukraine, responsible for the ideology portfolio, until his immediate superior was promoted to Moscow by Mikhail Gorbachev. Kravchuk was elected chairman of the Verkhovna Rada in July 1990 on the votes of the "Bloc of 239," a group of hard-line Communists also known as "For Soviet Ukraine." In August 1991 the Soviet Union was shaken to its foundations by an attempted coup. Kravchuk took a cautious position, refraining from criticizing the coup's instigators until it was clear they had failed, which prompted the Ukrainian Popular Rukh movement to call for his ouster. He changed his position quickly afterward, however, resigning from the Communist Party, and managed to get in front of the inexorable movement for a free Ukraine. He called a presidential election for December 1 and won a solid majority of 62 percent of the vote. As the establishment candidate running on a pro-independence platform with no widely recognized competitors, he was almost unassailable. No candidate entered to challenge him on the Left, and the Popular Rukh opposition movement was too disorganized to support a single candidate.

From the beginning, however, Kravchuk's hold on power was much more fragile than the election result would imply. His initial support bloc in the parliament evaporated along with the Soviet state and the Communist Party that had supported it, and Kravchuk had no popular mandate as an anti-establishment hero in the mold of Boris Yeltsin. He moved to conciliate the nationalist sentiments of Popular Rukh by striking a tough bargaining posture with Russia. However, resigning from the Party and breaking with Moscow cost him the support of the Communists, and the Communist Party of Ukraine, re-created under Oleksandr Moroz as the Socialist Party of Ukraine, remained the largest bloc of votes in parliament. Kravchuk's major objective appears to have been to hold onto power, and he regarded promoting economic reforms as a risky strategy. Instead, he attempted to consolidate a centrist coalition including nationalists, industrialists, moderate former Communists, and some reformers.

The first prime minister of independent Ukraine, nominated by Kravchuk a month before the Soviet Union disintegrated in December 1991, was Vitol'd Fokin. Fokin had been chairman of Gosplan Ukraine, the Ukrainian branch of the central planning agency that managed the Soviet economy, and had served for fifteen years as the director of a huge coal mining operation in Sverdlovsk. His appointment was a tangible signal that Kravchuk and the parliament had agreed on an agenda of minimal reform. Fokin's government liberalized most prices in January 1992, but in this it followed Moscow's lead rather than pushing a reform agenda. Once Russia had liberalized retail prices, its major trading partners had to follow suit or face disastrous shortages as the population scrambled to exploit opportunities for arbitrage. Many wholesale prices remained fixed, however, notably including those of oil and electricity. Fokin raised coal prices, which aided the depressed coal industry (and his political base there), but the effect of subsidizing petroleum while raising the price of coal was to create an artificial shift to oil-intensive production, which further eroded Ukraine's trade balance and increased pressure on the state budget. The price ratio of a ton of oil to a ton of coal fell from 2.67 in 1991 to .37 in the first quarter of 1992, and even further to .22 in the second quarter.[4]

Inflation remained repressed during 1992 for several reasons. First, many prices remained under state control. Second, for the first few months the National Bank of Ukraine was technically unable to print money or issue credits, so the state was forced to limit its spending. This obstacle to inflation was quickly overcome, however, with the karbovanets, a temporary currency introduced initially as a rationing coupon to be used along with Russian rubles but that soon became legal tender. In May the National Bank of Ukraine (NBU) doubled the level of credit to state enterprises. Furthermore, Ukraine ran up a trade deficit with Russia that spurred the Central Bank of Russia to issue credits to the NBU in the summer of 1992 in order to relieve Russian enterprises, and this allowed the NBU to expand its activities. In June and July it issued credits of 300 billion rubles, or 8 percent of estimated GDP. Third, although Ukraine remained within the ruble zone until November 1992, its supply of rubles steadily dropped as they were exported to Russia to cover the trade deficit. This put downward pressure on demand. Finally, although the karbovanets was formally fixed at 1 karbovanets to 1 ruble, there was a de facto devaluation of the karbovanets in the course of 1992, so that by fall it was trading at 1.3 to 1.4 to the ruble. This internal devaluation of the karbovanets substituted for ruble inflation. Once Ukraine left the ruble zone in the fall and began financing its budget by printing karbovantsi, however, inflation accelerated dramatically. In 1993-94 Ukraine had the worst inflationary experience in the former Soviet Union and hovered on the brink of hyperinflation.

As inflation rose and production fell in the second half of 1992, pressure built on President Kravchuk to change the government. In September a coalition of opposition parties and groups including Popular Rukh called for new parliamentary elections. To forestall this, Kravchuk dismissed the Fokin government and nominated Leonid Kuchma as prime minister. Kuchma was the former director of the Soviet Union's largest missile factory and seemed to be an ideal establishment candidate with a strong managerial background. Kuchma declared to parliament, "Ukraine's economy has come to the brink of collapse and needs emergency rescue." He announced a coalition cabinet of economists and managers, and sought to redefine the division of powers to keep the president at arms length from economic policy. The Verkhovna Rada approved his nomination and granted him extraordinary decree powers for six months in order to carry out economic reform. Kuchma brought Viktor Pynzenyk, a liberal economist from Western Ukraine, into the government as

[4]IMF calculations, cited in Banaian 1999, p. 19.

deputy prime minister, and gave him broad authority over economic policy. Pynzenyk moved quickly to try to restore macroeconomic balance. He aggressively sequestered payments, reducing the budget deficit to 1 percent of GDP in the first quarter of 1993, which was down from 29 percent of GDP in 1992.

The Ministry of Finance began work on a budget, and the initial requests from regions, ministries, and state organizations amounted to two to three times the projected revenues. The Ministry of Finance cut the requests by an average of 50 percent, and put together a budget with no deficit. This was discussed by the Cabinet of Ministers, and the draft budget came under sharp criticism; nevertheless, Pynzenyk and Kuchma succeeded in maintaining the principle that additional expenditures had to be matched with additional income. In the end, the Cabinet of Ministers made only minor changes. When the budget was presented to parliament, however, there was an uproar. Each deputy represented a particular region, and in every region some critical economic organization—collective farm, factory and the like—had been written out of the budget. When the Verkhovna Rada examined the budget, it sent the expenditures for each sector to the relevant specialized committee; the result was a classic logroll: The Verkhovna Rada returned a budget with expenditures increased by approximately 40 percent. A deputy finance minister at the time recalled, "I don't remember any case in parliament where someone made a suggestion to reduce expenditures or increase income."[5] After a great deal of haggling, the budget that was passed in April still cut spending by 4 percent from its 1992 level and raised revenues by 22 percent. However, the deficit remained 6 percent of GDP, and it had to be financed by direct credits from the central bank because Ukraine had developed no capacity to borrow domestically and had no access to international capital markets.

Meanwhile, reforms were beginning at the National Bank of Ukraine. It was not until Viktor Yushchenko was appointed Chairman of the NBU in 1993 that it began to take on the most important functions of a modern central bank, such as controlling the money supply. The NBU began life as one of Gosbank USSR's regional branches, whose functions were to lobby the center for credits for Ukrainian enterprises, to participate in the process of central planning and administrative setting of prices, and to attract deposits and confiscate "excessive" cash balances from local enterprises. Several years passed before it developed the expertise to intervene on currency markets and conduct open-market operations (i.e., buy and sell government bonds). Given its prior experience, the first function the NBU assumed was that of clearinghouse and advocate for direct government credits to enterprises. Until the beginning of 1996 Ukraine continued the Soviet practice of making important decisions

[5]Interview with Petro Hermanchuk, March 22, 2000. Hermanchuk was deputy minister of finance from February 1992 to July 1993, first deputy minister of finance from July 1993 to July 1995, and minister of finance from July 1995 to June 1996. When interviewed in 2000, he had been reappointed deputy minister of finance in the Yushchenko government.

about credit rationing in the Council of Ministers, rather than in the central bank. A Currency and Credit Council, consisting of fifteen to seventeen ministers, bank officials, and enterprise managers and chaired by the first deputy premier, discussed applications from enterprises for directed credits. If the credits were approved, they were automatically provided by the NBU.[6] Nevertheless, Yushchenko, who was an advocate of a tight credit policy, was able to make some decisions in the first part of 1993 that tightened monetary policy considerably. In March the NBU raised commercial bank reserve requirements (the portion of deposits that must be held at the National Bank) to 25 percent, and in May the NBU introduced credit auctions and suspended the practice of offering preferential interest rates to enterprises in priority sectors of the economy, such as military industries.

However, Pynzenyk and Yushchenko quickly found their policies undercut by President Kravchuk. When he sought to dismantle the system of state purchases, Pynzenyk was countermanded by Kravchuk, who insisted on maintaining state orders for six hundred categories of products. Meanwhile, the tight money policy was undermined by decisions in December 1992 to clear enterprise arrears with the other states of the former Soviet Union (which cost the NBU 500 billion karbovantsi in credits) and then in February to clear domestic interenterprise arrears (another 600 billion karbovantsi). These decisions gave the initial impetus to rising inflation, which rose steadily from 20 percent per month in January to 28 percent in June. In June, when Kuchma's decree powers expired, he offered to resign as a gambit to have them extended. Instead, the parliament refused his resignation and also refused to extend the extraordinary powers. Kravchuk declared emergency powers for himself but had no intention of using them to accelerate economic reform. In the spring and summer, pressure mounted on the NBU to expand credit to agricultural collectives. Pynzenyk and Yushchenko were categorically opposed to expanding these credits, but they were constantly dragged before the Verkhovna Rada to explain why they were not doing anything to avert a catastrophic collapse of the economy in the countryside. It might have been impossible to resist this pressure even with strong support from the president, but the Kuchma government was helpless without it.[7] Total NBU credit rose 44 percent in June, 37 percent in July, and 49 percent in August. The result was raging inflation. Kuchma again offered his resignation in September in an effort to force the parliament to renew his powers, but this time his resignation was accepted. This turned out to be a political stroke of luck on Kuchma's part, since he became associated in the public imagination with efforts to fight inflation rather than with the disastrous results of inflation that followed in November and December.

---

[6]Interviews with Serov, July 2, 1998; Lysytskyi, July 1, 1998; Hermanchuk, March 22, 2000.
[7]Interview with Hermanchuk, March 22, 2000.

In response to the deteriorating economic situation and the seeming paralysis of the government, 26 political groups—parties, labor unions, and public organizations—signed an agreement in September for joint action against the "pro-Communist regime." They called for early parliamentary elections and a referendum on non-confidence in the president. Miners in the Donbass staged strikes, and the opposition picketed the parliament and organized a general strike and a civil disobedience campaign. At the end of the month, the Verkhovna Rada bowed to public pressure and voted to hold parliamentary elections in March and presidential elections in July to head off momentum for a referendum. It then adjourned until after the election. With the parliament adjourned, Kravchuk now had the opportunity to carry out reforms, had he been inclined to do so. Instead, he apparently calculated that the social cost of reforms would undermine his chances of reelection.[8] Inflation rose in December to an annualized rate of 10,200 percent, and the karbovanets became practically worthless. Goods disappeared from store shelves. Almost as quickly as it had gathered strength, the inflationary storm spent itself, as the rapid escalation of the price level contracted the real money supply and the NBU refused to print money to keep up with inflation. In its wake, however, inflation left a severe depression: By one estimate, real GDP contracted by as much as 74 percent in the first quarter of 1994.[9] Anyone who had savings in cash karbovantsi lost them, and wages and pensions were dramatically slashed in real terms. After the economic mismanagement of 1993, Ukraine was a profoundly impoverished nation.

No candidate won a majority of votes in the first round of elections in July, and in the second round Ukrainians faced a choice between their unsuccessful president and their unsuccessful former prime minister. Kravchuk narrowly lost to Kuchma. Kravchuk led Kuchma in the first round of voting by 7 points and was widely expected to win the second round. However, in a choice that surely came back to haunt him years later, the third-place finisher, Communist parliament speaker Oleksandr Moroz, threw his support to Kuchma. King Banaian shows convincingly that this endorsement helped Kuchma to win a majority in the second round: The correlation between the Moroz vote share by region in the first round and increase in support for Kuchma between the two rounds is a highly significant .74.[10] The voting was sharply delineated along regional lines: Kiev and the nationalist West Ukraine voted heavily for Kravchuk, whereas Kuchma carried the Russian areas of the East and South—especially Crimea—by promising to improve relations with Russia.

[8] Kuzio 1997, p. 49.
[9] Banaian 1999.
[10] Ibid., 67.

7.2 THE SYSTEMIC TRANSFORMATION FACILITY, 1994

Ukraine benefited from the concession that the IMF made to Russia in 1993 by creating the Systemic Transformation Facility as a means of aiding post-Communist countries that were unable to meet the usual stringent requirements for IMF Stand-by Arrangements. Under the STF, Ukraine was able to qualify for funding in spite of a very high inflation rate, its lack of the technical capacity to collect quality economic data, and an extraordinarily uncertain political situation. Visiting Kiev in May, an IMF Mission found that Ukraine had not met the prior conditions to launch an STF program for $700 million. After the presidential election, however, the leaders of the G-7 countries announced at their annual summit meeting in July that Ukraine could qualify for $4 billion in aid if it launched serious reforms. Preparations began in earnest for an IMF-supported program, which was finally approved in October.

The IMF's caution in Ukraine proved to be justified. The new parliament was not much more inclined to support reform than the previous one. More than half the new deputies were independents, most of whom were well-connected members of the former Communist *nomenklatura,* and once again the largest party was the Socialist Party led by Oleksandr Moroz. Only a handful of deputies were elected as representatives of reformist parties. In addition, under Ukraine's system of single-member district representation, regionally concentrated interest groups had a significant voice in the newly elected parliament.[11] This gave substantial weight to the interests of two groups that were in constant need of government support: coal miners and collective farms. As they had in the past two years, these interests lobbied intensely for credits from the National Bank to support their enterprises. The result was an inconsistent central bank policy of doling out preferential credits with one hand, while trying to restrain the growth of the money supply with the other. In the summer of 1994 the new president repeated his predecessor's policy, and ordered the government to issue credits to cover the debts of the collective farms, which led to a significant increase in the volume of net claims on the government in the third quarter of the year.

The increase in credits to agriculture in the summer led to a sharp upward spike in inflation, and the karbovanets fell 38 percent in September and another 184 percent in October. This galvanized President Kuchma, who, in October, announced the beginning of "radical market reform." The NBU quickly introduced a series of new regulations. It replaced the two-tiered exchange rate system, which had been designed to subsidize imports by state enterprises, with a unified exchange rate, and replaced the foreign currency rationing system, which had become a focus of corruption, with a system of open currency auctions. The NBU imposed credit ceilings on individual banks and abolished

[11] Weingast, Shepsle and Johnsen 1981.

the practice of refinancing banks at preferential interest rates. Meanwhile, the government announced (not for the last time) that it would abolish energy subsidies, apartment subsidies, and export restrictions. The STF was approved in spite of the NBU's indiscretions in the summer and the resurgence of inflation in the fall. Kuchma appeared to be launching a serious reform effort on all fronts. In October he brought Viktor Pynzenyk back into the government as first deputy prime minister, and in January the government launched a voucher mass privatization program.[12]

The Verkhovna Rada opposed many of these initiatives. In response, Kuchma launched what became an eighteen-month campaign to revise the Ukrainian constitution to strengthen his powers and allow him to force reforms on a reluctant legislative branch. The first salvo in his offensive was a new draft law that he submitted to the Verkhovna Rada in December, giving the president sweeping decree powers and removing the parliament's authority to approve and remove individual cabinet ministers. Speaker Moroz and a solid majority of parliament deputies staunchly opposed this proposal, but under the threat that Kuchma would call a national referendum, the draft passed the first reading in parliament. The Verkhovna Rada subsequently delayed action on the required second and third readings.

In March the government and the IMF reached a preliminary agreement on a Stand-by program for 1995 that revised the government's inflation target for the year from 210 percent to 389 percent as a result of events in the fall.[13] However, the program still called for serious fiscal tightening: The budget deficit was programmed to decline from 8.6 percent of GDP in 1994 to 3.3 percent in 1995. Note that Ukraine's fiscal problems in 1994 were quite different from Russia's at the same time, since Ukraine had collected an increasing share of GDP in taxes throughout the period of near-hyperinflation. Among the post-Communist countries, only slow reformers such as Ukraine and Belarus had succeeded in doing this, and their relatively strong fiscal performance on the income side was apparently the result of postponing structural reforms. Since tax collection was already a burdensome share of GDP in Ukraine, the fiscal adjustment foreseen in the Stand-by Arrangement was to be accomplished by cutting expenditures, especially subsidies and price supports. In addition, the program called for further liberalizing prices and reducing restrictions on

---

[12]Privatization was a primary objective of the IMF, which encouraged the use of voucher privatization in Ukraine, as it had in Russia. Privatization suffered from many of the same pitfalls in Ukraine as it had in Russia. First, the rules of privatization were stacked in favor of insiders, particularly management, while foreigners were not permitted to participate. Second, under conditions of high inflation and political rationing of credit, any form of mass privatization was bound to lead to a very inegalitarian distribution of assets. In retrospect, it clearly would have been preferable to delay privatization until financial markets stabilized and to sell firms piecemeal rather than privatizing them en masse. As in Russia, privatization in Ukraine created a narrow, powerful elite that was interested in preserving the new status quo rather than proceeding with further reforms.

[13]Banaian 1999, p. 100.

grain exports. "It is a comprehensive, strong and courageous program," Michel Camdessus announced. "If implemented rigorously, it will constitute a decisive break with the past that Ukraine sorely needs and that the international community will surely welcome."[14] Leftist deputies in the Verkhovna Rada focused on the IMF as the villain, arguing that the IMF program, in effect, obliged them to dismantle the system of social protection that they had campaigned to protect. The IMF approved the Stand-by program in April, and parliament voted to dismiss the government.

This brought to a head the confrontation between Kuchma and the parliament. In a pointed signal to the parliament, the president appointed the former head of the Ukrainian secret police, Yevhen Marchuk, as acting prime minister. Marchuk announced plans to form a cabinet of "professionals," which suggested that reforms would be pursued. Meanwhile, Kuchma renewed his calls for the parliament to pass the "Law on Power," and, when there had been no progress by the end of May, he announced a referendum on confidence in the president and the parliament for June 28. "The further coexistence of the parliament and the president with the current legal status is impossible," he said in a televised address. "The political confrontation between the branches of power is unacceptable in this moment of crisis." A week later the parliament resolved the crisis by passing the measure, and Kuchma used his new powers to appoint Marchuk Prime Minister.

7.3 THE FIRST STAND-BY, 1995

The centerpiece of the government's policy was to introduce Ukraine's long-awaited permanent currency, the hryvnia, which had been expected since 1992. When the karbovanets was introduced, it was intended as a temporary currency; the notes were not printed on high-quality paper, because they were only expected to circulate for six months. The temporary currency created some nervousness in the population, both because the government's commitment to defending a temporary currency might be weak, and because the only currency reforms they had ever experienced had been confiscatory. Introducing the permanent currency was expected to increase confidence, dampen inflationary expectations, and improve the investment climate. However, the new currency could only be introduced once, and it seemed critical to do it at a time that minimized the risks of rapid devaluation.[15] As a result, although the notes had been printed and were lying in the National Bank vaults, the NBU kept waiting for the money market to stabilize. In 1995 the government and the NBU lobbied the IMF to provide a substantial fund to stabilize the hryvnia and minimize these risks, and negotiations dragged on into the summer. The Ger-

---

[14]"Ukraine Signs IMF Stand-by Accord," *Financial Times,* March 4-5, 1995, 3.

[15]Interview with Hermanchuk, March 22, 2000.

man executive director opposed the idea of a stabilization fund in principle, arguing that the central bank's monetary policy should demonstrate the hryvnia's credibility: You can't have a Deutschmark without a Bundesbank.[16] While discussions continued without resolution in Washington, decisions made in Kiev undermined the stability of the exchange market.

The first sign that Kuchma was deviating from his reform program came in June, when he announced a "correction" to the reform program. He set a monthly inflation target of 4-5 percent instead of 1-2 percent, and he denounced the policy of targeting the exchange rate, which was a condition of the IMF program. He had decided that the period of high inflation had come to an end, and he believed that "moderate" inflation would be tolerable and would soften the social impact of reforms. Viktor Pynzenyk resigned in protest, and Kuchma replaced him as deputy premier with Roman Shpek, whom Kravchuk had appointed as minister of the economy. Kuchma told Radio Ukraine that this did not portend the end of reform but, instead, signaled a shift from strict monetarism to a new focus on deep restructuring of industry (which, in practice, meant increasing subsidies to the ailing industrial sector). Pynzenyk was reappointed in August, during a visit by the IMF Mission to Kiev to monitor progress under the Stand-by Arrangement, which suggested that his appointment was made primarily to smooth relations with the Fund.

In the course of the summer of 1995 the government bowed to pressure from the agriculture and energy lobbies to increase subsidies and directed credits. The seasonal effect was less pronounced than in previous years, but National Bank domestic credit increased by 23.5 percent in July, and by September inflation had again spiked to 15 percent per month. Meanwhile, the government budget deficit again spiraled out of control. Introducing the hryvnia had to be put off into the indefinite future. As the NBU official charged with maintaining contacts with the IMF explained:

> Our leaders did not expect to actually have to fulfill the commitments that they assumed. Their attitude was, "We'll agree to anything; if you think we can fulfill the conditions, fine." The IMF team drafted the agreements, and the Ukrainian side didn't understand that fulfilling them was deadly serious. It didn't even really argue about the details, but just happily agreed to a number of conditions in the Memorandum. They didn't realize that there would be monitoring, and that you couldn't manipulate the figures.[17]

After this interview it came to light how weak the monitoring had been and how often the NBU had, in fact, manipulated the figures, but this only serves to underscore the point.

[16]Interview with Oleg Rybachuk, July 3, 1998. Rybachuk had been director of the International Department, National Bank of Ukraine, since May 1992.

[17]Interview with Rybachuk, July 3, 1998.

Events seemed to confirm the German position: It was impossible to introduce a solid currency in the absence of any independent central banking authority. In 1995, when the government ran a budget deficit, the National Bank of Ukraine was legally obliged to issue direct credit—in effect, to print money—to cover it. Furthermore, the NBU was still obligated to implement programs of directed credits determined by the Council of Ministers. The NBU senior staff complained that these programs were worked out "under conditions of secrecy" by the apparatus of the Council of Ministers and the managers of industry, and that the National Bank remained, in effect, an old-fashioned Soviet "transmission belt" that distributed credits without any control over where they went.[18] The NBU expanded domestic credit at less than the rate of inflation for almost all of 1995, but it made several expansionary policy changes under political pressure that undermined its tight monetary policy and destabilized the foreign exchange market. As a result, the National Bank was compelled to intervene on the exchange market to absorb excess liquidity and to prevent a dramatic currency devaluation, running down its foreign reserves. The level of foreign reserves, meanwhile, was replenished by loans from the IMF (see Figure 7.1). In effect, IMF credits financed a monetary policy that was less contractionary than would have been feasible without them. Ukraine presumably could have reduced the size of the devaluation that occurred in 1995 had it possessed a large fund of additional reserves to defend the currency, but it is likely that its economic policy would have been even more profligate.

In September Pavlo Lazarenko was appointed first deputy premier and given the task of reversing the slide in agricultural and industrial production, which further undermined the reformers' position in the cabinet. The finance minister at the time did not see this as a deliberate policy adjustment on Kuchma's part but, rather, as an unintended consequence of his general effort to improve the management of parts of the economy that were obviously performing poorly.

> I don't think the president thought about it [Lazarenko's appointment] as a tactical retreat. It is another question that Pavel Ivanovich was a person who worked directly with the real sector, he knew it better than macroeconomic processes, and he made decisions based on his experience. There was huge pressure to raise expenditures in the agriculture and coal sectors. He compromised the NBU credit policy in the coal sector. He simply called in the [commercial] bankers and told them how much to give to the coal industry.[19]

One of Lazarenko's first actions was to induce the NBU to introduce rules allowing commercial banks that made loans to the coal and agriculture industries

---

[18]Interview with Lysytskyi, July 1, 1998. At the time, Viktor Lysytskyi was head of the group of economic advisers to Viktor Yushchenko, the chairman of the NBU. In 2000 he became state secretary of the government under Yushchenko, a position ranking higher than minister.

[19]Interview with Hermanchuk, March 22, 2000.

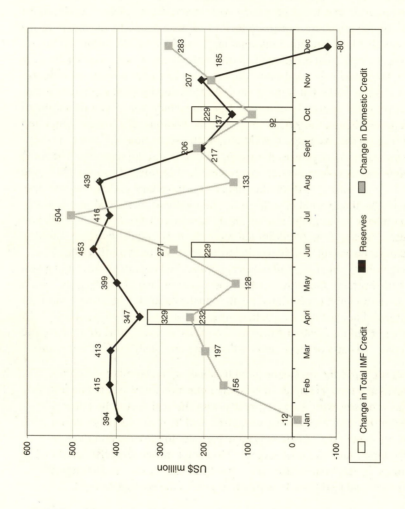

Figure 7.1: IMF Financing, NBU Reserves and Domestic Credit in 1995. IMF credits received in 1995 are not included in NBU reserves.

a complete offset against their reserve requirements. Since it is costly to hold reserves, the opportunity cost to the banks of making these loans was negative, and credits to the coal industry increased by an estimated 5-8 trillion karbovantsi ($25-40 million) as a result.[20] The effect on the money supply was the same as if the NBU had made the loans itself. The third tranche of the Stand-by was delayed for two months, and pressure built against the karbovanets. In order to stabilize the currency—which was a condition of the Stand-by program, since the currency was being used as a nominal anchor for the stabilization program—the NBU had to raise the discount rate to 95 percent in October, and then to 110 percent in November.[21] The IMF disbursed the third tranche in October. Miners went on strike in the middle of November, and the government promised to pay the miners 5 trillion of the 20 trillion karbovantsi that it owed in back wages. Prime Minister Marchuk promised that this would be accomplished without printing money or raising taxes, but it was clear that this was impossible. In fact, the NBU was compelled to issue credits to cover the deal, and the IMF suspended the program in January because the NBU had exceeded its credit ceiling.

7.4 THE SECOND STAND-BY, 1996

The prospects for negotiating a new Stand-by arrangement seemed dim in early 1996. Ukraine had failed to implement the soft conditions of its first STF and had then failed to fulfill its first Stand-by. The political system was unstable, the parliament was dominated by Communists, the president was clearly more concerned with political expediency than with reform, the government was mildly anti-reformist, and the central bank was a tool of special interests. All the evidence seemed to show that IMF loans to Ukraine were like pouring water into a leaking bucket. IMF loans simply allowed the central bank to expand credit without suffering a disastrous rise in the exchange rate; they did not seem to provide significant impetus to reform. IMF officials found some things to celebrate, notably the stabilization of the currency and the dramatic decline of inflation; nevertheless, Ukrainian economic policy left much to be desired. According to the head of the IMF Mission to Ukraine,

> They did the most obvious things on the stabilization side, but then ran into the most difficult problems. There are a lot of measures that we identified in 1995 that still have not been implemented. We faced a choice: do you withdraw and look after the credibility of the Fund with the rest of the world, or stay engaged? If the political

[20] Banaian 1999, p. 131-32.

[21] The discount rate had gradually fallen from its high of 300 percent in October 1994 to a low of 60 percent in July.

world and the capital market want you to be there? If the G-7 is on record that it wants us to be there?[22]

As this quotation indicates, the international significance of Ukraine was undergoing an important shift. As relations between the United States and Russia began to chill, the geopolitical significance of an independent and democratic Ukraine became increasingly obvious in Washington. Meanwhile, the Clinton administration was committing itself to the process of NATO expansion, so geopolitical maps were being redrawn all over Eastern Europe. As part of the deal in which it gave up its nuclear weapons, Ukraine became the third largest recipient of U.S. foreign aid ($330 million).[23] As if to underscore the new priority placed on Ukraine, Warren Christopher rearranged his schedule to meet President Kuchma in Helsinki before he met Russian Foreign Minister Yevgennyi Primakov. In the meeting he pledged U.S. support for Ukraine in its effort to obtain a new Stand-by agreement with the IMF. After this, negotiations moved forward quickly, despite the continuing deterioration of Ukraine's macroeconomic policy. In April the IMF granted Ukraine a waiver to allow the NBU to purchase 34 trillion karbovantsi worth of government bonds, which pushed it considerably above the limit for net domestic assets in its previous program. In May the executive board approved a new Stand-by program for 598.2 million SDRs.

Meanwhile, president Kuchma renewed his offensive against the Verkhovna Rada, which he accused of blocking progress in economic reform because it had shielded important enterprises from being privatized and had passed a series of laws that contradicted presidential and government decrees. Kuchma promoted a revised constitution that stripped the parliament of its levers of control over the government and expanded his power to issue decrees with the force of law, and the parliament developed an alternative plan that abolished the office of president. A compromise was finally worked out in the spring that shifted significant powers to the president but stopped short of Kuchma's proposal to introduce a bicameral legislature, but the parliament failed to approve it. In May Kuchma set a date for a referendum on the constitution—his own preferred version. Fearing that the president's referendum would pass, Speaker Moroz mobilized his supporters to pass the compromise version, and, in a twenty-four hour session of parliament, he finally managed to overcome the opposition.

Observers of Ukraine expected the president's victory in June to be followed by a rapid consolidation of reform; after all, Kuchma had campaigned on a reform platform, he had attempted to implement reform as prime minister under Kravchuk, and he had repeatedly clashed with the parliament over

---

[22]Interview with Shadman-Valavi, May 4, 2000.

[23]Aid appropriated by the U.S. Congress for Ukraine totaled $225 million in 1998 and $195 million in 1999 as the payments for dismantling nuclear weapons declined.

reform. With parliamentary power severely reduced by the new presidential constitution, Kuchma was finally poised to implement his preferred program. Instead, he vacillated. Having achieved his primary objective of consolidating presidential authority, Kuchma moved back to the center of the political spectrum by appointing Pavlo Lazarenko prime minister. Lazarenko's promotion marked the beginning of a significant shift in political patronage, as he convinced Kuchma to fire Marchuk's ministers and then appointed officials who had been close to him when he was administrator of the industrial region of Dnipropetrovsk. Lazarenko's special area of expertise was importing Russian natural gas, and, already in 1995, he had shown a startling ability to induce Russia to run up large, unfinanced trade surpluses while simultaneously extracting gas shipments as payment for use of the pipelines that ran across Ukrainian territory. In part, these gas exports represented an element of Russian foreign policy, which continued to try to build closer economic ties with Ukraine within the context of the Commonwealth of Independent States, and they were indirectly subsidized by the Russian government. In great measure, however, they reflected Lazarenko's skill at using a combination of creative financing, bribery, and outright extortion to extract subsidies from Gazprom officials who, in any case, faced a soft budget constraint.[24] In 1995 a portion of this debt was converted into $1.4 billion worth of long-term Ukrainian government-backed bonds known as "gazpromovki," which were regularly serviced by the Ministry of Finance until they were rescheduled along with other Ukrainian debts in March 2000. On several occasions the National Bank of Ukraine accepted these bonds as collateral for unguaranteed deposits of foreign reserves with Credit-Suisse First Boston (Cyprus), presumably as a pledge of Ukrainian good faith to service the debt.[25] Starting in 1995 Lazarenko used a

[24] The circumstances of Russia's accumulation of receivables for gas exports in the 1990s are very similar to those of the Soviet Union's indirect trade subsidies to its satellites during the Cold War. As I argued elsewhere, the Soviet Union was aware that it was subsidizing its allies, but the subsidies arose largely because the system of central planning left Soviet officials little incentive to minimize them. See Stone (1996). The institutional context was very different in the mid-1990s, but the soft budget constraints that Russian domestic policy allowed Gazprom RAO presented a similar principal-agent problem. Indeed, the problem was much more severe, since bribery was a realistic option for Lazarenko, but not for the Soviet satellites. By 1998 and 1999 the intermediary for gas sales, which sold about one-third of the gas consumed in Ukraine, was a Florida-registered company, Itera, which is believed to be controlled by Lev Viakhirev, the former chairman of Gazprom.

[25] Stenogram of speech by Viktor Suslov to the Verkhovna Rada on the findings of the Temporary Investigative Committee on the use of NBU reserves, which he chaired, on May 6, 1999. It was published under the title, "Pravitel'stvo Yushchenko nakanune otstavki," *Svoboda* (2) (March 13, 2000): 9. Suslov confirmed that the stenogram was accurate (interview with Suslov, March 15, 2000). Suslov regarded this as an unjustifiably risky operation to conduct with foreign reserves and considered this prima facie evidence of corruption. The amount of $100 million that was on deposit with CSFB (Cyprus) was not returned when the deadline arrived in September 1998 (probably because of the Russian financial crisis), a time when Ukraine was in desperate need of liquid foreign reserves, and Ukraine was compelled to extend the contract for another ten months.

complex web of murky financial transactions involving the import and resale of Russian natural gas to accumulate political influence and large offshore bank deposits. He was eventually charged with corruption in Ukraine and laundering $72 million in Switzerland, and was held in custody in the United States fighting extradition. Meanwhile, his family lived in a forty-one-room California mansion that had formerly belonged to Eddie Murphy, which he had purchased for $6.75 million in cash. A close aide to Kuchma, Oleksander Volkov, was also charged with money laundering, and $3 million of his deposits were frozen in Belgian banks.[26]

In short, Lazarenko was a poor choice for prime minister in 1996, and his agenda had nothing in common with promoting reform, at least in the gas sector. Meanwhile, the parliament continued to block progress on structural reform, and the powerful agrarian lobby in parliament succeeded in passing a law in July that blocked privatization of collective farms by delegating considerable responsibility for conducting privatization to the collectives themselves. The collective farms were unprofitable and subsisted on government support, and their chairmen had an interest in preserving the hierarchical structures that gave them economic and political power.

In 1996 the Ministry of Finance introduced a successful market in government securities, and this led to a dramatic increase in foreign investment in Ukraine, as international portfolio investors searched emerging markets for high-yield investments. The reader will recall that foreign investment began to surge in the Russian bond market at the same time; this was the origin of the boom-and-bust cycle that eventually overtook Turkey, Brazil, and Argentina, as well. The nonresident purchases of government bonds made it possible for the government to finance its deficit and bring down inflation, and also allowed the NBU to rebuild its foreign reserves late in 1996 and early in 1997. The stabilization of financial markets allowed the National Bank successfully to introduce its permanent currency, the hryvnia, in September. After some initial concern that a confiscatory monetary reform might accompany the new currency, the foreign exchange market calmed and demand for money increased. However, as in Russia, the effect of the dramatic flow of resources into Ukraine in 1996 and early 1997 was to soften the government's budget constraint. As time went on, the government granted more and more tax privileges and allowed an increasing share of tax payments to be made in barter. This undermined incentives for enterprises to restructure and made government finance

---

It was imprudent and a technical violation of NBU internal regulations to use reserves in this way. Meanwhile, the encumbered reserves were counted by the NBU toward its target for NIR, which was deceptive and may have led the IMF to disburse tranches that otherwise would have been withheld. However, the money was not stolen. The nominal value of the bonds that secured the deposit was $145 million in gazpromovki, the bonds were in fact being serviced by Ukraine, and the deposit was finally returned in September 1999.

[26]"Former PM alleges $613 m Ukraine fraud," *Financial Times,* January 28, 2000, 1, 2.

increasingly dependent on continued inflows of foreign capital, which set the stage for a significant downturn in the economy when these flows reversed two years later.

The second Stand-by program gives the appearance of having been completed successfully, since all the tranches were eventually released, albeit with some delays. However, a Ministry of Finance official insists that Ukraine was in violation of the major conditions of the program after the first two months.[27] The most important conditions were for the budget deficit, for government commitments, for central bank net domestic assets (NDA), and for central bank net international reserves (NIR). The most serious problems arose in the budget and government commitments. Oleg Sheiko, who had the job of monitoring compliance with the IMF conditions in the Ministry of Finance, recalls that the monthly targets were typically violated in the first week of each month.

The IMF staff report that accompanied Ukraine's application for the 1997 Stand-by hailed the introduction of an effective treasury in 1996 as a major institutional accomplishment and regarded the government obligations in the budgetary sphere as successfully fulfilled in 1996. According to another Ukrainian official, however, the IMF assessment in 1996 was too optimistic. The treasury that was established in 1996 was not effective because it was understaffed, was not equipped with computers, and could not attract competent professionals. At the same time, its mission of controlling budget expenditures was not yet supported even within the Ministry of Finance, much less in the Council of Ministers or branch ministries. Consequently, it was not able to exert any real control over expenditures. Budgetary organizations retained the de facto right to make direct expenditures and contract for services without clearing them with the treasury, and enterprises did not demand immediate payment, so the Ministry of Finance was unable to control the rate of expenditure. The 1996 budget looked fine on paper, but that was because of tremendous accounting legerdemain. The majority of tax receipts were never actually received but instead took place in the form of barter transactions and mutual clearing of accounts between the Ministry of Finance, taxpaying organizations, and budgetary organizations that contracted for services. A whole industry of barter middlemen arose to service the budget by finding government debts to offset tax payments.[28] Paying taxes in barter was advantageous for enterprises, since it often allowed them to charge higher prices for their products than they could receive on the open market, it did not cut into their cash profits because they had large inventories of goods that could not be sold, and it allowed them to expand turnover. For the government, of course, the real value of tax collections in barter was substantially below the nominal value, so it represented

---

[27] Interview with Oleg L. Sheiko, Department Head, Budget Policy and Macroeconomic Analysis Department, Ministry of Finance of Ukraine, March 16, 2000.

[28] Interview with Marina Shapovalova, July 2, 1998.

an implicit subsidy to privileged enterprises. Sheiko insists that barter collection of taxes was always a political issue, rather than an economic one; the variations from month to month in the extent to which taxes were collected in cash depended on political decisions rather than on variations in economic fundamentals.[29]

The most promising reform development in 1996 was a program of tax reforms promoted by Viktor Pynzenyk. Reappointed deputy prime minister, Pynzenyk gathered a small group of advisers, including Jeffrey Sachs and the staff of the Harvard Institute for International Development (HIID) from its office in Ukraine, and began work on a package of draft laws to change Ukraine's tax structure. The guiding principle of the proposed reforms was that Ukraine's tax system imposed a crushing burden that prevented the development of the private sector and pushed what little development arose into the shadow economy. To stimulate growth, it was necessary to scale back taxes drastically, especially payroll taxes, so that small businesses could operate profitably and legally. Indeed, Ukraine continued to collect a much higher share of GDP in taxes than other post-Communist countries in 1996. The main points of the program were to reduce the highest income tax rate from 40 percent to 30 percent, the payroll tax for the cleanup of the Chernobyl disaster from 12 percent to 6 percent; the payroll tax for the unemployment fund from 2 percent to 1 percent; the payroll tax for the pension fund from 32 percent to 25 percent, and the tax on salaries paid by businesses from 52 percent to 32 percent. In addition, the VAT was to be reduced. Pynzenyk intended to make up part of the lost revenues by reducing benefits and incorporating the Social Security and Pension funds into the state budget, and by increasing the administered prices for energy and utilities. However, the plan anticipated a substantial one-year increase in the budget deficit; thereafter, it was hoped, the effect of stimulating small-business development and bringing businesses back into the open economy would cause revenues to rebound. If ever there were a case to be made for supply-side economics, surely Ukraine was the place to do it. Even after the proposed reforms, payroll and wage taxes would remain a crushing 94 percent of the nominal wage bill, but the tax burden would be reduced from 138 percent.

The IMF staunchly opposed the tax reform plan, arguing that Ukraine's macroeconomic stabilization was too fragile to allow a major expansion of the budget deficit, and that Pynzenyk's estimates of GDP growth were too optimistic. While agreeing that tax rates were high, the Fund representatives insisted that tax cuts had to be matched by expenditure cuts of equal magnitude.[30] Pynzenyk, however, was convinced that linking the plan to expenditure cuts of that size would make it impossible to pass any tax reform in the

[29]Interview with Sheiko, March 16, 2000.
[30]Interview with Mohammed Shadman-Valavi, May 4, 2000.

Verkhovna Rada. This brought negotiations to a standstill for a three-year Extended Fund Facility, which Ukraine had hoped to use to consolidate the gains under its first two Stand-by programs.

It was not the IMF's opposition, however, that killed the Pynzenyk plan. The program was jeopardized from the outset because the prime minister and the president were not firmly committed to seeing it through the parliament. The executive branch had sufficient resources to prevail in a test of wills had it been united, but in this case the deputy prime minister quickly found himself isolated. Pynzenyk's position was further undermined because Lazarenko pushed the pace of development of the package when he gave it his endorsement on a Thursday and promised that it would be ready by Monday. As a result, there was no time for wide-ranging consultations or coalition building, and many of the provisions of the hastily drafted laws contradicted one another, existing legislation, and Ukrainian accounting practices. Opponents of the legislation, or simply opponents of the government, easily found flaws in the proposed legislation and denounced it as poor-quality work. A consensus quickly emerged that the draft laws had to be sent to committee for extensive revision. Pynzenyk attempted to marshal the resources of the executive branch to pressure the deputies to accept the legislation, and he even persuaded Prime Minister Lazarenko to withhold submission of the state budget to the parliament until the acts were passed. In the end, two of the laws were passed with significant amendments. Viktor Suslov, who spearheaded the opposition to the laws and chaired the Committee on Economic Issues that worked on them, said that he opposed even the final versions of the two laws that passed, but he finally gave in to tremendous pressure from the government.[31] For his efforts, he was appointed minister of economy in the Pustovoitenko government that Kuchma formed in the summer.

The fight over the Pynzenyk program delayed passage of the 1997 budget until June, and, as a result, the next Stand-by was delayed in February and only approved in August 1997. Simultaneously, negotiations continued for an EFF program. Although the IMF was not ready to approve a long-term program, detailed drafts of performance criteria and prior conditions were negotiated, which eventually became the basis for the EFF program criteria that were approved in 1998. In the process, dogged negotiating by Pynzenyk finally persuaded the IMF staff to adopt all the major points of his tax reform program as prior conditions or performance criteria. (Of course, the IMF staff were never opposed to cutting taxes per se; they simply wanted to maintain fiscal balance, and it was easier to imagine offsetting big tax cuts in the context of a three-year program to be implemented some time in the future than to write them into the current year's budget.) Pynzenyk resigned from the government in the spring, since he was unable to accomplish his program without substantial presiden-

---

[31] Interview with Suslov, March 15, 2000.

tial support, and he believed he was spending his political capital by remaining in the government as a lame duck. Meanwhile, there was turnover in the IMF staff. When the EFF was finally approved in 1998, the IMF staff members who were responsible for conducting the negotiations adopted the draft conditions that had been agreed on in 1997 as the basis for negotiating the program and, in effect, pushed the Pustovoitenko government to adopt the Pynzenyk program.

7.5 THE THIRD STAND-BY, 1997

Against this dismal background, the IMF approved a third Stand-by Arrangement in August 1997. According to the head of the IMF Mission to Ukraine, Mohammed Shadman-Valavi, the Fund felt that it was not a viable option to remain aloof from Ukraine. The Fund tried to hold out for a package of long-term structural reforms to be embodied in an EFF, but when it became clear that Ukraine was not ready to adopt far-reaching reforms, it agreed to Ukrainian pressure to adopt an SBA as a "holding operation to give more time for a political consensus to emerge."

> In the middle of the nineties the executive board and the creditors to this institution accepted the fact that these countries were going through a revolution, implementing dramatic changes, and institutions had to be built. We didn't consider nonperformance on some conditions of a loan as a reason to withdraw from a country. We put the emphasis on staying involved. The board of directors continued to complain about poor performance, but, at the same time, the board kept approving what we proposed. Targets were readjusted and waivers were granted.
>
> In 1994-'95 the board wanted to be engaged in all of these countries, but in a large country that is obviously on everybody's mind. Obviously, that has an influence. 1997 was the beginning of concern about contagion, Russia was facing serious difficulties, and there was concern that compounding these problems with developments in Ukraine would be very dangerous. All of the countries of the former Soviet Union had a lot of trade with Russia and Ukraine, so we had to take a regional view as well.[32]

When the first tremors of the Asian crisis struck, Ukraine insisted on signing an immediate Stand-by Arrangement, and the Fund agreed.

It became clear within months that the government was not meeting its budget deficit target. Many problems that had been hidden in 1996 rose to the surface and became obvious, in large part because the decline in inflation made the

[32]Interview with Shadman-Valavi, May 4, 2000.

budget more transparent.[33] For example, local authorities retained substantial spending authority, and it was difficult for the Ministry of Finance to prevent them from running up arrears. It was not until the second quarter of 1998 that line ministries became subject to monthly budgetary monitoring, and it still remained possible for them to make unplanned commitments. Extrabudgetary funds retained significant discretion, and the 1997 budget made the unrealistic assumption that one key fund, which had become a focus of corruption in 1996, the Government Reserve Fund, would run a surplus in 1997. Finally, even as late as 1998 there remained a tremendous amount of murkiness in the budget process, which made it impossible to trace all the financial flows and to account for expenditure in detail. The Ministry of Finance refused to open its accounts to the light of day, because a full accounting would reveal the depths of corruption and misappropriation of funds that routinely took place.[34]

According to the minister of the economy at the time, Viktor Suslov, it was a series of political decisions that violated IMF conditions.

> That was the Pustovoitenko government, and it was typical of his relations with the IMF.... As prime minister he never took the IMF conditions seriously. He simply didn't like them. He would sign any memorandum in order to get money, but he never tried to implement the agreements. The reason for canceling the [1997] program was the significant non-implementation of its conditions. The budget deficit, privatization of Khlebukraina [the state-owned grain distribution monopoly] —the prime minister had signed an agreement to do it, but in fact he slowed the process down. This was a prime minister who didn't want to implement the agreements that he signed. I always thought that when Ukraine didn't implement its conditions, the IMF Mission almost always compromised and took a flexible position.[35]

The contrast with the Polish case could not be made clearer: Ukraine missed its targets deliberately and expected the IMF to adjust them.

Tax receipts declined precipitously as the budget became caught up in the frenetic race for the March 1998 parliamentary elections, and the government, president, and parliamentary factions found themselves bidding for the support of important industrial lobbies. In the rush to close the books on the 1997 budget, the government approved sweeping clearing agreements with the gas and electricity monopolies, which canceled their tax obligations and the utilities arrears of government organizations. As a result, the percentage of tax

[33] Interview with Shapovalova, July 2, 1998.

[34] Author's notes from the "Open budget" project meeting, Mizhnarodnyi Tsentr Perspektivnikh Doslidzhen', July 1, 1998. Participants: Victor Pynzenik, Marina Shapovalova, Vira Nanivska, Inna Lunina, Mikhail Kukhar.

[35] Interview with Suslov, March 15, 2000.

revenues collected in the form of barter rose to 42 percent in November and to 68 percent in December.[36]

Since the program was weak on the income side, the financial side became all the more critical. However, nonresidents gradually began to withdraw from the treasury bill market after the first tremors of the Asian crisis in August, and cash shortfalls to the budget forced the National Bank to buy government bonds. Meanwhile, the position of Ukraine's international reserves became desperate. The NBU had committed itself to maintaining a range of 1.7 to 1.9 hryvnia to the dollar in 1997, and pressure on the exchange market compelled the NBU to intervene to support that corridor. As a result, Ukraine's reserves rapidly became depleted. The NBU was able to place Eurobonds in order to replenish its reserves, but the key IMF condition was for net international reserves (NIR)—that is, gross reserves minus central bank foreign liabilities. As the March elections drew nearer, this figure rapidly declined. The floor for NIR was $60 million for November and $150 million for December.[37] When December arrived, the NBU found itself with negative net reserves. Missing the target dramatically would almost certainly mean suspension of the Stand-by program, which would make it more difficult to sustain the declared exchange rate corridor and meet budget obligations in advance of the elections. Under the circumstances, the NBU leadership decided to misrepresent the level of its foreign reserves in order to win disbursement of the December tranche. Viktor Suslov, who later chaired an investigative committee of the Verkhovna Rada charged with determining whether NBU reserves had been misused, explained how this was done in his report:

> The National Bank of Ukraine instructed the bank, Credit Suisse First Boston (Cyprus), Ltd., to issue a credit of 150 million U.S. dollars to the Ukrainian Bank, Pervyi Ukrainskii Mezhdunarodnyi Bank, with a maturity of six months at 5 percent annual interest from the foreign currency reserve resources of Ukraine.
>
> The aforementioned Ukrainian bank was obligated to place these resources on deposit at the National Bank of Ukraine, which it did.... In this case, the National Bank explains the purpose of the operation with the fact that it allowed it to increase the nominal size of its foreign reserves by counting its reserves twice. That is, the reserves were counted once as a deposit in the Cyprus bank, and a second time the same money was counted as a deposit in the National Bank of Ukraine. Apparently, thanks to this we successfully

[36]"Koefitsient zbiraemisti podatkiv ta zboriv," Budget Policy and Macroeconomic Analysis Department, Ministry of Finance, July 1998.

[37]Staff Report for the 1997 Article IV Consultation and Request for Stand-By Arrangement, Attachment I, Table 2, "Ukraine: Quantitative Performance Criteria and Financial Benchmarks under the 1997-98 Stand-By Arrangement," 82.

fulfilled the normative indicator for the size of foreign reserves and received additional credits from the International Monetary Fund.[38]

The December disbursement was based on November statistics, so the relevant NIR target was $60 million. Ukraine reported NIR of $107 million, so the tranche was disbursed. However, the actual figure was $6 million.[39] When the details of the transaction came to light in the spring of 1999, the IMF altered the definition of NIR used in agreements with Ukraine specifically to exclude foreign currency deposits of domestic banks so that this maneuver could not be repeated.[40]

The flow of foreign capital from the bond market became a rush in January. Between November 1997 and July 1998 the NBU concluded contracts with Credit Suisse First Boston (CSFB) (Cyprus) in which it deposited $613 million in foreign reserves with the Cyprus bank as collateral for purchases by CSFB (Cyprus) of Ukrainian treasury bills through Pervyi Ukrainskii Mezhdunarodnyi Bank, apparently in an effort to support the bond market without making it obvious to market participants that the NBU was the only agent in the market buying bonds instead of selling them.[41] The NBU also facilitated a purchase of $600 million in treasury bills syndicated by Merrill Lynch by

[38] Stenogram of speech by Viktor Suslov to the Verkhovna Rada, May 6, 1999. "Pravitel'stvo Yushchenko nakanune otstavki," *Svoboda* (2) (March 13, 2000), 9. The NBU subsequently acknowledged in a report to the Verkhovna Rada that this was indeed the purpose of this transaction.

[39] PricewaterhouseCoopers 2000a, p. 9. See Table 7.1

[40] The new language said, "Finally, the definition excludes international reserves that correspond to deposits of commercial banks held in foreign currency at the NBU, as well as any international reserves that are (a) encumbered, (b) pledged as collateral for foreign loans, (c) frozen (d) pledged through derivative contracts." Letter of Intent of the government of Ukraine requesting completion of the Third Review under the EFF, Technical Memorandum, August 26, 1999. Compare this to the language used in 1997: "This definition excludes all NBU claims in foreign currency on resident institutions and international reserves pledged as collateral for foreign loans." Memorandum of Economic Policies of the Government of Ukraine for July 1997-June 1998, A1, Table 2, "Ukraine: Quantitative Performance Criteria and Financial Benchmarks under the 1997-98 Stand-By Arrangement." Although formally addressed from the country and signed by the prime minister and chairman of the National Bank, these documents are prepared by IMF staff.

[41] This came to light because of an investigation of NBU activities conducted by the Ukrainian secret service (SBU) after the election. The letter reporting the results of the investigation by the head of the SBU, Leonid Derkach, to the chairman of the Verkhovna Rada, Oleksandr Tkachenko, was published in a Ukrainian newspaper: "SBU proslukhovue telefonny rozmovi golovi Natsbanku: tse I bagato shto inshe viznaet'sia v taemnomu listi Leonida Derkacha," *Polityka,* (31) (October 21, 1998): 1-2. NBU officials do not deny that the transactions took place, but they insist that they were reported to the IMF at the time. An independent audit by Price Waterhouse Coopers of the state of NBU reserves released in 2000 found discrepancies with the official NBU figures on the order of $700 million to $800 million (see Table 7.1). Another question is what happened to the profits from the transactions. The NBU deposit with CSFB (Cyprus) was at 6 percent, and the NBU assumed all the risk for the investment. Meanwhile, the return on bonds in the secondary market had reached 60-70 percent. Since most of the bonds issued had maturities of one to three months, the bank making the investment could have made a substantial gain on arbitrage by rolling the bonds over and then defaulting on the principal when the government defaulted on the bonds in September.

Table 7.1: PriceWaterhouseCoopers Audits of Reported NBU Reserves.

| | 1996 | | 1997 | | | | | | | | | | | | 1998 |
	Nov	Dec	Jan	Feb	Mar	Apr	May	Jun	Jul	Aug	Sep	Oct	Nov	Dec	Jan
IMF NIR[a]	(768)	(270)	(193)	(131)	(191)	(99)	(154)	61	134	677	248	203	107	(18)	(418)
Tech. Adj.[b]	(44)	(26)	(18)	(28)	(35)	(34)	(13)	(45)	(53)	(102)	(102)	(36)	(101)	(88)	1
PWC NIR[c]	(812)	(296)	(211)	(159)	(226)	(133)	(167)	16	81	575	146	167	6	(106)	(417)
Encum. Adj.[d]	—	(182)	(111)	(109)	(119)	(116)	(147)	(146)	(116)	(116)	(116)	(116)	(266)	(266)	(166)
NIR Net[e]	(812)	(478)	(322)	(268)	(345)	(249)	(314)	(130)	(35)	459	30	51	(260)	(372)	(583)
Other[f]	(186)	(317)	(294)	(263)	(243)	(306)	(336)	(304)	(333)	(319)	(275)	(380)	(401)	(447)	(547)
Adj. NIR Net[g]	(998)	(795)	(616)	(531)	(588)	(555)	(650)	(434)	(368)	140	(245)	(329)	(661)	(819)	(1130)

[a] NIR reported to the IMF per NBU records.
[b] Adjustment to reflect the calculation method specified in the Technical Memorandum.
[c] NIR calculated by PriceWaterhouseCoopers.
[d] Adjustments to reflect encumbrances of fiduciary deposits.
[e] NIR net of fiduciary deposits.
[f] Total other encumbrances.
[g] Adjusted NIR net of encumbrances.

Source: PriceWaterhouseCoopers, "Agreed-Upon Procedures: Report of Findings for Publication Purposes," April (2000*b*), p. 9, and July (2000*a*), p. 9.

Note: all figures in millions of U.S. dollars.

selling a swap contract to repurchase the bonds for dollars in October. In addition, the NBU made open purchases of substantial quantities of treasury bills and ran down its international reserves to defend the hryvnia as the exiting capital made its way to the exchange market. In January the IMF suspended the Stand-by Arrangement because the NBU had missed its targets. However, in a memorandum dated January 23, the Fund agreed to significantly relaxed targets, and in February the IMF disbursed one final tranche. The head of the IMF Mission described the Fund's dilemma:

> They were facing a parliamentary election in March, and the situation was becoming increasingly political. What do we do? Interrupt the program, or go on with a holding operation? We knew that if we didn't make this decision early enough, we would be accused of trying to influence the election one way or the other. We had to make a choice, and we discussed two options with the president and the government. One was to get firm commitments on immediate reforms right after the election; the other was to get an agreement on an EFF now by pushing the decisions through now. They did make firm promises.... Of course, we all knew, including all the decision makers here, that this was going to be a difficult quarter for them because they had a parliamentary election and externally had to pay off a lot of debt.[42]

IMF support was important to the government, since Pustovoitenko's party was expected to be very close to the 4 percent threshold for making it into the parliament under Ukraine's new, half proportional representation, half single-member district system, and deterioration of the economy shortly before the election could easily make the difference between success and failure. The revised target for net international reserves allowed the NBU to spend another $200 million supporting the currency and the bond market in the run-up to the election. However, these transactions severely reduced the NBU's flexibility in the event of a crisis of confidence in the hryvnia, significantly increasing the risks in an already risky international environment. The evident political motivations behind the transactions in the first three months of 1998 demonstrate the National Bank of Ukraine's lack of institutional independence. Just before the March election, Ukraine succeeded in placing its last Eurobond for 500 million Euros at 14.75 percent, an unprecedented interest rate for Eurobonds. This indicates the level of risk that the market foresaw in Ukraine; it is also a sign of the degree to which spending the NBU's reserves had weakened its market position and how desperate the central bank was to replenish them.

The IMF suspended the Stand-by Arrangement in March. "After the board approval," an IMF official noted, "the Ukrainians decided it was important to

[42]Interview with Shadman-Valavi, May 4, 2000.

win the parliamentary elections, so they went on a spending spree in the first quarter of '98, and the fiscal program went way off track."[43] The projected budget deficit for 1998 had risen from 2.5 percent of GDP to over 8 percent of GDP, and it was clear that Ukraine would miss its program targets across the board.

7.6 THE EXTENDED FUND FACILITY, 1998

In spite of the budget crisis, negotiations continued for a three-year EFF program for approximately 2 billion Special Drawing Rights (SDRs). Interviewed in June, the chief of the NBU department for international relations explained that, since the Stand-by was frozen and it appeared unrealistic to revive it by meeting the original conditions, the government had decided to push for an EFF instead. This was an audacious move, but a calculated risk. Ordinarily, an EFF can only be signed after the successful conclusion of a Stand-by. It signals the transition from short-term, crisis-management measures to long-term structural reforms. However, in 1998 Ukrainian authorities calculated that, with growing financial instability in Russia and significant pressure on the Fund from the U.S. administration to take a proactive role in preventing looming financial crises, it would be difficult for the IMF to refuse to offer an EFF if it did not have the backup option of offering a Stand-by instead.[44] Furthermore, the program had been under discussion for two years, and the basic preparation for the EFF had been done the year before. For their part, IMF officials were convinced that Ukraine's main problems were structural, and they saw the negotiation of an EFF as an opportunity to break the logjam of parliamentary opposition to far-reaching reforms. The Fund, too, decided to hold out for an EFF when it canceled the Stand-by in the spring, instead of offering to negotiate another Stand-by.[45]

Visiting Kiev in June, Stanley Fischer spoke optimistically about the prospects of reaching agreement. In return for approving the EFF, however, the IMF insisted that a series of prior conditions be met: removing legislative obstacles to privatization, reforming the tax system, revising the 1998 budget, and making a large number of structural changes in the Ukrainian economy. The IMF perceived that its influence was at a high point. It is instructive to compare the conditions for the 1998 EFF to those for the Russian emergency rescue package of the same year; the Ukrainian conditions are much more ambitious. Russia had progressed much further than Ukraine in terms of structural reform, but it was never asked to address such a wide range of issues so rapidly, nor to bend its constitution quite so far in the process.

---

[43] Ibid.

[44] Interview with Rybachuk, July 3, 1998.

[45] Interview with Shadman-Valavi, May 4, 2000.

The results of the parliamentary elections in March 1998 did nothing to smooth the passage of the legislation demanded by the IMF. If anything, the new parliament was more strongly opposed to the president's pro-market approach than the previous one. Furthermore, the parliament spent several months embroiled in conflict over who should become the next chairman, during which time it was unable to produce any legislation at all. Meanwhile, as tension built on the Russian bond market, foreign investors accelerated their withdrawal from the Ukrainian market as well. The Ukrainian government came to feel that time was running out and that an agreement with the IMF was needed immediately to stem the contagion of market panic. Ukraine had become much more vulnerable to international currency market movements because of the increased exposure of the market for government bonds to foreign investors.

What followed is remarkable as an example of IMF influence at the highest levels of government. Kuchma announced in a televised address in June that he would reform the economy by decree, and within a few days he published fifteen decrees (*ukazy*) that lowered the current 20 percent VAT, simplified tax procedures for small businesses, and introduced a fixed tax rate on agricultural products. He announced, further, that the government planned to lay off 112,000 employees by the end of 1998. In the following weeks he issued decrees that fulfilled all the major IMF prior conditions for signing an EFF program and overruled the objections of the Verkhovna Rada on almost every point. Most dramatically, a decree revised the 1998 budget expenditures downward by 30 percent, and another overruled restrictions that the Verkhovna Rada had placed on privatizing many of Ukraine's most important enterprises. Almost all these decrees were unconstitutional. The Ukrainian Constitution of 1996 specifies that the president had the right for three years to sign "decrees (*ukazy*) on economic questions that are not regulated by laws" (point 4, Part 15, "On Transitional Arrangements"). Furthermore, Article 92 of the Basic Law (part of the Constitution) specified that taxation and budgetary issues were to be regulated "exclusively by laws." Almost all the decrees signed in June superseded existing laws, and the decrees that changed the tax system and revised the budget contradicted Article 92.

When asked whether the IMF was concerned about the legality of the president's decrees, an IMF official answered, "Absolutely."

> But first parliament couldn't elect a speaker, and once it had one, it was clear nothing could go through parliament. What could we do? One, we could withdraw; or two, we could push reforms that we thought would be delivered, knowing that all kinds of risks were attached.... There was a transitional authority for the president to take decisions in areas where the parliament had not spoken.... The G-7 was insisting they should have a program. The Ukrainians offered to do these things through presidential decrees. We accepted, with all the caveats you are thinking of.... The decision was made

because the risks of withdrawal were very high for Ukraine and for Russia.[46]

In July the NBU informed the IMF that a large portion of its reserves was in fact encumbered or tied up in illiquid assets. It is unclear exactly which NBU transactions were revealed at this point, and the IMF subsequently charged that it had been misled about transactions that took place between 1996 and 1998 that totaled approximately $1 billion. However, it must have become impossible to hide the existence of large movements of NBU reserves into the bond market. Meanwhile, by July the threat of a currency crisis in Russia had become very real, and the NBU was aware that it was in no position to defend the hryvnia in the event the ruble crashed. The IMF expressed its disappointment with the NBU's management of its reserves, but it decided not to cancel preparations for the EFF. The IMF, like the NBU, found itself with very little room for maneuver. The consequence of canceling the EFF would be to bring on a run on the bond market and the hryvnia, and the IMF very much wanted to contain the impact of the Asian financial crisis on the post-Communist countries. In addition, the concessions Ukraine had made in negotiations for the EFF had appeared to offer the first real progress on restructuring the Ukrainian economy. If implemented, these conditions would have dramatically improved the business climate and laid the groundwork for future growth.

According to the key IMF negotiator, the EFF was a calculated risk taken in full cognizance of the mounting evidence that Ukraine had failed to implement key conditions of previous agreements and had deceived the IMF in an effort to cover its tracks. IMF officials believed that the seriousness of the international financial situation in the summer of 1998 and the importance of Ukraine made the balance of risks justifiable.

> From my point of view it is absolutely silly to pretend the IMF and the G-7 didn't know what they were doing in Ukraine. Certainly the EFF was approved with the full knowledge of these things— well, not full knowledge—but everyone knew there was corruption in Ukraine. The EFF did make an effort to tighten up the definitions, and we started to audit the National Bank accounts at a time when this was not fashionable.... Suppose we had known about the $150 million [the double counting of reserves in December 1997] at the time of the EFF, would that have changed the decision? I think it is very unlikely. What is good for the country, for the region, for this institution—you have to balance these pitfalls.[47]

Ukraine's politics quickly reverted to form, so the apparent breakthrough reached in the summer turned out to be considerably less impressive than it initially

[46]Ibid.
[47]Ibid.

appeared. Once the parliament chose a new speaker, leader of the Agrarian Party Oleksandr Tkachenko, it quickly set about reversing many of the presidential decrees. Some of the decrees that were not reversed were actually profoundly antireformist measures that the presidential administration had slipped in along with the barrage of edicts that fulfilled IMF prior conditions. Some of the decrees desired by the IMF survived but were poorly implemented by the bureaucracy, so they ended up having little or no effect. A survey of managers of small and medium-sized private enterprises illustrates the difficulties. For example, the survey found that, by 2000, 96 percent of respondents knew about the presidential decree, "On a simplified system of taxation, accounting, and reporting for small business entities," signed July 3, 1998, and a majority believed that using the simplified tax system would have saved them time and allowed them to pay lower taxes, but only 16 percent had actually made the switch. Most of those who failed to change to the simplified system cited ambiguities in the rules or bureaucratic delays as the reason. Seventy-six percent of the respondents were aware of the decree, "On certain measures to deregulate entrepreneurial activities," which was intended to reduce corruption by regularizing procedures for conducting regulatory and tax inspections (typically opportunities for inspectors to collect bribes). However, the majority of respondents reported that inspecting agencies such as the State Tax Administration, the State Pension Fund, the Customs Agency, and the State Treasury routinely violated the rules by conducting inspections more than once per year, failing to conduct multiple required inspections of a single enterprise simultaneously, and failing to provide the mandated advance warnings about inspections.[48] The 1999 IMF Country Report for Ukraine acknowledges that measures to reform the coal sector and introduce a transparent market in natural gas had not been implemented and that agriculture remained "hampered by extensive formal and informal state controls."[49]

If, in the end, the president's decrees had little more than symbolic meaning, however, the urgency of the fiscal crisis allowed the Ministry of Finance finally to achieve reforms it had been pursuing for several years. In the middle of 1998, for the first time the Ministry of Finance became an effective veto-player for most government expenditures. It introduced a "budget within the budget," which was based on an estimate of the minimum necessary tax receipts and minimum necessary expenditures for salaries (nonpayment of which would violate the EFF agreement), national defense, and basic government functions. Line ministries were allowed to make commitments only for items detailed in this minimal budget. The Ministry of Finance, meanwhile, introduced several levels of priorities within the remainder of the budget, and released funds on

---

[48] The survey was conducted by the International Center for Policy Studies, and polled managers of twenty-two hundred nonstate enterprises (*ICPS Newsletter,* February 14, 2000, 1).

[49] "Ukraine: Recent Economic Developments," IMF Staff Country Report No. 99/42, May 1999, 11.

a monthly basis to meet those priorities only if the funds were available. As a result, budget expenditures were significantly curtailed. This measure reduced barter tax receipts as well, since now local authorities were unable to make spending commitments that were not backed by authorization from the Ministry of Finance. Inevitably exceptions were made and the system was much more complex in practice than in principle, but substantial progress was made and budget expenditures stayed within the EFF targets throughout the year.[50]

Inflation ran at an annual rate of 7 percent for the first eight months of the year, and for the first time GDP had ceased its long slide. However, the collapse of the Russian bond market in August, the crash of the ruble, and the declaration of default that followed shattered confidence in the Ukrainian bond market as well. As a result, the Ministry of Finance was unable to refinance bonds as they came due and had to turn to the National Bank for credits. These credits expanded the money supply, and investors fled to the exchange market to repatriate their capital while the exchange window remained open. The National Bank intervened furiously on the exchange market to slow the hryvnia's fall, drawing down its reserves by $1.4 billion. The market calmed dramatically when the first tranche of the EFF was disbursed in September, and this slowed the slide. Nevertheless, the hryvnia fell 54.4 percent in September. As a result, annual inflation amounted to 20 percent, and GDP declined by 2 percent.

In the beginning of October Ukraine was compelled to default. When investors attempted to exercise their right to convert a bond into foreign currency when it matured, the National Bank declared that it was not obligated to comply.[51] The IMF supported the NBU position by declaring that paying $70 million to redeem the bond would violate IMF conditions for net international reserves. Standard and Poor's declared that this amounted to a default. When the exchange market stabilized after two weeks, however, the NBU fulfilled its obligation to convert the bond to dollars. The financial crisis provoked heated discussions in the parliament about dismissing the government, but Kuchma stood by the government, and the new chairman of the Verkhovna Rada, Oleksandr Tkachenko of the Agrarian Party, urged parliament not to provoke a political crisis that would worsen the financial one. Pustovoitenko's government narrowly survived a vote of no-confidence: 206 of the required 226 deputies voted in favor of dissolving the government.

The effort to defend the hryvnia and prevent the government from defaulting as the bond market melted down caused the National Bank to violate its

[50]Interview with Sheiko, March 16, 2000.

[51]The bond in question was syndicated by Merrill Lynch in December 1997 and consisted of short-term treasury bonds bought by the First Ukrainian International Bank, with a nominal annual return of 44 percent. To make the bonds more attractive to international investors, the NBU sold a swap to the First Ukrainian International Bank to convert them to dollars at an annual return of 22 percent. This was one of the ways in which NBU reserves were encumbered that apparently was not initially revealed to the IMF. The NBU at first refused to honor the terms of the swap.

IMF conditions for net domestic assets and international reserves. In addition, a number of commercial banks that had invested in government bonds were bailed out, which cost the NBU another billion hryvnia of credit. Cash payments to the budget fell in the general crisis, causing the government to miss its targets for the deficit and for tax collection; in addition, salaries were not paid on time, violating another EFF condition. Furthermore, there had been no movement on a whole series of structural conditions: privatization, the level of sales of Russian gas on auctions (as opposed to closed sales to political cronies), transportation and housing payments, reforming the agricultural sector, abolishing the monopoly on wholesale distribution of grain, and abolishing tax privileges for particular enterprises and sectors, such as mining and shipbuilding. The IMF granted a waiver for cash collection of taxes, but the accumulation of missed targets on every front was too glaring to overlook. In December the IMF suspended disbursements under the EFF and took the position that the program could be brought back on track if the parliament passed a realistic budget for 1999. However, the parliament immediately rejected the government's draft budget, sending it back to the Budget Commission for amendments.

In January President Kuchma issued a decree forbidding the payment of taxes in barter, which was one of the terms the IMF had insisted on including in the EFF schedule of conditions. The effect was dramatic: The level of taxes collected in cash rose 17 percent in the first quarter. This confirmed Ministry of Finance officials in their conviction that what was necessary to solve the barter problem was a credible commitment from the government. "Tax collection," Oleg Sheiko argued, "is completely determined at the political level."[52] As if to prove the point, when the Verkhovna Rada passed the 1999 budget in March—making it possible for the IMF to resume disbursements under the EFF program—it included an amendment that made exceptions to the rule against barter payment of taxes for certain military industries that had very high energy debts. This sent a signal to enterprises that exceptions would, in fact, be made, and cash collection of taxes again fell drastically in April. As a result, the NBU—by now the only buyer of government treasury bills—was compelled to expand its purchases, which caused it to violate its targets for net domestic assets. By August Ukraine was compelled to appeal to the IMF for a waiver of its targets for cash collection of taxes through June and a modification of the targets for tax collections and net domestic assets for September.[53]

Throughout 1999 the Ukrainian economy gradually recovered from the crash of 1998. Tax collection recovered, and inflation fell: The price index had risen

---

[52]Interview with Sheiko, March 16, 2000.

[53]Letter of Intent of the government of Ukraine requesting completion of the Third Review under the EFF, August 26, 1999.

more than 20 percent in the six months from August 1998 to February 1999, and it rose only 6 percent in the next six months. As it gradually became clear that Ukraine had missed the worst of the Russian financial crisis, confidence in the hryvnia returned. However, three years of heavy borrowing had left Ukraine with substantial foreign debts, and the capital inflows that had helped the government to service them had evaporated. As a result, the NBU embarked on a crash program to accumulate foreign reserves, and its heavy purchases of foreign currency led to a 40 percent increase in broad money and a 48 percent depreciation of the hryvnia during the year. The government, for its part, substantially tightened fiscal policy on both the income and expenditure side. By the end of the year 97.9 percent of taxes anticipated in the budget had actually been collected. Since GDP declined by only .5 percent instead of the expected 1 percent in 1999, collections of income and profit taxes significantly exceeded the budgeted amounts. In a curious reversal of the electoral cycle, political pressure to collect taxes intensified as the presidential elections in October approached, because the insolvent government was unable to finance salaries and pensions without collecting taxes, and the arrears in salaries and pensions had become president Kuchma's greatest electoral liability. According to Ministry of Finance officials, the tax collection effort actually subsided immediately after the election, as the bureaucracy breathed a collective sigh of relief at Kuchma's reelection.[54] The most remarkable piece of election-year politics was the payment by Ukrgazprom, the Ukrainian gas distribution monopoly, of 150.7 million hryvnia ($33.7 million) to the budget in September for gas transit fees—a budget item in which it is rare to collect better than 20 percent of planned revenues, and 95 percent of that in barter—just in time to relieve the government's straitened financial circumstances before the election. A portion of this payment was an advance to the government, since 58 million hryvnia ($13 million) were returned to Ukrgazprom in November.[55] A number of important nontax revenue sources fell sharply below the budgeted levels, however, mainly because of the sharp decline of trade with Russia. The government dramatically overspent in some categories of expenditure and economized in others; the net result was a budget deficit of 2.14 percent of GDP, compared to a planned deficit of under 1 percent. Ordinarily, 2.14 percent of GDP is not an excessive budget deficit. However, Ukraine's room for fiscal maneuver was narrow because of the withdrawal of foreign financing and large impending debt repayments. The government made substantial progress in paying down the level of arrears in both salaries and pensions, but this was almost entirely financed by purchases of treasury bills by the NBU, which amounted to credits to the government. By the end of the year it became

---

[54]Interview with Sheiko, March 16, 2000.

[55]1999 Budget Revenues Execution Report, Fiscal Analysis Office, Verkhovna Rada Budget Committee, 4.

clear that Ukraine would not be able to service its debt in 2000 and would have to rely on creditors' self-interest to restructure the debt voluntarily and keep them from declaring Ukraine in default.

Throughout 1999 the stalemate persisted between the Verkhovna Rada and the government on structural reform. All of Kuchma's serious competitors for the presidency were members of the parliament, and none of them were inclined to make his reelection effort easier by handing him political victories, so work on legislation to fulfill IMF structural reform conditions ground to a halt. Meanwhile, President Kuchma and Prime Minister Pustovoitenko seemed uninterested in pushing through the administrative measures that they could use to meet other program criteria, such as raising apartment rents, utilities, and transportation costs. Each of these measures was bound to be unpopular, and in an election season it seemed wiser to put them off. In fact, the government spent four times the amount authorized in the budget for housing and utility subsidies. The extra 900 million hryvnia amounted to .7 percent of GDP, or 60 percent of the unplanned budget deficit. Far from exerting himself to promote reform, Kuchma introduced a series of populist measures to promote his election chances. Because his three-year grant of decree power under the constitution ran out in June, he rushed to declare a number of regions of Ukraine "free economic zones," which freed them from paying VAT and even entitled them to refunds of VAT paid in other regions. Only two of these zones were actually established, in Donetsk and Transcarpathia, and the rest were put on indefinite hold after the election. In an election year, however, this was a popular way of doling out tax privileges, and it helped to solidify Kuchma's support among the local elites. The IMF granted Ukraine a waiver on tax collection and adjusted some other indicators in order to release the September tranche of the EFF, but afterward it quietly informed the government that it was suspending the EFF program for a second time.

Summarizing conclusions from its visit to Ukraine in December, the IMF Mission wrote, "The government's program for stabilization and structural reform, which is financed by the Extended Fund Facility (EFF), has gone off course to a significant degree." The budget situation had "worsened dramatically" in the last two months because of low levels of cash income and excessive expenditures, and the budget deficit exceeded the criterion for November by 744 million hryvnia. As a result, the budget had depended on large credits from the NBU, which "put significant pressure on prices and the exchange rate." It cited failure to implement several structural reforms: raising charges for utilities, increasing the level of payment for electricity in cash, and abolishing an export tax on sunflower seeds. It went on to list a series of measures required for release of the fourth tranche, including adoption of a "realistic" budget, adoption of a privatization program with a goal of bringing income of $500 million in 2000 and $3 billion by 2002, and formulation of a comprehensive strategy for servicing the national debt. The Mission regarded the budget adopted in the first reading by the parliament as based on unrealistic income estimates and insisted that the budget for 2000 must have a deficit no greater than 1 percent of GDP, with income of 36.2 million hryvnia (24 percent of projected GDP) and expenses of 37.7 million hryvnia (25 percent of GDP). The document emphasized that implementing these measures would require "firm political will and decisive and determined actions."[56]

The Ukrainian constitution requires formation of a new government after election of the president, and the Verkhovna Rada rejected Kuchma's renomination of Valerii Pustovoitenko as prime minister. Kuchma at first blustered and threatened, but a group of parliament deputies convinced him to nominate the reformist chairman of the National Bank, Viktor Yushchenko, to be the next prime minister. Kuchma consented, and Yuschenko was overwhelmingly elected. Under pressure from Kuchma, who was reinvigorated by his reelection victory and threatened a national referendum to dissolve the parliament, the Verkhovna Rada formed, for the first time, a "pro-government majority" under the auspices, startlingly, of Leonid Kravchuk. Speaker Tkachenko initially used parliamentary maneuvers to defeat attempts to remove him and reform the parliament's rules of procedure, but, after a month of scandals in which two separate parliaments met simultaneously in different buildings and declared each other illegal, he eventually gave in. The Verkhovna Rada resumed functioning and rapidly passed a series of reformist draft laws proposed by the Yushchenko government.

The issue of rescheduling Ukrainian foreign debts became urgent at the beginning of 2000. Ukraine faced $2.7 billion of debt payments in 2000, and, after the political season in the fall, the NBU had only $1 billion remaining in reserves. The IMF made successful restructuring a necessary condition for resuming support. This last point may seem odd; indeed, it seemed to many well-informed Ukrainian observers, including officials of the Ministry of Finance, that the IMF was abandoning Ukraine in its moment of greatest need. However, the Fund's strategy was to place responsibility for restructuring Ukraine's debt firmly on the private sector. By failing to provide resources that would help to repay the debt, the Fund strengthened Ukraine's hand in negotiating with its creditors; by making restructuring a condition for future support, it rendered credible the Ukrainian position that it had no option but to declare default if restructuring failed. This was the same position the IMF had taken in September 1998 and June 1999, when Ukraine successfully restructured debt to international creditors.[57] However, in the earlier efforts the IMF had played a very active role in lobbying creditors and mid-level IMF managers had participated in conference calls with the Ukrainian government and

---

[56]Mizhnarodnii valiutnii fond, "Ukraina—Pam'iatna zapiska," December 16, 1999, 1-4. Translations from Ukrainian by the author.

[57]Interview with Shadman-Valavi, May 4, 2000.

international investors, but in March 2000 it took a less active role.[58]

Nevertheless, in March Ukraine succeeded in an unprecedented rescheduling of Eurobonds. The conventional wisdom had been that it is impossible to reschedule Eurobonds, because their dispersed ownership and cross-default clauses make collective action extremely difficult. This was, of course, one of the attractive features of Eurobonds from an investor's perspective; the threat that someone would sue for default in the event of nonpayment seemed very credible, and that is one reason why Eurobonds carried lower interest rates than other forms of sovereign debt. The Ministry of Finance estimated that the $2.7 billion of foreign debt that it attempted to reschedule in March was held by more than 100,000 individuals and organizations, any one of which could legally sue Ukraine for default. However, Ukraine succeeded in proving that the transaction costs that prevent large-scale coordination are indeed fungible. Ukraine offered Euro notes at 10 percent or U.S. dollar notes at 11 percent, both due in 2007, for five different instruments denominated in dollars, Euros, and Deutschmarks that were coming due in 2000 and 2001. The Ministry of Finance recruited ING Barings as lead manager of the effort, Commerzbank and Credit Suisse First Boston to manage various segments of the Eurobond market, and Salomon Smith Barney International to manage the effort in the United States. These agents, in turn, recruited numerous other banks and financial organizations as retail representatives, and they received commissions from Ukraine for convincing investors to roll over their bonds. Vitalii Lisovenko, the director of the Department for Foreign Debt at the Ministry of Finance, reports that the total cost of the operation, including commissions, fees, legal costs, and foreign travel, was less than the 1.75 percent commission paid to the original managers of the bond offerings in 1998. He did not expect that the effort would be nearly as successful as it turned out to be, however; he said that he expected a rollover of about 80 percent. By March 22, 98.1 percent of the offers to convert the bonds had been accepted.[59]

The final blow that delayed the resumption of the EFF was publication of an article in the *Financial Times* that discussed former prime minister Pavlo Lazarenko's charges of corruption in the use of NBU reserves received as IMF tranches.[60] Lazarenko's specific charges were inaccurate. He claimed that $613 million of NBU reserves were illicitly invested in the Ukrainian bond market in December 1997, and that $200 million in proceeds were illegally distributed to Kuchma's supporters. The $613 million figure came from a report by the Security Service of Ukraine(SBU) in the fall of 1998 and a subsequent investigation by the Verkhovna Rada, and it included five purchases of

[58]Interview with Vitalii Lisovenko, March 22, 2000. Lisovenko had been director of the Department of Foreign Debt, Ministry of Finance, since early 1997.

[59]Interview with Lisovenko, March 22, 2000.

[60]"Former PM alleges $613 m Ukraine fraud," *Financial Times,* January 28, 2000, 1.

Ukrainian treasury bills between November 1997 and July 1998 in which NBU reserves were used to support the bond market when it was collapsing because of the withdrawal of nonresidents. There is some prima facie evidence of corruption, since the transactions were carried out through a bank with close ties to Yushchenko, though it was probably on a smaller scale than Lazarenko alleges, since the entire sum was not invested at once and only the bonds that were rolled over before the default earned interest.[61]

On March 14, 2000, the IMF officially accused the NBU of intentionally misrepresenting its reserves in a series of transactions from 1996 to 1998. According to the Fund, "These transactions might have caused the IMF to disburse money earlier or in larger amounts than it otherwise would have done."[62] To the contrary, officials of the NBU and Ministry of Finance insist that the IMF was informed about all of them. Table 7.1 (p. 194) summarizes the main findings of the Price Waterhouse Coopers audits that came out in the summer of 2000.

The evidence of corruption tarnished the image of Ukraine's leading reformer at a critical juncture. Viktor Yushchenko seemed poised in early 2000 to carry out sweeping reforms; the parliament finally appeared to be united behind this agenda (if only under considerable duress); the newly reelected president was in a strong position to promote reform, and finally seemed committed to doing so. The charges against the NBU, however, forced the IMF to delay resumption of the EFF while a second independent audit of the transactions involved took place. The IMF was vulnerable to charges that its funds had been misused after the revelations from Russia in the previous year, and it was very sensitive to the uses that might be made of the new charges in the American presidential campaign in 2000.[63] As a result, the legacy of years of economic mismanagement and the political subservience of the National Bank came home to roost at precisely the time when Ukraine's political system had finally resolved to pursue serious economic reform. In March Yushchenko canceled a scheduled trip to the United States to lobby for resumption of the IMF loan, apparently because senior U.S. administration members were unwilling to meet with him. Further revelations were even more damaging. Audio tapes—apparently genuine—captured President Kuchma's express orders to kill a journalist and revealed lurid details of the rampant corruption in the upper echelons of government. The "cassette crisis" paralyzed government, spurred mass street protests, and led to widespread calls for Kuchma to resign.

---

[61]"Pravitel'stvo Yushchenko nakanune otstavki," *Svoboda,* 3 (March 20, 2000): 10. The article is the conclusion of the stenogram of Viktor Suslov's speech to the Verkhovna Rada on May 6, 1999.

[62]"IMF Scandal Heats Up," *Kyiv Post* 6 (12): March 23, 2000, 1.

[63]During a televised presidential debate on October 11, 2000, George W. Bush charged that Viktor Chernomyrdin had embezzled IMF funds lent to Russia, and Al Gore responded by saying that the IMF had made several questionable decisions. Ukraine escaped notice.

Sensing in Yushchenko a powerful new rival, Kuchma fired him in 2001, and apparently dropped his efforts to carry out extensive economic reforms.

These revelations, coming as they did during a U.S. election year, drove a wedge into the special relationship that had developed between Ukraine and the United States. While it is too early at this writing to be certain, it appears that the cooling of United States-Ukrainian relations has made the IMF less solicitous of Ukraine as well. Like Russia a few years earlier, Ukraine may have graduated into the status of a "normal" country, whose economic policies are subject to the full rigor of IMF scrutiny.

7.7 CONCLUSIONS

Ukraine is the hardest case for demonstrating the influence of the IMF. It is a country that has pursued disastrous economic policies throughout the transition period, that has suffered from sustained periods of high inflation as a result, and that has failed to introduce substantial microeconomic reforms. It ranks among the most corrupt, impoverished, and poorly administered post-Communist countries. The Ukrainian authorities have generally failed to fulfill the obligations that they had accepted under Fund programs, and every program has been revised to weaken its conditions substantially. In spite of this lenient treatment, the Ukrainian authorities found it expedient to deceive the IMF about the level of central bank reserves over a period of several years. In ways that were sometimes spectacular, the Ukrainian authorities managed to blunt the edges of IMF programs and circumvent conditions through accounting legerdemain or outright fraud.

This is, of course, exactly what the theoretical model outlined in Chapter 2 predicted: Large, powerful, strategically important countries should be hard to deter from inflationary policies, because they cannot expect to be subject to rigorous enforcement of the rules. As a corollary, they violate their programs' conditions more frequently and are subject to more frequent program interruptions—indeed, every Ukrainian program was interrupted at least once. Instead of rigorously holding the line and insisting that Ukraine achieve its old targets before resuming funding, however, the IMF flexibly adjusted the conditions to the circumstances. Some program interruptions were fairly lengthy, as in 1997 and again after 1999, but this was because Ukraine defected repeatedly, not because the Fund refused to adjust its targets. Throughout the story, Ukraine's international prominence is an important factor. Ukraine was able to get U.S. officials to support its position vis-à-viz the Fund in public, and the G-7 made it clear that it expected the IMF to reach some pragmatic accommodation with the recalcitrant Ukrainian authorities. The IMF's board of directors repeatedly bent the rules in Ukraine's favor. However, Ukraine's international prominence was not a fixed asset; it was a variable that increased over time, particularly after 1995, and the constraints on IMF decision makers became correspondingly tighter.

However, this is a case in which failure was overdetermined. Ukraine has been cursed with political stalemate, fragmented parliamentary institutions, and unclear division of powers between the legislative and executive branches. Its governments have never been wholeheartedly committed to economic reform, and what they have attempted to achieve has been effectively blocked by the parliamentary opposition. A lengthy period of failed transition entrenched the interests arrayed against reform and raised the political costs of balancing the budget. Even the consolidation of presidential powers failed to alleviate the problem. As in Russia, the more powerful the Ukrainian president became, the more reluctant he became to identify himself too closely with the reform agenda. Furthermore, election campaigns led to dramatic swings in macroeconomic policy. The IMF was often the only voice in Ukraine lobbying for reform. Nevertheless, Ukrainian observers and IMF officials believe that the IMF exercised an influence; indeed, they believe that without the incentives the IMF provided, inflation might have been far worse and the little progress that has been made in structural reforms might never have materialized.

In Ukraine, more than in other countries, observers can find much to fault in the Fund's tactical decisions. On the other hand, Ukraine, better than any other post-Communist country that has avoided the ravages of war, is a living illustration of the basic correctness of the Fund's main objectives: to accelerate the wide spectrum of market reforms and to lead with macroeconomic stabilization and liberalization. Ukraine failed to reform rapidly, then failed to reform gradually, and finally failed to reform at all. The result is an impoverished society, a debilitated state, an economy in decline, and a thoroughly corrupt political system.

8

Bulgaria

BULGARIA'S experience with economic transition has been one of repeated false starts. Bulgaria had eight governments between 1990 and 1999, and only three of these enjoyed majority support in the parliament. Every government announced its allegiance to some vision of economic reform, and most signed agreements with the IMF. Several managed to engineer at least a short-lived improvement in macroeconomic policy, but competing priorities and political instability soon undermined the commitment to tight budgets, and structural reform remained a mirage. None of the IMF-supported programs was successfully implemented during the first six years of the transition. However, in 1997 Bulgaria executed a dramatic about-face. Economic mismanagement had led to a run on the currency, rampant inflation, and the collapse of the banking sector. Popular unrest compelled the government to step down and call new elections, which returned a solid right-wing majority to the parliament. The new government implemented a currency board, supported by the Fund, and rapidly restored confidence in the Bulgarian economy. Corruption continues to be ubiquitous, but Bulgaria has become a showcase of successful exchange rate-based stabilization.

The case of Bulgaria shows several important commonalities with the other cases in this study that support features of the model, and one significant difference from Russia and Ukraine that underlines the importance of the variable sizes of states. First, as in the other countries in this study, Bulgarian governments clearly faced variable levels of temptation to defect from IMF agreements. During their initial months in office, new governments were generally willing to accept and implement painful adjustment measures, but, as time went on, they became less willing to pay the political costs of adjustment. Second, international capital markets played a key role in leveraging the influence of the IMF. At several key turning points—March 1994, April 1995, and December 1996—sharp capital movements and dramatic increases of the exchange rate pushed governments to accept IMF conditions they had previously rejected as unacceptable. Third, the Bulgarian case supports the model's expectation that the size and strategic importance of the recipient country should affect the IMF's bargaining posture. The difference between Bulgaria and the other cases is palpable. As more than one official whom I interviewed protested, "You can't compare Bulgaria and Russia!" If Ukraine and Poland had significantly less leverage in the international arena than their powerful Eastern neighbor, Bulgaria had much less than they. As a result, Bulgaria consistently found itself subjected to the full rigor of IMF supervision. The credibility of IMF threats to suspend aid and hold out for significant improvements in policy was never in question.

8.1 FALSE STARTS, 1990-1994

At the time Bulgaria joined the IMF in September 1990, the future of Bulgarian democracy seemed very much in question. As it had twice before in this century, Bulgaria had quickly changed its government when the tides of international fortune swung against its ruling party in 1989. The eighteen-year rule of Todor Zhivkov was swept away almost without protest, and Andrei Lukanov became prime minister. Lukanov, a reform-Communist with a distinct preference for social democracy, called rapid elections for a Grand National Assembly, whose primary task was to write a new, post-Communist constitution and govern the country in the interim. Lukanov's Bulgarian Socialist Party (BSP) won the June 1990 elections handily with 47 percent of the vote, and, under the single-member-district voting rule, captured 57 percent of the seats in the Assembly. Lukanov formed a government, calling for a wide coalition, but the opposition parties refused to join. As a concession to the opposition, the Assembly elected the leader of the Union of Democratic Forces (UDF), Zhelyu Zhelev, to be Bulgaria's first democratically elected president. By fall, however, the country was beginning to appear ungovernable. The capital was rocked by strikes and protests, and the economy was deteriorating. In November Lukanov resigned.

Zhelev, who was legally charged with nominating the next prime minister, faced a difficult conundrum. Only the BSP had the votes in the Assembly to support a government, but popular opinion found the BSP unacceptable. In the end, Zhelev chose a judge with no particular political pedigree, Dimitar Popov, to form a nonpartisan interim government. Popov himself was opposed to a strategy of "shock therapy," and, indeed, it had no influential proponents in Bulgaria in 1990. As Popov explained years later:

> Bulgaria has specific conditions: There are 2.5 million pensioners, and the electorate is 6.5 million. No one can accept conditions from the IMF that would put 40 percent of the electorate under the subsistence level. We had to carry on a war with the IMF to make it possible to interpret the agreement in a more acceptable way. I am quite familiar with the mechanisms of the IMF, but, for better or

worse, agreements have been signed by different governments, and I think the conditions are very harsh.[1]

Still, there was consensus that reform was necessary and that the eventual goal was a regulated market economy. In addition, there was great hope that substantial aid might be forthcoming from the international community. As one of his first acts, Prime Minister Popov announced that he was opening negotiations with the IMF and that he hoped to receive $3 billion in credits. As he soon discovered, this was an utterly unrealistic goal, given the size of Bulgaria's quota in the Fund.

> The West has been more generous to some. Poland got much larger credits. I had a conversation with Walesa when we signed the abolition of the Warsaw Pact. He said, "Mr. Prime Minister, our friends are not helping." I said, "One month ago they forgave your debt." He said, "They forgive what they know I'll never pay back. I want real money." I said, "I get nothing forgiven." I cannot state my disappointment. It is a question of politics. You never get economic aid or debt forgiveness for itself; it is all based on political considerations and calculations.... It is not lucky to be a small nation, a small state, or the leader of such if you are not the favorite of a big power that wants to help you and make a lot of guarantees.[2]

After two months of negotiations with the IMF, in February the government lifted almost all price controls, and some prices rose as much as 500 to 1,000 percent. In February the Fund approved 60.6 million SDRs under the Contingent and Compensatory Financing Facility to compensate for the collapse in trade in the CMEA, and in March it approved an eighteen-month Stand-by agreement for 279 million SDRs and disbursed the first quarterly tranche.

Popov saw his task primarily as one of guiding Bulgaria through the task of constructing workable democratic institutions. He had firm opinions on numerous issues of constitutional law, and he participated vigorously in the Assembly's work on the constitution. On economic issues, however, his grasp was much less firm. Years later he recounted with pride that his had been a government of consensus, composed of experts rather than politicians, and including representatives from all the major forces in the Assembly: the BSP, the Agrarian Party, and the UDF.[3] With such a heterogeneous group of ministers, no clear reform strategy, and a commitment to govern by consensus, it is unremarkable that very little progress was made in economic reform.

Indeed, the process of economic reform was significantly delayed by the emphasis Popov's government placed on passing a new constitution. This

---

[1] Interview with Dimitar Popov, May 11, 1999.
[2] Ibid.
[3] Ibid.

is an interesting contrast to the cases of Poland and Russia, where constitutional reform was explicitly put off in order to concentrate on economic reform. In those cases, delaying constitutional reform prepared the way for constitutional crises that would later destabilize the economy. In Bulgaria, by contrast, all political efforts in 1991 revolved around the constitutional debate. Whereas other countries went ahead and privatized industry, pausing only later to rewrite their constitutions, Popov was convinced that implementing any of the long-term structural conditions of the IMF program presupposed a legal, constitutional basis. The debate over the constitution in the summer proved long and contentious. The UDF split, and the majority withdrew its support from the government and called for disbanding the Assembly and holding early elections. Each UDF faction accused the other of falling under the influence of the formerly communist BSP. Twenty-three members of the UDF parliamentary delegation declared a hunger strike to protest the new constitution and set up tents outside the Aleksandr Nevsky Cathedral. Quipped Popov:

> I was nominated to be Prime Minister by the UDF. What if I had
> left the government to sit in a tent? Where would we be then? That
> was a fairy tale; it was naïve. The same people now rule the state
> with the same constitution. The question is not whether it was a
> perfect constitution, but how to use it to govern. Thank God we
> stayed to run the country. If we had left, the constitution would not
> have been ratified, there would have been no law on elections, no
> elections, the government would have fallen, and who would have
> been left to govern? Civil war or dictatorship. We remained, passed
> the constitution, the law on elections, and the UDF won and started
> governing.[4]

The Assembly became a lame duck body after the passage of the constitution in July and refused to act on a package of economic reform measures. Elections were held at the end of October under a proportional representation system with a 4 percent threshold, and of the thirty-eight registered parties, three won seats. The UDF, which remained a loose alliance of sixteen political groups, won 110 seats; the BSP, 106; and the Movement for Rights and Freedom (MRF), a liberal Turkish minority party, 24. The UDF formed a minority government with the tacit support of the MRF.

In the fall of 1991, Bulgaria fell behind the conditions of its IMF program. Bulgaria was broadly in line with its macroeconomic targets, but had agreed to begin privatization and introduce a comprehensive system of prudential banking regulations, and no progress had been made on either front. However, the IMF waived the structural conditions in order to give the new Dimitrov government time to come into compliance. Dimitrov announced that his government

[4]Ibid.

would be the "government of privatization." According to Dimitar Kostov, who was then deputy finance minister responsible for relations with the IMF:

> The Fund was always encouraged when there was a change of government in Bulgaria, hoping that the new government would finally carry out some of the difficult measures.... There were promises made to increase the price of electricity, and about oversight in the banking system. The Fund was ready to accept these assurances because there was a new government with sufficient support, which the coalition government had not had. In such a situation it is easier to negotiate with the Fund. I know from experience that when there was a political change, that gave us one more argument to use with the Fund. That solved everything.[5]

Within a few months, however, it became apparent that the Dimitrov government was no more capable of introducing rapid reform than the Popov government had been. It was handicapped by the lack of a majority in parliament and a lack of cohesion among its own deputies. The IMF suspended the Stand-by agreement but immediately began negotiations to launch another one.[6]

In April the IMF approved a new Stand-by and Enlarged Access to Fund resources totaling 124 million SDRs, and began negotiations for a more far-reaching program of reform to be supported by an Extended Fund Facility. Agreement was reached in principle, but the key obstacle to fulfilling the prior conditions for the EFF was that financial discipline be imposed on Bulgarian enterprises in the summer of 1992. Until this point, enterprises had continued to subsist on generous subsidies from the national budget and credits from subsidiaries of the National Bank that were dedicated to servicing their branches of industry. When austerity measures began to be felt in the summer, the unions went out on strike, and the strike rapidly became a national protest movement. The UDF's leadership split on how to respond, and the MRF's support for the government was shaken. The IMF continued to support the government's policies and disbursed a 31 million SDR tranche two months early in August in order to facilitate an agreement between Bulgaria and its creditors. Bulgaria began partial payment of interest in September as a sign of good will and launched negotiations with the London Club to reschedule its $10 billion of commercial debts. When the Dimitrov government fell in October, however, the IMF suspended the Stand-by and discussions about an EFF.[7]

---

[5]Interview with Dimitar Kostov, May 10, 1999.

[6]This is not apparent from the tempo of disbursements, since there was a disbursement in March and another in April when the new program was announced. However, Dimitar Kostov recalls that the IMF suspended the program in an effort to accelerate reform (interview with Kostov, May 10, 1999).

[7]Again, the record of disbursements obscures the causal relationship, since the last disbursement was recorded in January 1993. For technical reasons, disbursements are sometimes made

For the next two months, political life in Bulgaria became a standoff, as neither the UDF nor the BSP was able to form a government. Finally, in December the MRF nominated Lyuben Berov to form another nonpartisan government. Berov had been an economic adviser of President Zhelev, and the president suggested him to the MRF as a possible compromise candidate. The MRF calculated that it would have more influence over a weaker government than over the high-handed UDF government, and it suited the BSP to pull the government's strings quietly and bide its time until it judged that it had a chance to gain from parliamentary elections. Consequently, although Berov was a former member of the UDF, his parliamentary support came primarily from the BSP and the MRF. Seven UDF deputies broke ranks to vote for Berov, and in February the UDF expelled them from the party. Eleven more deputies resigned from the parliamentary faction in protest, and the eighteen former UDF deputies formed the New Union for Democracy, which also supported Berov.

The Berov government was severely constrained, because there was no party it could call its own, and it was forced to cobble together an alliance of convenience. Berov had no political base, so he had no electoral resources with which to threaten or reward his parliamentary supporters. Nor could he use the threat of early elections to compel them to support him, because the Bulgarian constitution did not give him the power to call early elections by resigning. Consequently, Berov pursued a policy of consensus: No important decision was made without the support of all three parliamentary blocs that supported him. As Berov put it, "I never expected an agreement from only one [party faction]. I always had the consent of all three. If just one group said no, the question was closed. I tried to reach consensus on every policy."[8] Since the Berov government's parliamentary support came primarily from the left side of the Bulgarian political spectrum, this meant that economic reform ground to a halt.

Discussions continued between Bulgaria and the IMF, but their positions were far apart. The new finance minister, Stoyan Alexandrov, postured and insisted that Bulgaria would not be dictated to. Berov described this as "just a way for the prime minister to get the word out without actually saying it himself."[9] He pointed to labor activism and demands for wage indexation that would have fueled higher inflation, and he regarded the fact that severe strikes and demonstrations had been avoided as one of his government's main

---

several months after they are approved (interview with Kostov, May 10, 1999). Some of the reasons for the government's fall had nothing to do with economic policy: In October the parliament censured the government for alleged arms sales to Macedonia, and this triggered the vote of no-confidence that brought the government down on October 28. The government fell because the MRF withdrew its support, in part because it had been slighted by the UDF, which refused to bring it into the governing coalition, and in part because of misgivings over the government's austerity program launched in the summer.

[8] Interview with Lyuben Berov, May 15, 1999.

[9] Ibid.

accomplishments. Meanwhile, although the government had inherited a draft budget proposed by the Dimitrov government and was nominally supported by the other two parties in parliament, it took three months of bitter debate finally to pass a budget in June with a deficit of 7.9 percent of GDP. This significantly exceeded the conditions set forth in the IMF program of the previous year.

The main victim of the extended period of instability in Bulgarian politics was the infant Bulgaria reform of banking system in the country, which never developed into a well-regulated or transparent commercial banking sector. The capital requirements to launch a commercial bank were trivial—as low as 5,000 lev, or $150—and the Bulgarian National Bank (BNB) had no capacity to regulate these banks effectively or impose reserve requirements. This, consequently, became the weak link in the economy and the focus of political corruption. Anyone with political influence formed a bank and quickly obtained credits from the BNB; many of these were never repaid. Banks sprang up to manage transactions between state-owned enterprises, and privatization ground to a standstill because it was much more profitable to provide the enterprises' inputs than to privatize them and bear the burden of their weak balance sheets and inefficient production. Political influence allowed the banks to skim the profits from the most profitable enterprises. The banks, in turn, could be turned into hollow shells, and the profits exported as capital flight. As Prime Minister Berov later admitted, "The policy of the BNB was not very normal, but it was very useful if you wanted to become rich: Just take a credit refinanced by the BNB and never pay it back. I don't want to mention names, but I know at least twenty people who made lots of money that way."[10]

At the center of the system of mismanagement and abuse were the and its governor, Todor Vulchev. The BNB had nominal responsibility for supervising the commercial banking sector, and it conducted the policy of refinancing the insolvent state-owned banks and extending lucrative credits to the well connected, including supporters of BSP leader Zhan Videnov. The BNB exceeded the IMF targets for net domestic assets in 1993, putting pressure on the exchange rate and contributing to inflationary pressure. The BNB, however, was in no sense an independent actor in Bulgarian politics. Prime Minister Berov's description of how important decisions were made in monetary policy is instructive, if somewhat misleading:

> The Bank was independent in its policy. I could not order [Vulchev] to do anything, it was entirely up to him whether he wanted to obey. I could only give advice, say what would be good to do; but we were friends, it was not necessary to give him orders.... Every ten days or every week we held a so-called wise men's council. That meeting was between myself, the minister of finance, the head of BNB, the head of Bulbank [the Bank of Foreign Trade], and three or four

[10]Ibid.

other people, perhaps ten people altogether. At those meetings we discussed monetary policy and the state of the market.[11]

The chairman of the BNB could be removed by a vote of parliament. Consequently, that the prime minister consulted with him about monetary policy every ten days suggests that the government had very close control over monetary policy. The atmosphere was collegial, and the influence was exercised gently, but this does not at all imply that the BNB was independent. Rather, it indicates that Vulchev's policy preferences coincided closely with the government's immediate needs, so the government never had to exercise overt coercion.

After the 1992 Stand-by lapsed, more than a year passed without an agreement between Bulgaria and the IMF. Finally, however, an agreement was reached in April 1994. The crucial motivating factor on the Bulgarian side was the need to reschedule the growing national debt. Most of Bulgaria's debt was held by commercial banks, so agreement on rescheduling had to be negotiated with the London Club, and a necessary condition for such an agreement was that Bulgaria make a substantial payment on its interest arrears. Since Bulgaria did not have sufficient international reserves to make such a payment, the linchpin of the agreement had to be international financing from the IMF. As a result, the weak and left-leaning Berov government managed to pass a more austere budget in 1994. With this result in hand, the IMF approved a Stand-by Arrangement for 70 million SDRs and a Systemic Transformation Facility for 116 million SDRs. A currency crisis in the spring of 1994 threatened to derail the agreement, but it does not seem to have served as the political impetus for the agreement, which had been worked out earlier. In June the Berov government survived a vote of no-confidence, and in July it signed an agreement with the London Club to reschedule $8.3 billion of its debt and reduce the principal of the loans by 46 percent.

A few weeks after the agreement was signed, the Berov government resigned. There were reports that IMF officials were furious; the Stand-by and STF presumed a return to political and economic stability, and the London Club agreement had been premised on the assumption that the IMF program would undergird a macroeconomic policy that would gradually return Bulgaria to creditworthiness.[12] Evidently, however, Berov had no choice but to step down. Since at least May his government had been living on borrowed time and had been able to hold off a no-confidence motion only by pointing to the fragility of the debt-rescheduling negotiations. Naturally, these uncertainties had not been shared with the bankers or the Fund. According to Berov:

> The BSP had changed its position. I cannot say I had a spy, but I had my ears in the party and I knew at any moment what had been

[11] Ibid.

[12] Interview with Martin Zaimov, deputy governor, Bulgarian National Bank, May 14, 1999.

discussed at the party conference the previous day. So in April or May 1994 there was a serious change in the position of the BSP: They wanted to take power. A very strong section of the party said "enough of this government, we want to govern by ourselves." The second parliamentary group that supported us—the former members of SDS [UDF]—was very disorganized right from the beginning, so I could not rely much on them. Also, I felt a change in the MRF. In July I was told that there were secret negotiations going on between the Turks [MRF] and SDS. So all three parliamentary groups had changed. There were negotiations about a future vote of no-confidence and it was planned for around the tenth to the fifteenth of September. I was not sure of the support of BSP, SDS, or MRF. So I could tell my task was over. I did not stay and wait for a vote of no-confidence.[13]

From the Fund's perspective, the Berov government had negotiated in bad faith. Nevertheless, the IMF disbursed 93 million SDRs in September to facilitate the complex transactions involved in the debt rescheduling. Immediately thereafter, it suspended Bulgaria's program, and waited to see what elections and a new government would bring to the bargaining table.

8.2 THE ORIGINS OF THE CRISIS, 1995-1996

Again, three months were lost in the campaign for parliamentary elections, in which time the caretaker government of Reneta Indzhova was able to accomplish very little. The elections on December 18 returned a solid majority for the BSP and its allies, the Bulgarian Agrarian Party and the social democratic environmentalist party, Ecoglasnost. Many of the top leaders of the UDF stepped down after their failure at the polls, and this set the stage for the former UDF finance minister, Ivan Kostov, to begin building a cohesive party around a policy of radical economic reform. In the meantime, however, the Bulgarian Socialist Party had returned to power with a solid majority and a four-year mandate. The party leader, thirty-five-year-old Zhan Videnov, became Bulgaria's youngest prime minister. Rumen Gechev, a dedicated Keynesian, became deputy premier and the minister for economic development, and Dimitar Kostov (no relation to Ivan Kostov, but a pragmatic, reform-minded technocrat) was promoted from within the Finance Ministry to be minister of finance. Bulgaria remained firmly committed to the West, pledging to maintain ties with the international financial institutions and continue servicing the national debt. On the other hand, the new government's economic policies were severely constrained by public opinion. Videnov was in no small degree a prisoner of his own successful electoral campaign, since he had run on a populist program

[13]Interview with Berov, May 15, 1999.

and had promised to halt the deterioration of living standards. In January Videnov announced an "anti-crisis" program, which was a union of opposites: He would lower inflation while cutting unemployment, and speed privatization and agricultural reform while strengthening industrial policy. Furthermore, Kostov found that even when he was able to win Videnov's support for fiscal restraint, this failed to guarantee support in parliament. Although it had a majority, the BSP consisted of numerous factions whose economic policy inclinations ran the gamut from reluctant reform to doctrinaire central planning. There was no effective party discipline, so the prime minister was reduced to lobbying his own supporters or inducing them to cooperate with dubious or illegal blandishments.

Minister of Finance Kostov regarded the BSP's electoral program as "populism," full of promises that were "excessively generous." In January these promises were carried over into the initial drafts of the government program. He clashed repeatedly with Gechev but later remarked that even Gechev "was subconsciously aware that the promises were too generous." As a result, the government was willing to make some compromises. "When the government was formed I saw the initial drafts of the government program. What was left at the end was less than one-third of what was originally promised, and it was still too much." The economic policy that Videnov and Gechev promoted looks neo-Keynesian in retrospect, but Kostov emphasizes that when the key decisions were made, the considerations were pragmatic, not ideological. "There is no government in the world," Kostov maintained, "in which theoretical aspects are discussed." The relevant questions were what public opinion would stand for, how severe the economic imbalances were, and how long the government could safely put off painful measures. It was difficult to make the case for urgent reforms, because the Ministry of Finance statistics were one to two quarters behind, "so by the time you got an accurate picture of the situation, it was too late."[14]

Rather than following a conscious economic strategy, the Videnov policy emerged as a series of contradictory compromises. The IMF insisted on liquidating banks and enterprises with weak balance sheets, cutting off loss-making enterprises from state and BNB credits, and cutting the fiscal deficit. The government refused to accept the painful measures the IMF proposed; instead, it continued to pump liquidity into the economy and cushion state-owned enterprises (SOEs) from the consequences of their inefficiency. The labor unions lobbied for higher wages, and the managers of SOEs had no incentive to resist. The inevitable result was that aggregate demand rose, and so did prices. On the other hand, the government had come into office with promises to stop inflation, and price controls were the only instrument that remained to accomplish that. It was not the case, however, that anyone in the government seriously

[14]Interview with Dimitar Kostov, May 10, 1999.

believed that, in the long term, one could overheat the economy and control inflation with price controls.

> This was a political compromise, mainly. Everyone believed that in the transition to a market economy, administered prices wouldn't work. For example, electricity prices had to be doubled in 1995, and we increased them by 20-30 percent. The same happened with the grain harvest. There was fear in the beginning of 1995 that the price of bread would increase from 20 to 50 leva, so there was a decision to import grain and subsidize it. This decision was populist.[15]

The government did not reject dialogue with the IMF; in fact, the dialogue with the new government began immediately and continued throughout the Videnov period. The Videnov government hoped to receive financial support from the IMF just as all previous Bulgarian governments had since 1990. However, in 1995 the government was not willing to compromise enough to reach an agreement, and the IMF insisted on a very dramatic program of structural and fiscal reform as a precondition for agreement. As Kostov explained,

> I think at that time the government was not ready to pay the political price for the necessary measures, because the problems were not yet catastrophic. There was an illusion that it was possible to postpone these measures and negotiate a longer timetable with the IMF. Two or three weeks after the government was formed there was a roundtable with the IMF, the World Bank, and the EBRD, and a discussion of the economy and possible measures. All the problems that led to the crisis a year later were on the table. All [the measures proposed] were met with the argument that they did not satisfy the criterion of political acceptability.[16]

Negotiations with the Fund continued, but Bulgaria was far from meeting the targets of the 1994 program and the IMF was not inclined to revise them. By the end of 1995 the IMF's assessment was that no progress had been made in Bulgaria. The agenda for reform remained essentially as it had been a year before, but privatization and liquidation of inefficient industrial enterprises had become more urgent: These measures were now essential in order to balance the budget and stabilize the currency. The corruption in the banking sector that had been a serious problem under Berov worsened considerably under Videnov, as members of the boards of commercial banks stripped their assets by taking out credits for themselves or their companies that they never intended to repay. As an official in the Ministry of Finance at the time put it:

[15]Ibid.
[16]Ibid.

There had been no real restructuring, the losses of SOEs were refinanced by credits from the commercial banks, and the bad debt
worsened the position of the commercial banks. The more important reason for the bankruptcy was that the banks had been partially
robbed by their shareholders and companies owned by their shareholders. This is to state the matter boldly. They made loans to
shareholders who turned out to be unable to repay the loans; some
of them had never intended to. The reasons were weak financial
discipline, soft budget constraints for SOEs, access to loans from
commercial banks, and ultimately refinancing for the commercial
banks from the BNB. The monetary mass kept increasing, and inflation exceeded forecasts.[17]

Far from making any concrete progress, the parliament was still debating privatization, bank reform, and enterprise restructuring at the end of the year.

For most of 1995 Bulgaria's economic performance seemed to be rebound-
ing, in large part because of the substantial devaluation in the previous year.
By the fall, however, the government's policy of controlling grain prices led
to severe shortages. Meanwhile, the government's high budget deficit drove
up interest rates, forcing it to resort to ever larger amounts of borrowing to
service the debt. The National Bank injected liquidity into the banking system
and bought bonds to support the government, and this put pressure on the market for foreign exchange. Parliamentary debates were held about the country's
"economic crisis," and the opposition pushed motions of no-confidence. Videnov came to the conclusion that Bulgaria had to reach an agreement with the
IMF in order to avert a financial meltdown, and serious negotiations began in
the spring of 1996.

As a condition for a loan, the Fund insisted that a series of steps be taken
to reduce the government's quasi-fiscal deficit, the losses that were made by
state-owned enterprises and covered by state subsidies or bank credits. These
measures formed the cornerstone of the program, because the credits that financed these losses were a major factor that drove the expansionary monetary
policy that had destabilized Bulgarian financial markets. Prominent banks and
enterprises were targeted for closure, and a World Bank Structural Adjustment
Loan that was negotiated in tandem with the IMF program was designed to
finance programs to address the social costs of liquidating them. The World
Bank and the IMF do not always work together smoothly, but in this case they
cooperated closely and presented a common front. In addition, the IMF required that a group of large, state-owned enterprises that were responsible for
making 50 percent of the losses be put on a regime of "isolation." These enterprises would be relieved of the burden of servicing their debts but would be

---

[17]Interview with Plamen Oresharski, May 13, 1999. Oresharski joined the Ministry in 1993 as
Head of the Treasury Department, and has been deputy minister of finance since 1997.

prohibited from receiving any new credits during a one-year "rehabilitation" period. Thereafter, they would be closed if they failed to show a profit.

Financial turmoil worsened during the spring. Lines reappeared for bread for the first time since 1990, and they swiftly spread to banks as panicked citizens raced to withdraw their savings. In May 1996 a serious tremor shook the exchange market. This spurred Videnov to compromise, and he granted authority to negotiate an agreement to an economic adviser, Ivan Angelov, who was sympathetic to the IMF's recommendations. Angelov had become disaffected with the Videnov government as it became increasingly clear that his proposals to speed the pace of reform were being politely ignored, but he stayed on to finish the negotiations because he felt that, without an agreement, Bulgarian financial markets would melt down within weeks. He did not, however, have any expectation that the agreement would be fulfilled. "Videnov led an imitation of reform," he explained. "It was clear to me that the agreement would not be implemented."[18] The IMF's assessment was more optimistic: Anne McGuirk, the head of the IMF Mission to Bulgaria, believed at the time that Videnov was trying to make the necessary changes, but he could not get the support of his party.[19] As if to underscore their unwillingness to commit to the program, all the leading ministers in the government made themselves scarce during the final phase of the negotiations. Videnov himself flew to China for a prearranged state visit. McGuirk cornered Angelov after an unproductive meeting at the BNB and told him that they had a flight booked for 6:00 P.M. the following day. Was there anything further for them to do in Bulgaria? Angelov invited her to a last-minute meeting at the prime minister's office the next morning. He was unable to find a single minister who was able and willing to attend, however.

> I asked the minister of finance to come, but he said he was busy.
> I asked deputy prime minister Gechev, who was supposed to be
> coordinating these meetings, and he said he was leaving in an hour
> for Moscow for a celebration of cultural cooperation. I asked the
> minister of labor and social affairs, and his secretary said he was in
> Cyprus for the opening of a trade fair. I talked to the governor of
> the National Bank, and he said he was leaving for his district to go
> to a secondary school reunion. I was not a minister or a government
> official, but a civil servant, nothing more. I thought that a couple
> people would come from the Fund; I was shocked when twelve or
> thirteen people came from the IMF and the World Bank. I was
> going to meet them in my office, but I found a conference room,
> and we started. Here the country that was supposed to be desperate
> for foreign funding was represented by one person, and he not a

[18] Interview with Ivan Angelov, May 12, 1999.
[19] Interview with Anne McGuirk, May 3, 2000.

government official. Those who were supposed to help us—whom the hardliners called agents of the CIA and world imperialism— were more eager to help us than we were to be helped.[20]

Angelov readily agreed to the IMF's proposals, and he kept Videnov apprised of his progress by telephone, but the cabinet never made a commitment to the agreement. The largest privatization initiative, for example, was to be the Sodi-Devnia Factory, and the minister of industry, Kliment Vuchev, told Angelov at the time that if it were privatized, it would be over his dead body. Considering the dramatic departure from the BSP's program that the agreement represented, it is surprising that the Fund accepted an agreement that had such weak government support. Angelov himself resigned his position as adviser to Videnov the day after the program was signed.[21] Kostov approved of the program, describing it as "intentionally ambitious"; it was intended to restore market confidence, and it was hoped that restored confidence would give the government a breathing space to carry out the necessary reforms. According to Kostov, however, the Fund was not very optimistic that the program would succeed.

> I spoke with Michael Deppler on the phone right after the board voted to approve the program. . . . The assessment of the Fund was that the program had a 50-50 chance of success, but they were will-ing to go ahead with it and give it a chance.[22]

It soon became clear that although the government was willing to accept the program under duress, it was not at all committed to implementing it. The key condition in the 1996 Stand-by agreement was the government's commitment to impose "isolation" on a list of major loss-making enterprises. The deadline for beginning the isolation process was in July, and the government refused to implement it.[23] Meanwhile, the BNB refinanced an ailing bank that had been slated for liquidation.

As if this were not enough, in July the worsening financial crisis forced the Ministry of Finance to take unscheduled credits from the BNB, shattering the IMF condition for central bank net domestic assets. The domestic market for government bonds had been jittery since the crisis in May. The main customers for government bonds were commercial banks, and they received their liquidity from the BNB, so when the BNB contracted liquidity it effectively withdrew

---

[20] Interview with Angelov, May 12, 1999.

[21] Videnov flew to China on May 19. The meeting in the BNB occurred on the next day, Monday, May 20. Angelov's meetings with the IMF Mission began on Tuesday, May 21, and the agreement was signed on Monday, May 27. He resigned the next day, May 28. Angelov's memory for these details is vivid, including the days of the week and the corresponding dates.

[22] Interview with Dimitar Kostov, May 10, 1999.

[23] Interview with Angelov, May 12, 1999.

support from the government bond market. On the other hand, lack of confidence in the exchange rate led holders of hard-currency deposits to withdraw them, which forced the banks to sell bonds to buy foreign currency. Consequently, increasing liquidity also created a drain on the bond market. This would not have been disastrous had it not been for two major foreign loans that came due in July: 200 million Deutschmarks on July 15, and a Brady Bond coupon for $140 million on July 28. The minister of finance, desperate for funds, overrode the objections of the specialists who managed the domestic bond market and flooded the market with bonds. The result was a panic, which prevented the government from selling any more bonds until the end of September. The government's only remaining options were to default on the debts as they came due or borrow from the BNB, so it took a credit from the BNB and violated the program for net domestic assets.[24] At the next review of the program in September, the Fund withheld the second tranche of the Stand-by Arrangement. This triggered the World Bank's decision to reject Bulgaria's application for the Structural Adjustment Loan. According to McGuirk, the Fund might have granted a waiver of the macroeconomic target had Bulgaria been making progress on its structural reform commitments, but the failure on both fronts left no alternative but to suspend the program.[25]

Even as it suspended the 1996 Stand-by, the Fund advanced a bold new proposal for dealing with the Bulgarian crisis: a currency board. A currency board is an institution designed to reinforce a commitment to a fixed exchange rate and to a monetary policy that is completely subordinated to the goal of defending that exchange rate. In principle, adopting a currency board means that the monetary authority is committed to maintaining sufficient international reserves to back the entire domestic money supply at the fixed exchange rate. The only way to increase the money supply under a currency board is to increase international reserves, which can only happen if there are net capital inflows. Operational control over the money supply, the international reserves, and the foreign-exchange market is typically turned over to an independent body, and central bank intervention to support banks and buy government bonds is strictly limited, if permitted at all.

It is an interesting story how the IMF came to promote the idea of a currency board in 1996. Until this point, the Fund's position throughout the 1990s had been very cautious about fixed-exchange-rate regimes. It took the general view that a fixed exchange rate can be a useful tool as a nominal anchor for a dramatic stabilization effort when other nominal targets—such as the money supply and interest rates—are moving too fast to serve. However, fixed exchange rates should eventually give way to sliding pegs and then to managed floating rates. There are two serious problems with fixed exchange rates. First,

---

[24]Interview with Oresharski, May 13, 1999.
[25]Interview with McGuirk, May 3, 2000.

they increase the fragility of a country's financial structure. Fixed exchange rates are used by high-inflation countries to tie their currencies to those of low-inflation countries, so they tend to become overvalued. This increases the risk of holding nominal assets in the fixed currency, so capital can only be attracted by offering high returns. The result is a financial pyramid that can tumble if market confidence is shaken, as investors scramble to convert their assets to foreign currency before the exchange rate changes. Second, fixed rates lead to long-term real exchange rate misalignments if inflation remains higher in the fixed-rate country than abroad; that is, domestic goods and services become uncompetitive if the exchange rate remains fixed and domestic inflation is higher than foreign inflation.[26] For both reasons, Deputy Managing Director Stanley Fischer was critical of fixed-exchange-rate regimes. However, experience had gradually convinced Fund officials that fixed exchange rates were potent tools for stabilization in extreme circumstances. The Fund had initially discouraged Estonia from instituting a currency board regime, but Estonia persisted and subsequently emerged as one of the most successful reformers in Eastern Europe. After facing hyperinflation, Argentina had just completed a successful stabilization under President Menem by adopting a currency board (an example that appeared more convincing in the mid-nineties than it does in 2002). In 1996 Russia's experiment with a fixed exchange rate had dramatically reduced inflation and appeared to be a success. Still, the Fund was not ready to push Bulgaria to adopt a currency board in September. Fund officials floated the idea at a seminar during the Annual Meeting of the IMF and the World Bank, and Dimitar Kostov's impression at the time was that Michael Deppler, the head of the IMF's Europe II department, was cautiously open to the idea rather than actively supportive.

> Originally we had an informal meeting with the head of the European II department. Alan someone—a deputy of Russo's—had worked in Estonia, and he made a presentation. We had questions about the currency board. How will it work? How will it change our policy instruments? Russo and Deppler had similar questions. At one point, Deppler said to me, "You understand, this is new for us, too, but we would like to explore it."[27]

McGuirk describes the position of Michael Deppler and the Europe I division rather differently: They fully supported the proposal at this point, but there

---

[26]If the lev is fixed to the Deutschmark and the domestic price level in Bulgaria has risen faster than the price level in Germany, then, correcting for inflation, the lev has appreciated in value against the Deutschmark. This is called a real exchange rate appreciation. This has, in fact, occurred since 1997.

[27]Interview with Dimitar Kostov, May 10, 1999. The person who made the presentation was Adam Bennett, who had been the IMF resident representative in Estonia when it adopted a currency board (interview with McGuirk, May 3, 2000).

was not yet complete consensus within the IMF. The main resistance within the Fund came from the Monetary and Exchange Department (MAE), which argued that the Bulgaria!banking crisis had to be resolved before a currency board could be introduced, since the currency board contained no provision for a lender of last resort. The Europe I Department, on the other hand, argued that it was impossible to clean up the banking system until a credible budget constraint was imposed, and this would be impossible without a currency board. In the end, the currency board was set up to allow the BNB to engage in a limited amount of intervention in the banking sector and a limited amount of financing for the state sector.[28]

Initially the Bulgarian reaction to the currency board proposal was vigorous opposition from all sides of the political spectrum. Dimitar Kostov went on to say, "I talked on the phone with Videnov right after that. He said, 'We are not a government to be involved with a currency board.' It would mean a loss of sovereignty over monetary policy. It had historically been used in colonial countries."[29] The UDF leader, Ivan Kostov, had the same initial reaction.[30] Bulgarians of all political stripes are now eager to claim credit for the currency board, so it is difficult to untangle the self-promoting stories. A few details, however, are clear. Dimitar Kostov came to support the idea early on, and it was he who convinced Gechev and Videnov to accept it.[31] He had become convinced that Bulgaria did not have the foreign or fiscal reserves to weather the crisis without a dramatic improvement in market expectations, which could only be brought about by adopting a currency board, and that trying to halt the crisis simply by tightening monetary policy would devastate the banking sector. Furthermore, he saw the currency board as the only way to tie the parliament's hands and compel it to exercise fiscal restraint. Early in the fall Michael Deppler became convinced that a currency board was the only way to reverse the Bulgarian lev's slide, and he formally proposed it in a visit to Sofia in October. By the following month it had become a condition for large-scale IMF support, and it appears that Kostov's support within the government convinced the IMF that it could insist on the adoption of a currency board. Several members of the board of the BNB also supported the proposal. In Kostov's view, Videnov was swayed by the argument that the IMF would not support

[28] Interview with McGuirk, May 3, 2000.

[29] Interview with Dimitar Kostov, May 10, 1999.

[30] Ivan Kostov came to support the proposal within months, and the currency board became a central plank of the opposition program in January. His initial opposition, however, reflected the suspicion that the current government would simply discredit the idea of a currency board because of the way it would implement it, and may also have been colored by the instinctive response of the opposition to all government proposals. It is significant, however, that the currency board was accepted by the BSP and would have been adopted by any of the possible Bulgarian governments in 1997–Videnov's, Dobrev's, Sofiyanski's, or Kostov's.

[31] Interviews with Dimitar Kostov, May 10, 1999; with Oresharski, May 13, 1999; and with McGuirk, May 3, 2000.

Bulgaria unless a currency board were adopted, but he finally came to support it when he decided it was the only way to save the BSP government, which had become increasingly precarious as the crisis deepened. By adopting a currency board the government could implement the necessary measures to alleviate the economic crisis, and Videnov hoped it would be possible to distance the government from some of the political fallout by delegating power.[32] For practical purposes, the decision to adopt a currency board had been made by the BSP government, and the opposition only took up the cry afterward. When it was finally implemented, therefore, the currency board had the support of every major political actor in the country.

In the late fall the strategy of controlling inflation with price controls struck back with a vengeance. Subsidized prices, short supplies of basic foodstuffs because of a poor harvest, and self-fulfilling fears of shortages led to hoarding and the disappearance of important consumer goods from store shelves. The harsh winter of 1996-97 prompted the coining of a new term in Bulgarian, the *Videnov winter*. Market confidence plunged, and in November and December the lev fell from 240 to the dollar to 500 to the dollar. Inflation surged to an annual rate of 311 percent. His popularity in tatters, Videnov now found that his support within the BSP had quietly melted away. Preempting the inevitable, he resigned from his government and party posts at a party conference in December. It quickly proved impossible for the BSP to contain the damage by changing leaders, however. For the second time the BSP found itself armed with a solid parliamentary majority but helpless in the face of a population in uproar. The opposition in the parliament introduced a motion calling for a "Declaration of National Salvation," which would dismiss the board of the BNB, launch negotiations with the IMF to set up a currency board, dissolve the parliament, and hold early elections. As many as 40,000 demonstrators gathered outside the parliament, and demonstrations spread across the country within days. When the BSP blocked a vote on the Declaration, the UDF, People's Union, and MRF walked out of the parliament, and the demonstrators reacted by surrounding and then attempting to storm the parliament building. The newly elected president, Petar Stoyanov, at first seemed to refuse to offer the BSP a mandate to form a government—which would have been a violation of the constitution, since the BSP was the largest party in the parliament—and then finally offered a mandate but urged the BSP not to exercise it. Meanwhile, daily protests had grown to include as many as 200,000 demonstrators. Nikolay Dobrev, the new BSP leader, went as far as announcing a lineup for his new proposed government before finally agreeing to call early elections and allow Stoyanov to appoint a caretaker government. As political uncertainty continued to prevail, the lev fell from 500 to the dollar in January to 1,600 to the dollar in February.

[32]Interview with Dimitar Kostov, May 10, 1999.

8.3 CONSOLIDATION UNDER THE CURRENCY BOARD

The appointment of Sofia's mayor, Stefan Sofiyanski (UDF), as a caretaker prime minister and the announcement of the imminent creation of a currency board to manage Bulgarian monetary policy stabilized the situation with shocking suddenness. By March 15 the BNB was able to declare that the lev was fixed at 1,000 to the German mark, and the market stopped testing its resolve. The Sofiyanski government carried out the negotiations with the IMF for a new Stand-by Arrangement and implemented many of the necessary prior conditions. The IMF ordinarily refuses to negotiate with caretaker governments, since they have limited tenure and no guarantee of parliamentary support. In this case, however, it was clear that a unique breakthrough had occurred in Bulgarian politics and that swift action would be required to capitalize on the opportunity before the deepening crisis swept it away. In addition, it seemed clear that the UDF would carry the elections in April, and the Sofiyanski government was working closely with the UDF. The deputy premier assigned to negotiate the Stand-by Arrangement, Krassimir Angarski, had worked in the Ministry of Finance under Ivan Kostov in the Dimitrov government, and they had maintained a close working relationship. Angarski reported that he kept Kostov apprised of the progress of the negotiations and included him in two delegations to Washington.

> We became collaborators. When we were designing the currency board arrangement, he had full trust in me, and accepted everything that I suggested.... This was a very important part of guaranteeing that the then-opposition party would fully accept the currency board arrangement. We gave such guarantees. The SDS [UDF] made a preelection statement of support for a currency board. Otherwise, the Fund would not have agreed.[33]

The Sofiyanski government operated in a unique environment in Bulgarian politics. The sense of crisis in early 1997 was so intense that old enemies found themselves agreeing on radical reforms that neither the Left nor the Right would have proposed a year before. Virtually every week the new government made a decision that satisfied one of the Fund's thirteen prior conditions for an agreement. Angarski recalls that the IMF resident representative to Bulgaria was in his office every day, and that every major government decision was immediately transmitted to the Fund.

For a brief time it seemed that ordinary political constraints did not apply, and momentous decisions were rushed through in a feverish atmosphere.

> Three lawyers and I met in my office every day from 9:00 A.M. to 9:00 P.M., and we wrote the ninety-nine articles of the law [on the

[33] Interview with Krassimir Angarski, May 14, 1999.

Currency Board]. We wrote another law with fifty-six articles on the BNB. They passed unanimously, with one abstention. There are no other cases of laws passing this way. These were contentious issues, and we were heavily attacked, but I convinced all the advisers in the parliament—the professors—and also consulted a wide range of representatives of all the political forces. The politicians were more concerned with the upcoming elections. When they started to attack me in the parliament, I said, "Talk to your own experts, they have signed on."[34]

Meanwhile, Ivan Kostov capitalized on the sense of crisis in the country to reorganize the UDF into a cohesive, programmatic party and, after a brief campaign, won an overwhelming victory in April. The National Assembly's first act was to approve the Declaration of National Salvation, which called for a currency board, restitution of land, opening secret police files, and membership in the European Union and NATO. In May Kostov formed the first Bulgarian government with a majority in parliament and a programmatic commitment to reform.

The Kostov government introduced sweeping changes in macroeconomic policy. In order to make the currency board work, the government had to achieve a substantial primary surplus—that is, a government budget surplus before paying interest on the national debt—and the combination of the highly charged atmosphere of 1997, the UDF majority, and the new cohesiveness of the party made this feasible. The reduced supply of government bonds and the symbolic commitment to the fixed lev, meanwhile, pushed down interest rates on domestic borrowing. As a result, the government was able to collect a surplus of 1 percent of GDP in 1998, which it deposited in the BNB. The BNB's policy shifted dramatically, as well. The institutional provisions of the Law on the Currency Board would not really prevent the BNB from manipulating the money supply were it so inclined. For one thing, it could manipulate reserve requirements for commercial banks to inject liquidity into the economy. There are various ways to move accounts around which, although formally permissible, would inflate the economy. There were still state-owned banks, and these could be used to issue credits to favored enterprises. To the IMF representative in Sofia, it was clear that there were plenty of loopholes that a wily banker could use to sabotage the system.[35] However, the psychological effect of introducing the currency board had been to convince everyone in Bulgarian politics that these levers were no longer available. By publicly betting the stability of the economy on a fixed lev, the government and the BNB had found a commitment device that was credible. Although technically capable

[34] Ibid.

[35] Interview with Peter Stella, May 12, 1999. Stella had been IMF resident representative to Bulgaria since January 1998.

of cheating, they were deterred by the enormity of the consequences if it ever became impossible to defend the fixed rate. The result would not simply be a devaluation—which in itself might or might not be desirable—but the shattering of the hard-won credibility of the National Bank and of the program of the governing party.

The IMF representative in Bulgaria gave the country's macroeconomic policy high marks.

> We have made a lot of mistakes, and right now Bulgaria looks like a shining example of success. It's really the Bulgarians' success, but we are happy to take some of the credit. Their performance has really been very good, though. If you compare Bulgaria to Russia, Bulgaria looks great. It's not barely meeting, or failing to meet, symbolic conditions; it has really ambitious conditions, and it is meeting them pretty consistently, and overshooting in some cases. If we were to suspend a tranche right now, it would be for tactical reasons, because we were trying to underscore the importance of some area of disagreement, not for strategic reasons.[36]

Even the new government, however, found it impossible to move rapidly to privatize key loss-making enterprises. Deputy Prime Minister Alexander Bozhkov boasted, on taking office, that 40 percent of state enterprises would be privatized by the end of 1997. However, Kostov decided to proceed more slowly. He calculated that the government could get better prices for enterprises after a period of macroeconomic consolidation, since a period of stability under the currency board would reduce the exchange-rate risk involved in investing in Bulgaria.[37]   A more important consideration, however, was that a key component of the UDF coalition was the Podkrepa labor union, whose leadership adamantly opposed privatization because it would lead to downsizing, liquidation, and an end to subsidized wages. As it turned out, however, waiting even a few months in the summer of 1997 could prove to be a serious mistake. By August the first tremors of the Asian crisis were being felt in emerging markets around the world, and investor interest in Bulgaria dried up. As the year rolled on the international economic news went from bad to worse, and in 1998 the Russian crisis cast a new pall over post-Communist markets.

The economic results for 1997 appeared disastrous even by the end of the year: GDP was down 7.4 percent, unemployment reached 13.7 percent, and inflation for the year was 579 percent. The crisis did its damage in the beginning of the year, however. After May the government closed the budget deficit and launched a series of initiatives to promote structural reform, and stability reasserted itself. All the conditions of the Stand-by agreement were fully met.

---

[36] Ibid.
[37] Interview with Angarski, May 14, 1999.

In September 1998 the IMF ratified Bulgaria's progress by approving a three-year Extended Fund Facility for 627 million SDRs. The program's conditions were extraordinarily ambitious. They required that the fiscal deficit remain below 2 percent of GDP and the current account deficit below 3 percent of GDP for 1999 through 2001, that banks and enterprises be privatized, that annual inflation drop to 5 percent by 2001, that public and foreign debt decline, and that Bulgaria liberalize its energy and agriculture sectors and foreign trade. Finally, Bulgaria agreed to adopt Article VIII obligations to liberalize its current account. Within six months, however, it became clear that Bulgaria would not meet all the conditions of the program. Privatization and bankruptcy proceedings lagged far behind schedule. The otherwise sanguine IMF representative worried that the failure to restructure industry in 1997 and 1998, when the political and economic costs were lower, might yet destabilize the Bulgarian economy.

> Restructuring is the major problem. Much of it still has not been tackled. There are lots of inefficient enterprises. They need to privatize them. We aren't arguing much about the price now, because the budget doesn't really need the funds anymore; they just need to bring in effective owners. Then there will be downsizing, and a lot of jobs will be lost, and there will be a painful transition period, but in the end you will have productive firms. If this is not done soon— well, it should have been done a year ago, but let's talk about the present—then it will be too late. Right now the government has the funds; they can even compensate for restructuring by making infrastructure investments and paying severance, because there is a budget surplus up through April. In a couple of years the losses will be a lot higher, and they won't have the money anymore. Then there will be an economic crash, and the currency board will turn out to be a failure and not a success after all.[38]

For most of 1999, foreign investment was largely frozen by the uncertainty surrounding the NATO bombing of Serbia over Kosovo, with all its potential for instability to spill over into neighboring countries in the Balkans. The case of the Kremikovtsi steelworks on the outskirts of Sofia is typical. The government was compelled to reduce its asking price repeatedly, until by 1999 it was offering to sell the enterprise to a Turkish consortium for 1 lev and bargaining about whether the consortium would be obligated to repay any of the enterprise's debts. Meanwhile, workers demonstrated against the deal, and the government's bargaining position was constantly in flux. Two years later, the enterprise was finally sold to another consortium under approximately the same terms.

[38] Interview with Stella, May 12, 1999.

Looking back from the perspective of 2002, the IMF resident representative's warning appears prophetic. The currency board succeeded in its immediate objective of stabilizing the currency and sharply reducing inflation. However, over the next four years, the majority UDF government made only slow progress in privatizing state-owned enterprises, restructuring industry, and reforming the banking sector, and made no progress at all in reducing corruption. Indeed, Bozhkov himself was fired amidst allegations of widespread corruption. Meanwhile, the inevitable consequences of fixed exchange rates caught up with Bulgaria: The exchange rate became overvalued in real terms, Bulgarian industry lost competitiveness, and the economy moved into recession. Elections in 2001 rendered a negative verdict on both the UDF and the BSP, and brought the Bulgarian King Simeon back from exile to be prime minister. Like Ukraine and Russia, Bulgaria demonstrates how recalcitrant the challenge of structural reform becomes when it is repeatedly delayed. Politically expedient decisions made early in the transition sow the seeds of intractable dilemmas that emerge later.

8.4 CONCLUSIONS

Bulgaria's transition was extended and painful because its fractious parliament was unable to form a majority government until 1995, and its largest party until 1997 was the rather unreformed Bulgarian Socialist Party. The BSP was much further to the Left than the post-Communist parties of Poland and Hungary, and its major economic policy objective was to prevent dramatic restructuring of Bulgarian industry. It was not until the financial crisis of 1996 that Bulgaria was finally able to break the cycle of partial reform. The crisis brought down the Videnov government and destroyed the BSP's electoral base. It galvanized Bulgarian elites to rally around economic reform, making it possible in 1997—indeed, almost unavoidable—for the parliament to adopt a highly restrictive currency board arrangement and insulate the Bulgarian National Bank from political manipulation. The crisis allowed Ivan Kostov to build the UDF into a new political party, which for the first time had a unified program and internal discipline, which made it possible to implement politically costly reforms. Bulgaria's success after 1997 was as overdetermined as its failure before.

Throughout the story, Bulgaria's economic policy was a hostage to financial markets. It was the need to reopen access to international capital flows that drove successive reluctant Bulgarian governments to embrace IMF agreements, which were a precondition for rescheduling Bulgaria's foreign debt. Crises on the currency market drove the Berov and Videnov governments to compromises with the Fund that they had never contemplated and finally created the consensus that a currency board was needed to commit Bulgaria to macroeconomic orthodoxy. Bulgarian policy has been much more tightly constrained under the currency board, because a small shift in fiscal or monetary policy could lead to a rapid erosion of foreign reserves and a run on the currency. Since the nominal value of the lev figures so prominently in Bulgarian policy, the impact on market expectations of a currency crisis would be severe, leading to a burst of inflation and perhaps forcing a dramatic correction in the exchange rate. The consequence has been a stunning reversal of Bulgarian economic policy.

The fractious parliament and left-leaning governments of Bulgaria were never committed to reform efforts; instead, they were dragged along by market pressure and the need for international aid. Consequently, it was not until 1997 that an IMF program was fully implemented. Even then, the persistent opposition to structural reform continually threatened to derail the program and may yet jeopardize its outcome. The Fund exercised some influence in Bulgaria all along the way, however, and the constraints it imposed on fiscal policy helped Bulgaria to avoid hyperinflation. When Bulgarian programs went offtrack, the Fund was very consistent in its policy and suspended them. There were two cases where it appears that political instability itself entered into the Fund's calculations, causing the IMF to suspend programs that were in the gray area after the Dimitrov and Berov governments fell. On the whole, however, the evidence is that the Fund was able to play a nonpartisan, technocratic role in Bulgaria that it never achieved in some of the other countries in this study. The payoff for this consistency came in 1997, in the dramatic response of the foreign exchange market to the Fund-supported currency board. Fund intervention in Russia and Ukraine in 1998 was on a much larger scale, but was less effective because it had become clear that IMF programs did not significantly change the governments' incentives in those countries.

9

Conclusion

THERE WAS NO policy issue facing the leaders of former Communist countries in the 1990s more important than inflation. As the previous chapters have shown, the politics of inflation—with all its budgetary implications, distributional consequences and financial ramifications—occupies center stage during the transition. In turn, the alliances forged and the choices made during the struggle that all these countries have waged against inflation have imprinted themselves on the political systems of the region. From starting points that were more remarkable for their similarities than for their differences, the post-Communist countries have developed into democracies, authoritarian dictatorships, and numerous chimerical hybrids that are not quite either. In some countries economic crisis has helped to consolidate strong democratic institutions, and in others it has undermined them. The former Communist countries have become prosperous, rapidly growing success stories, and shambling, stagnating backwaters. In the end, everyone managed to control inflation. In the meantime, some of the post-Communist states reduced their populations to poverty and opened vast gulfs between the newly wealthy and the newly impoverished, while others laid the groundwork for rapid growth, raised their peoples' living standards, and maintained much greater parity between rich and poor.

This book maintains that an international institution, the International Monetary Fund, played a key role in shaping these fateful choices. Fund staff made tactical errors at times, but the overall thrust of IMF advice was sound: Prioritize the fight against inflation. The countries that did so suffered smaller declines in output, resumed growing sooner, attracted more foreign investment, improved living standards, and maintained more equal distributions of income. The result was more stable and civil political systems and the consolidation of democracy. One has only to compare Russia to Poland, or Ukraine to Russia, to see the costs of deferring the struggle to reduce inflation.

Inflation arises primarily because policymakers succumb to the temptation to defer hard choices. International capital markets punish inflationary policies, so there are long-term incentives to avoid them. However, the pressure of short-term considerations can be overwhelming, particularly when elections draw near or coalition partners grow restive. In this context, the International Monetary Fund is able to exert a striking influence over countries' domestic policies by shifting the balance of incentives to favor long-term strategies and leveraging the weight of international capital markets. The Fund is influential because countries that turn to it do not perceive it as compelling them to act against their interests; rather, they believe that it induces them to pursue their long-term interests rather than the short-term interests of their ruling coalitions. When the proper conjunction of circumstances arises, the IMF can exert a very strong influence over the choice of national economic policies.

This applies with one very substantial caveat: The IMF is itself a flawed institution, whose deliberations are politicized and subject to ratification by its major donor countries. Consequently, the credibility of its threat to enforce countries' policy commitments is subject to question and political manipulation. Since countries with significant leverage in the international system are able to appeal the IMF's decisions to higher authority, their commitments are less binding; the IMF is therefore less able to shift the balance of incentives toward fiscal and monetary restraint, and international investors are more cautious about becoming involved. This implies, ironically, that the IMF will be least effective precisely in the countries that are most important.

This book argues that the IMF can lend credibility in spite of its own credibility problem. Human society contains nothing but flawed institutions; yet some of them exert tremendous influence in spite of their imperfections. However, it is essential to take the IMF's credibility problem into account in order to understand the effects of its intervention. If we look for a uniform effect across countries, we are unlikely to find one. Looking for an effect that varies as a function of the IMF's credibility, however, I find striking evidence that the IMF influences the policies of the countries with which it interacts.

9.1 RESEARCH DESIGN

I argued in chapter 1 that it is insufficient to catalogue the instances of compliance with Fund conditions and deviation from them or to compare levels of inflation before and after Fund programs in order to assess the IMF's impact. In order to do that, we have to construct a counterfactual: What would have happened in the absence of the IMF? Since we cannot rerun history, I argued that the best way to construct this counterfactual is to combine several modes of analysis that answer different parts of the question. First, I used a game-theoretic model to formalize my intuitions about how the IMF can exert influence, how the presence of international investors magnifies that influence, and how credibility concerns influence the strategies of the IMF, the borrowers, and the investors. The model answers the questions, "Is it possible for the IMF to exert influence without being able to send credible signals?" and "Is it possible to apply different enforcement regimes to different countries in order to maintain a reputation for enforcing rules?" Second, I used statistical analysis of twenty-six countries over time to test key hypotheses drawn from the model. Statistical analysis answers the questions, "Are the theoretical expectations of the model consistent with empirical evidence?" and "Are the conclusions generalizable?" Third, I conducted participant interviews in four countries and at the IMF with officials directly involved in the negotiation, implementation, and monitoring of conditionality agreements. Wide-ranging interviews allowed me to explore the actors' expectations and the logic of strategic interaction, and to compare the participants' experiences to the strategies and expectations specified in the game-theoretic model. In addition, they allowed me to determine what the actors believed to be the effects of the central causal variables in my analysis. Qualitative research, then, answers the question, "Is the causal story represented by the theoretical model and the statistical correlations plausible to those who are in the best position to know?"

Without any one of these methodological supports, social science research becomes unreliable, like a stool with only two legs. Statistical analysis not guided by theory is unreliable, because relationships are misspecified and there are no strong prior beliefs about the direction of causation. Qualitative analysis by itself can generate a prima facie case for causation by tracing the causal pathways and teasing out causal stories that fit a few cases, but it cannot establish the generality of its conclusions, and it cannot falsify hypotheses. Formal theory without empirical testing can only generate hypotheses and establish the logical consistency of conclusions with assumptions; it cannot establish the empirical validity of the assumptions or the real-world relevance of the results. Furthermore, without contextual knowledge, formal theory and statistical analysis may miss the key causal variables, making their conclusions unreliable in the best case and irrelevant in the worst. When they are combined, however, these three modes of inquiry supply one another's defects. The result is a rigorous, testable, generalizable social science that is relevant to real-world concerns, because it is grounded in the details of real cases.

Part I: Models and Data

The microfoundations of the theory are rational actors making choices based on the best available information. The IMF, the borrowing governments, and international investors all have objectives they seek to achieve, form rational expectations about how the others will seek to achieve their objectives, and choose strategies that will allow them to achieve their objectives to the greatest extent possible. This is necessarily a simplification of the real world. For example, in the model it is impossible for anyone to be naïve (although it is possible for someone to be tricked). However, this simplification is justifiable, because it makes it possible to use the tools of game theory to analyze the complex strategic interactions that arise among borrowing countries, the IMF, and international investors. Historical actors often do not make optimal choices; but the best way to analyze strategic interaction is to model what happens when they do. The results represent the best possible way to play the game, which is the best available approximation of what an experienced and talented politician might decide to do when the stakes are high.

The model has a number of novel results. It makes very conservative assumptions about the IMF's resources: In particular, it gives the IMF no information advantage over international investors and does not allow the Fund to send meaningful signals, so the only resource at the IMF's disposal is the value of the loans it can disburse or withhold. Furthermore, by assuming that it is costly to withhold loans, it builds a credibility problem into the Fund's commitment to enforce conditionality. Nevertheless, the model finds that the IMF is able to build a reputation for enforcing commitments to anti-inflationary policies. The IMF finds that it cannot credibly threaten to punish large countries for as long as it can punish small countries, so it uses different punishment regimes. Nevertheless, despite the fact that countries often cheat, and that the IMF treats larger countries more leniently than smaller ones, the Fund often does deter inflationary policies. Furthermore, international investors adapt their investment decisions to the IMF's strategies even though they know that the Fund does not have any information that they do not share. The most striking prediction of the model is that smaller countries will be subject to longer punishment periods than larger countries, but that larger countries, since they are harder to deter, will cheat more often and consequently be punished more often than smaller ones.

To date, the quantitative research on the effectiveness of IMF programs has all been based on one fallacious assumption: that the IMF exerts its influence when a program is in place, and not otherwise. Consequently, a large literature has grown up around before-after and control-group comparisons that take the negotiation of an IMF program as a treatment. The game-theoretic model I develop makes no such assumption; rather, a game-theoretic perspective turns attention to the incentives a country has to please the IMF before an agreement is reached or while an agreement is in abeyance, as well as when an agreement is in place. Consequently, a before-after or control-group approach would not be an appropriate test of the model. Fortunately, the model identifies another dimension of variation that should affect countries' policies: the credibility of IMF threats to enforce long punishments. The quantitative analysis reported in chapter 4 demonstrates that measures of a country's international influence, particularly commitments of U.S. foreign aid, are strongly associated with shorter punishment intervals and more frequent punishments. Moreover, it shows that countries that receive more U.S. foreign aid and that are subject to shorter punishment intervals suffer higher inflation rates, expand liquidity more rapidly, and experience more exchange-rate devaluation. These results are statistically significant and substantively very strong, from which we may infer that the IMF exerts a very important downward pressure on inflation when it is able to credibly commit to enforcing its conditions and that its inability to enforce agreements with some of the largest post-Communist countries was an important reason for their high levels of inflation. In addition, the results support counterintuitive implications of the model: that policy deteriorates when the IMF suspends a program, and that this effect is most striking for the smaller, less influential countries that the IMF ordinarily is best able to deter. The quantitative evidence strongly supports the expectations of the game-theoretic model.

Part II: History

The stories told in the last four chapters of the book form a rich melange of institutions, individuals, and forces operating at numerous levels of causation: in transition economies, on international capital markets, within domestic public opinion, and among the G-7 countries. On center stage are the interactions among the IMF, the borrowing countries, and international capital markets, with the major donor countries playing an important role in the background. Clearly, however, the complexity of the stories points to elements that are left out in the stylized formal model with which this book began and in the similarly simplified statistical model that was developed to test it. For example, the formal model assumes that a unitary rational actor chooses economic policy; the case studies, on the other hand, direct attention to executive-legislative relations and important interest groups. Whether this is a problem depends on how one views the purpose of a model. The model assumes that there are domestic constraints but does not attempt to explain where they come from, so they are simply represented by parameters. Instead, the model is designed to shed light on the strategic interaction among borrowing countries, the IMF, and capital markets. It does this well; I leave for the future the task of modeling the domestic level of the interaction explicitly.

The four country cases provide a wide range on the central independent variable, international influence. The theoretical expectation was that the process of negotiation with the IMF should vary according to the international status of the borrowing country, and should be very different in Russia and Ukraine than in Poland and Bulgaria. This was strongly borne out by the case studies. Russia, and Ukraine by 1996, were able to avoid the rigorous application of IMF conditionality. Program suspensions occurred frequently but were very brief, and they were generally resolved by IMF concessions on conditions rather than by dramatic new policy corrections on the part of the countries. Because the IMF applied its standards inconsistently, Russian and Ukrainian officials perceived that they could afford to defer policy adjustments that would be politically damaging or harmful to influential lobbies. Furthermore, both Russian and Ukrainian officials pointed to their special relationship with the United States as the key reason why they could afford to flout IMF conditions. The case studies also highlighted an evolution over time in the IMF's relations with the two largest countries: As U.S. relations with Russia gradually soured, particularly in 1999, the IMF began taking a firmer line, and as U.S. relations with Ukraine warmed after the agreement on dismantling the Ukrainian nuclear arsenal in 1995, the IMF became more lenient. Poland and Bulgaria, on the other hand, never doubted that they would be subject to the full force of IMF conditionality, and when they deviated from their program targets, the Fund insisted that they achieve them before it would renew financing. Officials from both countries believed it was unrealistic to expect the United States to intervene with the IMF on their behalf, although they were quite aware that it did so for Russia and Ukraine. As a result, Polish and Bulgarian officials perceived the IMF as a much more tangible constraint on their economic policies.

The case studies suggest that the theoretical model has the main calculations and strategies of the players right. For IMF officials, suspending a program was always a painful decision. A country's ability to repay the Fund never figured significantly in the decision, except insofar as that was one of the considerations involved in designing a program with coherent conditions. Consequently, renewing a program could not be interpreted as taking a risk, so it could not constitute a costly signal. Furthermore, IMF officials were aware that if they suspended a program, the country's response in the short term would likely be to adopt worse policies rather than better ones. However, Fund officials were acutely aware of their credibility problem, so decisions to suspend or renew programs were generally cast in that light. IMF officials thought in terms of the effects of their strategies on third countries, and they frequently referred to the danger that leniency toward one country could become a precedent for others.

The case studies also serve to underscore the importance of the relationship between the IMF and international capital markets. Russia, Ukraine, and Bulgaria each faced financial crises, and in each case dramatic exchange-rate movements became the impetus for sweeping reforms. The role of the IMF was generally recognized as catalytic: It helped to reinforce and render credible the authorities' desire to push forward with reform, but the primary impetus for reform was to attract the favor of international capital markets and staunch the export of capital by residents. Those markets, in turn, did indeed respond to IMF intervention, as the model predicts: Countries have increased incentives to restrain inflation when a program is in good standing, and markets update their expectations about the likelihood of inflationary policies to reflect this. Moreover, as the model predicts, this effect was much more potent in Bulgaria than in Russia or Ukraine, where extraordinary levels of intervention in 1998 could not forestall the meltdown of financial markets. In contrast, IMF support for the introduction of a currency board in Bulgaria in 1997 reversed the trend of market expectations virtually overnight.

Finally, the case studies cast some of the conclusions of the quantitative analysis in a different light. It seemed puzzling that the left-right policy preferences of governments did not have the strong effect expected on economic policy; however, the case studies generally upheld this conclusion. Left-wing governments were not much more profligate than right-wing governments. Poland is an extraordinary example of continuity, but, in fact, continuity has been the rule rather than the exception when coalitions changed. The most dramatic contrary example was in Bulgaria, but there economic crisis, a majority-party government, and dramatic institutional changes in the National Bank coincided with the shift to conservative power, so it is hard to ascribe the shift in policy in 1997 to a single factor.

9.2 POLICY IMPLICATIONS

The analysis and evidence presented in this book lead to three conclusions that cut against the grain of commonly accepted assumptions. The first concerns strategies of economic reform; the second concerns the role of international institutions in U.S. foreign policy; and the third concerns the appropriate reforms to the international institutions, particularly the IMF.

Strategies of Economic Reform

It has become fashionable to view the spectacular decline of Russia in the 1990s as an indictment of the strategy of "shock therapy," of a U.S. foreign policy based on encouraging rapid market reforms, and of the neoliberal advice offered by international institutions. As chapter 6 shows, this analysis is based on the mistaken assumption that Russia pursued shock therapy. In fact, Russia never consistently followed neoliberal policy advice, whether from the IMF, the U.S. government, or any other source. The initial stabilization policies were only pursued for four months in the beginning of 1992; thereafter, Russian policy oscillated between periods of reckless inflationary policies and short-lived policy corrections to avert hyperinflation. The result was the worst of both worlds: all the decline, poverty, and inequality associated with high inflation and all the social and political instability associated with efforts to contain inflation. When Russia finally stabilized its prices and exchange rate in 1995, it ignored IMF advice to rein in its budget deficit, a decision that ultimately led to the financial crash of 1998. As the country comparisons show, other paths could have been taken, some better than Russia's, some worse. A decade of experience in twenty-six post-Communist countries makes it clear that countries that brought inflation down rapidly during the transition suffered less economic decline and resumed growing faster, attracted more foreign investment, maintained higher living standards for their populations, and developed less inequality. The jury is in on economic reform, and the verdict is, the faster the better.

International Institutions

Can an international institution like the IMF be an effective instrument for encouraging sovereign nations to adopt a particular kind of economic policy? The evidence shows that it can, with one important caveat: The Fund cannot credibly commit to enforcing rigorous conditionality on influential countries. The quantitative evidence on the effects of Fund intervention presented in Chapter 4 demonstrates the effects of variations in Fund credibility on macroeconomic variables. It shows, for example, that inflation is much higher in countries where the IMF cannot credibly enforce a lengthy punishment interval in the event of a deviation from program conditions. This sounds like an indictment of an institutional strategy, and, indeed, it points out its key weakness: The IMF is least effective in the countries that are most important. The converse, however, is also true: The finding that the IMF is less effective in deterring inflationary policies in large, important countries means that it is more effective in smaller, more ordinary countries. The magnitude of the effects is substantial. As a result, we can confidently conclude that the successful negotiation of the transition in many countries in Eastern Europe and the former Soviet Union owes a great deal to Fund intervention.

The detailed case studies of Poland, Russia, Ukraine, and Bulgaria made it possible to trace out the influences of Fund intervention, and again the evidence suggests that the Fund played an important role. That role was most pronounced in Poland and Bulgaria, where the credibility of IMF enforcement of conditionality was never in question. Even in cases like Russia and Ukraine, however, where the IMF was less able to enforce its conditions credibly, Fund intervention nudged public policy onto a more reformist track on numerous occasions. This suggests that I actually understate the Fund's influence when I measure it in terms of differences between high- and low-credibility countries, because the Fund had an effect that was not negligible even in the worst cases. The cases show that Fund resources were not always used wisely by the recipient countries; sometimes they were embezzled. However, to the extent that interaction with the Fund reduced the excesses of economic mismanagement, accelerated the process of macroeconomic stabilization, and improved the chances that these countries could return to a path of sustainable growth, this was money well spent. The scale of the resources involved is trivial compared to the costs of economic mismanagement, particularly if mismanagement leads eventually to political instability and international conflict.

Reforming the IMF

Numerous proposals have been advanced for reforming the IMF in the wake of the Asian financial crisis of 1997 and the disappointing results of reforms in many post-Communist countries. Critics from both ends of the political spectrum have proposed abolishing the Fund or drastically curtailing its activities.

Even some moderate critics have called for the Fund to refocus its lending on the short-term balance of payments disequilibria that it was originally created to address, and to abandon the broader policy-based lending that it developed to deal with problems of underdevelopment in the developing world and transition in post-Communist countries. Critics on the Left and the Right view the Fund as too powerful and too independent of national authorities.

I believe that a careful analysis of the experience of the post-Communist countries with the IMF suggests very different conclusions. We should not conclude from recent experience that international financial institutions are less necessary than we once believed or that their advice is less sound. To the contrary, the volatility of global capital markets means that devices that coordinate market expectations are needed more than ever, and that unwise macroeconomic policies will be punished more severely. The function of the IMF is to tip the balance of incentives that governments face in favor of policies of fiscal and monetary restraint. A credible IMF stabilization plan provides a focus for market expectations, which allows decentralized actors to coordinate their behavior. Coordinated markets provide strong incentives for governments to step back from the brink; uncoordinated markets offer them nothing. This study shows that the IMF can change the market's expectations—but only when it can extract policy improvements in return for support.

The analysis put forward in this book also suggests a significant reform of the IMF, but one with a radically different premise. The IMF's Achilles' heel is its credibility. As this study shows, countries that are influential—in particular, countries that receive large amounts of U.S. foreign aid—are not subject to the full force of IMF conditionality. As the case studies showed, the form this takes is that the IMF is more willing to revise its conditions when more important countries miss their targets. In effect, U.S. clients and allies are offered the dubious benefits of social promotion when they fail their reading tests.

As investors and economists have long recognized, monetary and fiscal restraint at the national level depends on the existence of institutions that create the proper incentives. In domestic policymaking, the existence of an independent central bank—one that is autonomous from interference by elected officials—is a necessary condition. Independence is crucial, because there are always short-term incentives to deviate from optimal long-term plans. The institutional capacity to ensure independence from political authority, however, is something that is lacking in all but the most consolidated democracies. For other countries, some other institution must fill the gap, and the best available candidate is the IMF. The problem, of course, is that the IMF is not an *independent* central bank. Because the IMF is controlled by its member states—in particular, by the handful of countries that control the majority of votes on its Board of Directors—the IMF is unable to substitute for an independent central bank for influential countries.

Two possible policies could be urged to resolve this problem. First, the United States and other members of the G-7 could resolve not to interfere in the enforcement of conditionality programs. However, this proposal runs into the same credibility problems it is intended to resolve: It is simply not credible for the United States to claim that it will always refrain from responding when an influential country calls for assistance in dealing with the IMF. Second, the IMF could be reformed: It could be made an independent agency in the same way that central banks are made independent, by guaranteeing the long tenure and autonomy of the leading officials of the institution. Governments may be loath to delegate such wide authority to an international institution; this argument has not prevented them from recognizing the wisdom of delegating much broader authority to domestic central banks, however. Decisions about institutional design are often made for short-term reasons, but they can be based on long-term calculations, and they can be used to resolve credibility problems that would be intractable if decisions were made on a case-by-case basis. While the leading donors derive a short-term benefit from being able to influence the IMF, and trading that influence for concessions on other issues from borrowing countries, they suffer in the long run from their inability to commit to refraining from exercising that influence. Their credibility problem becomes their agent's credibility problem—the Fund's—and undermines the effectiveness of their main instrument for assuring international stability and prosperity.

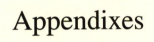

Appendixes

A

Data

The data set for this study, The Post-Communist Politics and Economics Database (PCPED), includes monthly data for twenty-six countries from January 1990 through December 1999. The replication data set for this study is available on the author's web page, as is a continuously updated data set including additional variables. The sample contains all former Soviet republics, Hungary, Poland, Czechoslovakia (before January 1993), the Czech and Slovak republics (since January 1993), Croatia, Macedonia, Slovenia, Albania, Bulgaria, Romania, and Mongolia.[1]

DOMESTIC POLITICAL VARIABLES

GOVERNMENT DURATION counts the number of months the current government has been in office. Changes in prime minister or in the main party of the ruling coalition are coded as fall of government.[2] No change of government is coded when a junior partner leaves the coalition but the prime minister and the main coalition partner remain the same.

MONTHS TO ELECTION counts the number of months till the next scheduled parliamentary election. Any changes in the date of elections during the term of the parliament have been noted, and the count has been updated from the

---

[1] The Czech Republic is coded as the continuation of Czechoslovakia after December 1992.

[2] In the few cases when a prime minister dies unexpectedly (e.g. homicide or accident), the government is coded as continuing. The exception is Kyrgyzstan's Prime Minister Djumabek Ibraimov, who died in Bishkek on April 4, 1999, after a long struggle with cancer – I assume that this condition was common knowledge. In Armenia, after Prime Minister Vazgen Sargsian was shot on October 27, 1999, the president temporarily performed his duties and later appointed a new prime minister. In this case, the count for the months the government had been in office continued uninterrupted since these were unanticipated events, the same party remained in government, and the same program was being implemented. In Hungary, after the death of Prime Minister Jozsef Antall on December 12,1993, the count continued uninterrupted.

month the changes were made. In order to account for the uncertainty that generally prevailed in these countries immediately after an election, while coalitions were being put together and new governments were in the process of formation, the variable is coded 0 for the first three months after a parliamentary election.

NUMBER OF COALITION MEMBERS is the number of parties in the governing coalition. Parties that informally support the government are not ordinarily included. However, in cases where the government does not have majority support in the parliament, a party is included in the number of parties even if it only informally supports the government without having ministerial positions, if the secondary literature or press reports indicate that it plays an influential role in the bargaining over legislation (e.g., Bulgaria, November 1991). A large group of unaffiliated deputies that support the government is counted as one party in the coalition.[3]

PARLIAMENTARY SUPPORT is the percentage of seats controlled by the largest party in the government. In cases where the parliament has been disbanded or too few deputies have been elected to form a legislative quorum, parliamentary support is assumed to be 100 percent (the parliament is not constraining).[4] When a government falls and it takes a few months to form a new one, the old one is assumed to act as a caretaker, and parliamentary support is unchanged for that period unless new elections resulted in a change in seats. In cases where there have been new elections, the support for the caretaker parties is coded using the new election results.

LEFT-RIGHT SCALE is the ideology score for the largest party in the government. This variable ranges from -10 (extreme Left on economic issues) to 10 (extreme Right on economic issues).

EXECUTIVE POWER SCORE is a coding for formal presidential powers based on the Hellman-Tucker Executive Powers score, modified in a few places to reflect coding disagreements and updated from 1996-99 to reflect constitutional and extraconstitutional changes that took place after the original data were gathered. The coding scheme generally follows the one created by Matthew Shugart and John Carey (1992) but was modified by Joel Hellman and Joshua Tucker. Both coding systems are reproduced in the codebook for the replication dataset.

---

[3]The Armenian coalition Masniutiun is coded as one party here and for seat percentage purposes (see Parliamentary Support, below) although it is in fact a coalition of two parties. The same coding applies to Bulgaria's Union of Democratic Forces (UDF) and Lithuania's Sajudis coalition (February 1990 - November 1992).

[4]The majority controlled by the Armenian National Movement in the parliament formed after the August 1990 election is based on the investiture vote for the prime minister.

AUTHORITARIAN is an index created by adding the Freedom House scores for political rights and civil liberties. The score for each measure ranges from 1 (most democratic) to 7 (least democratic). In the dataset, the index ranges from 3 to 14.

IMF VARIABLES

IMF QUOTA is the country's quota in the IMF, in millions of Special Drawing Rights (SDR). This represents the size of a country's contribution to the IMF, the scale of financing for which it is eligible, and its vote share. Quotas are determined by a system of formulas involving variables such as GDP, trade volume, and foreign reserves, and are revised periodically.

IMF STATUS is an indicator variable with value 1 when the country is in punishment status (i.e., its program has been suspended or a tranche has been delayed because it did not fulfill IMF conditions for disbursement, or it is not currently eligible to draw credit from the IMF because it has not fulfilled the necessary prior conditions) and 0 when the country is eligible to draw on IMF credits.

APPLICANT is an indicator variable with value 1 if the country has not yet participated in an IMF program and 0 otherwise.

PARTICIPANT is an indicator variable with value 1 if the country has participated in one or more IMF programs and continues to do so.

GRADUATE is an indicator variable with value 1 if the country has participated in one or more IMF programs but is no longer actively participating. Graduates have succeeded in stabilizing their macroeconomic variables, and would be eligible to draw on IMF funding, but do not currently have programs in place and are not involved in negotiations with the IMF to begin programs.

MACROECONOMIC DATA

The series are from the March 2000 version of the IMF CD-ROM publication *International Financial Statistics (IFS)*, supplemented with data from *Russian Economic Trends* and *Quarterly Predictions: Ukrainian Economic Survey*.

CHANGE IN EXCHANGE RATE is the percentage change in the nominal exchange rate.

INFLATION is the monthly percentage change in the Consumer Price Index (CPI) supplemented with de-annualized monthly inflation data when data in the CPI series were missing.

CHANGE IN DOMESTIC CREDIT is the percentage change in domestic credit issued by the central bank.

CHANGE IN RESERVES is the percentage change in gross reserves of the central bank.

FOREIGN AID DATA

U.S. AID (APPROPRIATIONS) is U.S. military and economic aid, taken from annual congressional presentations by USAID published in ASI. I used appropriations figures for 1992-99, and requests for 2000. This variable is reported in fiscal years. Economic items are Development Assistance, Economic Support fund, and programs under the Support for Eastern European Democracy Act (SEED), Food for Peace Titles II and III, Narcotics, and the Peace Corps. Military items include Foreign Military Financing Loans and International Military Education and Training (IMET).

U.S. ODA is U.S. economic aid data from the OECD *International Development Statistics* 2000 CD-ROM. It includes Total Gross Official Development Assistance (ODA) and Official Assistance (OA) (grants and loans that are undertaken by the official sector with promotion of economic development and welfare as the main objective, at concessional financial terms, and including a grant element of at least 25 percent) and ODA/OA Commitments (these are based on agreements or equivalent contracts undertaken by governments, official agencies of the reporting country, or international organizations). Regional figures that were not disaggregated by country were not included. The Czech and Slovak figures were summed for Czechoslovakia for the period 1990 to 1992. The coverage is for 1990-98, in calendar years.

NON-U.S. OECD AID is total economic aid from all members of the OECD excluding the United States. It is taken from the OECD *International Development Statistics* 2000 CD-ROM and calculated in the same way as U.S. ODA.

U.S. MILITARY AID is reported by the Federation of American Scientists (FAS) website (www.fas.org). The items covered are International Military Education and Training (IMET) Programs and Deliveries, including Service Funded Military Assistance and Emergency Drawdowns, and the Foreign Military Financing Program. The data are in fiscal years, for 1990-1998. The data for Czechoslovakia 1993 were allocated to the 3 remaining months of calendar 1992, and the Czech and Slovak FY 1993 data were allocated over 9 months for calendar 1993.

U.S. AID (DISBURSEMENTS) is the total of U.S. ODA and U.S. Military Aid. The data are for calendar years.

WORLD BANK represents the same categories of aid as OECD Aid, as measured and reported by the World Bank in *World Development Indicators* (2000).

Table A.1: Correlations of U.S. and non-U.S. Foreign Aid.

	U.S. Appr.	U.S. Disb.	World Bank	WB minus U.S.	OECD	OECD minus U.S.
U.S. Appr.	1.0000					
U.S. Disb.	.4129	1.0000				
World Bank	.2394	.5894	1.0000			
WB − U.S.	−.0070	−.0052	.8047	1.0000		
OECD	.4164	.7263	.9362	.6252	1.0000	
OECD − U.S.	.3162	.3875	.9098	.8415	.9151	1.0000

B

Statistical Methods

Coauthored with Timothy Carter, Christopher Kam and Kalina Popova

B.1 MULTIPLE IMPUTATION

Assumptions

All imputation methods depend on assumptions about how data come to be missing. Denote partially observed variable(s) as Y, fully observed variables as X, a missing/observed indicator matrix as M, and let the subscripts "obs" and "miss" signify observed and missing data respectively. The implications of various missingness assumptions for using listwise deletion (LD) and multiple imputation (MI) are summarized in Table B.1.

Intuition

The imputation strategy is not to maximize any objective function but, rather, to generate imputations that reflect as accurately as possible the process that generated the original data. Consider incomplete data generated by flipping an unbalanced coin that lands "heads" with probability .6. One could minimize the error between the "real" (but unobserved) data and any imputations by setting the missing values equal to "heads." However, this would be an inferior method to an imputation technique that emulated the original data-generating process by imputing "heads" with probability .6 and "tails" with probability .4, because setting all the missing values to "heads" would bias the point estimates.[1]

Rubin (1977) uses a simple regression approach to motivate MI. Imagine a simple linear relationship between Y and X:

$$E\left[\bar{Y}_{\text{obs}}\right] = \alpha_{\text{obs}} + \beta_{\text{obs}}\bar{X}'$$
$$E\left[\bar{Y}_{\text{miss}}\right] = \alpha_{\text{miss}} + \beta_{\text{miss}}\bar{X}'$$

---

[1] Rubin 1996, p. 475.

Table B.1: Assumptions and Implications of Missing Data.

Missingness Assumption	Statistical Interpretation	Substantive Interpretation	Consequences of LD and MI
Missing Completely at Random (MCAR)	$E[Y_{\text{obs}}]$ $=E[Y_{\text{miss}}]$	Missing and observed Ys come from the same distribution.	LD is inefficient, MI is efficient.
Missing at Random (MAR)	$E[Y_{\text{miss}}|X,M]$ $=E[Y_{\text{miss}}|X]$	The values of Y_{miss} may depend on the values of the background variables, X, but are independent of the missingness mechanism. Once the Xs are accounted for, the Y values (missing and observed) contain no information about M.	LD is inefficient and leads to bias in both parameter and standard error estimates. MI is superior.
Non-ignorable	$E[Y_{\text{miss}}|X,M]$ $\neq E[Y_{\text{miss}}|X]$	The Y values contain information about M even after controlling for X, so the missingness mechanism should be modeled explicitly. Non-ignorability cannot be diagnosed with the observed data.	LD is inefficient, MI and LD are biased. LD may outperform MI if there are there are very few missing observations *and* X contain little information about Y_{miss}. Otherwise MI is preferable.

Source: adapted from King et al. (2001).

MI is a method of drawing inferences about the unobserved parameters, α_{miss} and β_{miss}, from α_{obs} and β_{obs}, which can be estimated from the observed data. This does not involve an assumption that that $\alpha_{\text{obs}} = \alpha_{\text{miss}}$ or $\beta_{\text{obs}} = \beta_{\text{miss}}$. Rather, we assume that the observed data allow us to make reasonable probability statements about the likely values of α_{miss} and β_{miss}. To be more precise, the 95 percent confidence interval of the unobserved parameters is taken to be $\alpha_{\text{miss}} = \alpha_{\text{obs}}(1 \pm 2\theta_1)$ and $\beta_{\text{miss}} = \beta_{\text{obs}}(1 \pm 2\theta_2)$, where the θs are "standard errors" that are estimated from the observed data and that express our uncertainty about how similar α_{miss} and β_{miss} are to α_{obs} and β_{obs}. Our uncertainty in this regard takes account of the residual variance, $\hat{\sigma}^2_{\text{obs}}$, produced by the regression of Y_{obs} on X; the greater $\hat{\sigma}^2_{\text{obs}}$ is, the greater our uncertainty.

Common Imputation Methods

Several approaches to imputation are frequently employed in political science and economics, but each has serious deficiencies when compared to multiple imputation.

- *Mean Imputation:*

$$Y_{\text{miss}(i)} = \text{E}\,[Y_{\text{obs}}]$$

Y_{miss} is assumed to be nonstochastic, implying that we have underestimated the variance (i.e., uncertainty) in the mode. We have also failed to consider the possibility that Y varies with X.

- *Conditional Mean Imputation:*

$$Y_{\text{miss}(i)} = \text{E}\,[Y_{\text{obs}}|X] = a_{\text{obs}} + b_{\text{obs}}X'$$

Y_{miss} is allowed to vary with X but is still nonstochastic (a and b denote estimates of α and β).

- *Regression with Random Error:*

$$Y_{\text{miss}(i)} = \text{E}\,[Y_{\text{obs}}|X] = a_{\text{obs}} + b_{\text{obs}}X' + e_i$$

Y_{miss} is stochastic, but we have still understated its variance because this imputation model does not capture the fact that: (1) the estimates of the regression parameters are drawn from a distribution; and (2) the unobserved parameters, α_{miss} and β_{miss}, may not equal the observed parameters, α_{obs} and β_{obs}.

- *Multiple Imputation:*

$$Y_{\text{miss}(i)} = \text{E}\,[Y] = \hat{\alpha}_k + \hat{\beta}_k \bar{X}' + e_i$$

This approach corrects the mistakes outlined above by adding a random error to the imputations and making multiple draws of the regression parameters from a probability distribution. The product of imputation is several data sets with varying values for the imputed data. The correct point estimates and standard errors for the analysis model take into account the estimates and standard errors obtained from each data set and the variance across them. The advantage of MI relative to naïve imputation techniques (such as mean imputation or listwise deletion) is that it explicitly incorporates uncertainty about the missing data into the statistical model. Single imputation methods (i.e., imputing one value for each missing datum) do not do this, so tests based on single imputation data return smaller (and incorrect) standard errors and hence lead to more Type I errors.

Amelia and Multiple Imputation Issues

There are two general types of multiple-imputation algorithms, Imputation-Posterior (IP) and Expectation-Maximization (EM). IP generates the entire distribution of α_{miss} and β_{miss}, whereas EM returns only the maximum likelihood estimates of α_{miss} and β_{miss}. IP is computationally intensive, and it is difficult to diagnose convergence; EM is fast, but biases standard errors downwards. The problem with estimating only the MLEs of α_{miss} and β_{miss} is that it suggests that we know α_{miss} and β_{miss} with certainty when, in fact, we do not—it ignores estimation uncertainty. King et al.'s (2001) solution is to add uncertainty to the EM-based MLEs of α_{miss} and β_{miss}, and therefore to the resulting imputations.

Multiple imputation uses multiple guesses to fill in the blanks, so the best point estimate is an average, and standard errors take into account the variance of the point estimates and the number of imputed trials. The algorithm used is described in detail in King et al. (2001).[2]

- E$[Y]$ is estimated as the mean of the mean of Y in each (of the m) imputed data sets:

$$\mathrm{E}[Y] = \frac{1}{m} \sum_m^1 \bar{Y}_m$$

- V$[Y]$ is the mean of variances of each data set plus the variance between those variances, so letting V$[Y_m]$ denote the variance of Y in data set m, we have

$$\mathrm{V}[Y] = \frac{1}{m} \sum_m^1 \mathrm{V}[Y_m] + \mathrm{V}[\mathrm{V}[Y_m]]$$

[2]I used the Windows version of *Amelia: A Program for Missing Data* (Honaker et al. 1999), to generate imputed data.

The formula for the standard errors is

$$\text{SE}(q)^2 = \frac{1}{m} \sum_{j=1}^{m} \text{SE}(q_j)^2 + Sq^2 \left(1 + \frac{1}{m}\right)$$

where q is the point estimate of interest, Sq^2 is the sample variance of q across the m point estimates, m is the number of imputed datasets, and $\text{SE}(q_j)$ is the estimated standard error of q from dataset j.[3]

B.2 DURATION MODELS

The most appropriate method to analyze the duration of events, here the duration of governments and IMF program status, is to use a hazard model, also known as a survival model, duration model, or event history model. Analyzing the duration of events using Ordinary Least Squares (OLS) is inappropriate, because the underlying process that generates duration data does not fit the distributional assumptions of OLS. Logit and probit are inappropriate because they do not model the timing of events.[4]

Hazard models estimate a hazard rate, which is the instantaneous rate at which an event ends, for example, a government falls or the IMF status changes, at duration t, given that it has lasted until time t. More technically, the hazard rate is the relative likelihood that an event will end in an interval of time $t + \Delta t$, as the interval goes to 0, given that the event has survived up to or beyond some time t.[5] The hazard rate is thus defined as

$$h(t) = \lim_{\Delta t \to 0} \frac{\Pr(t \leq T \leq t + \Delta t | T \geq t)}{\Delta t}$$

Here, hazard models estimate the instantaneous rate at which events occur, that is, transitions from one government to the next or from one IMF status to another, as a function of independent variables, including time. Hazard rates are not necessarily constant over time. Some duration models, such as those employed here, can identify the duration dependence of a process. If the hazard rate increases over time (has positive duration dependence), for example, then the instantaneous probability that the event occurs increases over time.

In these analyses, I used a Weibull specification to model the duration processes. The basic functional form of the hazard rate $h(t)$ using a Weibull specification is

$$h(t) = \lambda p(t)^{p-1}$$

[3]The Stata .do files to replicate my analyses can be downloaded along with the replication data sets. They incorporate this algorithm.

[4]Box-Steffensmeier and Jones 2002, pp. 30-3.

[5]Box-Steffensmeier and Jones 2002, pp. 23-8.

Here, the parameter p represents the duration-dependence estimate. Also known as the shape parameter, it determines the shape of the hazard function. When $p = 1$, there is no duration dependence; when $0 < p < 1$, the hazard rate decreases monotonically with time; when $p > 1$, the hazard rate increases monotonically with time.

Covariates can be added to the model as influences on the hazard rate by parameterizing λ as follows[6]

$$\lambda = e^{\beta X}$$

In duration models, in contrast to linear models, it is difficult to interpret the coefficients directly. The effect of unit changes in the independent variables, or covariates, on the hazard rate or the duration are not constant over the range of the independent variables, as they are in an OLS model. Their effects depend both on the independent variable in question and the values of the other independent variables.

In addition, estimating predicted durations for hazard models is more complicated than in an OLS model. The mean duration time, or the expected value of the random variable T, for a Weibull model can be found using the following formula, where Γ is the gamma function.[7]

$$E[T] = \frac{\Gamma \left(1 + \frac{1}{p}\right)}{\lambda}$$

Model Selection

The primary choice to be made in modeling a duration process is between nonparametric models such as the Cox model and parametric models such as the Weibull model.[8] The Cox model is very flexible, and, unlike the Weibull, which is also a proportional hazards model, it is not limited to a monotonic hazard rate. For some purposes, this may be advantageous.[9] However, if the theory's parameterization is correct, a parametric model will provide more precise estimates than would a nonparametric model.[10] In addition, it is preferable to use a parametric distribution if one has some theoretical interest in the shape of the hazard rate. In this case the theory is precise about the type of distribution that is needed to relate the covariates to the rate of events: The probability of the event should be monotonically increasing. The analysis of government durations is a well-developed literature and there is a broad consensus that the hazard rate is increasing, so finding an increasing hazard rate increases my

---

[6]There are many different ways to parameterize λ, I use that discussed by Box-Steffensmeier and Jones (2002).

[7]Box-Steffensmeier and Jones 2002, p. 59, Lawless 1982, p. 16.

[8]Box-Steffensmeier and Jones 2002, Chap. 4.

[9]Ibid., 148.

[10]Ibid., 44.

confidence in the results. I also expect an increasing hazard rate in my IMF status models. Both punishment periods and good status periods are designed to last more than a few months. Subsequently, the probability of lasting additional months should decrease as a set period of punishment comes to an end and as small deviations from program parameters accumulate and increase the pressures to violate IMF conditions.

Government Duration Model

The government duration model I use differs from previous studies in that I do not include cabinets that failed the investiture vote, that is, were never formed, while King et al. (1990) do. The inclusion of such cabinets in their model causes the hazard to be steeply decreasing at the beginning of a government's tenure. By excluding these cases, I focus attention on factors leading to instability of sitting governments, which is an issue distinct from cabinet formation. Warwick and Easton (1992) argue, in agreement with previous research, that when the incumbent government wins an election, it should be considered a new government because the composition of the parliament and thus the conditions for survival tend to change, often drastically, after an election. I have followed this approach as well.

I agree with Martin's (2000), Warwick's (1992), and Warwick and Easton's (1992) criticisms of King et al.'s (1990) usage of an exponential model, which assumes no time dependence in the hazard rate. In fact, since they use no time-varying covariates, their model assumes that the probability that a government will fall at a particular point in time is constant throughout its term in office. It is more reasonable to expect the hazard rate to be increasing as governments move farther away from the circumstances that produced their electoral mandates and take responsibility for more unpopular decisions. The Weibull model I used allows for a monotonic hazard rate, and the increasing hazard rate I find is in line with the findings in the government duration literature.[11] Given the multitude of models proposed in the literature, I also estimated a Cox proportional model.[12] The results were substantively the same as those from a Weibull model, and the plot of the hazards supported the assumption of an increasing hazard rate.

Results

The model of government duration and the resulting coefficients and standard errors, corrected for the effects of imputation, are presented as Table B.2. The tables of coefficients and standard errors for the analyses of the duration of IMF programs in good standing and of punishment intervals described in Chapter 4 follow as Tables B.3 and B.4.

---

[11] Warwick 1992; Diermeier and Stevenson 1999.
[12] King et al. 1990; Warwick and Easton 1992.

Table B.2: Government Duration Models.

	Weibull			Cox		
	Coeff.	Hazard		Coeff.	Hazard	
Baltic	.8022	2.2304	***	.6680	1.9503	**
	(.3193)			(.3659)		
Balkan	.4672	1.5955		.3842	1.4684	
	(.3272)			(.3435)		
Central Asia	.7939	2.2120	**	.6899	1.9934	
	(.3937)			(.4320)		
Rest of the	1.0737	2.9262	***	.9149	2.4966	**
Former USSR	(.3614)			(.4089)		
Up to 1993	.5242	1.6892	***	.4482	1.5654	*
	(.1879)			(.2300)		
Interim	.6429	1.9019	*	.6110	1.8422	*
	(.3476)			(.3148)		
No. of Coalition	.1228	1.1306	*	.1128	1.1194	*
Partners	(.0741)			(.0628)		
Support in	−.7449	.4748		−.6677	.5129	
Parliament	(.5613)			(.5092)		
Left-right Scale	.0118	1.0119		.0028	1.0028	
	(.0181)			(.0163)		
War	.5787	1.7838	*	.5493	1.7320	*
	(.3439)			(.3315)		
Executive	−.0731	.9295	**	−.0794	.9237	**
Power Score	(.0359)			(.0395)		
Authoritarian	−.0054	.9947		−.0052	.9948	
	(.0544)			(.0579)		
Months	−.0558	.9457	***	−.0645	.9375	***
to Election	(.0140)			(.0137)		
Executive	.0027	1.0027	**	.0030	1.0030	***
× Months	(.0012)			(.0013)		
IMF Status $(t-1)$	.1875	1.2062		.2106	1.2345	
	(.1976)			(.2194)		
Constant	−4.1309		***			
	(.6563)					
Baseline Hazard	.3750					

$^{*}p < .1; \, ^{**}p < .05; \, ^{***}p < .01$

Table B.3: Analysis of Duration of Programs in Good Standing.

	Model 1		Model 2		Model 3		Model 4	
	Coeff.	Hazard	Coeff.	Hazard	Coeff.	Hazard	Coeff.	Hazard
IMF Quota	-7.48×10^{-6} (9.72×10^{-5})	1.0000	-3.21×10^{-5} (1.04×10^{-4})	1.0000	5.39×10^{-5} (1.22×10^{-4})	1.0001	9.37×10^{-5} (1.13×10^{-4})	1.0001
U.S. Aid Appropriations	9.28×10^{-5} (2.65×10^{-5})	1.0001***	9.25×10^{-5} (3.42×10^{-5})	1.0001***	7.20×10^{-5} (3.70×10^{-5})	1.0001*	8.48×10^{-5} (3.87×10^{-5})	1.0001**
U.S. Aid Disbursements	5.03×10^{-6} (2.16×10^{-6})	1.0000**	5.14×10^{-6} (2.13×10^{-6})	1.0000**	4.54×10^{-6} (2.17×10^{-6})	1.0000**	3.78×10^{-6} (3.00×10^{-6})	1.0000
Non-U.S. OECD Aid	-1.42×10^{-6} (2.83×10^{-6})	1.0000	-3.94×10^{-6} (2.83×10^{-6})	1.0000	-1.55×10^{-8} (2.80×10^{-6})	1.0000	3.77×10^{-7} (2.77×10^{-6})	1.0000
Inflation $(t-1)$	.00325 (.00775)	1.0033	6.24×10^{-4} (.00700)	1.0006	.00103 (.00713)	1.0010	2.38×10^{-4} (.00753)	1.0002
Inflation $(t-6)$	-4.39×10^{-4} (.00634)	.9996	$-.00257$ (.00641)	.9974	$-.00277$ (.00671)	.9972	$-.00359$ (.00656)	.9964
% Ch. Domestic Credit $(t-1)$	.00861 (.00429)	1.0086**	.00670 (.00403)	1.0067*	.00695 (.00416)	1.0070*	.00791 (.00436)	1.0079*
% Ch. Reserves $(t-1)$	-6.05×10^{-4} (7.75×10^{-4})	.9994	-6.15×10^{-4} (6.93×10^{-4})	.9994	-6.89×10^{-4} (7.29×10^{-4})	.9993	-6.52×10^{-4} (7.17×10^{-4})	.9993
IMF Status	.54479 (.36397)	1.7242	1.44019 (.66654)	4.2215**	1.49437 (.76154)	4.4565**	2.30239 (1.41703)	9.9980

$* p < .1; ** p < .05; *** p < .01$ (two-tailed tests)

Table B.3 continued from previous page

	Model 1		Model 2		Model 3		Model 4	
	Coeff.	Hazard	Coeff.	Hazard	Coeff.	Hazard	Coeff.	Hazard
Authoritarian			.10097	1.1062**	.12408	1.1321***	.11776	1.1250**
			(.04280)		(.04658)		.05251	.9938
Parliamentary Election			−.00657	.9935	−.00757	.9925	−.00619	
			(.00542)		(.00532)		(.00615)	
Fragmentation					.12373	1.1317*	.14359	1.1544**
					(.07002)		(.06817)	
Left-Right Scale					-4.34×10^{-4}	.9996	.02710	1.0275
					(.02361)		(.02830)	
Parliamentary Support							.49615	1.6424
							(.84389)	
Pr(Gov't Fall)							.60350	1.8285
							(3.17873)	
Left-Right× Pr(Gov't Fall)							−.63758	.5286**
							(.31566)	
Constant	−3.01491***		−3.66266***		−4.09101***		−4.44641***	
	(.29554)		(.50352)		(.49691)		(.70499)	

* p < .1; ** p < .05; *** p < .01 (two-tailed tests)

Table B.4: Analysis of Duration of Punishment Intervals.

	Model 1		Model 2		Model 3		Model 4	
	Coeff.	Hazard	Coeff.	Hazard	Coeff.	Hazard	Coeff.	Hazard
IMF Quota	-1.27×10^{-4}	.9999	-4.86×10^{-5}	1.0000	4.65×10^{-5}	1.0000	5.21×10^{-6}	1.0000
	(2.01×10^{-4})		(1.97×10^{-4})		(2.47×10^{-4})		(2.43×10^{-4})	
U.S. Aid Appropriations	6.19×10^{-5}	1.0001^{**}	6.44×10^{-5}	1.0001^{**}	5.61×10^{-5}	1.0001^{**}	4.39×10^{-5}	1.0000
	(2.81×10^{-5})		(2.54×10^{-5})		(2.85×10^{-5})		(3.49×10^{-5})	
U.S. Aid Disbursements	9.69×10^{-7}	1.0000	1.90×10^{-6}	1.0000	1.10×10^{-6}	1.0000	1.52×10^{-6}	1.0000
	(3.16×10^{-6})		(3.17×10^{-6})		(3.81×10^{-6})		(3.31×10^{-6})	
Non-U.S. OECD Aid	4.47×10^{-6}	1.0000	1.10×10^{-7}	1.0000	-6.60×10^{-8}	1.0000	-2.15×10^{-7}	1.0000
	(4.46×10^{-6})		(4.36×10^{-6})		(5.56×10^{-6})		(5.49×10^{-6})	
Inflation $(t-1)$	.00621	1.0062	.00896	1.0009	.00974	1.0098	.00956	1.0096
	(.00852)		(.00975)		(.00930)		(.00789)	
Inflation $(t-6)$	.00857	1.0086^{*}	.01265	1.0127^{**}	.01272	1.0128^{**}	.01143	1.0115^{**}
	(.00510)		(.00514)		(.00505)		(.00503)	
% Ch. Domestic Credit $(t-1)$	$-.00438$	.9956	-2.97×10^{-4}	.9997	1.99×10^{-5}	1.0000	3.86×10^{-4}	1.0004
	(.01530)		(.01286)		(.01495)		(.01588)	
% Ch. Reserves $(t-1)$	1.32×10^{-4}	1.0001	2.17×10^{-4}	1.0002	2.52×10^{-4}	1.0003	2.53×10^{-4}	1.0003
	(9.14×10^{-4})		(9.06×10^{-4})		(9.18×10^{-4})		(9.69×10^{-4})	
IMF Status	$-.54479$	.5800	-1.44019	$.2369^{**}$	-1.49437	$.2244^{**}$	-2.30239	.1000
	(.36397)		(.66654)		(.76154)		(1.41703)	

$^{*}\,p < .1;\ ^{**}\,p < .05;\ ^{***}\,p < .01$ (two-tailed tests)

Table B.4 continued from previous page

	Model 1		Model 2		Model 3		Model 4	
	Coeff.	Hazard	Coeff.	Hazard	Coeff.	Hazard	Coeff.	Hazard
Authoritarian			−.10036	.9045*	−.08384	.9196	−.06475	.9373
			(.05589)		(.06536)		(.06569)	
Parliamentary Election			.01576	1.0159**	.01557	1.0157**	.01511	1.0152
			(.00637)		(.00625)		(.00988)	
Fragmentation					.10898	1.1151	.05004	1.0513
					(.07084)		(.08529)	
Left-Right Scale					−.00634	.9937	−.00388	.9961
					(.03150)		(.03977)	
Parliamentary Support							−.86414	.4214
							(.92385)	
Pr(Gov't Fall)							.72877	2.0725
							(4.75643)	
Left-Right× Pr(Gov't Fall)							−.07795	.9250
							(.46580)	
Constant	−2.47013***		−2.22247***		−2.59664***		−2.14403***	
	(.33570)		(.46526)		(.61619)		(1.04816)	

* $p < .1$; ** $p < .05$; *** $p < .01$ (two-tailed tests)

C

List of Interviews

BULGARIA

Krassimir Angarski, Associate Professor, Head of the Sofia Tax Division, Ministry of Finance, 1990-94; Director of the Bank Consolidation Company, 1994-95; Deputy Prime Minister and Minister of Economic Policy, February-May 1997

Ivan Angelov, Professor, Economic Adviser to Prime Minister Zhan Videnov, 1995-96

Roumen Avramov, Professor, Member of the Board of the Bulgarian National Bank, 1997-

Ivan Batchvarov, Head of the Foreign Financing and Financial Projects Division, Bulgarian National Bank

Gergana Beremska, Head of the Analysis and Forecast Division, Government Debt Department, Ministry of Finance

Lyuben Berov, Professor, Prime Minister, 1993-94; Chairman of the joint-stock company "Agroproduct-B"

Ivan Buchvarov, Head of the International Dept, Bulgarian National Bank

Liubomir Datsov, various positions, Ministry of Finance, 1992-97; Head of the Macroeconomic Policy Department, Ministry of Finance, 1997-99

Encho Dimitrov, Head of the Government Debt Issuance Division, Ministry of Finance

Tsacho Filkov, Vice President, Foreign Trade Bank of Bulgaria until 1993, Chairman, Slaviani Bank, 1993-2000

Dimitar Kostov, Deputy Minister of Finance, 1990-95, Minister of Finance, 1995-96; Executive Director of the Central Cooperative Bank, 1996-

Anne McGuirk, Head of the IMF Mission to Bulgaria,1995-98

Mileti Mladenov, Member of the Board of the Bulgarian National Bank, January 1991-June 1996; Chairman of the Deposit Insurance Fund, 1996-

Mariela Nenova, Director of the Agency for Economic Analysis and Prognosis, Ministry of Finance

Plamen Oresharski, Head of the Treasury Department, Ministry of Finance, 1993-97; Deputy Minister of Finance, 1997-

Georgi Petrov, Professor, Member of the Board of the Bulgarian National Bank, 1997-
Dimitar Popov, Prime Minister, December 1990-October 1991
Olga Raeva, Public Relations Adviser to the Minister of Finance
Peter Stella, IMF Resident Representative to Bulgaria
Krassen Stanchev, Director of the Institute for Market Economics
Martin Zaimov, Deputy Governor of the Bulgarian National Bank

POLAND

Mark Allen, IMF Senior Resident Representative to Poland, March 1990-February 1993; Deputy Director of the Policy Development and Review Department, IMF
Leszek Balcerowicz, Professor, Minister of Finance and First Deputy Prime Minister, 1989-93; 1997-2000
Andrzej Chmiel, Deputy Director of the Foreign Department, Ministry of Finance
Pawel Durjasz, Deputy Director of the Research Department, National Bank of Poland
Jerzy Hylewski, Director of the Department for International Financial Institutions, and Member of the Board, National Bank of Poland
Grzegorz Kolodko, Professor, Deputy Prime Minister and Minister of Finance, 1994-97
Stefan Kawalec, Head of group of consultants, Ministry of Finance, September 1989-91, Deputy Minister of Finance with responsibility for relations with international organizations, 1991-94
Jerzy Osiatynski, Minister of Finance, 1993-94; Deputy to Sejm (Unia Wolnosci), 1995-97
George T. Park, Senior Operations Officer of The World Bank, Poland
Markus H. Rodlauer, Senior Resident Representative in Poland, IMF
Dariusz Rosati, Director, Foreign Trade Institute, Ministry of International Cooperation; Minister of Foreign Affairs, 1995-97
Jerzy Rutkowski, Deputy Director, Department of Economic Analysis, Ministry of the Economy
Wieslaw Szczuka, Director, Foreign Department, Ministry of Finance, until 1997; Governor and Deputy Director, IMF, 1997-1999
Lidia Wilk, Deputy Director of the Department of Financial Policy and Analysis, Ministry of Finance

RUSSIA

Sergei V. Aleksashenko, Deputy Minister of Finance, 1992-93; First Deputy Minister of Finance, 1994; First Deputy Chairman of the Central Bank of Russia, 1995-98

Igor' L. Bubnov, Director of the Research Institute of the Central Bank of Russia

Sergei K. Dubinin, First Deputy Minister of Finance, 1993; Minister of Finance, 1994; Chairman of the Central Bank of Russia, 1996-98

Andrei A. Filev, Director of the Division (Upravlenie) for Relations with International Financial Organizations, Ministry of Finance, early 1993 to March 1997

Yegor Gaidar, Acting Prime Minister, 1992; First Deputy Prime Minister, September 1993-January 1994

Leonid M. Grigoriev, Deputy Minister of Finance, 1992; Director of the Bureau of Economic Analysis

Ernesto Hernandez-Cata, Head of the IMF Mission to Russia, 1992-95

Yusuke Horiguchi, Head of the IMF Mission to Russia, 1995-97; Associate Director, IMF

Aleksandr A. Khandruev, Deputy Chairman of the Central Bank of Russia, 1992-98

Alexander Ya. Livshits, Adviser to Yeltsin, 1992-, Finance Minister and Deputy Prime Minister, August 1996-March 1997

Vladimir A. Mau, Director of the Working Center for Economic Reform of the Russian government

Michael Mussa, Economic Counsellor and Director of the Research Department of the International Monetary Fund

Aleksandr D. Nekipelov, Professor, Academik; Director of the Institute of International Economic and Political Studies

Vitalii M. Novikov, Head of the Monetary Policy Division of the Research Institute of the Central Bank

Brian Pinto, Chief Economist, World Bank, Russia, 1998-

Aleksandr I. Potemkin, Head of the Foreign Exchange Department of the Central Bank of Russia, 1992-98

Ivan I. Rodionov, Director, AIG Brunswick Capital Management, LTD, Russia

Andrei P. Vavilov, Deputy Minister of Finance, 1992-93; First Deputy Minister of Finance, 1994-97

Yevgenii Yasin, Minister of the Economy, October 1994-98; Acting Minister without portfolio, March-September 1998

Ruben N. Yevstigneiev, Professor, Deputy Director of the Institute of International Economic and Political Studies

Viatcheslav S. Zakharov, Executive Vice President of the Association of Russian Banks

UKRAINE

Darwin Beck, U.S. Department of the Treasury Resident Adviser, National Bank of Ukraine, 1998-

Petro K. Germanchuk, First Deputy Minister of Finance; Minister of Finance; First Deputy Minister of Finance, 2000

Vitalii Lisovenko, Director, Department of Foreign Debt, Ministry of Finance

Viktor Lysytskyi, Head of Group of Advisers to the Governor of the National Bank of Ukraine, 1995-99; Secretary of the Government, 2000

Vira Nanivska, Director of the International Center for Policy Studies, Kyiv

Oleg Rybachuk, Director of the International Department of the National Bank of Ukraine, 1992-

Petr Serov, Chairman of the Council of Ministers Commission for Foreign Economic Relations, and Director of the Department of the Council of Ministers for Foreign Economic Ties, 1990-93; President of AO Torgovyi Dom, 1993-97; Consultant to the Communist Party Faction, Verkhovna Rada, January 1997-

Mohammed Shadman-Valavi, Head of IMF Mission to Ukraine, 1997-2000

Marina M. Shapovalova, Head of the Budget Policy and Macroeconomic Analysis Department, Ministry of Finance

Oleg L. Sheiko, Deputy Head of the Budget Policy and Macroeconomic Analysis Department, Ministry of Finance

Ihor O. Shpak, Director of the Fiscal Analysis Office, Verkhovna Rada Budget Committee

David Snelbecker, Adviser at the Harvard Institute for International Development, Kyiv

Khwaja Sultan, Senior Adviser at the Harvard Institute for International Development, Kyiv

Viktor Suslov, Adviser to President Kravchuk; Adviser to Prime Minister Kuchma; Verkhovna Rada Deputy 1994-, Minister of the Economy, July 1997-April 1998; Chairman of the Commission for Economic Questions, Verkhovna Rada, March 1998-

Wayne Thirsk, Barents Group LLC

Harry Trines, Deputy Head of IMF Mission to Ukraine, 1996-2000

Yuriy G. Yakusha, Alternate Executive Director, IMF

Bibliography

Aleksashenko, Sergei. 1999. *Bitva za rubl'*. Moscow: Alma Mater.

Alesina, Alberto. 1987. "Macroeconomic Policy in a Two-party System as a Repeated Game." *Quarterly Journal of Economics* 102: 651–78.

Alesina, Alberto and Allen Drazen. 1991. "Why Are Stabilizations Delayed?" *The American Economic Review* 81: 1170–88.

Alesina, Alberto and Howard Rosenthal. 1995. *Partisan Politics, Divided Government, and the Economy*. Cambridge: Cambridge University Press.

Alesina, Alberto, Nouriel Roubini and Gerald D. Cohen. 1997. *Political Cycles and the Macroeconomy*. Cambridge: The M.I.T. Press.

Alesina, Alberto and Roberto Perotti. 1995. "The Political Economy of Budget Deficits." *IMF Staff Papers* 42 (1): 1–31.

Alvarez, Michael R., Geoffrey Garrett and Peter Lange. 1991. "Government Partisanship, Labor Organization, and Macroeconomic Performance." *The American Political Science Review* 85 (June): 539–56.

Andres, Javier and Ignacio Hernando. 1997. "Does Inflation Harm Economic Growth? Evidence for the OECD." NBER Working Pape Series 6062 (June).

Andres, Javier, R. Domenech and C. Molinas. 1996. "Macroeconomic Performance and Convergence in OECD Countries." *European Economic Review* 40: 1683–1704.

Åslund, Anders. 1995. *How Russia Became a Market Economy*. Washington, D.C.: The Brookings Institution.

Bagci, Pinar and William Perraudin. 1997. "The Impact of IMF Programmes." Working Paper 35, Institute for Financial Research, Birkbeck College, University of London.

Balcerowicz, Leszek. 1992. *800 Dni: Szok kontrolowany*. Warsaw: Polska Oficyna Wydawnicza "BGW".

Balcerowicz, Leszek. 1995. *Socialism, Capitalism, Transformation*. Budapest: Central European University Press.

Banaian, King. 1999. *The Ukrainian Economy since Independence*. Northhampton, MA: Edward Elgar Publishing, Inc.

Barro, Robert J. 1991. "Inflation and Economic Growth." Bank of England Economic Bulletin, 1-11.

Barro, Robert J. and David B. Gordon. 1983. "Rules, Discretion, and Reputation in a Model of Monetary Policy." *Journal of Monetary Economics* 12: 101–20.

Bawn, Kathleen. 1999. "Money and Majorities in the Federal Republic of Germany: Evidence for a Veto Players Model of Government Spending." *American Journal of Political Science* 43: 707–36.

Beck, Nathaniel and Jonathan N. Katz. 1995. "What to do (and not to do) with Time-series Cross-section Data." *The American Political Science Review* 89: 634–647.

Beck, Nathaniel and Jonathan N. Katz. 1996. "Nuisance vs. Substance: Specifying and Estimating Time-series Cross-section Models." *Political Analysis* 6: 1–36.

Bennett, Adam, Maria Carkovic and Louis Dicks-Mireaux. 1995. "Record of Fiscal Adjustment." In Schadler et al., *IMF Conditionality: Experience under Stand-by and Extended Arrangements. Part I: Key Issues and Findings,* and *Part II: Background papers* pp. 6–35. IMF Occasional Paper 129.

Berg, Andrew. 1994. "Does Macroeconomic Reform Cause Structural Adjustment? Lessons from Poland." *Journal of Comparative Economics* 18: 376–409.

Bernhard, William T. 1998. "A Political Explanation of Variations in Central Bank Independence." *American Political Science Review* 92 (June): 311–28.

Biersteker, Thomas, ed. 1993. *Dealing with Debt: International Financial Negotiations and Adjustment Bargaining.* Boulder: Westview Press.

Bird, Graham. 1995. *IMF Lending to Developing Countries: Issues and Evidence.* London: Routledge.

Bird, Graham. 1996. "The International Monetary Fund and Developing Countries: A Review of the Evidence and Policy Options." *International Organization* 50 (3): 477–511.

Bird, Graham and Tony Killick. 1995. "The Bretton Woods Institutions: A Commonwealth Perspective." Commonwealth Economic Papers, No. 24. London: Commonwealth Secretariat.

Bjork, James. 1995. "The Uses of Conditionality: Poland and the IMF." *East European Quarterly* 29 (1): 89–124.

Blanchard, Olivier Jean. 1994. "Transition in Poland." *The Economic Journal* 104: 1169–77.

Bordo, M. D. and B. Eichengreen, eds. 1993. *A Retrospective on the Bretton Woods System: Lessons for International Monetary Reform.* Chicago: University of Chicago Press.

Bordo, Michael and Anna J. Schwartz. 2000. "Measuring Real Economic Effects of Bailouts: Historical Perspectives on How Countries in Financial Distress Have Fared with and without Bailouts." National Bureau of Economic Research: NBER Working Paper No. 7701.

Box-Steffensmeier, Janet M. and Bradford S. Jones. 1997. "Time is of the Essence: Event History Models in Political Science." *American Journal of Political Science* 41 (4): 1414–61.

Box-Steffensmeier, Janet M. and Bradford S. Jones. 2002. *Timing and Political Change: Event History Modeling in Political Science.* Ann Arbor: University of Michigan Press. Forthcoming.

Bruno, Michael and William Easterly. 1996. "Inflation and Growth: In Search of a Stable Relationship." *Federal Reserve Bank of St. Louis Review* 78 (May/June): 139–46.

Budge, Ian, David Robertson and Derek Hearl, eds. 1987. *Ideology, Strategy, and Party Change: Spatial Analyses of Post-War Election Programmes in Nineteen Democracies.* Cambridge: Cambridge University Press.

Bukowski, Charles and Barnabas Racz, eds. 1999. *The Return of the Left in Postcommunist States.* Northampton, MA: Edward Elgar Publishing, Inc.

Bulow, Jeremy, Kenneth Rogoff and Afonso S. Bevilaqua. 1992. "Official Creditor Seniority and Burden-sharing in the Former Soviet Bloc." *Brookings Papers on Economic Activity* 1: 195-233.

Central Intelligence Agency. 1990-1999. *World Fact Book.* Washington, D.C.: C.I.A.

Chung, Ching-Fan, Peter Schmidt and Ann D. Witte. 1991. "Survival Analysis: A Survey." *Journal of Quantitative Criminology* 7 (1): 59–98.

Clark, William Roberts and Mark Hallerberg. 2000. "Mobile Capital, Domestic Institutions, and Electorally Induced Monetary and Fiscal Policy." *The American Political Science Review* 94 (2): 323–46.

Cohen, Benjamin J. 1996. "Phoenix Risen: The Resurrection of Global Finance." *World Politics* 48 (2): 168–96.

Collier, Peter. 1999. "Consensus-building, Knowledge, and Conditionality." Paper prepared for presentation at the International Symposium on Global Finance and Development, Tokyo, March 1-2.

Colton, Timothy J. 2000. *Transitional Citizens: Voters and What Influences Them in the New Russia.* Cambridge: Harvard University Press.

Connors, T. 1979. "The Apparent Effects of Recent IMF Stabilization Programs." Federal Reserve Board, Washington, DC: International Finance Discussion Paper No. 135.

Conway, Patrick. 1994. "IMF Lending Programs: Participation and Impact." *Journal of Development Economics* 45 (2): 365–91.

Conway, Patrick. 1999. "Evaluating Fund Programs." Manuscript, Department of Economics University of North Carolina, 4 January.

Conway, Patrick. 2000. "IMF Programs and Economic Crisis: An Empirical Study of Transition." Working Paper, University of North Carolina, Third revision, 5 January.

Crawford, Keith. 1996. *East Central European Politics Today.* New York: Manchester University Press.

Crisp, Brian F. and Michael J. Kelly. 1999. "The Socioeconomic Impacts of Structural Adjustment." *International Studies Quarterly* 43 (September): 533–52.

Csaba, Laszlo. 1995. "Hungary and the IMF: The Experience of a Cordial Discord." *Journal of Comparative Economics* 20: 211–34.

Dawisha, Karen and Bruce Parrott. 1997. *Democratic Changes and Authoritarian Reactions in Russia, Ukraine, Belarus, and Moldova.* New York: Cambridge University Press.

De Gregorio, J. 1992. "Economic Growth in Latin America." *Journal of Development Economics* 39: 59–84.

Dhonte, Pierre. 1997. "Conditionality as an Instrument of Borrower Credibility." International Monetary Fund: Paper on Policy Analysis and Assessment, PPAA 97/2 (February).

Diaz-Alejandro, Carlos. 1981. "Southern Cone Stabilization Plans." In William R. Cline and Sidney Weintraub, eds. *Economic Stabilization in Developing Countries.* Washington, D.C.: The Brookings Institution pp. 119–41.

Dicks-Mireaux, Louis, Mauro Mecagni and Susan Schadler. 2000. "Evaluating the Effect of IMF Lending to Low-income Countries." *Journal of Development Economics* 61: 495–526.

Diermeier, Daniel and Randall T. Stevenson. 1999. "Cabinet Survival and Competing Risks." *American Journal of Political Science* 43 (4): 1051–68.

Donovan, Donal J. 1981. "Real Responses Associated with Exchange Rate Action in Selected Upper Credit Tranche Stabilization Programs." IMF Staff Papers 28: 698-727.

Donovan, Donal J. 1982. "Macroeconomic Performance and Adjustment under Fund-supported Programs: The Experience of the Seventies." IMF Staff Papers 29: 171-203.

Doroodian, Khosrow. 1993. "Macroeconomic Performance and Adjustment under Policies Commonly Supported by the International Monetary Fund." *Economic Development and Cultural Change* 41 (4): 849–64.

Drabek, Zdenek. 1995. "IMF and IBRD Policies in the Former Czechoslovakia." *Journal of Comparative Economics* 20: 235–64.

Edwards, Sebastian. 1989. "The International Monetary Fund and the Developing Countries: A Critical Evaluation." Carnegie Rochester Conference Series on Public Policy 31 North Holland.

Edwards, Sebastian and Julio A. Santaella. 1993. "Devaluation Controversies in the Developing Countries: Lessons from the Bretton Woods Era." *In* Bordo and Eichengreen (1993) pp. 405–455.

Fedorov, Boris. 1999. *10 Bezumnykh Let: Pochemu v Rossii ne sostoialis' reformy.* Moscow: Sovershenno Sekretno.

Feldstein, Martin. 1998. "Refocusing the IMF." *Foreign Affairs* 77 (2): 20–33.

Ferejohn, John. 1986. "Incumbent Performance and Electoral Control." *Public Choice* 50: 5–26.

Fernandez, Raquel and Dani Rodrik. 1991. "Resistance to Reform: Status Quo Bias in the Presence of Individual-Specific Uncertainty." *The American Economic Review* 81: 1146–55.

Fischer, Stanley, Ratna Sahay and Carlos A. Vegh. 1996. "Stabilization and Growth in Transition Economies: The Early Experience." *The Journal of Economic Perspectives* 10 (Spring): 45–66.

Franklin, James. 1997. "IMF Conditionality, Threat Perception, and Political Repression: A Cross-national Analysis." *Comparative Political Studies* 30 (5): 576–606.

Franzese, Robert J. Jr. 2002. *Macroeconomic Policies of Developed Democracies.* Cambridge: Cambridge University Press.

Fudenberg, Drew and David K. Levine. 1989. "Reputation and Equilibrium Selection in Games with a Patient Player." *Econometrica* 57 (4): 759–778.

Fudenberg, Drew and Jean Tirole. 1991. *Game Theory.* Cambridge: The M.I.T. Press.

Gabel, Matthew J. and John D. Huber. 2000. "Putting Parties in Their Place: Inferring Party Left-Right Ideological Positions from Manifestos Data." *American Journal of Political Science* 44: 94–103.

Gaidar, Yegor. 1997. "Applied Economics in Action: The International Monetary Fund. The IMF and Russia." *AEA Papers and Proceedings* May (May): 13–16.

Garrett, Geoffrey. 1995. "Capital Mobility, Trade, and the Domestic Politics of Economic Policy." *International Organization* 49 (Autumn): 657–88.

Garrett, Geoffrey. 1998. *Partisan Politics in the Global Economy*. New York: Cambridge University Press.

Garrett, Geoffrey and Peter Lange. 1995. "Internationalization, Institutions, and Political Change." *International Organization* 49 (Autumn): 627–56.

Garuda, Gopal. 2000. "The Distributional Effects of IMF Programs: A Cross-country Analysis." *World Development* 28 (6): 1031–51.

Giavazzi, Francesco and Marco Pagano. 1988. "The Advantage of Tying One's Hands: EMS Discipline and Central Bank Credibility." *European Economic Review* 32: 1055–1082.

Goldgeier, James M. 1999. *Not Whether But When: The U.S. Decision to Enlarge NATO*. Washington, D.C.: The Brookings Institution.

Goldstein, Morris and Peter Montiel. 1986. "Evaluating Fund Stabilization Programs with Multicountry Data: Some Methodological Pitfalls." IMF Staff Papers 33: 304-44.

Gomulka, Stanislaw. 1993. "Poland: Glass Half Full." In Richard Portes, ed. *Economic Transformation in Central Europe: A Progress Report*. London: Center for Economic Policy Research.

Gomulka, Stanislaw. 1995. "The IMF-Supported Programs of Poland and Russia, 1990-1994: Principles, Errors, and Results." *Journal of Comparative Economics* 20: 316–46.

Grier, K. and G. Tullock. 1989. "An Empirical Analysis of Cross-National Economic Growth 1951-80." *Journal of Monetary Economics* 24 (2): 259–76.

Grossman, Gene M. and Elhanan Helpman. 1994. "Protection For Sale." *The American Economic Review* 84 (September): 833–50.

Gubina, Irina and Maksim Rubchenko. 1997. "Anatomiia Kodeksa." *Ekspert* 22 (June): 18–23.

Guitian, Manuel. 1995. "Conditionality: Past, Present, Future." *IMF Staff Papers* 42 (4): 792–835.

Gylfasson, Thorvaldur. 1987. "Credit Policy and Economic Activity in Developing Countries with IMF Stabilization Programs." Princeton Studies in International Finance, No. 60.

Gylfasson, Thorvaldur and Tryggvi T. Herbertsson. 1996. "Does Inflation Matter for Growth?" Centre for Economic Policy Research, London, Discussion Paper 1503.

Haggard, Stephan. 1986. "The Politics of Adjustment: Lessons from the IMF's Extended Fund Facility." In Miles Kahler, ed. *The Politics of International Debt*. Ithaca, N.Y.: Cornell University Press.

Haggard, Stephan, Chung H. Lee and Sylvia Maxfield. 1993. *The Politics of Finance in Developing Countries*. Ithaca, N.Y.: Cornell University Press.

Haggard, Stephan and Robert R. Kaufman. 1995. *The Political Economy of Democratic Transitions*. Princeton: Princeton University Press.

Halligan, Liam and Pavel Teplukhin. 1996. "Investment Disincentives in Russia." *Communist Economies and Economic Transformation* 8 (1): 29–51.

Haque, Badrul M. and Charles R. Wartenberg. 1992. "Direct Effects of Debt Overhang and IMF Programs." *Review of Financial Economics* 1 (2): 30–39.

Heckman, James J. 1979. "Sample Selection Bias as a Specification Error." *Econometrica* 47 (January): 153–61.

Helleiner, Eric. 1994. *States and the Reemergence of Global Finance: From Bretton Woods to the 1990s*. Ithaca, N.Y.: Cornell University Press.

Hellman, Joel. 1998. "Winners Take All: The Politics of Partial Reform in Post-Communist Transitions." *World Politics* 50 (January).

Hibbs, Douglas A. 1977. "Political Parties and Macroeconomic Policy." *The American Political Science Review* 71 (December): 1467–87.

Hills, Carla A., Peter G. Peterson and Morris Goldstein. 1999. *Safeguarding Prosperity in a Global Financial System: The Future International Financial Architecture*. Washington, DC: Council on Foreign Relations and Institute for International Economics.

Holmes, Stephen. 1993. "Superpresidentialism and its Problems." *East European Constitutional Review* 2 (4): 123–26. Continued in Volume 3, Number 1.

Honaker, James, Anne Joseph, Gary King, Kenneth Scheve and Naunihal Singh. 1999. "Amelia: A Program for Missing Data (Windows version)." Cambridge: Harvard University, http://Gking.Harvard.edu/.

Huber, John D. 1989. "Values and Partisanship in Left-Right Orientations: Measuring Ideology." *European Journal of Political Research* 17: 599–621.

Huber, John D. and G. Bingham Powell, Jr. 1994. "Congruence between Citizens and Policymakers in Two Visions of Liberal Democracy." *World Politics* 46: 291–326.

Huber, John D. and Ronald Inglehart. 1995. "Expert Interpretations of Party Space and Party Locations in 42 Societies." *Party Politics* 1 (1): 73–111.

Inglehart, Ronald. 1990. *Culture Shift in Advanced Industrial Democracy*. Princeton: Princeton University Press.

International Monetary Fund. 1990. "Staff Report for the 1989 Article IV Consultation and Request for a Stand-by Arrangement." January 17, 1990, Attachment.

International Monetary Fund. 1997. "The ESAF at Ten Years: Economic Adjustment and Reform in Low-Income Countries." International Monetary Fund Occasional paper No. 156.

International Monetary Fund. 1998. *Financial Organization and Operations of the IMF*. Washington, D.C.: The International Monetary Fund.

International Monetary Fund. 2000*a*. *IMF Survey*. Vols. 18-29 (1989-2000).

International Monetary Fund. 2000*b*. *International Financial Statistics*. CD-ROM.

International Monetary Fund. 2000*c*. "Staff Report for the 2000 Article IV Consultation." August 23, 2000.

Iversen, Torben. 1999. *Contested Economic Institutions: The Politics of Macroeconomics and Wage Bargaining in Advanced Democracies*. Cambridge: Cambridge University Press.

James, Harold. 1996. *International Monetary Cooperation since Bretton Woods*. New York and Oxford: The IMF and Oxford University Press.

Johnson, Juliet. 2000. *A Fistful of Rubles: The Rise and Fall of the Russian Banking System*. Ithaca, NY: Cornell University Press.

Jones, Michael. 1987. "IMF Surveillance, Policy Coordination, and Time Consistency." *International Economic Review* 28 (1): 135–58.

Kahler, Miles. 1992. "External Influence, Conditionality, and the Politics of Adjustment." In Stephan Haggard and Robert R. Kaufman, eds. *The Politics of Economic Adjustment: International Constraints, Distributive Conflicts, and the State*. Princeton: Princeton University Press.

Kapur, Ishan and Emmanuel van der Mensbrugghe. 1997. "External Borrowing by the Baltics, Russia and Other Countries of the Former Soviet Union: Developments and Policy Issues." International Monetary Fund: Working Paper, WP/97/72.

Karatnycky, Adrian, Alezander Motyl and Charles Graybow. 1998. *Nations in Transit*. New Brunswick (U.S.A.): Transitions Publisher.

Keesing's Record of World Events. 1990-1999. London: Longman.

Kelly, Margaret R. 1982. "Fiscal Adjustment and Fund-Supported Programs, 1971-1980." *IMF Staff Papers* 29: 561–602.

Keohane, Robert and Helen V. Milner. 1996. *Internationalization and Domestic Politics*. Cambridge: Cambridge University Press.

Khan, Mohsin S. 1990. "The Macroeconomic Effects of Fund-Supported Adjustment Programs." *IMF Staff Papers* 37 (2): 195–231.

Khan, Mohsin S. and Malcolm D. Knight. 1985. "Fund-Supported Programs and Economic Growth." Washington, D.C.: International Monetary Fund Occasional Paper No. 41.

Khan, Mohsin S. and Malcolm Knight. 1981. "Stabilization Programs in Developing Countries: A Formal Framework." *IMF Staff Papers* 28: 1–53.

Killick, Tony. 1984. *The Quest for Economic Stabilization: The IMF and the Third World*. New York: St. Martin's Press.

Killick, Tony. 1995. *IMF Programmes in Developing Countries: Design and Impact*. London: Routledge.

Killick, Tony and Moazzam Malik. 1992. "Country Experiences with IMF Programmes in the 1980s." *The World Economy* 15 (4): 599–632.

Killick, Tony, Moazzam Malik and Marcus Manuel. 1992. "What Can We Know about the Effects of IMF Programs?" *The World Economy* 15 (4): 575–97.

King, Gary. 1989. *Unifying Political Methodology: The Likelihood Theory of Statistical Inference*. New York: Cambridge University Press.

King, Gary, James E. Alt, Nancy Elizabeth Burns and Michael Laver. 1990. "A Unified Model of Cabinet Dissolution in Parliamentary Democracies." *American Journal of Political Science* 34 (3): 846–71.

King, Gary, Joseph Honaker, Anne Joseph and Kenneth Scheve. 2001. "Analyzing Incomplete Political Science Data: An Alternative Algorithm for Multiple Imputation." *The American Political Science Review* 95 (March): 49–70.

Kirkpatrick, Colin and Ziya Onis. 1985. "Industrialization as a Structural Determinant of Inflation Performance in IMF Stabilisation Programmes in Less Developed Countries." *Journal of Development Studies* 21: 347–61.

Kitschelt, Herbert, Zdenka Mansfeldova, Radoslaw Markowski and Gabor Toka. 1999. *Post-Communist Party Systems: Competition, Representation, and Inter-Party Cooperation*. Cambridge: Cambridge University Press.

Knight, Malcom and Julio A. Santaella. 1994. "Economic Determinants of Fund Financial Arrangements." Washington, D.C.: International Monetary Fund Working Paper No. WP/94/36.

Kolodko, Grzegorz W. 1996. *Poland 2000: The New Economic Strategy*. Warszawa: Poltext.

Kolodko, Grzegorz W. 2000*a*. *From Shock to Therapy: The Political Economy of Post-socialist Transformation*. Oxford: Oxford University Press.

Kolodko, Grzegorz W. 2000*b*. *Post-Communist Transition: The Thorny Road*. Rochester, NY: University of Rochester Press.

Kolodko, Grzegorz W. and D. Mario Nuti. 1997. "The Polish Alternative: Old Myths, Hard Facts and New Strategies in the Successful Transformation of the Polish Economy." Helsinki: UNU World Institute for Development Economics Research (WIDER).

Kormendi, Roger C. and Phillip G. Meguire. 1985. "Macroeconomic Determinants of Growth. Cross-Country Evidence." *Journal of Monetary Economics* 16 (2): 141–63.

Krueger, Anne. 1998. "Wither the World Bank and the IMF?" *Journal of Economic Literature* 36 (4): 1983–2020.

Kuzio, Taras. 1997. *Ukraine under Kuchma: Political Reform, Economic Transformation and Security Policy in Independent Ukraine*. New York: St. Martin's Press.

Kuzio, Taras. 1998. *Contemporary Ukraine: Dynamics of Post-Soviet Transformation*. Armonk, NY: M. E. Sharpe.

Kuzio, Taras, Robert S. Kravchuk and Paul D'Anieri, eds. 1999. *State and Institution Building in Ukraine*. New York: St. Martin's Press.

Kydland, Finn E. and Edward C. Prescott. 1977. "Rules Rather than Discretion: The Inconsistency of Optimal Plans." *Journal of Political Economy* 85 (3): 437–91.

Lawless, J. F. 1982. *Statistical Models and Methods for Lifetime Data*. New York: John Wiley and Sons.

Lee, Jong-Wha and Changyong Rhee. 2000. "Macroeconomic Impacts of the Korean Financial Crisis: Comparison with the Cross-country Patterns." Rochester Center for Economic Research Working Paper No. 471.

Levine and Renelt. 1992. "A Sensitivity Analysis of Cross-Country Growth Regressions." *The American Economic Review* 82 (4): 942–63.

Lipson, Charles. 1986. "Bankers' Dilemmas: Private Cooperation in Rescheduling Sovereign Debts." In Kenneth A. Oye, ed. *Cooperation Under Anarchy*. Princeton: Princeton University Press.

Little, Roderick J.A. and Donald Rubin. 1987. *Statistical Analysis with Missing Data*. New York: Wiley & Sons.

Lohmann, Susanne. 1998. "An Information Rationale for the Power of Special Interests." *The American Political Science Review* 92 (December): 809–28.

Loxley, John. 1984. *The IMF and the Poorest Countries: The Performance of the Least Developed Countries under IMF Stand-by Arrangements*. Ottawa, CA: The North-South Institute.

Martin, Lanny W. 2000. "Public Opinion Shocks and Government Termination." Paper presented at the Annual Meeting of the American Political Science Association, Washington D.C., August 31-September 3.

Maxfield, Sylvia. 1997. *Gatekeepers of Growth: The International Political Economy of Central Banking in Developing Countries.* Princeton: Princeton University Press.

McCauley, Robert N. 1985. "IMF Managed Lending." In Michael P. Claudon, ed. *World Debt Crisis: International Lending on Trial.* Cambridge, MA: Ballinger Publishing Co.

McFaul, Michael, Nikolai Petrov and Andrei Ryabov, eds. 1999. *Primer on Russia's 1999 Duma Elections.* Washington, D.C.: Carnegie Endowment for International Peace.

Meng, Xiao-Li. 1994. "Multiple Imputation with Uncongenial Sources of Input." *Statistical Science* 9 (4): 538–573.

Millar, James R. 2000. "New Leadership and Direction at the IMF: Prospects for the Transition States." *Problems of Post-Communism* 47 (5): 38–47.

Mosley, Paul. 1987. "Conditionality as Bargaining Process: Structural-adjustment Lending, 1980-86." Princeton Essays in International Finance. No. 168. Department of Economics, Princeton University.

Naray, Peter. 2001. *Russia and the World Trade Organization.* New York: Palgrave.

Nelson, Joan, ed. 1990. *Economic Crisis and Policy Choice: The Politics of Adjustment in Developing Countries.* Princeton: Princeton University Press.

Nordhaus, William D. 1975. "The Political Business Cycle." *Review of Economic Studies* 42 (April): 169–90.

Oatley, Thomas. 1999. "How Constraining is Capital Mobility? The Partisan Hypothesis in an Open Economy." *American Journal of Political Science* 43 (October): 1003–27.

Organization for Economic Cooperation and Development (OECD) Development Assistance Committee. 2000. *International Development Statistics.* CD-ROM.

Orphanides, A. and R. Solow. 1990. "Money, Inflation and Growth." In Benjamin M. Friedman and Frank H. Hahn, eds. *Handbook of Monetary Economics, Volume 1.* Amsterdam: Noth-Holland.

Pastor, Manuel. 1987. "The Effects of IMF Programs in the Third World: Debate and Evidence from Latin America." *World Development* 15 (2): 249–62.

Persson, Torsten and Guido Tabellini, eds. 1994. *Monetary and Fiscal Policy.* Cambridge: The M.I.T. Press. 2 volumes.

Pindyck, Robert S. and Andres Solimano. 1993. "Economic Instability and Aggregate Investment." *NBER Macroeconomic Annual* 8: 259–302.

Powell, G. Bingham Jr. 1982. *Contemporary Democracies: Participation, Stability and Violence.* Cambridge: Harvard University Press.

Powell, G. Bingham Jr. 2000. *Elections as Instruments of Democracy: Majoritarian and Proportional Visions.* New Haven: Yale University Press.

Powell, Robert. 1987. "Crisis Bargaining, Escalation, and MAD." *The American Political Science Review* 81 (September): 717–35.

Powell, Robert. 1999. *In the Shadow of Power: States and Strategies in International Politics.* Princeton: Princeton University Press.

PricewaterhouseCoopers. 1999. *Report on Relations between the Central Bank of Russia and the Financial Management Company Ltd (FIMACO).* Washington, D.C.: International Monetary Fund, August.

PricewaterhouseCoopers. 2000*a*. *National Bank of Ukraine Agreed-upon Procedures: Report of Findings for Publication Purposes.* Washington, D.C.: International Monetary Fund, July.

PricewaterhouseCoopers. 2000*b*. *National Bank of Ukraine Agreed-upon Procedures: Report of Findings for Publication Purposes.* Washington, D.C.: International Monetary Fund, April.

Przeworski, Adam. 1991. *Democracy and the Market: Political and Economic Reforms in Eastern Europe and Latin America.* New York: Cambridge University Press.

Przeworski, Adam and James Raymond Vreeland. 2000. "The Effects of IMF Programs on Economic Growth." *Journal of Development Economics* 62 (2): 385–421.

Putnam, Robert. 1988. "Diplomacy and Domestic Politics." *International Organization* 42 (Summer): 427–61.

Reichmann, Thomas M. 1978. "The Fund's Conditional Assistance and the Problems of Adjustment, 1973-75." *Finance and Development* 15: 38–41.

Reichmann, Thomas M. and Richard T. Stillson. 1978. "Experience with Programs of Balance of Payments Adjustment: Stand-by Arrangements in the Higher Credit Tranches, 1963-72." *IMF Staff Papers* 25 (2): 293–309.

Remmer, Karen L. 1986. "The Politics of Economic Stabilization: IMF Standby Programs in Latin America, 1954-1984." *Comparative Politics* 19 (1): 1–24.

Riker, William H. 1980. "Implications from the Disequilibrium of Majority Rule for the Study of Institutions." *The American Political Science Review* 74 (June): 432–46.

Riker, William H. 1982. *Liberalism against Populism: A Confrontation between the Theory of Democracy and the Theory of Social Choice.* Prospect Heights: Waveland Press, Inc.

Rodlauer, Marcus. 1995. "The Experience with IMF-supported Reform Programs in Central and Eastern Europe." *Journal of Comparative Economics* 20: 95–115.

Rodrik, Dani. 1997. *Has globalization gone too far?* Washington, DC: Institute for International Economics.

Rogoff, Kenneth. 1985. "The Optimal Degree of Commitment to an Intermediate Monetary Target." *Quarterly Journal of Economics* 100: 1169–1190.

Rogoff, Kenneth and Anne Sibert. 1988. "Elections and Macroeconomic Policy Cycles." *Review of Economic Studies* 55 (January): 1–16.

Rogov, Sergei M. 1998. "The Russian Crash of 1998." Center for Naval Analyses, CIM 585 (October).

Romer, Thomas and Howard Rosenthal. 1978. "Political Resource Allocation, Controlled Agendas, and the Status Quo." *Public Choice* 33: 27–43.

Rosati, Dariusz. 1993. "Poland: Glass Half Empty." In Richard Portes, ed. *Economic Transformation in Central Europe: A Progress Report.* London: Centre for Economic Policy Research.

Roubini, Nouriel and Xavier Sala-i-Martin. 1992. "Financial Repression and Economic Growth." *Journal of Development Economics* 39: 5–30.

Roubini, Nouriel and Xavier Sala-i-Martin. 1995. "A Growth Model of Inflation, Tax Evasion and Financial Repression." *Journal of Monetary Economics* 35: 275– 301.

Rowlands, Dane. 1996. "New Lending to Less Developed Countries: The Effect of the IMF." *Canadian Journal of Economics* 29 (Supplemental): S443–47.

Rubin, Donald B. 1977. "Formalizing Subjective Notions about the Effect of Nonrespondents in Sample Surveys." *Journal of The American Statistical Association* 72 (359): 538–543.

Rubin, Donald B. 1987. *Multiple Imputation for Nonresponse in Surveys.* New York: Wiley & Sons.

Rubin, Donald B. 1996. "Multiple Imputation After 18+ Years." *Journal of The American Statistical Association* 91 (434): 473–489.

Rubin, Donald B. and Nathaniel Schenker. 1986. "Multiple Imputation for Interval Estimation From Simple Random Samples With Ignorable Nonresponse." *Journal of The American Statistical Association* 81 (394): 366–374.

Sanford, Goerge. 1999. *Poland: The Conquest of History.* Amsterdam: Harwood Academic Publishers.

Santaella, Julio A. 1995. "Four Decades of Fund Arrangements: Macroeconomic Stylized Facts before the Adjustment Arograms." Washington, D.C.: International Monetary Fund Working Paper No. WP/95/74.

Schadler, Susan, Adam Bennett, Maria Carkovic, Louis Dicks-Mireaux, Mauro Mecagni, James H. J. Morsink and Miguel A. Savastano. 1995. *IMF Conditionality: Experience under Stand-by and Extended Arrangements. Part I: Key Issues and Findings,* and *Part II: Background papers.* Washington, D.C.: IMF Occasional Papers No. 128 and 129.

Schadler, Susan, Franek Rozadowski, Siddharth Tiwari and David O. Robinson. 1993. "Economic Adjustment in Low-Income Countries: Experience Under the Enhanced Structural Adjustment Facility." Washington, D.C.: International Monetary Fund Occasional Paper No. 106.

Schafer, Joseph L. 1997. *Analysis of Incomplete Multivariate Data.* London: Chapman & Hall.

Shi, Min and Jakob Svensson. 2000. "Conditional Political Business Cycles: Theory and Evidence." W. Allen Wallis Institute of Political Economy, University of Rochester.

Shugart, Matthew Soberg and John M. Carey. 1992. *Presidents and Assemblies: Constitutional Design and Electoral Dynamics.* Cambridge: Cambridge University Press.

Simmons, Beth A. 1994. *Who Adjusts? Domestic Sources of Foreign Economic Policy during the Interwar Years.* Princeton: Princeton University Press.

Smith, Steven S. and Thomas F. Remington. 2000. *The Politics of Institutional Choice: The Formation of the Russian State Duma.* Princeton: Princeton University Press.

Smyslov, Dimitrii V. 1999. "MVF na rubezhe stoletii. Rossiiskii aspekt." *Den'gi i Kredit* (October).

Sobel, Andrew. 1997. "State Institutions, Economic Risk and Uncertainty, and Global Capital." Presented at the American Political Science Association Annual Meeting, Washington, D.C.

Spraos, John. 1986. "IMF Conditionality: Ineffectual, Inefficient, Mistargeted." Princeton Essays in International Finance No. 166.

Stallings, Barbara. 1992. "International Influence on Economic Policy: Debt, Stabilization, and Structural Reform." In Stephan Haggard and Robert R. Kaufman, eds. *The Politics of Economic Adjustment.* Princeton: Princeton University Press.

Stiglitz, Joseph E. 1999. "Whither Reform? Ten Years of the Transition." World Bank Annual Conference on Development Economics, Keynote Address.

Stone, Randall W. 1996. *Satellites and Commissars: Strategy and Conflict in the Politics of Soviet-Bloc Trade.* Princeton: Princeton University Press.

Stone, Randall W. 1997. "The IMF and the Post-Communist Transition: Reputation, Bargaining, and Institutions." Presented at the 93rd Annual Meeting of the American Political Science Association.

Stone, Randall W. 1998. "The IMF, the Market, and Credibility: A Formal Model with Empirical Tests on 27 Post-Communist Countries." Presented at the 94th Annual Meeting of the American Political Science Association.

Stone, Randall W. 1999. "Russia: The IMF, Private Finance, and External Constraints on a Fragile Polity." In Leslie Elliott Armijo, ed. *Financial Globalization and Democracy in Emerging Markets.* New York: St. Martin's Press.

Swoboda, Alexander. 1982. "Exchange Rate Regimes and European-U.S. Policy Interdependence." IMF Staff Papers 30.

Taagepera, Rein and Matthew Soberg Shugart. 1989. *Seats and Votes: The Effects and Determinants of Electoral Systems.* New Haven: Yale University Press.

Thacker, Strom C. 1999. "The High Politics of IMF Lending." *World Politics* 52 (October): 38–75.

Tiongson, Erwin R. 1997. "Poland and IMF Conditionality Programs: 1990-1995." *East European Quarterly* 31 (1): 55–68.

Treisman, Daniel S. 1998. "Fighting Inflation in a Transitional Regime: Russia's Anomalous Stabilization." *World Politics* 50 (January): 235–65.

Tsebelis, George. 1990. *Nested Games: Rational Choice in Comparative Politics.* Berkeley: University of California Press.

Tsebelis, George. 1995. "Decision Making in Political Systems: Veto Players in Presidentialism, Parliamentarism, Multicameralism and Multipartyism." *British Journal of Political Science* 25: 289–325.

Tufte, Edward R. 1978. *Political Control of the Economy.* Princeton: Princeton University Press.

Ul Haque, Nadeem and Mohsin S. Khan. 1998. "Do IMF-Supported Programs Work? A Survey of the Cross-Country Empirical Evidence." IMF Working Paper, WP/98/169.

United States Agency for International Development (USAID). 1992-1999. "Congressional Presentation, Summary Tables." In *American Statistics Index.* Washington, D.C.: Congressional Information Service.

Warwick, Paul and Stephen T. Easton. 1992. "The Cabinet Stability Controversy: New Perspectives on a Classic Problem." *American Journal of Political Science* 36 (1): 122–46.

Warwick, Paul V. 1992. "Rising Hazards: An Underlying Dynamic of Parliamentary Government." *American Journal of Political Science* 36 (November): 857–76.

Watson, James. 1996. "Foreign Investment in Russia: The Case of the Oil Industry." *Europe-Asia Studies* 48 (3): 429–55.

Weingast, Barry R., Kenneth A. Shepsle and Christopher Johnsen. 1981. "The Political Economy of Benefits and Costs: A Neoclassical Approach to Distributive Politics." *Journal of Political Economy* 89 (4): 642–64.

Wells, Robin. 1993. "Tolerance of Arrearages: How IMF Loan Policy Can Effect Debt Reduction." *The American Economic Review* 83: 621–33.

White, Stephen, Richard Rose and Ian McAllister. 1997. *How Russia Votes*. Chatham, NJ: Chatham House Publishers.

Williamson, John. 1994. *The Political Economy of Policy Reform*. Washington, D.C.: Institute for International Economics.

Wolf, Thomas and Emine Guergen. 2000. "Improving Governance and Fighting Corruption in the Baltic and CIS countries: The role of the IMF." IMF Working Paper, WP/00/1.

Woo, Wing Thye. 1994. "The Art of Reforming Centrally Planned Economies: Comparing China, Poland and Russia." *Journal of Comparative Economics* 18: 276–308.

World Bank. 2000. *World Development Indicators*. CD-ROM.

Zubek, Voytek. 1991. "Walesa's Leadership and Poland's Transition." *Problems of Communism* 40 (January-April): 69–83.

Zubek, Voytek. 1994. "The Reassertion of the Left in Post-communist Poland." *Europe-Asia Studies* 46 (5): 801–37.

Zubek, Voytek. 1995. "The Phoenix Out of the Ashes: The Rise to Power of Poland's Post-Communist SdRP." *Communist and Post-Communist Studies* 28 (3): 275–306.

Zulu, Justin B. and Saleh M. Nsouli. 1985. "Adjustment Programs in Africa: The Recent Experience." Washington, D.C.: International Monetary Fund Occasional Paper No. 34.

Index

Afghanistan, 163
Agrarian Party (Bulgaria), 217
Agrarian Party (Russia), 129
Agrarian Party (Ukraine), 199
Albright, Madeleine, 118, 158
Aleksashenko, Sergei, 132, 144, 145, 151
Alexandrov, Stoyan, 214
Alfonsin, Raul, 98
Alliance of the Democratic Left (SLD), 55, 103, 109–111, 113
Angarski, Krassimir, 227
Angelov, Ivan, 221, 222
Argentina, 8, 98, 186, 224
Article VIII, 147, 230
Asian financial crisis of 1997, 150, 190, 192, 198, 229, 240

Baka, Wladislaw, 93
Balcerowicz Plan, 90–96
Balcerowicz, Leszek, 90, 93, 97, 104, 105, 108, 113
Bank of New York, 160
barter
    in Russia, 121, 148, 150, 164
    in Ukraine, 169–170, 186–188, 192, 200–201
Belarus, 67, 71, 178
Berezovsky, Boris, 151
Berov, Lyuben, 214–216
Bielecki, Jan, 97, 102, 104, 107
Black Tuesday, 134, 135
bond market
    Bulgarian, 220
        1996 collapse, 223
    Russian, 136, 141–142, 147, 151–152, 154, 157
    Ukrainian, 170, 186, 193, 197, 198, 200, 206
Borowski, Marek, 111
Bosnia, 118, 158

Bozhkov, Alexander, 229, 231
Brazil, 8, 186
budget process, 191
Bulgaria, 19, 69
    and the London Club, 213, 216
    anti-crisis program, 218
    attitude toward a currency board, 225–226
    banking crisis, 219–222, 225
    Berov government, fall of, 216–217
    bond market, 220
        1996 collapse, 223
    capital flight, 209, 215
    central bank independence, 215–216
    constitution, 210, 211, 214, 226
    corruption, 209, 215, 219, 231
    currency board, 209, 223–229
    democracy, 210
    Extended Fund Facility, 213, 230
    fall of Dimitrov government, 213
    financial crisis of 1996, 221–223, 231
    fixed exchange rate, 209, 223, 224, 231
    fragmentation, 211, 214, 231
    Grand National Assembly, 210
    losses of state-owned enterprises, 219
    National Bank of, 215, 220
    parliament, 212
        elections, 212, 214
        elections of 1990, 210
        elections of 1991, 217
        elections of 2001, 231
        UDF calls for elections in 1991, 212
    price controls, 218, 220, 226
    privatization, 212, 213, 215, 218, 219, 229
    reform of banking system, 212, 215
    state-owned enterprises, 215, 218
        regime of isolation for, 220–222

Bulgarian National Bank, 215
Bulgarian Socialist Party, 210, 217
Bush administration, 119
Bush, George, 117
Bush, George W., 163, 206

Camdessus, Michel
and Poland, 95
and Russia, 120, 125, 130, 131, 136,
140, 159, 160
and Ukraine, 179
capital controls, 117, 147–148
capital flight
from Bulgaria, 209, 215
from Russia, 123, 131, 133, 141, 157,
166
from Ukraine, 193, 195, 197, 200
Center Alliance (PC), 104, 105
central bank independence, 11, 80
Bulgaria, 215–216
Russia, 135, 157–158
Ukraine, 181, 195
Central Bank of Russia, 120–123, 126, 133,
134, 141–144, 151, 153, 154,
157, 160
central banks
Bulgarian National Bank, 215, 220
Central Bank of Russia, 120–123, 126,
133, 134, 141–144, 151, 153,
154, 157, 160
National Bank of Poland, 95, 96, 98,
101
National Bank of Ukraine, 170, 173–
175, 177, 181, 200
central planning, 8
Chechnya, 134, 135, 137, 147, 158, 160,
164
Chernomyrdin, Viktor, 55, 69, 123, 125–
127, 129–131, 136, 140, 148,
151, 153, 154, 157, 206
Christian National Union, 105
Christopher, Warren, 118, 129, 184
Chubais, Anatolii, 135, 138, 146, 147, 151,
154
Clinton administration, 118, 129, 130, 147,
154, 158, 161
Clinton, William, 117, 124, 125, 140

CMEA, 97, 100, 211
Cold War, 1, 19, 117
commitment device, 228
commitment problems, 10, 16, 240
Commonwealth of Independent States (CIS),
122, 185
Communist Party of the Russian Federation (KPRF), 117, 129, 137, 148,
158
Confederation for an Independent Poland
(KPN), 105
constitution
Bulgarian, 210, 211, 214, 226
Polish, 108
Russian, 119, 128, 137, 156
Ukrainian, 178, 184, 197
corruption
in Bulgaria, 209, 215, 219, 231
in Ukraine, 186, 191, 198, 205, 206
Council for Mutual Economic Assistance,
97, 100, 211
credibility, xx, 3, 11, 17, 23, 26, 94–96,
99, 156, 210, 240, 241
Credit-Suisse First Boston (Cyprus), 185,
192, 193
currency board, 209, 223, 225, 227, 228,
231
currency crisis, 142, 216, 238
fear of, in Poland, 95
in Bulgaria, 221–223, 231
in Russia, 123, 133–134, 142, 153–
157
in Ukraine, 200–201

debt rescheduling, 204, 216, 231
forgiveness, 211
Declaration of National Salvation, 226, 228
democracy, xx, 63, 68, 71
and inflation, 6–10
in Bulgaria, 210
quality of, in Russia, 128, 129, 138,
155, 164
Democratic Union (UD), 103, 105
Deppler, Michael, 222, 224, 225
Dimitrov, Filip, 212
discount factors, 56
Dobrev, Nikolay, 226

Dubinin, Sergei, 122, 130, 131, 135, 142, 143, 151, 153, 157
duration models, 254–256
dynamic inconsistency, 16

Ecoglasnost, 217
elections
    effects on economic policy, 52–53, 63, 71
    parliamentary
        in Bulgaria, 210, 212, 214, 217, 231
        in Poland, 90, 102, 109
        in Russia, 128–129, 137–138, 159
        in Ukraine, 176, 195–197
    presidential
        in Poland, 97
        in Russia, 118, 138, 140, 142, 144, 163
        in Ukraine, 172, 176, 202, 203
electoral law, 109, 148, 171, 195
    proportional representation, 102, 212
    single-member districts, 177
Estonia, 224
Eurobank, 142, 143
Eurobonds, 146, 192, 195, 205
European Bank for Reconstruction and Development, 219
European Union, 57, 113, 119, 228
    Bulgarian aspiration to join, 228
exchange rate
    fixed (or pegged)
        as a commitment device, 228
        as a nominal anchor, 95
        Bulgaria, 209, 223, 224, 231
        criticism of, 155
        dangers of, 136–137, 224
        Poland, 95
        rationale for, in Russia, 156
        Russia, 133, 143, 151
        Ukraine, 192
    flexible, 40
    targeting of, 180
Extended Fund Facility
    in Bulgaria, 213, 230
    in Poland, 100, 101, 105
    in Russia, 125, 140, 142, 155

    in Ukraine, 170, 189, 190, 195–198, 201, 203, 205
Eysymontt, Jerzy, 104

Fedorov, Boris, 120, 124–127, 129, 165
FIMACO, 142–144, 160
First Ukrainian International Bank, 192–193
Fischer, Stanley, 143, 196, 224
Fokin, Vitol'd, 172
foreign aid, xx, 57
    from United States, 57, 62, 63, 70, 78, 84, 85, 184, 241
foreign direct investment, 6, 9
foreign investment, 186
Foreign Investment Management Company, 142–144, 160
fragmentation
    empirical effects, 61, 71, 79–80, 84
    in Bulgaria, 211, 214, 231
    in Poland, 102–104, 109, 114
    in theory, 53–54
    in Ukraine, 208
France, 140

Gaidar, Yegor, 120, 121, 123, 124, 129, 149
Gazprom, 154, 162, 185
gazpromovki, 185
Gechev, Rumen, 217, 225
Gerashchenko, Viktor, 120–122, 126, 135, 143, 157
Geremek, Bronislaw, 103
Germany, 119, 140, 180
GKO market, 141–142, 147, 151–152, 154, 157
Gorbachev, Mikhail, 157
Gore, Al, 129, 206
Gref, German, 161
Group of Seven (G-7), 119, 124, 130, 177, 184, 197, 207
growth, 6

hold the line, 25
hryvnia
    introduction of, 179, 180, 186
Human Development Index, 6, 7

Hungary
    compared to Bulgaria, 231

Ignatiev, Sergei, 121
IMF board of directors, 18, 190
IMF Programs
    effects on growth, 41–43
    effects on inflation, 40–41
    effects on international accounts, 40–41
    effects on policy variables, 40–41
IMF quotas, 57, 70
IMF seal of approval, 115
income inequality, 6, 7
Indonesia, 138, 155
Indzhova, Reneta, 217
inequality, 9, 10
inflation
    and democracy, 6–10
    and growth, 6–9
    surprise, 22, 53
institutions, 22
    as equilibria, 22
    democratic, 11
    international, 1, 2, 12, 240
interenterprise arrears, 121, 175
international institutions, 1, 2, 12, 240
investors, 21, 24
Iran, 118, 158
Iraq, 118, 158

J-curve, 6
Japan, 120, 124, 155
Jaruzelski, Wojciech, 93, 97

Kadannikov, Vladimir, 140
Kasyanov, Mikhail, 163
Khasbulatov, Ruslan, 119, 124
Kiriyenko, Sergei, 55, 153, 156, 159
Kohl, Helmut, 129
Kolodko, Grzegorz, 112
Kosovo, 118, 158, 161, 230
Kostov, Dimitar, 213, 217, 218, 224, 225
    clashes with Gechev, 218
Kostov, Ivan, 217, 225
    builds UDF into a cohesive party, 217
Kravchuk, Leonid, 169, 172, 173, 175, 176

Kuchma, Leonid, 173–181, 197, 200, 202–206
Kuron, Jacek, 93
Kwasniewski, Alexander, 110

Lake, Anthony, 118
Law on Power, 179
Lazarenko, Pavlo, 181, 185, 186, 189, 205, 206
Lebed', Aleksandr, 145, 147
Lewandowski, Janusz, 107
Liberal Democratic Congress (KLD), 104
Liberal-Democratic Party (LDPR), 129, 137, 149
life expectancy, 6, 7
Livshits, Aleksandr, 146, 149
Lobov, Oleg, 134
London Club
    and Bulgaria, 213, 216
    and Poland, 113, 115
    and Russia, 163
Lukanov, Andrei, 210
Lukashenka, Alyaksandr, 67, 71
Lutkowski, Karol, 105

Marchuk, Yevhen, 179, 183
Masliukov, Yurii, 157
Matyukin, Georgii, 122
Mazowiecki, Tadeusz, 90, 97, 104
Mexico, 19, 136
Michnik, Adam, 90
Miyazawa, Kiichi, 124
Moroz, Oleksandr, 172, 176–178, 184
Movement for Rights and Freedom, 212
Mulford, David, 95
multiple equilibria, 22, 23
multiple imputation, 250–254

National Bank of Bulgaria, 220
National Bank of Poland, 95, 96, 98, 101
National Bank of Ukraine, 170, 173–175, 177, 181, 200
NATO, 118, 158, 161, 228
    bombing of Serbia, 230
    Bulgarian aspiration to join, 228
    expansion of, 184
Nemtsov, Boris, 147

New Union for Democracy, 214
North American Free Trade Agreement, 19
North Korea, 158

oil pipeline to Caspian Sea, 158
oil prices, 159, 161, 162
Olechowski, Andrzej, 105
Olszewski, Jan, 104, 105
Organization for Economic Cooperation and Development (OECD), 52
Osiatynski, Jerzy, 107, 111
Our Home Is Russia, 137, 148

Paramonova, Tatyana, 135
Paris Club
    and Poland, 100–102, 107, 112, 115
    and Russia, 124, 163
parliamentary elections
    in Bulgaria, 210, 212, 214, 217, 231
    in Poland, 90, 102, 109
    in Russia, 128–129, 137–138, 159
    in Ukraine, 176, 195–197
partisanship, 16, 17, 54–56, 69
path dependence, 19
Pawlak, Waldemar, 106, 110, 111
Peasant Alliance (PL), 108
Pervyi Ukrainskii Mezhdunarodnyi Bank, 192–193
Philippines, 19
Podkrepa labor union, 229
Poland, 55, 67, 69, 71
    and the London Club, 113, 115
    and the Paris Club, 100–102, 107, 112, 115
    Bielecki government, 99
    compared to Bulgaria, 210, 212, 231
    compared to Russia, 121
    Extended Fund Facility, 100, 101, 105
    fear of currency crisis, 95
    fixed exchange rate, 95
    fragmentation, 102–104, 109, 114
    National Bank of, 95, 96, 98, 101
    Olszewski government, 104
    parliamentary elections, 90, 102, 109
    parliamentary elections of 1991, 102
    parliamentary elections of 1993, 109

    presidential election of 1990, 97
    presidential elections, 97
    privatization, 108, 111
    Small Constitution, 108
    Stand-by Arrangement of 1990, 98
    state-owned enterprises, 107
Polish Communist Party (PUWP), 111
Polish Peasant Party, 104
Polish Peasant Party (PSL), 55, 106, 109, 110, 113
Polish United Workers' Party, 90
popiwek, 93, 94, 98, 113
Popov, Dimitar, 210, 211
Popular Rukh, 172, 173
post-Communist parties
    Bulgarian Socialist Party, 210, 217
    Communist Party of the Russian Federation, 117, 129, 137, 148, 158
    Social Democracy of the Republic of Poland, 108, 111
    Socialist Party of Ukraine, 172, 177
Potemkin, Aleksandr, 134
presidential elections
    in Poland, 97
    in Russia, 118, 138, 140, 142, 144, 163
    in Ukraine, 172, 176, 202, 203
price controls, 218, 220, 226
Primakov, Yevgenyi, 55, 157, 159
privatization
    in Bulgaria, 212, 213, 215, 218, 219, 229
    in Poland, 108, 111
    in Russia, 130, 138, 140, 150, 162, 164
    in Ukraine, 178, 186, 191, 196, 201, 203
    mass, 108, 138, 178
    nomenklatura, 111
proportional representation, 102, 212
Przeworski, Adam, 6
Pustovoitenko, Valerii, 191, 195, 200, 203, 204
Putin, Vladimir, 160–162
Pynzenyk, Viktor, 173–175, 178, 180, 188, 189

Rakowski, Mieczyslaw, 90
rational expectations, 52
realism, 2
referendum, 178
Rosati, Dariusz, 112
Rubin, Robert, 147, 154
ruble zone, 122, 173
Russia, xx, 19, 26, 55, 69, 70, 78, 83
  and the London Club, 163
  and the Paris Club, 124, 163
  barter, 121, 148, 150, 164
  Black Tuesday, 134, 135
  bond market, 136, 152
  capital controls, 117, 147–148
  capital flight, 123, 131, 133, 141, 157, 166
  central bank independence, 135, 157–158
  Central Bank of, 9, 83, 120–123, 126, 133, 134, 141–144, 151, 153, 154, 157, 160
  Communist Party (KPRF), 117, 129, 137, 148, 158
  compared to Bulgaria, 210, 212, 229, 231
  compared to Ukraine, 170, 185, 196
  Congress of Peoples' Deputies, 118, 119, 123
  constitution, 119, 128, 137, 156
  coup attempt of 1991, 118
  Duma, 136, 137, 142, 148, 149, 153, 156, 157
    elections of 1993, 128–129
    elections of 1995, 137–138
    elections of 1999, 159
    threats to dissolve, 149, 153, 156, 157
  Extended Fund Facility, 125, 140, 142, 155
  financial crisis of 1998, 83, 147, 149, 153–158
    effects on Bulgaria, 229
    effects on Ukraine, 170, 196, 198, 200, 202
    policy implications of, 239
  fixed exchange rate, 133, 136–137, 143, 151

  GKO market, 141–142, 147, 151–152, 154, 157
  influence on IMF policy toward Ukraine, 190, 198, 206
  Near Abroad, 122
  presidential elections, 70, 83, 138, 140, 144
    election of 1996, 118
  privatization, 130, 138, 140, 150, 162, 164
  quality of democracy, 128, 129, 138, 155, 164
  referendum, 124–125, 128
  Supreme Soviet, 119, 127
    dissolution of, 128
    siege of, 128
  tax collection, 117, 132, 148, 149, 151, 155
  tax reform, 149, 153, 161
Russia's Choice, 129
Russo, Massimo, 224

Sakskoburggotski, Simeon, 231
Schroeder, Gerhard, 163
Serbia, 1, 159
  NATO bombing, 230
shock therapy, 90, 91, 116, 118, 210, 239
Shpek, Roman, 180
single-member districts, 177
Sochi conference, 133, 134
Social Democracy of the Republic of Poland (SdRP), 108, 111
Socialist Party of Ukraine, 172, 177
Sofiyanski, Stefan, 227
Solidarity, 90, 92, 94, 97, 109, 111
South Korea, 155
state-owned enterprises, 7
  in Bulgaria, 215, 218
    regime of isolation for, 220–222
  in Poland, 107
Stepashin, Sergei, 160
Stoyanov, Petar, 226
Strategy for Poland, 112
Suchocka, Hanna, 106, 109
Summers, Lawrence, 147, 153, 160
Suslov, Viktor, 185, 189, 191–193
Swiecicki, Marcin, 95

Systemic Transformation Facility (STF), 124, 125, 128–131, 177, 178, 216

Talbott, Strobe, 118, 129
tax collection
in Russia, 117, 132, 148, 149, 151, 155
in Ukraine, 178, 187, 192, 201, 203
tit for tat, 25
Tkachenko, Oleksandr, 199, 200, 204
Turkey, 186
Turkmenistan, 1
Tyminski, Stanislaw, 97

Ukraine, 69, 70, 78, 231
agrarian lobby, 186
barter, 186–188, 192, 200–202
bond market, 170, 186, 193, 197, 198, 200, 206
capital flight, 193, 195, 197, 200
cassette crisis, 206
central bank independence, 195
compared to Bulgaria, 210, 231
constitution, 178, 184, 197
referendum on, 184
corruption, 186, 191, 198, 205, 206
division of powers, 169, 171, 208
electoral law, 195
Extended Fund Facility, 170, 189, 190, 195–198, 201, 203, 205
financial crisis, 200–201
fragmentation, 208
IMF policy and Russia, 190
industrial lobbies, 191
Law on Power, 179
Ministry of Finance
reform of, 187, 199
misuse of international reserves, 186, 192, 198, 200, 205
National Bank of, 170, 173–175, 177, 181, 200
parliamentary elections, 176, 195–197
parliamentary opposition, 196
presidential decrees, 197, 199
presidential elections, 172, 176, 202, 203

privatization, 178, 186, 191, 196, 201, 203
tax collection, 178, 187, 192, 201, 203
tax reform, 188, 196
Verkhovna Rada, 175, 176, 178, 184
Ukrgazprom, 202
Unified Energy System (UES), 162
Union of Democratic Forces, 210, 212
parliamentary defections from, 214
split in 1991, 212
Union of Freedom (UW), 113
United Nations, 6, 7
United States, xx, 57, 70, 117, 119, 120, 164, 184
Congress, 155, 160
foreign aid, 57, 62, 63, 70, 78, 84, 85, 184, 241
presidential campaign of 2000, 206
presidential election, 162
pressure on the IMF, 119–120, 124–125, 129, 184, 196, 207
relations with Russia, 117–118, 158, 161, 238
relations with Ukraine, 184, 238
Uruguay Trade Round, 119
Uzbekistan, 67, 71

value-added tax, 107
Viakhirev, Lev, 185
Videnov winter, 226
Videnov, Zhan, 215, 217, 225
populist electoral program of, 217
resignation of, 226
Vietnam, 19
Volkov, Oleksander, 186
Vuchev, Kliment, 222
Vulchev, Todor, 215, 216

Walesa, Lech, 97, 98, 102, 103, 106, 211
Warsaw Pact, 97, 99
workers' councils, 108
World Bank, 113, 119, 131, 155, 219–221, 223
World Trade Organization, 163

Yabloko, 137, 148

Yasin, Yevgenyi, 150
Yavlinskii, Grigorii, 137, 148
Yeltsin, Boris, 19, 118–120, 122–124, 127,
        128, 135, 138, 139, 142, 145,
        149, 150, 153, 156, 160
Yushchenko, Viktor, 169, 174, 175, 204,
        206, 207

Zaire, 19
Zhelev, Zhelyu, 210, 214
Zhirinovskii, Vladimir, 129, 137, 149
Zhivkov, Todor, 210
zloty stabilization fund, 95
Zyuganov, Gennadyi, 137–139, 143, 145,
        148, 157